The Politics and Security of the Gulf

Since the nineteenth century the Gulf region has been an area of intense interest, having been shaped first by the British and more recently by the Americans. This book charts the changing security and political priorities of these two powers and how they have influenced the region.

Adopting a narrative approach, the author provides background history on British involvement from the nineteenth century and a detailed analysis of the years after World War II, when oil supply became more critical. He covers the growth of U.S. influence and the British withdrawal, and follows more recent changes as the U.S. built up its military presence following *Desert Storm* and the invasion of Iraq. Looking at the three enduring missions fulfilled by the British – maintaining interstate order, protecting the free flow of commerce, which later included petroleum, and keeping out other Great Powers – the book demonstrates how these had by 1991 been assumed almost entirely by the American leaders.

A comprehensive and thorough look at the history of the Gulf and the contemporary issues affecting the region, this will be essential reading for students of Middle East history, military history and diplomatic history.

Jeffrey R. Macris is a Permanent Military Professor at the U.S. Naval Academy in Annapolis, where he teaches Middle Eastern history and military history. A resident of the Persian Gulf for nearly three years, he has worked with military officers from most of the Arab states of the Gulf. He holds a PhD from Johns Hopkins University's School of Advanced International Studies as well as a linguist certificate in Arabic.

The Politics and Security of the Gulf

Anglo-American hegemony and
the shaping of a region

Jeffrey R. Macris

Routledge
Taylor & Francis Group

LONDON AND NEW YORK

First published 2010
by Routledge
2 Park Square, Milton Park, Abingdon, Oxon OX14 4RN

Simultaneously published in the USA and Canada
by Routledge
270 Madison Avenue, New York, NY 10016

*Routledge is an imprint of the Taylor & Francis Group,
an informa business*

© 2010 Jeffrey R. Macris

Typeset in Times by
RefineCatch Limited, Bungay, Suffolk
Printed and bound in Great Britain by
CPI Antony Rowe, Chippenham, Wiltshire

The opinions expressed in this work are those of the author and do not
necessarily reflect those of the U.S. Government, the U.S. Navy, or the
U.S. Naval Academy.

British Library Cataloguing in Publication Data
A catalogue record for this book is available
from the British Library

Library of Congress Cataloging-in-Publication Data
Macris, Jeffrey R.
  The politics and security of the Gulf : Anglo-American hegemony
  and the shaping of a region / Jeffrey R. Macris.
    p. cm.
  Includes bibliographical references and index.
  1. Persian Gulf Region—Strategic aspects—History. 2. British—
  Persian Gulf Region—History. 3. Americans—Persian Gulf
  Region—History. 4. Persian Gulf Region—Foreign relations—
  United States. 5. United States—Foreign relations—Persian Gulf
  Region. 6. Persian Gulf Region—Foreign relations—Great
  Britain. 7. Great Britain—Foreign relations—Persian Gulf
  Region I. Title.
  DS326.M246 2009
  355′.0330536—dc22   2009026905

ISBN10: 0–415–77870–0 (hbk)
ISBN10: 0–415–77871–9 (pbk)
ISBN13: 0–203–86189–2 (ebk)

ISBN13: 978–0–415–77870–1 (hbk)
ISBN13: 978–0–415–77871–8 (pbk)
ISBN13: 978–0–203–86189–9 (ebk)

Book Cover Bahraini palace guard renders a rifle salute, 1956.

> From Left to Right: Mr. Charles A. Gault, British Political Agent to Bahrain;
> Sheikh Sulman bin Hamad Al-Khalifa, Ruler of Bahrain; Rear Admiral John
> Quinn, Commander, U.S. Navy Middle East Force, 4 February 1956. (U.S. Navy
> Photo, U.S. Naval Institute.)

For Jenn

Contents

Acknowledgments

This book would not have been possible without the assistance and sage guidance of many. For inspiration, special thanks go to my two mentors at Johns Hopkins University's School of Advanced International Studies, Professors Fouad Ajami and Eliot A. Cohen, both of whom spent considerable energy directing the initial phases of this study. As well, during his time as a distinguished visiting professor at the U.S. Naval Academy, Victor Davis Hanson suggested that I try to "think big," and to choose subject material that appeals to, and is written toward, a wide general audience. Over a decade ago Admiral Tom Fargo, during his tenure as fleet commander in the Persian Gulf, allowed his young *aide de camp* to sit in on meetings with ambassadors, emirs, and future Kings, which changed the way that I think about the Gulf.

In Annapolis, the U.S. Naval Academy's History Department, under the leadership of its chairmen Professors Richard Abels and David Peeler, and the Center for Middle East and Islamic Studies, under the direction of Professor Brannon Wheeler, provided the time, freedom, and support to embark on my continued studies on the Great Powers and the Persian Gulf. Christie Mills and Connie Grigor offered support and assistance. Many other members of the History Department staff provided feedback through our works in progress series. Specifically, Professor Ernie Tucker, a dedicated friend, continually provides unvarnished and helpful advice on the study and teaching of the Middle Eastern history; Brian VanDeMark enthusiastically gave comments on the manuscript. Several librarians from the Naval Academy also proved indispensable, including Barbara Manvel, Barbara Breeden, and Flo Todd. Cindi Gallagher from the Multimedia Support Center assisted with photographs and graphics. At the U.S. Naval Institute, Ms. Janis Jorgensen and Mr. Tim Wooldridge opened the Institute's enormous photo archives for use in this book.

From outside of Annapolis, Dr. Saul Kelly at the U.K.'s Joint Services Command and Staff College – Britain's war college – and Professor Miriam Joyce of Purdue University Calumet read the entire manuscript and provided detailed commentary and encouragement. The archivists at the United States National Archives in College Park, particularly Mr. Tim Nenninger, head of Modern Military Records, and Mr. Herb Rawlings-Milton, coordinator of

Freedom of Information Act requests, helped immeasurably. Likewise, I must recognize the staff of the British National Archives in Kew, England, to whom I am deeply indebted. Great Britain's drive over the centuries to open the state's government records to the people stands as a noteworthy gift to humanity. Several organizations have graciously provided other photographs that accompany the text: the British Library, the Imperial War Museum, National Maritime Museum, Brown University's Library, the BP Photo Archives, Getty Images, and the U.S. Library of Congress.

I also offer thanks to Joe Whiting, Suzanne Richardson, and Abigail Humphries of the Routledge editorial staff, as well as to Patricia Alderman, Kirsty Holmes and Donna White who supervised the production of the manuscript. It was a pleasure to work with such professionals.

On a personal front, I would also like to recognize my parents John and Nancy Macris, and my brothers Greg and Andrew, from whom I developed a life-long passion for learning and exploring, as well as my parents-in-law, Don and Karen Neff, who provided the same for their beautiful daughter. Most importantly, I would like to thank my wife Jennifer and our loving children – John, Jamey, Joseph, Joy, and Jesse. The members of our extended Neff and Macris families – along with a deep and lasting love for the Lord – serve as the foundation upon which any modest professional success springs.

List of maps and photos

Maps

Photos

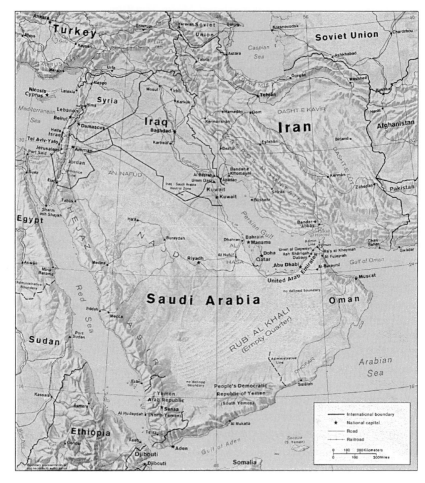

Map 1 Arabian Peninsula and vicinity.

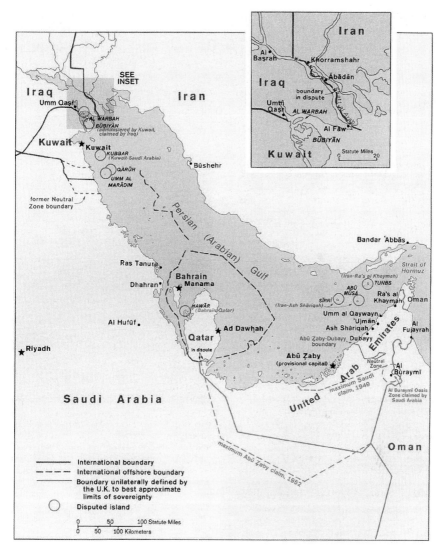

Map 2 Persian Gulf 1973 – with disputed borders.

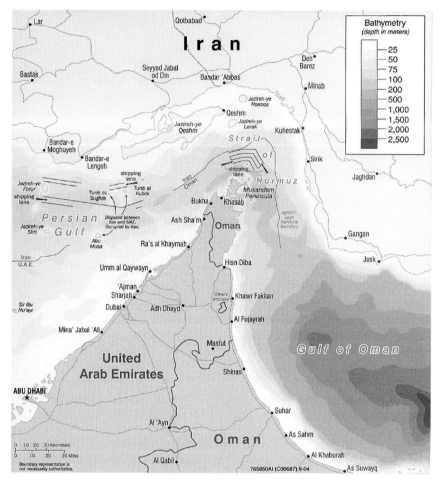

Map 3 Strait of Hormuz and disputed islands.

Introduction

A glance at a map of the Persian Gulf reveals a patchwork of small and large countries. Dotted along the southern coast lie a series of minor states: Kuwait, Bahrain, Qatar, the United Arab Emirates, and Oman. Towering over them stand Iran, Saudi Arabia, and Iraq, the Gulf's dominant local powers. None of the maps, however, reveal the two states that have shaped the modern history of the Gulf more than any other outside power: Great Britain and the United States. Sometimes working together, sometimes at odds with one another, and sometimes simply indifferent, leaders of these two Western superpowers have drawn borders in the region, determined issues of war and peace, kept commerce moving and oil flowing, and chosen which leaders will rule. They have bequeathed a language of diplomacy and commerce. Their militaries have maintained order there, kept out other Great Powers, and prevented perpetually squabbling parties from making war on each other. In their absence – from 1971 to 1991 – turmoil beset the Gulf.

The Politics and Security of the Gulf: Anglo-American Hegemony and the Shaping of a Region investigates the roots of Britain and America's involvement in the politics and security affairs of the Gulf. The book starts with an introductory chapter on Britain's early legacy, then stretches chronologically from World War II, the start of America's military involvement in the region, to Operation *Desert Storm,* the 1991 conflict that marked the beginning of America's permanent military presence there, to the present.

Several related research questions, then, drive this study. What brought Britain and America's military forces to the Gulf, and how have the superpowers used relatively modest doses of military power to maintain order and safeguard their interests there? Why did the British depart the region, and why did the Americans initially refuse to take over, only to reverse that decision after two decades of trouble there? And finally, throughout this drawn-out transition, when have Anglo-American aims in the region coincided, and when have they diverged?

A frequent criticism of modern scholarship is that authors today concentrate too much on too little, that is, there exists an overabundance of books that concentrate narrowly on specialized periods or subjects, at the expense of broader patterns or larger meaning. Rather than looking at a single issue – the 1956 Suez Crisis, the 1968 British announcement of departure from East of Suez, the 1973 worldwide oil crisis, for example – *The Politics and Security of the Gulf* looks at the broader issue of how the two superpowers, along with their armies and navies, have shaped the Gulf since the nineteenth century. Given the continuing hostilities and tension in the region, the author hopes that this work will provide for readers insight and historical context.

As one might expect, this account deals primarily with military and diplomatic affairs, which, as frequently happens, prove intertwined. Both Britain's and America's ability to influence events in the Gulf, after all, depended ultimately upon their ability to project force to the region, one of the most distant and difficult places for London and Washington's forces to reach, and one of the harshest and most remote places in the world in which to operate.

This study rests upon a combination of primary and secondary works, chiefly from British and American sources. The chapters draw heavily upon original diplomatic and military documents from Great Britain's National Archives in Kew, England (formerly the Public Records Office) and the U.S. National Archives in College Park, Maryland, as well as from published document collections. As we approach the present, however, the archival trail dries up. For the period from the 1980s to the present, therefore, the author uses Congressional proceedings, secondary sources, published firsthand accounts in journal articles, and to a lesser degree, open-source press reporting.

This topic straddles a number of different disciplines, including modern Middle Eastern history, strategic studies, military history, and American and British diplomatic history. A book that attempts to bridge these subject areas, and aims to cover such thematic and chronological ground, must sacrifice detail and depth. For this reason, *The Politics and Security of the Gulf* includes in the Notes and Bibliography valuable books and journal articles for more detailed study in a particular topic. The author hopes that this work will prove especially helpful to undergraduate and graduate students of modern Middle Eastern history, as well as diplomats, military personnel, and the curious general reader.

Author's interest

I remember clearly how I first became interested in the topic of Anglo-American hegemony in the Gulf. After almost two years studying Arabic full-time in the United States, I traveled for the first time to the Gulf to explore the feasibility of moving there with my newlywed California bride. After checking in to a Western-style hotel I boarded a hotel van and, anxious to exercise my language skills, in Arabic I asked the driver to take me to the souq, the old-fashioned bazaar that marks downtown in most Arab cities. When his brow furrowed I repeated my words: "Ila as-souq, min fidlak." Clearly not understanding, he turned around and in an erudite British accent that hinted of the Indian subcontinent, he eloquently requested, "Excuse me, sir, but I don't speak much Arabic. Kindly, would you please speak in English." As I found that day, the British clearly had left their mark on the region. As I found on my initial trip, speaking Arabic there proved a challenge, for most in the business and professional classes preferred to practice their English rather than Arabic. Everywhere I turned I saw vestiges of more than 150 years of British presence: the language, the traffic circles, the Anglican Church, the rugby clubs, and the bagpipes and beefeater hats that the Arab militaries sported – in 130 degree heat. Living subsequently in the Gulf for several years, I discovered that the British influence proved pervasive up and down the coastal emirates, from Kuwait to Oman.

The chapters

This historical narrative takes a largely chronological approach, with occasional thematic diversions, starting off with an initial chapter titled "Great Britain's legacy in the Persian Gulf." Beginning in the early 1800s, Britain's leaders found themselves, somewhat against their will, involved in the untidy affairs of this harsh and inhospitable realm. Unlike the bountiful lands of India and further east, the Arabian Peninsula and Iranian plateau offered to officials in London and Bombay few exotic spices or riches, but much sand, in-fighting, and brigandage. It was disarray that sucked in the Great Power. A general lack of order in the Gulf created conditions where piracy flourished, threatening the lucrative seaborne trade upon which the Empire prospered. Lack of effective central authority in the region also tempted Britain's other rivals, who coveted the rich Asian colonies to the east. The Persian Gulf's strategic location, furthermore, lying athwart the pathways connecting Europe, Africa, and Asia, made these environs particularly important to protect. In the nineteenth and early twentieth centuries Britain signed treaties with various Gulf leaders that established London as the arbiter of international relations in the region, while at the same time providing tacit and sometimes explicit British security guarantees to ruling families against external attack. These agreements served as part of Britain's "Great Game" against other European nations, first Russia and then Germany. London's development in the early twentieth century of the region's oil fields deepened Britain's involvement in the region. For approximately a century and a half, then, the British remained in these lands, standing guard, providing order, not quite colonizing, but certainly shaping the region, while denying access and use by foes.

To impose its will on the Persian Gulf region, Britain used a relatively small amount of force, mostly naval power, coupled with the daunting possession of a vast strategic reserve in India. Small numbers of Indian Navy and Royal Navy ships, tethered to bases on the subcontinent, plied the region's waters, showing the British flag, cannonading and blockading when necessary, and if needed, threatening further destruction from garrisons of

Indian ground troops. The British Resident in the Gulf, a political officer in the service of the Indian Government, worked with deployed naval and military leaders to ensure the protection of British interests. India, in both political and military affairs, cast a long shadow on British involvement in the Persian Gulf, serving as the *raison d'être* for British presence there, while at the same time providing a strategic reserve of military forces to safeguard those interests. The growth of the oil industry at the turn of the century, coupled with Britain's growing use of petroleum over coal in its military, led Great Britain to turn the Gulf into a major theater of operations in World War I. By the end of the conflict Britain reigned supreme throughout the Middle East, ruling even Mesopotamia, at the head of the Gulf, in addition to continuing its paternalistic control over the other coastal emirates that it had exerted since the mid 1800s.

Chapter 2 is entitled "World War II and the arrival of the Americans," for it is during these war years that the United States military gets drawn for the first time into the Persian Gulf. American forces originally arrived to assist the British in delivering Lend-Lease supplies to their Russian allies. Americans constructed new roads and railroads to the Soviet Republics through the western portion of Iran, built many aircraft and truck assembly plants, and helped to produce and transport petrochemicals. During the middle of the war approximately 60,000 American civilians and uniformed personnel served in the region. Despite this enormous supply effort, however, when the conflict ended these logistics troops quickly returned home. The more long-lasting American influence stemmed less from these transport efforts, Herculean as they were, than from the very small number of military advisors that gained in World War II the trust of the monarchs in Iran and Saudi Arabia. Following the war, both Iranian and Saudi rulers turned to the United States for assistance in modernizing their military forces, in large part to stand better on their own, and to obviate long-standing British strength in the region. The presence in the region of American advisors, and later of American aid and military supplies, looms large in the post-war history of the Gulf, and at first raised the ire of leaders in London.

Chapter 3, "The early Cold War, the loss of India, and Nasser's revolt against the British," deals with the region during the decade and a half after World War II. One could rightly say that the Cold War erupted in one of the states bordering the Persian Gulf. Despite war promises to the contrary, the Soviets in 1946 refused to withdraw their troops from Iran. Coupled with other hostile actions in Europe, Moscow's behavior toward Tehran prompted Winston Churchill to give his famous "Iron Curtain" speech. America's historic disdain for the British Empire, however, quickly gave way to Washington's realization that London could take the lead in maintaining order in the greater Indian Ocean region. Rather than pushing for London to reduce its influence in these reaches, as FDR did during the war, subsequent presidents encouraged it, and eventually came to welcome British leadership in the Indian Ocean region.

The independence of the Indian subcontinent following the war, however, would turn upside down British involvement in the Persian Gulf, and would set in motion a chain of events that would ultimately lead in the early 1970s to London's withdrawal. Without India, Britain lost at the same time the strategic rationale for its presence in the region, the bulk of its military forces to defend it, as well as a source of financial wealth to pay for it all. The independence of India would also spark similar calls throughout the empire, which would spread across the globe. The British suffered setbacks in Suez, where an enormously popular Egyptian President Nasser succeeded in nationalizing the Suez Canal and chasing the British from their immense base at Suez, which since the late 1940s – after India's independence – served as the chief repository of London's military might for the region. The loss of another of Britain's sympathetic regimes, in Iraq, served as another blow. In spite of these losses, throughout this period London officials patched together various military basing schemes to fulfill Britain's commitments to the Persian Gulf's leaders, eventually choosing the base at Aden as the location for the strategic military reserve that they had lost in India.

Chapter 4, "The British position in the Gulf under assault," begins in the late 1950s with two related events: the British acceding to Kuwait's requests for autonomy, and London's response to Iraq's threats toward an independent Kuwait. If the independence of India cracked the British foundation in the Gulf, the actual British retrenchment started over a dozen years later, when in 1961, with London's blessing, Kuwait broke free. Shortly thereafter, however, the British would undergo a test of their ability to fulfill their remaining military and political commitments to the leaders of the region, when leaders of the Iraqi state threatened an invasion of neighboring Kuwait. A quick British response, however, drawing upon reserves in Aden and elsewhere, showed that Britain could and would fulfill a security role in the region, despite the loss of basing rights in revolutionary Egypt and Iraq. The Iraqis backed down. This successful British military operation became a blueprint throughout the 1960s for London's war plans in the region.

A growing nationalist insurgency in the southern portion of the Arabian Peninsula, however, supported by Nasser's Egypt, crippled Britain's ability to use the garrison base at Aden. It also brought into question how long the British would remain in the area, and whether or not they could support their military commitments to an independent Kuwait and to the other Persian Gulf emirates.

As Britain's position in Aden came under fire in the mid 1960s, some prescient officials on both sides of the Atlantic foresaw the importance of a new Anglo-American military base on the Indian Ocean archipelago of Diego Garcia. Despite its 3,000 mile distance from the northern reaches of the Gulf, the existence of such a base would ensure that Anglo-American forces could stage military operations from their own sovereign lands, not needing to heed the dictates of unreliable or unfriendly Arab or Persian clients. In a reflection of an Anglo-American difference in geo-political objectives, however, the U.S. Secretary of Defense refused to fund it, believing it would foster in London the mistaken belief that Washington stood ready and willing to assume Britain's security commitments in the Indian Ocean. The island remained largely unimproved for several years, unprepared for service when in the early 1970s leaders from both countries needed it desperately.

The empire-weary Labour Government's January 1968 decision to withdraw from "East of Suez" marks the beginning of Chapter 5, "Britain births a new Gulf order," which details London and Washington's actions from 1968–1971. Though Labour Party leaders entered office boasting that they would remain engaged around the world, throughout the 1960s they wrestled in a series of defense studies with a daunting trade-off: protect what remained of Britain's once-mighty overseas empire, or concentrate resources in Europe. These penetrating studies concluded that – sometime in the future, likely in about a decade – London should jettison its commitments East of Suez, and as with Kuwait several years earlier, set free the emirates of the Gulf. A series of devastating financial crunches, however, drove Prime Minister Harold Wilson to expedite that schedule, announcing in January 1968 that Britain would terminate most security commitments East of Suez, including those in the Persian Gulf, before the end of 1971. The announcement turned the Gulf upside down, for it came with virtually no advance warning to Arab or American allies. The century and a half of British stewardship of the Gulf would soon end, and no one knew what would follow it.

This chapter also discusses Washington's actions during these three critical years. After a period of initial shock and intense outrage in Washington, the Anglo-American relationship from 1968–1971 proved candid and open. The chapter details the philosophic development of the Nixon Doctrine, and Washington's deputizing of Iran and Saudi Arabia as the "Twin Pillars" to safeguard America's vital interests. Facing their own financial and political crisis in Vietnam – the Tet Offensive commenced in the same month as the "East of Suez" announcement – American officials refused to consider deploying forces to the Persian Gulf, despite entreaties and financial offers from local sheikhs. No longer would the United States "bear any burden" around the world.

Chapter 6, "The chaotic interregnum: America cries enough," discusses the Persian Gulf from 1972 to 1991, the period following British departure during which neither London nor Washington shepherded over the Persian Gulf. This two-decade period coincides, not coincidentally given the power vacuum that emerged, with a tumultuous string of setbacks for the West. After each of four major crises the superpower took an incremental but unplanned step in the direction of assuming the role that the British had abdicated in 1971. First, during the 1973 oil crisis, the U.S. began to deploy its navy combatant ships to the region, and started to provide modest funds to improve the island base on the Indian Ocean atoll of Diego Garcia. The U.S. had shied away from funding such a project during the previous decade, believing it would precipitate a British withdrawal. But with that feared outcome now a reality, U.S. leaders began to build up the island. The second step came later in the 1970s, following the collapse of the Shah's regime. President Carter's Administration crafted a rapid reaction military force to project power to the region, and invested heavily in air and sea lift. In what would become known as the Carter Doctrine, following the Soviet invasion of Afghanistan the U.S. president declared that his country would oppose with military might any attack on the region by outside forces, a dramatic reversal of the Vietnam-induced hesitancy to engage military forces there.

President Reagan took a third step during the Iran–Iraq War with his deployment to the Gulf of armed naval combatants to escort oil tankers through the region's troubled waters. Despite the assistance proffered to local states, however, Arab leaders proved unwilling to welcome the Americans to their shores. The U.S. military operated largely from barges anchored offshore in the Persian Gulf. When the Iran–Iraq War dissipated, the bulk of U.S. forces quickly returned home, leaving behind only the Navy's modest Middle East Force that had been there since the 1940s. Congressional leaders, who had opposed the Reagan initiative, breathed a sigh of relief. In the late 1980s the Arabs still were not willing to permit, nor was the superpower ready to assume, a permanent American presence in the Gulf. The fourth and final American move into the Gulf, from which it never stepped back, took place following the Iraqi invasion of Kuwait in 1990. Operation *Desert Storm*, led by America with unwavering support from Great Britain and a host of other nations, swept Saddam out of Kuwait. Following *Desert Storm* U.S. forces stayed in the Gulf, marking finally the U.S. assumption of the role that the British had served for a century and a half: security guarantors for the region. America was there to stay.

Chapter 7 is entitled *Pax Americana–Bellum Americanum*, 1991–present. The decade and a half following *Desert Storm* featured deep American diplomatic and military penetration into the Gulf region. After a two-decade absence in which no Western superpower maintained order in the region, Washington by 1991 had effectively replaced Britain as the arbiter of war and peace in the region.

The first few years after 1991's *Desert Storm* saw the "bureaucratization" of a much-expanded U.S. military and diplomatic presence in the Gulf. Although prior to the war President George H.W. Bush promised that American forces would depart immediately after evicting Saddam's forces from Kuwait, for two reasons Washington chose to keep a formidable military presence there, and construct an administrative and logistics infrastructure that would keep it there well into the future. First, in an effort to capitalize on post-*Desert Storm* pro-American goodwill in the Arab world, U.S. leaders seized the opportunity to procure a military foothold in the region, which since the Iranian Revolution over a decade before had proven unattainable. The small Arab coastal emirates that for a century and a half had flourished under British protection and patronage warmly, if quietly, accepted America's growing presence in the region.

The second reason that America's leaders kept a large military presence in the Gulf after *Desert Storm* surrounded an unforeseen development: the need to fight a low-intensity war against Saddam. What started as a short-term, Anglo-American effort to protect Iraqi Shia and Kurds from Saddam's reprisals effectively morphed into a semi-permanent U.S.-led aircraft campaign to enforce no-fly zones over Iraq. Like fish caught in tidal pools at low tide, American military forces – predominantly aircraft and their crews – for years remained at their *Desert Storm* postings, sometimes in exceptionally high-visibility locations in very sensitive spots. In xenophobic Saudi Arabia, uniformed American service members walked through the streets of Riyadh and Dhahran, seemingly oblivious to the hostile reaction that their presence provoked from conservative elements of Saudi society.

Not surprisingly, throughout the 1990s, open opposition to America's military presence in the Persian Gulf grew. This reaction proved most pronounced in Saudi Arabia, where opponents to America's presence in the kingdom exploded bombs in 1995 and 1996, killing Americans. One of the most vocal advocates for driving America from Islam's holy lands was Osama bin Laden, leader of the terror group al-Qaeda. The genesis of a growing conservative backlash in the Gulf against America stemmed in part from the American decision to keep large numbers of troops in Saudi Arabia to fight the ongoing low-intensity conflict against Saddam.

The low-intensity conflict against Saddam became a high-intensity conflict in 2003 when Anglo-American forces invaded Iraq. The axis between London and Washington – as it had been since shortly after Britain's announcement of its abandoning the Gulf in 1968 – proved close and cooperative, with Prime Minister Tony Blair and President George W. Bush leading an international campaign to forcibly overthrow Saddam's regime. Neither side, however, entered the conflict envisioning the maladies that would beset them after their invasion; it took several years before a change of generals and the adoption of a new counter-insurgency military strategy quelled the unrest in Iraq. Noting the fact that since *Desert Storm* Washington has largely determined issues of war and peace in the Gulf region, the period following 1991 can rightfully be called a period of "Pax Americana–Bellum Americanum".

1 Great Britain's legacy in the Persian Gulf

The Persian Gulf is a remote body of water whose importance to Western powers over the centuries has vastly exceeded its size. An appendage of the Arabian Sea and the Indian Ocean, it stretches 600 miles in a northwesterly direction, from its mouth at the Strait of Hormuz to its headwaters at the Shatt al Arab, the river that separates Iran and Iraq. This Gulf separates two noble societies. To the south, on the Arabian Peninsula, live the Arabs. This is the holy land of Islam, the place in which the Prophet Muhammed in the 7th century CE received the revealed word of God, and from which – in an amazing display of faith and fury – his followers set out to conquer and convert what remained of the Roman and Persian empires. To the north live the Iranians, also Muslims, but of a different stock. Speaking an Indo-European rather than a Semitic tongue, the Iranians claim a proud Persian heritage that stretches back over two millennia to Kings Cyrus, Darius, and Xerxes. Although thought by some to be the Biblical Garden of Eden, today the Arab and Persian lands surrounding the Gulf are dusty, hot, and humid. Arable land is scarce. Salt flats and barren plains stretch for miles along the southern shore; forbidding mountains arise from the northern coast. The Arabs have been cheated of deep, navigable water on their side of the Gulf; the flatlands ashore stretch underwater for miles, providing a dearth of natural ports. Iranian sailors have fared somewhat better; the natural deepwater channel through the Gulf hugs their northern shore, for example, but they too lack abundant havens from the sea, and hundreds of miles pass between good ports. Despite this paucity of harbors, however, the Gulf region sits athwart the trade and communication routes that bind Europe, Africa, and Asia. For centuries this strategic location, coupled the past 100 years with the discovery of oil, has made the Gulf a possession over which Western nations tangled. The Europeans arrived over five centuries ago, however, not to capture oil, nor to conquer, but rather to guard and to police. And though others preceded them, it would be the British who would stay for years, profoundly shaping the Persian Gulf region, and using surprisingly little force to impose their will.

The first Europeans enter the Gulf

Europeans had known for centuries of the exotic lands and riches to the east. As that continent's residents awoke from the darkness of the Middle Ages, increasingly affluent buyers sought China's and India's fine silks, bright fabrics, enchanting jewels, and zesty spices. Portugal proved the first of several western nations that would dominate the Persian Gulf region. When Vasco da Gama rounded Africa's Cape of Good Hope and continued onward to India in 1498, he opened for Portugal a century and a half during which the tiny state played an imposing role in Asia and the Persian Gulf.[1]

In the century that followed, the Portuguese used their European technology and military might to dominate the Indian Ocean and Persian Gulf region. Throughout the sixteenth century the Portuguese set up trading posts and fortifications in the Persian Gulf region, stretching from the Yemeni coast, northward to Muscat, thence along the Gulf coast in what is now the United Arab Emirates, Bahrain, Saudi Arabia, and Iran. They imposed direct rule in parts of the region.[2]

As the larger Atlantic powers discovered the sea, however, Lisbon's power

Figure 1 Portuguese castle on Hormuz Island, Iran.

The Portuguese were the first Europeans to arrive in the Persian Gulf. The small Atlantic nation's early leadership in the Age of Discovery led Portuguese sailors to the Indian Ocean region in the late 1400s. During the 16th and 17th centuries the Portuguese constructed or rebuilt coastal fortifications like this one.

and influence in Asia came under attack. The English challenged the Portuguese, and in concert with Persian allies, drove them in the first half of the 1600s from their stronghold at Hormuz. As Portuguese power waned, the commercial activities of the English, Dutch, and French increased.

Britain prevails over European rivals in India. From the early seventeenth century European companies, tied closely to their home states, battled for primacy on the Indian subcontinent. In the 1600s the English, French, Dutch, Danes, and Swedes all had companies trading there.[3] The scope of operations of these companies exceeded what one might expect multi-national corporations to engage in today, and sometimes took on roles akin to sovereign states. They engaged in acts of diplomacy, and pursued exclusive economic treaties and political relationships with south Asia's rulers. They often hired and managed their own military forces, officered normally by Europeans but staffed by local hires. When necessary, the companies engaged in military action against Asian leaders or their European competitors. The companies' leaders ultimately received direction from shareholders as well as government officials back in Europe; the governance of these large trading companies became intertwined with the policies of the home state. In the seventeenth and eighteenth centuries the British gradually gained a paramount position in India.[4] Maintaining their supremacy there ultimately provided the philosophic rationale for the nation's entry into the Persian Gulf.

Britain secures approaches to India. Like the Portuguese who fortified the seaborne route to India, the British found themselves concerned with protecting the strategic flanks to their lucrative Indian colony. Commencing in the late 1700s the British took control of critical chokepoints leading to the Indian Ocean. In the 1790s, for example, they snatched from the Dutch the seaborne entryway from the Atlantic, South Africa's Cape Colony. Shortly thereafter they took the distant Pacific gate to India, Malacca, and several decades later established a colony and military garrison at Singapore. The possession of these distant chokepoints allowed Britain to prevent rivals from threatening India from the sea, while at the same time allowing London to influence and control travel and trade between the continents.

At about the same time, political events in Europe prompted the British to look toward the Persian Gulf region. Napoleon's invasion of Egypt in 1798 gave rise to fears in London that the French might move into the weak states of the Gulf region and, using the Persian Gulf and Red Sea routes, threaten India. The Arab lands bordering on the Persian Gulf, as well as Persia and Afghanistan began to loom large in British minds.

The Persian Gulf in the early 1800s proved a place of disorder. Arab and Persian notables there fought for primacy. On the eastern side, Qajar dynasty leaders proved weak, like their Arab neighbors across the Gulf. Wahhabi puritan zealots burst forth from their Arabian desert strongholds in what is now Saudi Arabia. Fighting spilled over into maritime attacks on shipping from India, and also disrupted the lucrative pearling season. Seaborne brigands exploited the lack of central authority in the region, and worked from the shallow waters of the southern Gulf, leading the British later to refer to the region as the "Pirate Coast."[5]

Into these troubled waters in the early 1800s sailed the ships of the Royal Navy and the British-run Indian Navy, ushering in a period of over a century and a half in which British rulers used a modest amount of military force – primarily naval – to suppress piracy and the slave trade, and to promote peace amongst the Gulf's warring factions, while at the same time keeping at bay Britain's Great Power foes who cast covetous eyes toward India.

The British maintain order with a small military and diplomatic force

With colonial interests and demands all over the world, the British for most of the nineteenth century deployed to the Persian Gulf region only a handful of naval ships.[6] Working hand-in-hand with a cadre of British diplomats representing the Indian Government, however, this combination proved able to suppress piracy and to enforce truces between the warring parties of the Arabian coast. How did they do it? With a mixture of good intelligence collection, skilled negotiations, credible naval deterrence, and gunboat diplomacy. When confronted by Great Power foes, furthermore, British leaders did not hesitate to employ the British Indian Army. Behind London's success

Figure 2 British military punitive raid against Arabian pirates, Ras al Khaima, 1809.

Sketch by Major R. Temple of H.M. 65th Regiment, illustrative of the forces employed on an expedition sent from Bombay against Arab pirates, November 1809.

in maintaining order in the Persian Gulf region, then, ultimately stood the forces of the Indian subcontinent.

Accounts of some early nineteenth century British naval journeys in the Persian Gulf illuminate roles the British military forces fulfilled. One account, for example, describes the value of the intelligence that naval forces collected, details how the British negotiated, and shows how little the British really coveted the region for its own sake. In an 1831 letter to a naval leader at sea, the British Resident in Bushire writes:

> The reports of the proceedings of the vessels of war which have visited the Arabian Coast within the last two months are highly satisfactory, and the intelligence communicated therein of the conclusion of a truce between the chiefs of Ras Al Khaymah and Aboothabi [Abu Dhabi] most gratifying. The amicable relations now entered into by those two powers will, by permitting their respective subjects to turn their entire attention to the pearl fishing, obviate all these evils which would unquestionably have arisen had the sole means of subsistence to so many thousand individuals been cut off by the continuance of hostilities . . .
>
> There can be no doubt that the vigilant watch maintained by our vessels of war, must give very considerable weight to the pacific opinions which I trust are gradually disseminating themselves in the minds of the Maritime Arabs.[7]

In most cases the British achieved their political goals with the simple presence of a man-o-war, although when that failed their naval crews occasionally applied more extreme forms of coercion. The port blockade served as one option, for example, which British crews could impose by force, using "such exertions . . . in enforcing it as you may deem practicable."[8] In other situations, when a local Arab had plundered a British commercial vessel, for example, the Resident directed the naval leaders to go ashore to apprehend the guilty party, or demand from the appropriate tribal leader a monetary sum.[9]

Should a foe ashore still not submit to Britain's will, however, the naval vessels might open fire. One 1820 letter discussed the optimal weapons for retaliating against a wayward Arab ashore who had offended the Crown, including "cruizers" with 10-pound long guns, "luggage boats to be fitted with gun and mortar boats," and 8 inch "howitzers."[10] At every step the British made a conscious effort to convince the Gulf locals that further reinforcement lay just over the horizon, and that any attempt to resist the will of the Crown would ultimately lead to their own destruction. Capturing the essence of this philosophy, the British Resident in 1832 makes clear that an offending Arab must be made to understand that "strong measures are sure to follow and that there is no release except in ultimate submission."[11]

The naval forces plying the Persian Gulf waters in the 1800s and early 1900s, of course, did not possess unlimited authority, and they operated with

Figure 3 Entrance to British Persian Gulf Residency at Bushire, Iran, c. 1870.

A Political Resident and his small staff working from the coastal town of Bushire, Iran (after World War II, from Bahrain), along with Political Agents throughout the region, aided Britain in maintaining order in the region and dissuading other Great Powers from entering. (The British Library Board. All Rights Reserved June 2009, 355/1(34) British Library).

guidance from British leaders in India and London. Overall strategic naval policy for the Persian Gulf emerged from a dialog between the Government of India, the Foreign Office, and the Admiralty. The Commander in Chief of the East Indies Station, in turn, controlled naval affairs over a vast expanse that stretched from the Red Sea to China.[12] Navy crews normally arrived in the Gulf with general orders from Bombay, but often accepted specific direction and tasking from the British Resident in Bushire, who provided intelligence targets, assigned ports to blockade, or identified individuals to apprehend.

The Gulf Resident in Bushire, then, played a critical role in military affairs of the Persian Gulf, and his duties proved expansive, akin in some respects to those of an ambassador.[13] The Resident served as a representative in the Persian Gulf of the British Government of India. He worked to protect commerce transiting to and from the subcontinent, to suppress piracy in the Persian Gulf, and to negotiate treaties with the coastal warring parties. The Resident, in other words, served as the Indian Government's chief official in the Gulf's littoral region. By the early twentieth century the Resident had two subordinate Agents, in Bahrain and Kuwait.[14] The Residents, however, were *not* ambassadors, and beginning in 1821 the British Government had both an ambassador in Tehran, who reported to the Foreign Office in London, as well as a Resident in Bushire who reported to India. Of the two, the Resident proved more involved than the ambassador in maritime Gulf affairs, and served as the principal official interacting with people on the Arab side of the Gulf. This system of Residents and Agents who reported back to India would prove a hallmark of British diplomacy in the Persian Gulf through World War II.

Aden. In the age of sail, a ship could journey largely independently, limited only by the provisions that her crew carried. With the advent of steam propulsion in the mid 1800s, however, oceanic travel required large numbers of coaling stations to feed the ships' steam plants. In 1839 the British took control of the port of Aden, on Yemen's southern shores.[15] The British facility over the next century and a half would play a critical role in the projection of European power to the Persian Gulf region. Later in the twentieth century, in the aftermath of India's independence, it would become Britain's strategic military garrison in the Indian Ocean. For the majority of the 1800s and early 1900s, however, it remained a coaling and refueling point, particularly important for ships transiting the Suez Canal.

Origin of the first treaties. Britain's close involvement in the Persian Gulf thus began in the first half of the 1800s, when Britain began to conclude treaties with Arab sheikhs. In 1820, for example, several sheikhs signed with Britain "General Treaties of Peace."[16] Further treaties followed: the "First Maritime Truce," signed by the Assistant Resident in 1835, mandated a "cessation of hostilities at sea between our respective subjects and dependents [or] we will immediately afford full redress. . . ."[17] It should be noted that the British proved most concerned with events on the seas, not ashore. Initially the British harbored no ambition, and actually aimed to steer clear of any entrapments on land that might involve having to favor one leader or group over another.[18]

Later in the nineteenth century and into the twentieth, Britain's involvement in the Persian Gulf grew, with the British providing security to favored ruling families in the region in return for submitting to London's will. The number of agreements with local leaders multiplied. The British signed pacts, for example, with the rulers of Bahrain in 1880, Kuwait in 1899, and Qatar in 1916.[19] What started in the first half of the 1800s as mediation between independent battling tribes had evolved by the early 1900s into British security guarantees to selected Arab rulers. Although the specifics of these agreements varied, sheikhs essentially passed to Britain the right to handle interstate diplomacy and military affairs, and in return received protection, under Britain's security umbrella, from attacks by their neighbors.

In 1903 Lord Curzon, Viceroy of India, visited the Persian Gulf for the first time, and formally annunciated Britain's policy toward the region: Great Britain did not aim to control the Gulf, but rather to maintain order there. Confessing self-interest, Lord Curzon explained to assembled Arab tribal chiefs:

Chiefs, your fathers and grandfathers before you have doubtless told you of the history of the past. You know that a hundred years ago there was constant trouble and fighting in the Gulf; almost every man was a marauder or a pirate; kidnapping and slave-trading flourished; fighting and bloodshed went on without stint or respite; no ship could put out to sea without fear of attack; the pearl fishery was a scene of annual conflict; and security of trade or peace there was none. Then it was that the British Government intervened and said that, in the interests of its own subjects and traders, and of its legitimate influence in the seas that wash the Indian coasts, this state of affairs must not continue. British flotillas appeared in these waters. British forces occupied the forts and towns on the coast that we see from this deck. ... In 1820 the first general Treaty was signed between the British government and the Chiefs; ... until the year 1853, when it was succeeded by the Treaty of Perpetual Peace that has lasted ever since. ... In the event of aggressions on any one by sea, the injured parties should not retaliate, but should refer the matter to the British Resident in the Persian Gulf; and that the British Government should watch over the peace of the Gulf and ensure at all times the observance of the Treaty. Chiefs, that Treaty has not, of course, prevented occasional trouble and conflict; it has sometimes been neglected or infringed; but on the whole it has well deserved its name; and under it has grown up a condition of affairs so peaceful and secure that the oldest among you can only remember as a dim story the events of the past, while the younger have never seen warfare or bloodshed on the seas. ...[20]

In short, as Curzon proclaimed in that speech, "The British Government should watch over the peace of the Gulf. ..."

Britain takes on other Great Powers in the Persian Gulf

Turkestan, Afghanistan, Transcapia, Persia – to many these names breathe only a sense of utter remoteness or a memory of strange vicissitudes and of moribund romance. To me, I confess, they are the pieces on a chessboard upon which is being played out a game for the dominion of the world.[21]

(Lord George Curzon, 1892)

The British in the late 1800s recognized that India served as the foundation of their empire's greatness, and that maintaining control of the subcontinent – and all its gateways, including the Persian Gulf – proved of paramount importance. As Lord Curzon suggested above, from the British vantage, the key to defending India lay in the Asian lands surrounding India; specifically, keeping those lands free of other Great Power rivals. The might of the vaunted Royal Navy could defend India on the high seas. But Great Britain

Figure 4 Lord Curzon's party arrives ashore in Kuwait on the backs of natives, 1903.

historically had not proved a land power. Afghanistan, Persia, and Anatolia thus became battlegrounds in the nineteenth century as Britain countered Russia and later Germany. The Persian Gulf region grew in importance, and suppressing piracy and protecting maritime trade to India became relatively less important than the growing grand military and strategic interstate contest for control of the states buffering India.

The Great Game against Russia. Russian forces in the middle 1800s moved southward into the Caucasus and Central Asia. Britain perceived this as a threat to their interests, particularly their primacy in India. Afghanistan, Persia, and the Ottoman Empire thus became British–Russian battlegrounds in what has become known as the "Great Game," a duel of diplomatic, strategic, and sometimes military confrontations.[22]

Persia became a key arena in the Great Game, and Britain took military action twice in the state in the nineteenth century to reduce Russia's influence there. In 1838, for example, the British deployed 500 Indian sepoys (troops) and Indian Navy ships to the Gulf to dissuade the Shah from moving his forces eastward into Herat, Afghanistan, which the British believed would further Russian interests. Although the British forces there never directly confronted those of the Czar, the prime motivation in the expedition surrounded the desire to contain Russian influence in the region.[23]

Almost two decades later, further Persian adventures evoked a similar, but more aggressive, British response. In the Persian War of 1856–57, a British

Figure 5 Arab sheikhs assemble to hear Lord Curzon, on board Royal Indian Marine
Ship (RIMS) *Argonaut*, in Sharjah, 1903.

The Indian Viceroy summarized British aims in the Persian Gulf: "The British
Government should watch over the peace of the Gulf.. . ." In 1903 the British Viceroy
in India visited the Persian Gulf for the first time, and stated that Britain's policy
toward the region was not to control it, but rather to maintain order there: "Chiefs,
your fathers and grandfathers before you have doubtless told you of the history of the
past. You know that a hundred years ago there was constant trouble and fighting in
the Gulf; almost every man was a marauder or a pirate; kidnapping and slave-trading
flourished; fighting and bloodshed went on without stint or respite; no ship could put
out to sea without fear of attack; the pearl fishery was a scene of annual conflict; and
security of trade or peace there was none. Then it was that the British Government
intervened . . . . " (© The British Library Board. All Rights Reserved June 2009,
49/1(7)).

Army general based in Bombay led more than 5,000 Indian and British
troops, transported in over 45 naval vessels, to Persia, aiming to stop the
Shah's continued military adventures in Afghanistan.[24] After an initial ren-
dezvous at Bandar Abbas, the force sailed up the Gulf and took Kharaq
Island without opposition, then put ashore a landing force to take Bushire.
Unlike the 1838 expedition, however, the British penetrated further inland,
in what has been called the first major campaigning in southern Persia by
a European army since Alexander the Great.[25] The British fought inland
to take Mohammerah and Abadan Island in northeastern Khuzistan (in
which British oil prospectors would later discover oil), fighting against the
forces of the Shah, who had proclaimed a *jihad* for the defense of Islam
against Christian invaders.[26] The Shah's forces fled, and a victorious Britain

successfully forced the Shah to renounce his claims on Herat, Afghanistan, leading to a negotiated peace in 1857.

The Ottoman Turks in the Gulf. In addition to the Great Game confrontation against the Russians, the British in the nineteenth century also squared off against their former allies the Ottoman Turks, who for centuries had maintained loose control over much of the Middle East, including Mesopotamia and the Red Sea littorals of the Arabian Peninsula. The Ottomans first burst into the greater Middle East in the 1400s and 1500s, establishing a multi-ethnic empire stretching from the coast of North Africa to the deserts of Iraq, from the forests of Austria to the sands and waters of the Red Sea and Persian Gulf. Inside the Gulf, Ottoman sway crept southward along the coast into the date-rich agricultural region of Hasa, brushing against the northern reaches of Portuguese influence.

Ottoman control proved uneven on the Arabian Peninsula, however, and outside of Mesopotamia and the Red Sea coast it proved in spots non-existent. South of Qatar on the Gulf coast, for example, Ottoman influence ended and that of Muscat and Oman prevailed. By the 1700s, of the local Gulf powers, Oman dominated the southern Gulf, occupying the Mussandem peninsula, the strategically valuable southern gate to the Strait of Hormuz, as well as Persia's premier port, Bandar Abbas; Oman's reach extended as far as Zanzibar on the African coast. Nor did the Ottomans control the sparsely populated Hadramaut region, on the Gulf of Aden between Yemen and Oman. Even in Hasa, on the Gulf coast between Qatar and Kuwait, Ottoman rule lacked deep roots. When the Portuguese challenge disintegrated in the mid 1600s Istanbul turned its attention elsewhere, and essentially ignored the Hasa region.[27] Ottoman power never held for more than temporary periods in the vast deserts of Arabia, where for centuries local and tribal leaders fought amongst themselves for power, riches, and control over water sources and trade routes. In practice, Ottoman authority in the Persian Gulf region extended only as far as the reach of the garrisons, and beyond that Istanbul's sway gave way to local control.

The interior of the inhospitable Arabian Peninsula, in particular, proved largely immune to Ottoman influence, and from its depths would spring a puritanical and militant movement that would supplant Ottoman rule there by the early 1900s. Wahhabi Islam rose in the sands of the Nejd desert, a region where Ottoman troops had never maintained control for extended periods of time. In the late 1700s a religious visionary, Muhammed Ibn Adul Wahhab, found in the Saud family a willing ally. Saudi warriors embraced the cleric's teachings of a unitary God, cleansed from centuries of accretions that included saint worship, and in return, the clerics provided religious justification to the expansionist Saudi state. In a partnership that continues today, the marriage of Saudi power with Wahhabi teachings proved a powerful unifying force, and after two setbacks in the 1800s, King Abdul Aziz, commonly known in the West as Ibn Saud, in the early 1900s reclaimed the Arabian Peninsula, driving out Ottomans and other Arab foes alike.

Once allied to London, Ottomans become British foes. At first glance, the British and the Ottomans would appear natural allies, for both shared a mutual interest in stopping Russia's southward march. Throughout the first half of the 1800s this alignment of interests led to Britain's general support for the Sublime Porte in Istanbul, and underlay London's alliance in the 1850s with the Ottomans in the Crimean War against a potent Russia, and again in the 1878 Russo-Turkish War. At the 1878 Berlin Conference Britain went so far as to promise to respect the territorial integrity of the Ottomans' Asiatic possessions. For several reasons, however, as the nineteenth century waned and the twentieth century approached, Istanbul's and London's interests diverged and tensions rose. Indebted Ottoman rulers, for example, along with other beleaguered leaders throughout the Muslim world, turned to English bankers for economic assistance. The financial constraints that accompanied Western lending, including control over customs duties, however, led to growing involvement in domestic affairs by Westerners, fueling resentment against the most visible lender, Britain.[28]

This Ottoman resentment against Britain was matched by Ottoman military efforts starting in the 1870s to re-claim Persian Gulf domains over which British control in the 1800s grew. Starting in that decade the Ottomans moved southward into the Persian Gulf's Hasa region, in an attempt to re-assert their authority over the coastal region as well as Kuwait, Bahrain, and Qatar. A growing fear of British power, as well as a desire to create a "bulwark" against foreign encroachment, underlay the move. The Ottoman effort began with the successful occupation of Hasa (modern-day Saudi Arabia's east coast) in 1871, but subsequent designs on the small emirates of the Gulf ultimately met with failure. Arab rulers of these small lands proved adept at playing the British against the Ottomans to their own advantage. Navies and armies from British India and Istanbul faced each other down but an all-out hot war between London and Istanbul did not erupt in the 1800s.

In the end, the ruling Sabah family of Kuwait, the Khalifah of Bahrain, and the Al-Thani of Qatar by the early twentieth century had chosen association with Britain rather than with their nominal Ottoman rulers. In the eyes of these Arabs, British leaders had proven over the course of several decades disinterested in administering affairs ashore, and they found this preferable to submission to Istanbul. Coastal Arab rulers concluded treaties with Britain, some secret and some public, that cemented London as the dominant power in nominally Ottoman lands, paradoxically while Britain still professed the territorial integrity of the Ottoman Empire, and while Kuwait, Bahrain, and Qatar remained nominally part of it. By the dawn of World War I, then, Ottoman claims to the coastal stretches of the Gulf proved hollow. The Ottoman Empire's cozying-up to Berlin, coupled with Britain's growing dependence upon oil, would bring London in World War I into a clash with Istanbul.

Britain and Germany in the Gulf. Great Powers rise and fall, sometimes with great speed. Up-and-coming nations often clamor for increased roles in the world commensurate with their growing economic and military power, eliciting opposition from existing powers.[29] Such was the case in the late 1800s as European leaders struggled to adjust to the explosive growth of Germany's power, whose bold leaders sought the spoils that other Great Powers enjoyed: colonies, favored trading blocs, and business opportunities, including railroad concessions around the world. Not surprisingly, Germany's hyperbolic climb in power met with fear, apprehension, and opposition in European capitals. In one of the great readjustments in world alliances of the past two centuries, in the late 1800s and early 1900s Britain, France, and Russia's mutual antagonisms began to fade as their new German foe grew stronger.

The growth of German power in the Persian Gulf manifested itself in part in a drive to construct railways in the region, stoking fears in London and India of Berlin's ultimate designs in one of the ancient gateways to India.[30] German businessmen aimed to construct several projects in the region, the most significant of which was a Berlin-to-Baghdad railroad, with a final terminus on the Persian Gulf coast in either Basra or Kuwait. The German railway projects were viewed by Britain as more significant than just transportation issues: they represented a threat to British hegemony in the Gulf region.

For their part, Ottoman leaders had concluded that their interests coincided with those of Germany over Britain. The Sultan and his advisors believed that granting a concession to Berlin for a rail line all the way to Kuwait might simultaneously strengthen Istanbul's claim on the emirate, while at the same time making it appreciably easier to bring troops to the region. Both sides believed it to be a mutually beneficial relationship. As historian Frederick Anscombe aptly concluded, "Just as the sultan hoped to use Germany to reattach Kuwait to his empire, the Germans and others wanted to use the Ottomans to confound the British."[31]

The British used their considerable financial power to forestall German penetration of the Persian Gulf. Ottoman financial woes had led to substantial borrowing from British lenders, who had earned a voice in setting tariff and customs duties, the only dependable sources of Ottoman revenue. In the case of the railroad, Ottoman officials needed British consent to raise funds. The British demanded substantial concessions, such as a large stake in the venture. Germany balked at Britain's demands, and the railway line to Kuwait was not built before World War I.

In addition to a growing presence on the western side of the Gulf, the British – along with their former arch-enemies the Russians – also moved into Persia, a nation paralyzed in the early 1900s by financial and political chaos.[32] The sclerotic Qajar dynasty was dying in Persia, and the Shah's regime proved unable to provide for its people the fruits of the modern world. Discontent grew. As it had in the Ottoman lands, the infusion into Persia of ideas like consensual government and elections had led to increasing calls for reforms. Coupled with general displeasure from both the Shia clerical class and the urban merchants, a movement arose to demand from the Shah a political assembly. When the Shah faced a political uprising in which thousands of subjects took refuge – *bast* – in Western consular offices, he ultimately relented. British officials helped to draft a new Persian Constitution, in which power – along the Western model – flowed from the people.[33] The leaders of the elected Majlis that emerged, however, could not possibly solve overnight decades of political fumbling and financial mismanagement. Public order and safety broke down. British diplomats reported bread riots in the streets.[34]

Into this disintegrating state British and Russian forces entered to maintain order, and to ensure that debts were paid. In previous years bankers from the two states had helped to keep the penurious Qajar regime solvent; these influential businessmen wielded power, and demanded a large voice in the affairs of the country. In the chaos and disruption that marked the first decade of the twentieth century in Persia, Britain and Russia in 1907 signed an "Anglo-Russian Convention," which essentially divided the country into a British zone in the southeast bordering India, a Russian zone in the north, and neutral zone in the south bordering the Persian Gulf.[35] From the British perspective this was not a conquest of a nation as much as a move to ensure the efficient collection of taxes, to retire the administration's debts.[36] It had, to be sure, the added benefit to Britain of expanding the buffer to India.

Thus, by the first years of the twentieth century the fear of Germany had driven three implacable foes, Britain, Russia and France, into alliance, as symbolized by 1907's Triple Entente. The Great Game contest between Britain and Russia in the Persian Gulf environs would ultimately become subsumed by the conflict that turned the world, and the Gulf region, upside down: World War I.

World War I ushers in greater British involvement in the Persian Gulf region

On the eve of World War I, then, Britain maintained a dominant position throughout the Persian Gulf region. In Persia, British bankers had lent previous rulers enormous sums of money, and had received a large voice in the affairs of state. Although not in military occupation of the country, Britain and Russia possessed complementing spheres of influence, in which the collection of revenues became a top priority. On the opposite shore of the Gulf, the British enjoyed preferred positions in the emirates of Kuwait, Bahrain, and Qatar, which remained nominally under Ottoman control but in practice more closely aligned with Britain. On the mainland, the forces of Ibn Saud challenged the Ottomans, and in the harsh desert interior of Nejd, Ottoman power proved virtually non-existent. On the western side of the peninsula, however, on the Red Sea coast, the Ottoman client rulers, the Hashemites, continued to rule. In Aden, as well as the surrounding Arabian lands between Yemen and Oman, the British dominated. And, throughout the region, the British continued to stem the growth of German influence.

During the first years of the twentieth century the British gained another reason to safeguard their position in the Gulf: oil. As steam engine technology developed throughout the 1800s, European and American engineers sought new ways to power larger vessels for further distances. The dominant fossil fuel, coal, proved heavy, and required strings of coaling stations around the world, like that at Aden. Experimental work in engines powered by liquid petroleum, however, offered promise of longer ship legs, lighter weight, additional speed, and smaller crew sizes.[37]

Royal Navy converts to oil. In the years before World War I Sir Winston Churchill, First Lord of the Admiralty, drawing upon the expertise of Sir Jackie Fisher, former First Sea Lord, successfully pushed to convert the Royal Navy's fleet to oil, which ultimately made the Persian Gulf a region of high value to Britain. As long as Royal Navy ships burned coal, the British had nothing to fear, for their coal reserves proved abundant. The discovery and development of oil by British concerns in the early years of the twentieth century in western Persia, therefore, was viewed as a way to maintain self-sufficiency in oil, of which Britain possessed very little. The British Government later snatched up a dominant interest in the Anglo-Persian Oil Company that controlled these reserves and oil fields, making possession of these lands at the head of the Persian Gulf an issue of vital strategic importance, above and beyond their historic significance as a gateway to India.

Figure 6 Knocking off time at Abadan refinery, Iran, c. 1910–1930.

The Persian Gulf's importance grew in early 20th century, due to Britain's burgeoning oil interests in western Persia. The oil fields north of Britain's refinery at Abadan (pictured above in the early 20th century) became a strategic British national interest, especially after the Royal Navy converted from coal to oil.

In November 1914, three months after Britain entered the war against Germany, London declared war on the Ottoman Empire,[38] whose leaders in Istanbul had thrown their lot in with Berlin. The British war against the Ottoman Empire played itself out in three principal theaters: an ultimately futile amphibious drive through the Dardenelles toward Istanbul, known as the Gallipoli campaign; a victorious push by General Allenby, starting from Egypt and moving northeastward into Palestine and Syria; and a Pyrrhic but ultimately successful three-year campaign from the Persian Gulf into Mesopotamia. This thrust into modern-day Iraq would shape subsequent British involvement in the Gulf for decades.

From the earliest days of World War I the British viewed as a necessity deploying forces from India to the Persian Gulf region.[39] Admiralty officials, in particular, felt it important to protect the nation's oil industry in western Persia, specifically the Anglo-Persian Oil Company's refinery on Abadan Island and the miles of pipelines that connected it to the oil fields in Shustar.[40] The Persian Gulf region, as it had through the nineteenth century, fell under the purview of the Indian Government. During the three months that the war raged in Europe prior to the entry of the Ottomans, however, the British Indian Government deemed it unwise to deploy troops to the Gulf, fearing that any outbreak of hostilities with the Muslim Ottomans might provoke a backlash amongst the Indian Muslim population. Immediately after the declaration of war with the Ottomans in November 1914, however, the British deployed an Indian force to the Persian Gulf and occupied the oil-rich lands in western Persia, as well as Basra in what is now southern Iraq, which in the mind of a British war officer stood as "the key to Mesopotamia."[41]

With the oil fields secured, many British officials believed that the mission in the Gulf was accomplished, and that the superpower should go no further. What would today be called "mission creep," however, set in, drawing the British into a long, costly, and controversial campaign to take Baghdad. Some prominent British leaders in the Persian Gulf, notably Colonel Percy Cox,[42] later a Major General instrumental in Britain's administration of wartime Iraq and later minister to Persia, argued that Britain must parlay victory in Basra into a successful march 500 miles northwards into the heart of Mesopotamia. Scarcely six of the Ottomans' 52 wartime divisions, however, rested in the Mesopotamian theater, making it highly unlikely that any British victory there would lead to a strategic triumph in the wider war. Despite this, the British embarked on what would turn out to be an enormously costly three-year campaign to seize Baghdad. The northward drive stumbled, and included a disastrous capitulation at Al Kut, one of the most humiliating setbacks in British military history. At the end of 1917 the British finally stormed Baghdad, but at an enormous cost: 60,000 British lives, and the efforts of over 300,000 men.[43] It also marked the beginning of over four decades in which London's influence dominated one of the large states of the Persian Gulf, its own creation known as Iraq.[44] During those years Britain used a combination of air power and tribal levies, in conjunction with political advisors, to shape the state.[45]

World War I also shaped the relationship between Britain and Abdul Aziz (Ibn Saud), the Saudi prince who had defeated both his tribal rivals in the desert and Ottoman foes in coastal Hasa. Because of his designs on Qatar and Bahrain, however, the British had proven wary of Ibn Saud. In spite of this concern, wartime necessity drove the British to secure alliances with several anti-Ottoman forces, and in a 1915 treaty with Ibn Saud, the British recognized his suzerainty over central and eastern Arabia, so long as he refrained from dallying with other European powers, and abstained from attacks on the coastal emirates that Britain dominated:

> The British Government does acknowledge and admit that Najd, El Hasa, Qataf and Jubail, and their dependencies and territories . . . and their ports on the shores of the Persian Gulf, are the countries of Bin Saud and of his fathers before him, and do hereby recognize the said Bin Saud as the Independent Ruler thereof and absolute Chief of their tribes, and after him his sons and descendants by inheritance . . . but with the proviso that he shall not be a person antagonistic to the British Government in any respect. . . .
>
> Bin Saud hereby agrees and promises to refrain from entering into

Figure 7 British-Indian troops in Mesopotamia man World War I anti-aircraft gun.

Although a small diplomatic and naval presence proved able to maintain order amongst the warring local parties in the Persian Gulf, defeating Great Powers in the region required the use of the Indian Army. Indian troops man a Lewis gun on an anti-aircraft mounting in Mesopotamia. Troops can be seen in the rear taking shelter in trenches.

any correspondence, agreement, or treaty, with any Foreign Nation or Power. . . .

Bin Saud undertakes, as his fathers did before him, to refrain from all aggression on, or interference with, the territories of Kuwait, Bahrain, and of the Shaikhs of Qatar and the Oman Coast, who are under the protection of the British Government. . . .[46]

The Anglo-Saudi relationship, however, would ultimately not prove as deep as Britain's relationships with other Gulf states. Although the British continued paying a subsidy to Ibn Saud for decades, and would increase it after World War I to soften his opposition to the establishment of Hashemite monarchies around him, the British military at no time occupied the expanding Saudi desert domain. In all of his dealings with the Great Powers, from World War I up to his death in 1953, the Saudi king would prove extremely shrewd, sensitive to any agreements or actions that would diminish sovereignty over his kingdom's territory. In part to curb the dominant power of the British in the region, Saudi King Abdul Aziz Ibn Saud, furthermore, in the early 1930s would choose the Americans over the British to develop the Kingdom's oil resources.

Mesopotamia was not the only British theater of operations in the Gulf in World War I, for British forces also fought and proved victorious in neighboring Persia, one of the less remembered theaters of World War I.[47] German agents and officers had penetrated the state, recruiting from the Persian population irregular forces, including many from the Swedish-officered "Gendarmerie," the national police force. While Russian forces entered the northern part of Persia to engage Turkish forces there, a British force under the direction of Sir Percy Sykes marched into Bandar Abbas in March 1916. Along with a mix of British, Indian, and locally recruited Persian forces, Sykes occupied many towns in the western portion of Persia, securing the eastern flanks of the British campaign in Mesopotamia.[48] When revolutionary Russia withdrew from World War I, Britain's forces moved northward, citing the need to prevent Turko-German moves toward Afghanistan and India.

Interwar British dominance in Persian Gulf region. World War I ended with Britain ascendant throughout most of the Middle East. In the Persian Gulf, London's shadow stretched inland in all directions from the coastal emirates, whose affairs they had long controlled.

In a series of conferences following World War I, Britain settled many outstanding issues in these former Ottoman lands,[49] adding to the map of the region several new states that they would administer. In Mesopotamia, British officials fused together under the name "Iraq" the former Ottoman provinces of Mosul, Baghdad, and Basra. After a heated debate over the shape of the new polity – whether Britain should rule directly, as in India, or exert influence through a proxy – the British ultimately selected as king a son of the Hashemite Sharif Hussein of Mecca, Britain's ally during World War I, Prince Faisal. Under the League of Nations mandate system Britain assumed official powers as the colonial authority overseeing the region's affairs, with an eye toward these nascent states eventually gaining independence. The war had ended with several hundred thousand British troops occupying Iraq. Post-war financial constraints, however, along with growing domestic opposition, forced London to pull back.[50] By the mid 1920s British power in Iraq lay largely in the form of squadrons of air bombers. British advisors served alongside key members of the Iraqi Government, and many influential members of the Iraqi parliament still showed sympathy toward London. Iraq in the 1920s remained largely in Britain's orbit.

In neighboring Arabia following World War I, British ally Ibn Saud continued his conquest of the Arabian Peninsula, pushing outward from his stronghold of Nejd to capture in 1925 the Hijaz. London officials did not stand in the way of his conquest of the Red Sea coast, despite Britain's close affiliation during the war with the Sharif of Mecca, whose ruling son Ali had fled into exile, initially to Cyprus on a Royal Navy warship,[51] thence onward to Baghdad. Ibn Saud, however, knew not to overstep his bounds, and exerted great efforts not to run afoul of Great Britain. When his Ikhwan warriors, tribal recruits comprised of Wahhab zealots, for example, threatened the British, Ibn Saud crushed the rebels. The king knew the limits beyond which not to push, and proved acutely aware that London would not tolerate Saudi interference in the coastal emirates over which Britain held sway. In that way, British power following World War I helped to shape the map of the Gulf: Great Britain's presence in Kuwait, Bahrain, Qatar, the Trucial States, and Oman prevented those lands from falling under the great Saudi push of the twentieth century. Only after British retrenchment from the region had begun, after World War II, did the Saudis dare challenge British might, and even then – in a dispute over an oasis called Buraimi, under which oil reportedly lay – the European power prevailed.

Across the Gulf in the course of World War I, Persia had collapsed even further into disorder. In a famine that accompanied the three major powers' battles in Persia, millions may have perished.[52] British Foreign Minister Lord Curzon, former Viceroy of India, placed a high priority on the reconstruction of the state, as a bulwark against a resurgence of Russian expansionism.[53] Despite the retrenchment of British military forces from all over the world after the Great War, the British crafted a plan to reconstruct the Persian state, involving British military equipment sales, British loans, and British cooperation in the construction of rail and communications facilities.[54] Although the move gained the approval of the weak and wary Shah, it failed to secure the approval of the Majlis. British leaders sought this approval, believing it would bolster the credibility of the regime in the eyes of the Persians as well as the rest of the world. Coming at the same time as an outreach by the Bolsheviks, who pledged an end to former colonial practices as well as a renunciation of Persian debts, nationalist critics in the Majlis lambasted the Anglo-Persian accord, which was to prove hollow in the end. Persian eyes increasingly viewed Russia, the former conqueror, as a deliverer from the British.[55]

Figure 8 Royal Navy ship in Persian Gulf or Red Sea, 1920s.

> Britain's financial condition deteriorated sharply after World War I, leading London
> to curtail its world-wide land army commitments. As it had since the mid 19th
> century, throughout the 1920s Britain drew upon naval power to assist in maintain-
> ing order in the littoral regions of the Persian Gulf. Above, the Flower class sloop
> HMS *Crocus* sails in 1922–23 at an undetermined location in the Red Sea or Persian
> Gulf.

As revolutionary Russia stoked anti-British fervor, leaders of the remaining
British forces in Persia assisted the rise of a military official who would later
take over the nation and unexpectedly turn against London. Major General
Edmund Ironside, thinking he had found a Persian leader who could craft a
viable state in the absence of either Russian or British power, installed as head
of the Cossack Brigade Reza Khan, an exceptionally capable officer and
military leader. The Cossack Brigade – originally formed by the Russians in
the late nineteenth century as a guard force for the Shah and a way for the
Russians to influence the Persian state – however, had increasingly come
under the influence of the British. A British Foreign Office official in 1905
described the influential unit:

> The Cossack brigade was established in 1879. It is composed of four
> Russian officers and five non-commissioned officers, whose services are
> lent by the Russian government, and about 1,500 Persian officers and
> men. It is the only part of the Persian army which is regularly paid and
> properly drilled and disciplined. It is the only force in Persia which can
> be, to some extent, relied on.[56]

Apparently without the approval of the British cabinet, Ironside orchestrated
plans for Reza Khan to rule Persia after the British departed.[57] He told Reza

Figure 9 RAF biplanes from No. 55 (Bomber) Squadron exercise with RAF armored
cars, Iraq, 1934

> While warships assisted in maintaining interstate order along the littorals, during the
> interwar years in Iraq, aircraft and tribal levies allowed Britain to influence events far
> ashore. Above, RAF biplanes from No. 55 (Bomber) Squadron exercise with RAF
> armored cars in the desert of Iraq.

Khan that the British would not interfere if he pulled off a *coup d'etat*, so
long as he did not overthrow the British-supported Shah. With tacit British
approval, then, Reza Khan took his Cossack Brigade into Tehran and installed
himself as head of the armed forces. Notwithstanding his pledge to keep the
Shah in power, Reza Khan engineered his own dramatic rise, naming himself
Minister of War, then Prime Minister in 1923, and ultimately Shah in 1925.
The new Shah spent much of the 1920s and 1930s centralizing control over
the state and reforming its bureaucracy and military, aiming as did Ataturk
in neighboring Turkey to thrust the former state into the modern world. He
also wanted the state, however, to function free of the domination by its
former masters in Britain and Russia.[58]

America's nascent involvement in the Gulf

In the first several decades of the twentieth century, the lands surrounding
the Persian Gulf remained a British domain, but America began to exert an
influence, albeit a small one, there. In addition to American missionaries who

Figure 10 His Majesty's Armoured Cars (HMAC) and British biplane on maneuvers in Iraqi desert, 1934.

had arrived there in small numbers in the nineteenth century, the first substantive American involvement in the states of the Gulf consisted of private individuals in the employ of the Persian regime, and came in response to financial challenges. Facing dire straits, members of Persia's constitutional assembly in 1911 turned to the American Government to help find independent civilian officials who might straighten out the ineffectual and outdated Persian national tax collection and financial system. They sought Americans specifically because they were "free from any European influence."[59] W. Morgan Shuster answered the call, but despite some initial headway in tackling the economic chaos, his efforts ultimately ran afoul of the Russians, still very much dominant in the state. Fearing an erosion of power in Persia, the Russians engineered his ouster.

In the next decade a new Shah, facing continued economic problems, turned once again to the United States for another financial advisor, and chose a team headed by Arthur C. Millspaugh. In a 1925 account he explained:

> The Persians looked upon America as a rich and powerful country whose government and people had already shown their humanitarian tendencies and their friendliness and sympathy for the Persian people. They did not doubt the disinterestedness of America; and entertained no fear that Americans, under cover of concessions or loans, would interfere in the politics of an Eastern country or attempt to dominate its government.[60]

Figure 11 Senior Naval Officer Persian Gulf, between Sheikh of Dubai and Sheikh of Henjam, c. 1920s.

The Senior Naval Officer Persian Gulf played a critical role in Britain's maintenance of order in the Persian Gulf region for much of the 19th and 20th centuries. Reporting to the Commander in Chief of the East Indies Station, a vast geographic expanse that at times included all of the waters from the Red Sea to the seas adjacent China, the Senior Naval Officer Persian Gulf brought naval force to bear in support of British interests in the region. Above, he is pictured in between two Arab leaders. Ten years after the conclusion of World War II, arguing for the maintenance of a robust naval force in the Gulf, the Senior Naval Officer wrote, "The Gulf is one of the last outposts of gunboat diplomacy."

Like Shuster before him, however, Millspaugh's initiatives ran afoul of entrenched interests, and in 1927 the Shah dismissed him after six years of service. A return invitation, however, led to another tour of duty there during World War II.[61]

The idea that America served as a new type of Great Power, free of colonial impulses and dedicated to an "open door" of free commerce for all, proved appealing to many locals, and President Woodrow Wilson's espousal of national self-determination based upon the consent of the governed attracted much favor and support in the Persian Gulf lands. According to the American Minister to Persia in 1918, many locals believed that the best route to independence from European control lay through Washington:

For the realization of their hopes Persians of all parties are looking more and more towards the United States for help. They would like to have the support at the peace conference of a strong disinterested power like the United States having no political interest in Persia, should Persian representatives be admitted there. . . .[62]

American growing oil interests. In the first half of the twentieth century a small but growing involvement in the petroleum industry also brought Americans into the Gulf region. Prior to World War I, oil production in Persia was very small, with the Anglo-Persian Oil Company comprising only 1 percent of total world production.[63] The promise of larger reserves, however, began to lure American oilmen to the region; Yankee businessmen vied for opportunities in Iraq in the mid 1920s. Standing in the way of the Americans, however, were the British, who before World War I had cemented tight agreements with many local Arab sheikhs. During negotiations in the 1920s, however, London eased its restrictions in the Gulf emirates to allow American oil development, although it mandated that the oil companies respect there the primacy of Great Britain. On the Arab side of the Gulf, it was the American-dominated Bahrain Petroleum Company that first struck oil in 1932.

Geologists believed that the Bahrain oil strike portended further discoveries in the Hasa region of Saudi Arabia, prompting American oilmen to compete with the British for Saudi Arabia's oil concession. After lengthy negotiations the oil concession went to a consortium of American companies. The 1933 agreement would prove enormously important, and would eventually give rise to a substantive American presence in the region to match the kingdom's unsurpassed oil resources.

But in the short term, however, America resisted increasing its official role in the region. Despite protestations from leaders of the American oil companies, the Roosevelt Administration declined to inaugurate a diplomatic mission to the kingdom, waiting until 1939 to accredit the U.S. minister in Cairo with responsibilities in Saudi Arabia. Only in the year following U.S. entry into World War II did Washington open a legation in the kingdom. It would be World War II, then, that marked the opening of the United States' large-scale involvement in the politics and security affairs of the Persian Gulf region.

2 World War II and the arrival of the Americans

Though the Persian Gulf remained but a side show in the worldwide fighting that took place in World War II from 1939–45, the theater proved important for several reasons. It provided to Great Britain and the allies a chief source of petroleum. By seizing the region, Axis leaders aimed to take those supplies, and use the greater Gulf area as an embarkation point for a possible attack into the Soviet Union's southern underbelly. Throughout the war the region remained important, as it had been for millennia, because of its strategic travel and communications route between Europe and Asia; the Allies would have found it much more difficult to move men and materiel between the Atlantic and Pacific theaters had they lost the Persian Gulf. And finally, the Gulf became a principal lifeline in Washington and London's strategic initiative to provide material aid to their beleaguered Russian ally. The Gulf region, in other words, held a strategic significance in World War II much greater than the dearth of fighting might otherwise suggest.

Early in the war, Britain attacks German-sympathetic regimes throughout the greater Middle East

The British spent the first 18 months of the war ridding the greater Middle East region of potentially hostile forces, recognizing early that they must do everything possible to prepare for the much more difficult duty that lay ahead: a probable German onslaught into the Persian Gulf region. The initial task, however, lay in figuring out what to do with several states that had fallen under the sway of the Axis powers. In Libya and Abyssinia (Ethiopia), for example, the 1940 entry of Mussolini into the war brought Italy to the Axis fold. In North Africa the Italians readied an invasion force poised for British-controlled Egypt, and in East Africa Italian forces in Ethiopia threatened the Red Sea approaches to Suez. In Iraq, a Berlin-leaning cabal of army officers had seized power and sent fleeing the regent of the British-installed monarchy. In neighboring Syria, the fall of France and its replacement by the puppet Vichy regime had made the leadership in Damascus suspect and potentially hostile to Allied interests. In Tehran, finally, nationalist Reza Shah – whom British officers ironically had assisted in grabbing the reins of national power the previous decade – had turned away from Britain in the 1930s and cavorted with the Germans. In all of these places, from 1939–41 the British led campaigns against Axis-sympathizing regimes, using forces often drawn from India, the strategic garrison that underlay Britain's ability to control the Persian Gulf as well as the greater Middle East.[1]

British knock out Italian force in Libya poised to invade Egypt. From London's perspective, Mussolini's entry into the war in June 1940 made it likely that Italy – working from bases in north Africa – would turn to the east to attack British forces in Egypt. According to Churchill's post-war account of the conflict, Mussolini harbored ambitions of "dominating the Mediterranean and rebuilding the former Roman Empire."[2] Although in summer 1940 the bulk of Britain's forces and attention were devoted to the defense of the home islands and defeating the German air "blitz," the War Cabinet proved "determined to defend Egypt against all comers with whatever resources could be spared from the decisive struggle at home." Churchill grew increasingly concerned at the large numbers of Italian forces gathered in the deserts of Libya. Accordingly, in December 1940 British forces based in Egypt attacked and decisively defeated the Italians at the battle of Sidi Barrani, just inside the Egyptian–Libyan border. Italian threats to the Middle East extended beyond Egypt, however, and would result in British–Italian clashes further south along the Red Sea coast.

British invade Italian Abyssinia. Since the mid 1930s the Italians had played a large role in East Africa, and Italy's membership in the Axis alliance inevitably transformed that region into a theater of conflict in World War II. In 1935 Italy conquered Abyssinia, modern-day Ethiopia, Eritrea, and parts of Somalia. Five years later, when Mussolini entered World War II allied with Nazi Germany, Italian presence on the Red Sea threatened British supply routes through the Suez Canal, and provided for the Axis powers sites for their garrisons of troops. In August 1940 the Italians used those troops to invade British Somaliland. Several months later, in October 1940, the Italians used an Eritrean air base to recover four aircraft bombers, launched from the occupied Mediterranean island of Rhodes, whose crews had dropped 200 bombs on oil installations in Dhahran, Saudi Arabia and Bahrain; the bombs apparently missed their targets and exploded harmlessly.[3] The British responded in February 1941 by invading Abyssinia in a campaign that again drew upon forces from India and Africa, with the assistance of Free French troops.[4] By November 1941 the Italian garrison at Gondar finally capitulated.[5]

British again invade Iraq. For over two decades Britain had played a dominant role in Iraq. Since British-Indian troops in 1914 first moved into Mesopotamia, London had proved the "ultimate guarantors of law and order in the country."[6] After the war the British withdrew the bulk of their occupying army, and used the services of local, hired levies, working in conjunction with Iraq-based Royal Air Force crews, to maintain order. That British presence, however, wasn't enough to tame the rough-and-tumble world of Mesopotamian politics, where through the 1920s and 1930s brutal beatings, coups, and assassinations proved commonplace. In the years immediately preceding World War II, for example, seven coups took place.[7] The British, however, during the interwar years safeguarded their interests. Despite granting nominal independence in 1932 to the Iraqi state following a dozen years of Mandate trusteeship, the British maintained advisors in critical positions of government. So when a group of Iraqi Army officers known as the "Golden Square" threatened in World War II to tilt the Iraqi state toward Germany, Great Britain quickly intervened.[8]

The proximate cause of British intervention in Iraq in World War II stemmed from a coup against the regency of young King Faisal II. The four-year-old boy in 1939 had assumed the throne following the death in an automobile accident of his father King Ghazi. Until reaching adulthood, according to King Ghazi's wishes, Ghazi's uncle Abdul Illah would handle royal affairs as a regent. On 1 April 1941, however, the Golden Square proclaimed a state of emergency, marched troops to Baghdad, and surrounded the royal palace. Abdul Illah fled, taking refuge for "some hours" with the American Minister to Iraq, who later drove him to the British air base at Habbaniya the next day. The British then evacuated him by air southward to Basra, hoping that Iraqis there would provide for Abdul Illah a "strong base

Figure 12 British troops looking at Baghdad, 1941.

At the beginning of World War II, British leaders aimed to restore friendly regimes in the greater Middle East.

of support."[9] In Basra, however, the rebel regime surrounded the regent's hotel, forcing him to take refuge on a series of Royal Navy ships.[10] British diplomats emphasized to the naval officers that their government must do everything possible to ensure that the regent ultimately prevailed; according to one naval war diary, "The regent must be backed with all our power and if he quitted the area of our cause would be irretrievably lost."[11]

The British military campaign that followed the Golden Square's refusal to step down took place in two parts of Iraq, Baghdad and Basra. In the center of the country, rebel Iraqi forces had surrounded Habbaniya, the mammoth British air base outside Baghdad. On 2 May 1941 Iraqi air forces attacked Habbaniya, and the British responded. Within a few weeks, however, the fight was over. British forces, including airborne troops drawn from India, broke free from the Iraqi cordon around Habbaniya and marched into Baghdad, reinstalling the regent. In the south in and around Basra, joint Navy–Royal Marine landings similarly resulted in British victories.[12] By the end of May 1941 the British had reclaimed Iraq from the Golden Square, and reestablished a military occupation of the nation.

British move into Vichy Syria and Lebanon. That same month, further west in Syria and Lebanon, the British moved into another Arab state to topple a German-sympathetic regime. When France fell to Germany in June 1940 and a puppet regime in Vichy took power, a question arose over the allegiance of France's overseas colonies and mandate territories. Did French colonial leaders abroad answer to Vichy, or to Free French forces led by General Charles de Gaulle, working initially from London and then Algiers? In Syria and Lebanon, leaders appeared sympathetic to Vichy, leaving open the eastern Mediterranean to the Germans, a condition that the British could not tolerate.

A combined British–Free French campaign to topple the Vichy regime in Syria and Lebanon began in May 1941. The force drew heavily upon Indian troops. Within two weeks Allied forces had entered Lebanon's southern coastal town of Tyre and penetrated Damascus, and within 34 days after commencing "Operation Exporter," Syria and Lebanon lay in the hands of the British and the Free French.

Britain and Russia move against Iran in August–September 1941. After Hitler's June 1941 invasion of Russia in Operation *Barbarossa*, both Churchill and Stalin grew anxious over Axis influence in Iran. Britain feared the safety of the oil fields at the head of the Gulf in Iran, as well as the potential loss of the Europe-to-Asia transit route through Mesopotamia toward the Gulf. Russia and Britain both feared the loss of a potential re-supply route to the western Soviet Union, to augment the beleaguered Arctic port of Murmansk, which increasingly came under attack from Nazi forces operating from Scandinavia. As well, the British and Russians feared the potential mischief that 5,000 Germans in Iran, many of whom occupied key technical posts,[13] might cause. On 17 August 1941, therefore, the British and Russians delivered to Iran a formal demand calling for the expulsion

Figure 13 British and Free French troops invade Syria, 1941.

> Great Britain moved against German-leaning regimes in the Middle East at the beginning of World War II, drawing upon the Indian Army. Great Britain's lines of communication to the Persian Gulf, India, and the Far East became threatened by Italy's forces in East Africa along the Red Sea Coast, prompting a British invasion. Allied interests were also threatened by Vichy control of Lebanon and Syria, eliciting an invasion by British and Free French forces. Above, Bren gun carriers manned by British Indian troops outside Damascus, 26 June 1941.

from Iran of most Germans, plus the identification of key German technicians who remained. The Allies also demanded the identification and surveillance of suspected German-sympathetic Iraqis who fled from Rashid Ali's revolt in neighboring Baghdad.

The Iranian Government's reply, however, proved unacceptable to London and Moscow officials, who deemed it full of "many conditions and qualifications,"[14] and within two weeks the first British and Russian forces moved into Iran, "almost unopposed."[15] In what would become known as Operation *Countenance*,[16] from positions in Basra, British units hailing from India moved eastward to take the enormous Anglo-Persian Oil Company's refinery on Abadan Island, as well as the Ahwaz oilfields to the north that fed it. Another British contingent from Baghdad captured the Khaniqin oil fields yet farther north.[17] A British naval flotilla captured the Gulf port of Bandar

Figure 14 British-Indian guard watches over wrecked flagship of Iranian Navy, 1941.

> The British government viewed with great concern the Iranian monarch Reza Shah's drift toward Germany at the beginning of World War II. When Reza Shah did not move fast enough to sever his ties with Berlin and evict German citizens, Britain and Russia attacked. Here a British-Indian soldier stands guard over the wreckage of the flagship of the Iranian Navy, the *Babr*, sunk by the British at Khorramshahr, near the Abadan refinery, in 1941. The Iranians in the 1970s purchased from Washington a U.S. Navy warship, and named it the "Babr."

Shahpur.[18] Much of the invading force hailed from India, emphasizing once again the importance of the subcontinent in Britain's ability to control the Persian Gulf region. At about the same time that British forces attacked from the west, Russian forces penetrated Iran from the north. Leading elements of the two European nations met in Senna and Kasvin, 75 miles northwest of Tehran, before the end of August. The Shah ordered a cease-fire.[19]

Despite the military action, the Iranian regime – in the eyes of the British and Russians – still dragged its feet in moving against the Germans, contributing to the two occupying powers taking more drastic action. British and Soviet troops marched onward into Tehran to occupy the capital. The British and Russians forced Reza Shah – whose rise to power two decades before British officers helped to engineer – to abdicate, and exiled the monarch first to British Mauritius, then to British South Africa, where he died in 1944. For their part, the Russians occupied the half of Iran that lay north of Tehran, into which other allied troops needed special permission to enter.[20] The British deported remaining Germans to Iraq, and interned them in the southern city of Basra.[21] With the ascent to the throne in September 1941 of Reza Shah's 21-year-old son Mohammed, the British and Russians had installed a compliant and subservient monarch. Although during the war he would not challenge directly either London or Moscow, young Mohammed Reza Pahlevi would nonetheless invite into his kingdom a force that would later stand up to British and Russian meddling there: the United States. That struggle would become apparent in the later phases of World War II. But in 1940 and 1941 neither British nor Soviet leaders concerned themselves with this tension with the Americans, for a much larger specter loomed: countering the inevitable onslaught of German troops heading toward the Middle East, seeking the rich oil fields of the Persian Gulf and Caspian Sea.

Britain's land and sea forces counter Axis designs on the Persian Gulf

Despite the 1940–41 Axis defeats in Africa, Syria, and Iraq, Germany still coveted the greater Middle East, as a route to the Soviet Union and for its Persian Gulf oil supplies. According to scholar Alexi Vassiliev, the first goal proved just as important as the second.[22] A key to German victory over Moscow, in this vein, lay in a drive through Iran, Afghanistan, and India, and thence north; to get there, however, they had to go through the Arab lands of the Gulf. In a curious twist of history, for over a century during the Great Game the British had fought against the Russians moving *southward* toward Iran and Afghanistan toward India; in World War II, however, the British had to defend against German forces attacking their former Russian foe through those same states, but in the opposite direction.

In addition to the desire to attack the Soviets from the south, of course, the Persian Gulf's oil supplies served as a strategic prize that the Germans desired. Although World War II still saw some limited use of horse-mounted cavalry and supply units, particularly on the German–Russian front, the worldwide conflict heralded the maturation of motorized and mechanized warfare, and the need for a seemingly endless supply of petroleum. This, essentially, underlay the second of Germany's strategic goals in its push into the Persian Gulf region: procuring oil, and denying that resource to Allied foes. Neither Germany nor Britain, after all, possessed at home substantial oil deposits, forcing the former to rely on captured fields in Rumania and to seek additional sources in the lands bordering the Caspian Sea and the Gulf. Of particular interest was Britain's Anglo-Persian Oil Company refinery at Abadan, the largest petroleum refinery in the world, which British naval forces – particularly those in Asia – depended upon. Fuel from Abadan would later prove critical in supplying the Soviets, particularly in 1942 and 1943 in their push westward from Stalingrad.

The Germans embarked on two strategic eastward offensives that would take them within striking distance of – but never reach – the Persian Gulf. In North Africa, following Britain's defeat in Libya of Italy's invasion force,

Figure 15 Indian rifleman guards oil pipeline in Iran, 1941.

> The Abadan refinery was the largest oil refinery in the world, and its protection
> represented a chief wartime goal for both Britons and Americans. This photo, taken
> shortly after the British attack on Iran in 1941, shows that the refinery was
> undamaged.

Hitler sent Field Marshall Erwin Rommel to move against Egypt. Rommel
aimed to take out the British garrisons and supply bases there, and secure the
Suez Canal, thus leaving open the road to the Levant nations, Mesopotamia,
and the Persian Gulf. In one of the great decisive battles of World War II,
however, Allied forces thwarted Hitler and Rommel's ambitions. At El
Alamein in western Egypt in fall 1942, British Lieutenant General Bernard
Montgomery soundly defeated Rommel's Afrika Korps, whose forces would
never again seriously threaten eastward. The British had thus stalled the
Germans in North Africa just as they had the Italians two years before at
Sidi Barrani.

In central and eastern Europe, Hitler's surprise June 1941 offensive against
the Soviet Union brought German forces the next year toward the Caucasus,
aiming – in Churchill's mind – for the "oilfields of Baku and the domination
of the Caspian area."[23] From the Caucasus the Germans could turn south
toward the Persian Gulf states of Iraq and Iran. The German offensive,
however, met with fierce resistance. In Stalingrad, a catastrophic battle commenced in summer 1942 that took more than two million lives before the

Figure 16 British and American forces defend Abadan complex, World War II.

The area around Abadan was important to the Allies not just because of the presence there of the world's largest oil refinery, but also because of the factories that assembled Lend-Lease aircraft for the Russians. Above, British and American MPs search and check civilians as they attempt to enter the Abadan perimeter.

Soviets repelled the Axis foes the next year. Just as the Battle of El Alamein marked the end of the Germans' approach from the west toward the Persian Gulf states and their oil, the Battle of Stalingrad marked the end of Hitler's approach from the north.

Britain's leaders directed their defense of the region from Cairo, headquarters of the Middle East Command, whose territory stretched from Libya eastward through Iran, and from Egypt southward through East Africa. As such, the commanding general faced many tall tasks, indeed. The Middle East Command had to manage several ongoing campaigns: countering the Italian and German assaults from Libya into Egypt, directing the British and French forays into Iraq and Syria, and managing the campaigns against the Italians in Africa. They did this while defending against air assaults from occupied Greece, and seaborne raids from Abyssinia on Red Sea and Persian Gulf shipping. Cairo thus served as the center of gravity for British activities throughout the greater Middle East. Of note, we see again in World War II the importance to the Middle East Command of British-Indian forces, who comprised the bulk of land soldiers in the Middle East theater in World War II, and without whom it would have proven exceptionally difficult for Britain to defend the region.

British air power contributed to the land forces, and worked from a number of air bases in the region.[24] From Iraq the Royal Air Force flew as they had since the 1920s, operating from a major base at Habbaniya, outside of Baghdad, and Shaiba, on the outskirts of Basra. Further down the coast in the British-dominated coastal emirates, British pilots used bases in Bahrain and Sharjah. In Oman, airmen working from Salalah and Masirah Island helped the British to defend Arabia's southern flank. These units operated in conjunction with others from Britain's extensive facilities at Aden, which during the interwar years had become a regional air base as well as a refueling station for Royal Navy ships. In addition to these larger bases, the Royal Air Force also flew from dozens of smaller air strips scattered throughout the region, although notably, normally not from mammoth Saudi Arabia, which dominated the Arabian Peninsula.

The Royal Navy's charge in the Persian Gulf and Red Sea in World War II involved keeping open these waterways, escorting convoys through them, and preventing the seaborne flow of contraband to Germany.[25] At the dawn of the war, working primarily from bases in Suez, Aden, and Bahrain, the British naval forces in 1939 received tasking to immobilize German merchant ships in the Persian Gulf,[26] a job that took less than a month. Drawing upon the four Royal Navy and Royal Indian Navy ships then on patrol in the Gulf, and augmented by reconnaissance aircraft from British forces in Iraq, British forces patrolled the Strait of Hormuz under orders not to allow any German merchant ships – the British believed that six lay inside the Gulf at the start of the war – to escape. The British located and "immobilized" five merchantmen in Bandar Shahpur, an Iranian port in the northern reaches of the Persian Gulf, in the vicinity of the strategic British oil facilities at Abadan, and shortly thereafter British intelligence located the last outside the region. British forces sank at least one Italian submarine in the Persian Gulf in June 1940,[27] and U.S. and British forces later in 1943–44 would report sightings of several German U-boats outside the Gulf, and capture the crews from at least one.[28] Also, the British expended considerable time and effort in checking transiting Persian Gulf merchant ship traffic for contraband headed to Germany. Intelligence sources indicated that the Axis leaders used dhows and other merchant vessels to transport rubber, tin, and other contraband through Iran and Iraq, thence onward to Europe. Despite all of these activities, however, the Persian Gulf largely remained a quiet naval theater throughout most of the war, with Allied Navy vessels escorting through it hundreds of supply ships. By autumn 1944, the Gulf region had become so quiet that the vast majority of tankers and merchants sailed independently, without the need for escorts.[29]

Likewise, in the Red Sea, the theater saw some armed conflict after Italy entered the war in June 1940, but following the defeat of the Italians in fall

1941 the waterway thereafter proved calm. On the opening day of the war with Italy, for example, British forces captured as prizes two Italian warships prior to their crews being able to scuttle them.[30] Over the next several months aircraft, presumably Italian, bombed Aden.[31] Italian submarines, furthermore, attacked allied merchant traffic transiting the Red Sea.[32] The Red Sea theater, however, quieted down after the British defeated the Italians ashore in fall 1941.

This ability of the Allies to move freely in the Red Sea, Persian Gulf, and Arabian Sea proved critical for three reasons: first, it allowed the Allies the use of the supply depot at Suez, and at times the Suez Canal itself, obviating the need for a Cape of Good Hope transit; second, it allowed petroleum products to flow *outbound* from the Persian Gulf; and third, it permitted manufactured goods to surge *inbound* toward Soviet Russia. The latter mission – delivering goods through the Persian Gulf to the beleaguered Russian forces – brought the United States and her military to the region for the first time. Although almost five decades passed before Washington leaders finally assumed the role of security guarantor that the British relinquished, World War II marked an entry into the Persian Gulf after which the superpower never entirely retreated. Although arriving as Britain's ally, America brought with it a set of ideals that clashed with its Atlantic partner, and before the war ended a substantial gulf had emerged between London and Washington, differences that would shape the region for years.

The Americans arrive in the Persian Gulf

After Hitler's June 1941 invasion of the Soviet Union, Roosevelt and Churchill both recognized that one of their chief duties lay in keeping the Soviet Union in the war to bloody the Nazis. The Anglo-American leaders aimed to prevent a repeat of World War I, during which revolutionary Russia essentially withdrew and capitulated, allowing Germany to redirect her might westward toward British, American, and French forces. Even before Pearl Harbor brought America into the war later in December of that year, Roosevelt had put in motion a program that flooded Russia with supplies; on 30 October 1941 he approved an expansion to Moscow of the Lend-Lease program.

Several routes emerged to supply European Russia with Lend-Lease equipment, but the Persian Gulf route proved among the most safe.[33] Ships transiting the northern seaborne path to the alternate Russian port of Murmansk often fell victim to German aircraft operating from Scandinavian bases. Likewise, a Black Sea route to Crimean bases necessitated a passage through the Dardanelles and Bosporus, close aboard Axis-occupied Greek islands. A corridor through the warm-water Persian Gulf, open all year, however, provided a relatively safe and direct path for Allies to deliver war materiel to Russian forces in Europe; the route became even more attractive after the eastern Mediterranean was reopened in 1943, allowing ships to transit the Suez Canal. Although an Alaskan route to the Soviet Asia east coast port of

Vladivostok became more productive in terms of gross tonnage processed,[34] for war stuffs destined for the Soviet–German front its use required a lengthy trans-continental transit. Before the end of 1941, then, the first American personnel arrived in the Persian Gulf to help set up what would become a monumental logistics endeavor: providing trucks, aircraft, petroleum products, foodstuffs, clothing, and other war materiel required by the Soviet Union in its battle with Germany. The first ship to leave the continental U.S. for the Gulf departed for Persia in November 1941, in what would be the first of thousands.

What the Americans did in Iran and Iraq. The vast bulk of the U.S. military effort in the Persian Gulf theater – at its peak numbering approximately 30,000 uniformed troops and an equal number of civilians – went to delivering goods through Iraq and Iran to Soviet handlers, who picked up shipments in the vicinity of Tehran and forwarded them to the Red Army further north. United States troops serving in the "Persian Gulf Command"[35] essentially took over three ports in the northern Persian Gulf, Bandar Shahpur[36] and

Figure 17 Unloading U.S. supply ship in Kermanshah port, Iran, World War II.

The U.S. Army's Persian Gulf Command's complement of soldiers and civilians, up to 60,000 in mid-war, delivered Lend-Lease gear from supply ships docked in Iranian and Iraqi ports to the beleaguered Soviets. Above, crated planes and truck equipment is unloaded at Kermanshah port in Iran during World War II. The equipment was transported several miles to Abadan for assembly.

Figure 18 Lend-Lease tanks on their way through Iran to Russia, World War II.

After being transported by sea from the United States, an American tank is being loaded onto a railroad car in Iran, en route to Russia during World War II. Delivering the Lend-Lease supplies to Russia involved many different types of transportation, primarily ships, trucks, and railroads.

Khorramshar in Iran, and Cheybassi in Iraq, and using large numbers of drafted stevedores, unloaded the contents of hundreds of "Liberty" supply ships onto trucks and trains destined northward. Over the 350 mile transit from the coast to the capital in Tehran lay some of the most inhospitable land on the planet: mountain ridges that topped 7,000 feet and arid plains upon which summer temperatures topped 140 degrees. Existing communication and transportation facilities, furthermore, proved primitive, forcing U.S. engineers to improve or construct from scratch rail and road links.[37] According to the historian who compiled the official U.S. post-war history of the supply effort in the Middle East theater, T.H. Vail Motter, an incredible 3.5 million long tons of goods destined for the Soviet Union arrived through U.S.-run Persian Gulf ports.

As part of this effort the U.S. constructed and operated aircraft and vehicle assembly plants in Iraq and Iran. The U.S. contracted with the Douglas Aircraft Company to help run an aircraft assembly operation at an airfield three miles north of Abadan Island. Of the 4,800 aircraft the U.S. delivered to the Russians from the Gulf, 3,879 were assembled or refitted there; the

Figure 19 U.S. Army truck convoy in Iranian snow storm, 1943.

A United States Army truck convoy carrying supplies to Russia stops to tighten loads before entering a dangerous, snowbound mountain pass.

balance were flown in.[38] The aircraft included A-20 Boston Bombers, B-25 bombers, P-39 fighters, and P-40 pursuit planes.[39] American leaders also set up truck assembly plants in the Iranian towns of Andimeshk and Khorramshar, both of which poured out enormous numbers of vehicles destined for the Soviet Union. Of over 409,000 Lend-Lease trucks that the U.S. delivered to the Soviets, about 45 percent of these arrived through the Persian Gulf corridor, and of those, 88 percent were assembled at Andimeshk and Khorramshar, or approximately 170,000 vehicles. Like the aircraft assembly operation, Washington officials contracted with a major U.S. industrial giant, General Motors, to help run the operation.

American war efforts also led to increased numbers of petroleum processing and transportation facilities in the region. As early as late 1941, at the very beginning of America's entry as a combatant into the war, the U.S. Army Air Forces aimed to increase the Middle East refinery capacity,[40] which up to that time was dominated by the Anglo-Iranian Oil Company's refineries in Abadan. To that end, the U.S. "expressed a paramount interest" in increasing oil production from Bahrain, particularly 100-octane gasoline. Although the emirate remained essentially a British protectorate, the Bahrain Petroleum

Figure 20 American, British, and Russian engineers in train in Iran, World War II.

Here, American, Russian and English engineers appear in the cab of a railroad locomotive engine. U.S. forces took primary responsibility for the construction of new roads and railroads from Iran's southern ports on the Persian Gulf, northward toward Tehran. In the vicinity of Tehran, Soviet forces picked-up war materiel and delivered it to the Red Army.

Company was a Canadian subsidiary of Standard Oil Company of California, and the U.S. War Department accordingly possessed some influence over the operations of the private company. The U.S. later posted to Bahrain personnel from its Air Transport Command to assist in providing security to the refinery. On the nearby east coast of Saudi Arabia, furthermore, the U.S. Government – acting upon the "urgent recommendation" of the Army–Navy Petroleum Board – proved instrumental in bringing about the expansion of the oil industry there. Accordingly, in 1943 the California Arabian Standard Oil Company (CASOC, the name changed to the Arabian-American Oil Company the next year) commenced construction of a mammoth refinery at Ras Tanura. By the end of the war Saudi oil production had increased substantially, although European concerns – in particular the British-owned Anglo-Iranian Oil Company – still possessed the bulk of the Persian Gulf's total known reserves;[41] the extent of Saudi Arabia's oil wealth was not yet fully known.

The U.S. maritime services also served in the Persian Gulf theater in World War II. Hundreds of American-built and American-staffed "Liberty" supply

Figure 21 American aircraft assembly plant in Iran, World War II.

U.S. workers assemble hundreds of aircraft in the Persian Gulf, and deliver them to their Soviet allies. Above, crated fighter aircraft wait to be unloaded at a new U.S.-built air base in western Iran.

ships sailed from the United States to the northern reaches of the Gulf,[42] for example, where American crews from the Persian Gulf Command unloaded their contents and shipped them onward to wartime ally Russia. Outside the Strait of Hormuz in the Gulf of Oman, U.S. Navy and Royal Navy ships and aircraft searched the waters of the Gulf of Oman for submarines, which in 1943 and 1944 attacked ships transiting to and from the Persian Gulf.[43] As the war drew to a close in Europe, however, the need in the Persian Gulf region for Allied anti-submarine warfare units diminished, along with merchant ship convoy and escort patrols, particularly after the Russians had fought further to the west, opening up additional supply routes through the Black Sea to the Red Army.

The United States also deployed airmen to the Persian Gulf as part of the Air Transport Command's "airbridge" to India and Asia. As well, airmen served as communications specialists throughout the theater.

The Persian Gulf Command, as well as Air Transport Command soldiers, U.S. Navy escorts, and other service-members dedicated to delivery of aircraft, trucks, petroleum, and other war materiel to Russia, then, constituted the largest bulk of American servicemen serving in the Persian Gulf theater. They were not the only U.S. service-members in the theater, however, and the others – uniformed officers serving as advisors and diplomats – played a more lasting role in the region. Their story, told in detail in the

Figure 22 Readying U.S. aircraft for delivery to Soviet Union – painting the white
American star a Soviet red color.

At a U.S. aircraft assembly plant in Iran in World War II, a native worker in Abadan,
Iran paints over the U.S. white star with red paint, prior to transfer to Russian
airmen, October 1943.

subsequent section, reflects the push by the United States to weaken spheres-
of-influence politics. This drive, understandably, gave rise to a widening gulf
between the U.S. and Britain, the latter of whom had been a chief architect of
the old system.

With respect to the Persian Gulf, the Atlantic Charter
represents a rift between Britain and America

Winston Churchill believed that the American mind, in war and in peace,
required a broad idea or a grand design upon which to build or fight a war.
He suggested that:

> In the military as in the commercial or production spheres the American
> mind runs naturally to broad, sweeping, logical conclusions on the
> largest scale. It is on these that they build their practical thought and
> action. They feel that once the foundation has been planned on true and

Figure 23 U.S. Air Transport Command aircraft in Salalah, Oman, World War II.

In addition to delivering aid to Russia, American personnel came to the Arabian Peninsula to assist in delivering materiel and personnel to India and beyond. Above, an Air Transport Command aircraft refuels in Salalah, Oman. The southern coast of the Arabian Peninsula was used as a transport route. A common path took aircraft from the United States to South America, across the Atlantic to Africa, then onward through Aden and Oman. Transiting aircraft sometimes reported submarine sightings to British naval forces outside the Strait of Hormuz. U.S. aircraft used a number of British-controlled air bases in the Persian Gulf region, including Bahrain, Sharjah, Masirah, and Aden.

comprehensive lines all other stages will follow naturally and almost inevitably. The British mind does not work quite in this way. We do not think that logic and clear-cut principles are necessarily the sole keys to what ought to be done in swiftly changing and indefinable situations. In war particularly we assign a larger importance to opportunism and improvisation, seeking rather to live and conquer in accordance with the unfolding event than to aspire to dominate it often by fundamental decisions. There is room for much argument about both views. The difference is one of emphasis, but it is deep-seated.[44]

Implicit in Churchill's words lay the notion that, prior to taking up arms, America needs a sweeping high moral principle for which to fight. It is not enough, in other words, for the United States to fight a war simply to win, there must be a grander cause.

Figure 24 Changing of the guards, U.S. Air Transport Command Ferry Squadron, Aden.

This facility served as another Air Transport Command stopover point for aircraft transiting to India.

The Atlantic Charter as America's Grand Design. If Churchill was correct, that America more than Britain or other European nations needs a substantial philosophical foundation upon which to justify a flight to arms, then the Atlantic Charter served as that grand design. As Churchill pleaded with Roosevelt to enter the war, the two hammered out the document during meetings off Argentia, Newfoundland in August 1941, several months before Pearl Harbor. The document envisioned how nations would interact after the cessation of hostilities, and talked of a world free from empires and preferential trading blocs that accompanied them:

> [Countries must] respect the right of all peoples to choose the form of government under which they will live; and that they wish to see sovereign rights and self-government restored to those who have been forcibly deprived of them. . . .

In this document, however, Roosevelt didn't envision just the end of the German and Italian empires, but that of their allies the British as well. Roosevelt, in fact, harbored particular antipathy toward Britain's continued

Figure 25 Sharjah Airfield, World War II.

> Sharjah airfield (in modern United Arab Emirates) was a primary air facility in World War II, from which British and American forces operated. A small sign adjacent to the door (to the left of the two workers in the distance) reads "British Overseas." British and American military aircraft used these remote facilities during the war.

colonial rule in India,[45] whose military forces over the past century had proved essential in ensuring British control over the Persian Gulf region. Roosevelt, in other words, aimed to bring self-representation to the world's peoples, and end the colonial practices of yore. Although he typically did not voice these goals with the soaring hyperbole and rhetoric that Woodrow Wilson did two decades before, President Roosevelt held "essentially the same outlook"[46] as had Wilson.

The negotiations over the Atlantic Charter, then, proved more contentious than often portrayed.[47] In them, America pushed for what amounted to a curbing of the prior practices of the British empire, and Britain predictably pushed back. From before the beginning of America's involvement in the war, then, a significant gulf had emerged in Anglo-American conceptions of a just post-war order. Britain, however, really had no choice but to acquiesce to Roosevelt's demands. Roosevelt's son Elliott – who served as aide de camp to the President for this and several subsequent leadership conferences,

Figure 26 Habbaniya, Iraq, World War II.

The Second U.S. Army Airways Communications Wing radio station at the British military base at Habbaniya, Iraq, near Baghdad.

Figure 27 Headquarters building of the Basra, Iraq detachment of the U.S. Persian Gulf Command, World War II.

Note the U.S. flag in the distance.

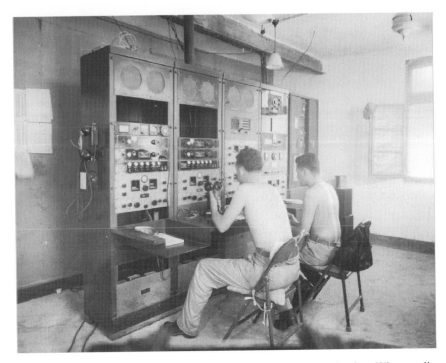

Figure 28 Members of the 2nd U.S. Army Airways Communication Wing, radio receiving station, Bahrain, World War II.

and as such sat in on many critical meetings – described Churchill's anger in Argentia:

> "Mr. President," he cried, "I believe you are trying to do away with the British Empire. Every idea you entertain about the structure of the postwar world demonstrates it. But in spite of that" – and his fore-finger waved – "in spite of that, we know that you constitute our only hope. And" – his voice sank dramatically – "*you* know that *we* know it. *You* know that *we* know that without America, the Empire won't stand."[48]

Other historians have confirmed the thrust of Elliott Roosevelt's argument: FDR at Argentia and throughout the war encouraged Britain to dismantle its worldwide empire.[49] In keeping with this overall vision, in the Persian Gulf region during the war Roosevelt worked to strengthen an independent Iran, and made efforts to free Saudi Arabia from its previous British orbit. On one level, then, while American military forces worked hand-in-hand with their British allies to fight the Axis foes, Washington and London's diplomats tussled over the future of Britain's empire. As one historian noted, "The wartime

Figure 29 British and American shared facilities in Bahrain, World War II.

The U.S. Air Forces Air Transport Command Office stands at left, with a U.S. Jeep; the sign in center says "Royal Air Force."

archives amply reveal that the sense of historic antagonism between Britain and the United States continued to exist along with the spirit of co-operation generated by the war."[50] This competition was apparent in the Persian Gulf.

Early in the war the U.S. pushed Britain and the Soviet Union for pledges of prompt post-war withdrawal from Iran. FDR had watched with concern the 1941 occupation of Iran by Great Britain and the Soviet Union. U.S. Secretary of State Cordell Hull became so dissatisfied with the terms of the occupation that he pushed for a formal Anglo-Soviet declaration that committed London and Moscow to a prompt post-war withdrawal from Iran.[51] With the Nazi war machine grinding down British and Russian forces, and fearful of alienating Washington, London and Moscow agreed, enshrined in the signing on 29 January 1942 at Tehran of a Tripartite Iranian-British-Soviet Treaty of Alliance. Article five stated that, "The forces of the Allied powers shall be withdrawn from Iranian territory not later than six months after all hostilities between the Allied powers and Germany and her associates have been suspended." Other passages called for the signatories to act in accordance with the principles enshrined in the Atlantic Charter.[52] FDR and Hull, in other words, had placed a stiff price tag on America's entry into the war to assist her new wartime allies: an end to the excesses of the Great Game in Persia. No longer would the British and Russians slug it out for dominance in Iran. For their part, the Iranians didn't hold much trust in the words or treaties of the British and the Russians, and had sought an American signature on agreement. The Americans, not yet ready to anger their new Allies, declined.[53] In a letter to FDR, the young Shah, however, made it clear that he was looking to the U.S. to ensure the independence of a post-war Iran: "In appending our signature to this document we rely upon the goodwill and the friendship which binds the United States to Iran and feel confident that your traditional attitude toward the basic principles involved will ensure the fulfillment of the pledges given and reserving for my country and people a brighter future of peaceful development within our borders."[54]

America desired a strong government in Tehran. In the early twentieth century Iranian leaders had invited several Americans to Tehran for assistance in fiscally and administratively running its affairs, free of British and Russian dominance. In World War II this tradition continued. Mr. Millspaugh, private advisor in the 1920s, accepted a return invitation. But whereas the prior efforts were limited to individual U.S. citizens working to improve Iran's administrative and financial systems, in World War II the assistance grew to include help from the very top reaches of the U.S. Government.[55]

President Roosevelt himself took an active role in encouraging the strengthening of Iran. Shortly after the Anglo-Russian occupation of Iran, for example, FDR sent a note to the Shah remarking that he had taken notice of London and Moscow's promises to honor the political independence and territorial integrity of Iran.[56] By mid 1943, members of the U.S. State Department's Division of Near Eastern Affairs talked of providing assistance to the Shah, to allow the state to become strong enough to rule itself, independent of the British and Russians: "What I have in mind is . . . full rehabilitation of Iranian self-government."[57] These words mirrored America's monumental wartime financial commitment to Iran, designating Iran in March 1942 – just three months after Pearl Harbor – as a recipient of Lend-Lease aid.[58] This represented the first time that Washington provided substantial direct aid to the Iranian state, as well as the first time that American officials involved themselves in the affairs of the Tehran Government.[59]

America, however, as new partners to the British and Russians in Iran, had a delicate act to play. Washington leaders' top priority, of course, remained the delivery of critical war materiel and supplies to Soviet Russia; America's own security interests depended on keeping Moscow in the war. But for practical as well as philosophical reasons, they also sought to bolster the power of Tehran's central government, for a weak central government fostered disorder. American soldiers had been dying in their delivery trucks in Iran, not from hostile fire, but from looting and brigandage. As one veteran of the Persian Gulf Command exclaimed, "It is one thing to be strafed by a legitimate enemy and quite another to be shot by some bushwacker out for a night's hijacking."[60] American leaders ultimately concluded that they could better deliver aid to Russia if the Iranian central government could accomplish several things on its own: controlling petty crime and brigandage, keeping its territory free from spies and German intruders, and fulfilling basic services like keeping the populace housed and fed. All of these functions, the Americans realized, were related. As historian T.H. Vail Motter concluded, "it [became] apparent that the political, economic, and military health of Iran, essential to the success of Russian-aid operations, was a matter of life or death for Iran itself; that . . . the problem of Iran was monolithic."[61] The American paradox, of course, rested in the fact that although strengthening Iran was an American goal, it wasn't necessarily shared by either Britain[62] or Russia. Those two states, in fact, had attacked Iran in 1941 precisely because it had grown *too* strong, *too* independent, and, of course, too closely affiliated with Germany.

In addition to supporting the Tripartite Treaty of Alliance of January 1942 that committed the large powers to withdraw within six months of the war's conclusion, and designating Iran as a Lend-Lease recipient, Washington leaders took another concrete step to strengthen Iran. At the November 1943 Tehran conference, FDR successfully pushed to get Britain and Russia to formally acknowledge Iran's future status as an independent nation in a "Declaration of the Three Powers Regarding Iran," which Roosevelt signed. At a protocol meeting between the President and the young Shah, whose very presence on the throne had been dictated by Britain and Russia, the subject of Iran's dominance by foreigners arose. FDR turned a sympathetic ear to the monarch, who complained of Britain's "economic grip" on the nation, including its oil wells and mineral wealth.[63] Apparently moved, after the meeting the President directed his ambassador-at-large General Hurley to "get to work drawing up a draft memorandum guaranteeing Iran's independence and her self-determination of her economic interests." The General worked with the President's staff and Iranian legation officials to compose such a document,[64] a revision of which Churchill, Stalin, and Roosevelt signed on 1 December 1943. In it, the three powers agreed to respect the "independence, sovereignty, and territorial integrity of Iran,"[65] which Britain and the Soviet Union, to be sure, had not honored for over a century. President Roosevelt considered this the most important part of the declaration,[66] which he chose to sign, unlike the Tripartite agreement of the year before.[67]

American military missions to Iran. Perhaps the most enduring example of America's drive to create a strong, independent Iran lay in the U.S. military advisory missions that the superpower set up during World War II. Long the pawns of Russia and Great Britain, whose military forces over the previous century had moved virtually at will in and out of Persia in the "Great Game," Iran's leaders in World War II found themselves under twin yokes: British forces occupied key points in the south of their country, and Russian troops in the north. According to a senior U.S. military officer writing at the time, Iranians "distrusted and disliked" these occupiers,[68] but welcomed the Americans who arrived to help transport logistics to Russia. The presence of the Americans, furthermore, sparked some hope amongst parliamentary leaders and the Shah that the newcomers might help Iran stand up for itself. Inspired in part by Wilsonian ideals of self-determination that appeared in the Atlantic Charter, top Iranian leaders viewed the Americans as honest brokers who might do for the Iranian Army what the American financial advisors three times in the twentieth century had attempted to do for their Treasury: modernize, provide for efficient central control, and allow national leaders one day to hold at bay British and Russian military might. At the request of the Iranian Government,[69] then, Washington began to send military advisors to that nation in World War II, first as supply experts, then as general advisors. Ultimately, two U.S. advisory commands emerged during World War II, one for the Iranian Army, and the second for its national police force, the "Gendarmerie." The Iranian armed forces, as the name implied, largely defended the nation's borders from external aggression, while the Gendarmerie served as a less powerful national police force, primarily for internal security.

Iran's leaders ask originally for military supply help, but expand the American mission. Iran's original request in World War II surrounded the need for expertise in supply issues, but it grew. Washington sent to the nation General

Figure 30 Shah with U.S. Persian Gulf Command's Commanding General, 1944.

Mohammed Reza Pahlevi, Shah of Iran, with Maj. Gen. Connolly in reconnaissance car during an inspection of U.S. Army Persian Gulf Command troops, 1 March 1944.

Figure 31 Shah plays ping pong with U.S. serviceman, 1945.

> In an informal moment with a U.S. soldier that reflects the growing intimacy of Iranian leaders and American service members, the Shah of Iran plays a game of ping pong with U.S. Army Sergeant Jack Cherry, in the Shah's Royal Palace, 1945.

C.S. Ridley, a top supply officer. It quickly became apparent to him, however, that Iran's leaders desired more than just guidance on their supply efforts, and sought instead a top-to-bottom overhaul of all their military forces. Writing in December 1942 Ridley explained:

> I know that originally, [an Iranian] request was made for an officer to be Intendent-General [a supply chief] of the Army. The ideas of the Shah and the Government have gone much beyond that and what is now desired is some-one to reorganize the entire Army with the assistance of other officers, in a Military mission. . . . Apparently I have been received with enthusiasm by the Shah and the Government and there seems to be no other idea in their minds but that I must stay here and "reorganize" the Army. . . .[70]

U.S. leaders consented to Iran's request, and expanded their scope of military operations. Within two years the U.S. staff had drawn up plans to reorganize Iran's entire operational Army, its finance department, the motor transport functions, its quartermaster department, and its finance department, virtually the entire armed force of the country.[71]

Before the end of World War II, then, U.S. diplomats had concluded that a "cornerstone" of U.S. policy in the region ought to be the creation of a strong Iranian military, capable of maintaining security "after foreign forces have been withdrawn."[72] In 1944, the commanding officer of the U.S. military trainers warned, however, that the Iranian military was not yet ready to face the task of maintaining order in the country after foreign forces pulled out, particularly in the Russian-occupied north where the army was "not free to operate . . . and are more or less on the order of token forces."[73] The presence in the Russian-occupied north of large numbers of Kurdish troops, Ridley believed, made it critical that worthy Iranian units must immediately replace the Russians on the latter's departure, lest an armed insurrection arise against Tehran's forces[74] and the Russians use the chaos as a pretext to remain.

Just as U.S. advisors assisted the Iranian Army, U.S. advisors working with

Figure 32 Col. Norman Schwarzkopf, Sr. trains the Iranian Gendarmerie, World War II.

Although the effort to deliver Lend-Lease equipment to the Soviets comprised the largest number of American personnel serving in Iran in World War II, American officers and soldiers also served as advisors to Iranian government officials and military leaders. Here, Col. H. Norman Schwarzkopf, Sr., the head of the U.S. Army's advisory mission to the Iranian Gendarmerie, a national police force, participates in a graduation ceremony. Col. Schwarzkopf was the father of U.S. General Norman Schwarzkopf, Jr., leader almost four decades later of Operation *Desert Storm*.

the Gendarmerie, under the direction of U.S. Army Colonel Norman Schwarzkopf (father of the Central Command general in *Desert Storm*), began to reform the internal security forces of the country. The military relationship between the two nations' security forces became formal with the signing of a written agreement, signed in Tehran with an effective date of 2 October 1942. The verbiage of the text reflected the start of the mission: it was originated by "request of the Government of Iran to the Government of the United States of America," and dealt with a mission to "advise and assist the Ministry of Interior of Iran in the reorganization of the Imperial Iranian Gendarmerie."[75] A similar agreement was later penned for the Army training mission.[76] Thus, American influence on the armed forces of Iran had begun to grow, and it would become pervasive over the next several decades. Although this growing U.S. role met with approval in Tehran, in London, not surprisingly, it met in World War II with derision.

London attempts to block America's efforts to strengthen Iran. Although close cooperation generally marked the Anglo-American military relationship in the field, in matters of Persian Gulf politics the two nations battled one another during World War II. One such clash involved U.S. assistance to Iran. In March 1944 British and American officials met for staff talks in Baghdad at the General Headquarters of Britain's Persia Iraq Force. The Americans revealed that the Iranians had requested guidance on crafting a robust army and national police force, and had accepted most of the U.S. proposals to do so. Although the British nodded at these steps, they desired strongly that the two allied nations *jointly* supervise all future Iranian military planning and expenditures. Britain's ranking officer in Baghdad explained London's desire not to cede Iranian internal affairs to the Americans:

> I have just received a telegram from London on this subject. It emphasizes the necessity of building up the Persian Army to a standard sufficient for the maintenance of law and order, and the importance of agreement between ourselves [Britain and America]. This will place us in a stronger position to resist any [Iranian] demand for a large and useless army and to insist on adequate support of, and adequate powers for your Mission. I understand that our Foreign Office is prepared to consider asking the United States Government to join in using all diplomatic influence on the Shah to accept our agreed proposals.[77]

To the Americans, these British requests to limit the potency of Iran's military smacked of colonial interference in the affairs of a sovereign state. Although this proposed British action may have been appropriate in a former imperial age, at least one American thought, they were not compatible with ideals enshrined in the Atlantic Charter. The commanding officer of the U.S. Military Mission with the Iranian Army grew offended at such British attempts to "impose their will on the Iranian Government with respect to its Army." In a reflection of how deeply American antipathy ran toward these

British imperial practices, Major General C.S. Ridley "felt very strongly" that he must have no part in such British designs, lest the Iranians completely lose trust in the Americans. According to Ridley, "If there is one thing that irks the Shah more than another it is to have outsiders meddling with the Army. If he thought for a moment that *I* was involved in such an agreement [with the British], my mission [should] just as well go home."[78]

Americans dragged into Iranian constitutional issues. As if these disputes with the British weren't unsettling enough to the Americans, Ridley also found his small U.S. military staff embroiled in an Iranian tug-of-war over the rightful leadership of Iran's military, with the Shah battling the Prime Minister over military funding and control of the forces in the field. According to the Western-inspired constitution that emerged during the Constitutional Revolution of the first decade of the twentieth century, the Parliament-appointed Minister of War controlled the Army's Chief of Staff, the top uniformed officer in Iran, who would then control forces in the field. The constitution thus provided a substantial role for Parliament, which in theory constrained the Shah's role as Commander in Chief. During the reign of Reza Shah, the nationalist monarch deposed by the British and Russians at the beginning of World War II, however, such constitutional formalities meant nothing, for he had ascribed to himself through "dictatorship, initiative, and terror"[79] virtually all state powers, starting with, naturally, those of the armed forces. But when the British and Soviets exiled Reza and put on the peacock throne his 21-year-old son, the Europeans inadvertently breathed new life into the moribund Persian constitutional movement. Parliamentary leaders, who for a quarter century had served as "yes men" to the whims and wishes of the former Cossack Brigade tyrant, perceived that they might constrain the young monarch. The new Shah, predictably, acted to preserve as many of his father's prerogatives as he could, particularly those relating to the armed forces. Control of the military, then, became a key struggle between the parliament and the monarch, and the Americans discovered quickly that they were in the middle of it. According to U.S. General Ridley:

> The Shah is apparently very jealous of his power as Commander of the Army. He apparently has visions of a large army comparable with that of Turkey. The Prime Minister and the Parliament apparently have other ideas more nearly apportioned to the country's capacity and economic status as well as the status quo produced by the British and Russian occupation.[80]

As war ends, Shah and U.S. State Department keep open the training missions. In late 1944, as Allied armies converged on Berlin, even the German U-boat campaign in the Gulf of Aden had essentially ceased. Not surprisingly, in an effort to divert resources toward the still-raging Pacific campaign against Japan, the War Department aimed to shut down the Army's advisory missions in Iran. As the head of the U.S. training mission stated:

The primary work of this Mission [in proposing potential reforms to the Iranian military] as described in the contract is practically finished. . . . If it were purely a military matter I would recommend that the Mission be withdrawn. However, it is apparently now a matter of public policy for decision by the State Department.[81]

The matter of whether or not to keep open the U.S. military advisory missions, however, *had* grown larger than a purely military matter, and at the end of the war, the Shah and the Department of State agreed to keep it open. As the American logistics force delivering aid to the Soviets withdrew, the small band of American military advisors remained, and provided for Washington a degree of influence in Iran, where at the end of the war the British and Russians still had occupying troops. The U.S. military missions in Iran would be renewed periodically by both sides over the subsequent decades. Although the two U.S. administrative commands would later be led by a single officer, two separate training organizations – one for the armed forces and the second for the Gendarmerie – would continue up through the Iranian Revolution of the 1970s.

Great Britain and the United States tussle over Saudi Arabia during the war

The United States entered World War II harboring few ambitions for the Persian Gulf, which Washington had long considered a dominion of the British. The United States started the war as a net exporter of oil,[82] after all, and Saudi supplies – over which U.S. companies possessed the rights – had not yet been fully revealed. Before the war ended, however, Washington's leaders found themselves in pitched bureaucratic battles over Saudi Arabia with their counterparts in London. Although Washington officials did not challenge London's control over British strongholds elsewhere – in Iraq and the coastal emirates, for example – in Iran and Saudi Arabia they did. Both sides attempted to curry favor with the staunchly independent Ibn Saud. For his part, the crafty monarch early in the conflict professed neutrality while simultaneously seeking arrangements with all of the parties, including the Nazis. Perhaps sensing Hitler's ultimate demise, however, the Saudi king abandoned his dalliance with the Germans and spent the war years shrewdly pitting the two English-speaking powers against each other. By war's end, although few in these three nations sensed it at the time, British power in Saudi Arabia, as well as the greater Persian Gulf, had begun to wane and that of America to wax.

Saudi neutrality. In 1940 Mr. H. St. John Philby, a British merchant and Arabist who for years served as a close advisor and confidant to Ibn Saud, told American diplomats that Arabs in Saudi Arabia desired strongly to stay out of the hostilities that then tore apart Europe. "The general feeling in Saudi Arabia," Philby explained, "is one of complete neutrality coupled with an intention not to become embroiled therein."[83] While the Saudis understood the "ruthlessness" of the Germans, Philby continued, the Nazis were just "too remote" to engender in the Arabs a desire to take up arms to defeat them.[84]

To the Saudis and other Arabs, the British represented a closer and more tangible threat. A "heavy weight averse to England" existed in Arab lands, according to Philby,[85] reflecting the widespread disdain held toward the British. Why? The displacement of Arabs in Palestine served as a complaint. Another was the French cession back to Turkey of the Syrian coastal territory of Alexandretta, which many Arabs suspected (correctly, it would turn out) stemmed largely from Anglo-French designs to ensure Turkey's neutrality in the war. But the largest factor that pushed many Arabs into the anti-British camp was the almost three-decade long domination by that Christian nation over the greater Middle East. The Arabs, many of whom in World War I looked to Britain to end the ascendancy of the Ottomans who had controlled the region since the 1500s, concluded that they had traded Istanbul's yoke for London's. Many Arabs felt trapped and enslaved. Even the generally accepted geographic term for their surroundings, the Middle East, stemmed from the West,[86] and it framed the Arabs' existence largely in terms of their relations to London, Paris, and their other colonies in the Far East.[87] Thus, whereas many in the Western world viewed, then and now, World War II as a moral fight that pitted good vs. evil, right vs. wrong, in many Arabs' eyes the conflict proved more of an opportunity for the defeat of their colonial enslaver, the British. To that end, in Iraq, Syria, Iran, as well as Saudi Arabia and the rest of the Middle East, Arab public opinion early in World War II often tended toward the Germans, not springing so much from an affinity with their ideas – although Hitler's anti-Semitism found some favor in some Arab camps – as the realization that victory of the Axis might mean the downfall of the British. Echoing these sentiments, a vice-president of the Bahrain Petroleum Company concluded:

> Practically speaking, the Arab people do not share our interest in [the Western principles of freedom and democracy]. They are already subject to domination, politically and commercially, and in greater or less degree, by foreign Powers, and their prime concern is not whether democracy or totalitarianism shall survive in the Western World but how they can gain or regain a greater degree of political and economic freedom for themselves.[88]

Ibn Saud, ever the pragmatist, attempted to squeeze from the Europeans and Americans sufficient funds to keep his insolvent regime afloat. During the first three decades of the twentieth century the king had built an empire on the Arabian Peninsula, the greatest amalgamation of territory and political might there since the era of the Prophet. But maintaining his realm – which stemmed in part from payments he made to his subordinate tribal leaders, along with strategically selected royal marriages – required cash, of which the monarch possessed little. Few oil revenues had materialized by the beginning of World War II; in fact, just the opposite: the king even *owed* money to Russia for imports in the 1930s of petroleum products![89] A modern style of tax collection simply did not exist in the state; although the king received some funds from "rudimentary" forms of revenue extraction, such as a "one-in-forty" collection of livestock, the bulk of his revenues came from the annual pilgrimage to holy sites in Mecca and Medina.[90] During the war, however, the annual flood of Muslim faithful had decreased almost 50 percent: from 59,627 pilgrims in 1939 to 32,288 the following year. The reduction in the king's revenues proved even more dramatic: from "4,000,000 gold sovereigns" before the war to only 25 percent of that in 1940.[91] The king needed cash, in other words, and he recognized that the principal combatants in World War II might provide it.

Early Saudi dalliance with the Nazis. Early in World War II it would have been difficult for Ibn Saud not to consider as probable a future where Germany played a large role in the Middle East. The Germans had intimidated the West into accepting an annexation of parts of Czechoslovakia. Berlin's forces had rolled into Poland, then Norway, the Netherlands, and France. German-sympathetic regimes ruled in Iraq and Syria. Into 1940, virtually all goals to which Hitler directed his forces he achieved with alacrity. As well, large numbers of Ibn Saud's own Arab population desired to see Great Britain lose, including pro-German members of his own inner circle of advisors.[92] Ibn Saud understandably envisioned, then, that he would likely have to deal with a strong Germany in the future.

Not surprisingly, the monarch developed a relationship with the German regime. The Saudi king's emissaries traveled to Germany to meet with Hitler.[93] The king met with the head of German operations in the Middle East, Dr. Fritz Grobba. In July 1939 Ibn Saud even agreed to a deal with Hitler that included 4,000 German rifles and ammunition, although he never took delivery of them.[94] But as the war progressed, particularly as the German war machine began to stall, the pragmatic king backed away from his dalliance with the Germans, toward the British and the Americans.

British–Saudi relationship in World War II. While the Saudis covertly flirted with the Axis powers, King Ibn Saud and his advisors maintained solid ties to the British, which paid off for the monarch. The Saudi king successfully pressed the British Government during the war for an increase in subsidies,[95] for example, which he had received regularly for over two decades. Against the will of a large number of his countrymen, furthermore, the king declared himself a "neutral" early in the war rather than what would have been a more popular, pro-German stance. Ibn Saud reportedly boasted that if he felt it necessary for the security of his kingdom to maintain his relationship in World War II with the British, against the will of the Saudi populace, it was his prerogative to do so: "it really does not matter much what anyone else in Saudi Arabia feels or thinks."[96] One of the king's close confidants, his political secretary Yussef Yassin, furthermore, went so far as to tell the British Minister in 1941 that the king felt that, "Great Britain is my friend and always has been. Great Britain is the friend of the Arabs and has so shown itself in the past. The Arab countries need a powerful European friend and Great Britain is undoubtedly preferable to any other country to fill that role."[97]

Although speaking in hyperbole, the king's deputy appeared to capture part of what made Ibn Saud such a powerful and long-lived, independent ruler: he understood and paid deference to the Great Powers, using their protection when it suited him, but all the while proving capable of maintaining independent control of his own realm. Although the king generally did not travel outside of his empire – his trip to meet FDR in Egypt was one of his first international forays – he seemed to grasp that his desert surroundings, as one of the cross-roads and critical chokepoints of the world, would inevitably bring the Great Powers to the region. Rather than fight this inevitability, Ibn Saud chose to turn it to his own ends, exploiting the Great Powers' insecurities, yet knowing all the while when to submit.

If in the course of the war Ibn Saud proved most interested in money, what did Britain want in return? First, London officials desperately wanted to keep him out of the Germans' camp, a goal that they essentially achieved. The British throughout the war, additionally, wanted to see the Saudi monarch declare war on the Axis powers. The king drew out this decision for years, however, giving to the British the impression, as early as January 1942, that Saudi Arabia might soon declare war on Germany.[98] The king managed to delay that decision for over three years, collecting all the while from London enhanced subsidies; finally in March 1945, as the outcome of the war was all but determined, Ibn Saud declared war on Germany and Japan.

Another goal of the British in Saudi Arabia surrounded the need to court favor with one of Islam's new leading figures. Many British and American diplomatic reports of the time mention the special leadership role that Ibn Saud enjoyed amongst the hundreds of millions of Muslims. As the new keeper of the holy sites, the king possessed an exalted position within the faithful. With tens of millions of Muslims as colonial subjects, British leaders proved keenly concerned with any tensions that might inflame their own Muslim populations within India and other parts of the Empire. Having the support of Ibn Saud, accordingly, would undoubtedly prove beneficial. Of note, the British did not need military bases in Saudi Arabia. Surrounded as it was by British interests – Palestine, Iraq, Kuwait, Bahrain, Qatar, Oman – the British had ample facilities in the region from which to work. The Americans, on the other hand, did not; later in the war the idea of constructing a military air base in Saudi Arabia, preferably near the American oil companies' interests in the east, would become a chief object of America's desires, and give rise to British attempts to thwart them.

To a certain degree, the British relationship with Saudi Arabia – that is to say, with Ibn Saud, in whose hands rested all major decision-making within the kingdom – was profoundly shaped by the arrival in the kingdom during World War II of the Americans. Although prior U.S. presidential administrations had chosen to shun a substantive diplomatic presence in the kingdom, shortly after the start of U.S. involvement in World War II Washington leaders recognized the strategic importance of the kingdom. The ensuing arrival of American influence and money in Saudi Arabia during World War II, however, was not greeted with enthusiasm in London. The story of the British–American relationship in Saudi Arabia, then, as it was in Iran, was one of sparring and competition, despite their tight military alliance on the battlefield.

America in Saudi Arabia in World War II. When America entered World War II, in December 1941, Washington officials had little experience working with Ibn Saud or his desert kingdom, for the superpower had never had a diplomatic post there. After shunning a 1928 Saudi request to commence diplomatic relations between the U.S. and the Saudi realm, Washington belatedly recognized the state in 1933.[99] Reflecting the lack of U.S. strategic interests in Arabia in the 1930s, however, the U.S. initially opted to forego opening a diplomatic post there, choosing instead to append Ibn Saud's kingdom to the portfolio of the U.S. ambassador in the Arab world's most weighty state at that time, Egypt.

With no permanent diplomats in the country, not surprisingly, American oilmen themselves frequently developed close relations with Saudi ruling family members, and sometimes fulfilled the roles of diplomats. American oil executives wrote political and economic analyses on the Persian Gulf region for U.S. State Department officials in 1940, for example, and forwarded up-to-date maps of the region for possible use in military contingency planning.[100] Even after the superpower opened a legation in Jeddah in 1942, top Saudi officials out of habit continued to turn for years to private American citizens living in the country instead of to the superpower's diplomats, which raised the ire of U.S. Foreign Service officials.[101]

World War II brings increased U.S. participation in Saudi state. Despite the oil concessions granted to American companies in the 1930s, Washington in the early 1940s still had little influence over affairs on the Arabian Peninsula. The kingdom's oil supplies still had not been proven, and production proved minimal. Within three years of Pearl Harbor, however, the United States had become the largest benefactor to King Ibn Saud, exceeding even Britain, and Washington would begin to rival London in its overall influence there. What happened to account for the enormous growth in U.S. interest in Saudi Arabia? First, a realization emerged in some Washington circles that a strong Saudi state benefited the United States. Second, powerful oil executives lobbied for a larger U.S. role in the state to counter British designs on the oil industry. Third, it became increasingly evident that Saudi oil fields might become quite prolific. And finally, increased American influence there matched FDR's desire to see the British monopoly in the Middle East challenged.

Figure 33 Saudi desert soldiers, 1943.

> America's first military involvement in Saudi Arabia came during World War II, when U.S. army trainers worked side-by-side with Saudi troops. Here is a U.S. Army Signal Corpsmen's May 1943 photo of Saudi soldiers in Riyadh. Jealous of America's growing presence and influence in the Kingdom, the British in World War II attempted to match man-for-man the number of American trainers and advisors. The legendary King Ibn Saud, however, disliked either western nation planting in his domain a large, foreign military force, and took every opportunity to assert his authority over them.

As early as spring 1941, a half-year before Pearl Harbor, there grew in some Washington circles a nascent realization that a strong Saudi Arabia served U.S. interests. Senator Warren R. Austin, for example, contacted Secretary of State Cordell Hull concerning the "importance of the position of Abdul Aziz Ibn Saud, King of Saudi Arabia."[102] The senator feared the repercussions of a potentially weak Ibn Saud who might fall victim to German designs. At the beginning of America's involvement in World War II, therefore, there existed at least some basic level of support for the idea of America backing the Saudi state.

The lobbying efforts of politically influential U.S. oilmen also contributed to the growing U.S. involvement in the kingdom at the beginning of World War II. Ibn Saud in 1942 began to warn U.S. oil executives that his regime was in financial jeopardy.[103] The British at that time provided to the monarch approximately $4 million annually, although the king stated he needed $10 million to prevent his regime from collapsing. Noting the shortfall, the king in turn requested loans totaling $6 million annually from the American oil company that controlled the concessions in the kingdom, but the company's leaders balked at sinking more money into their projects in

Figure 34 Saudi Princes Faisal and Khalid in U.S. aircraft, World War II.

World War II cements close personal relationships between Saudi royal family members and U.S. government officials. Prince Faisal and Prince Khalid, both future kings of Saudi Arabia, in a U.S. aircraft, November 29, 1943, enroute to Washington, D.C., during World War II.

the kingdom for which they still had "little to show."[104] These executives, author Anthony Cave Brown asserts, turned to Washington and told American officials that should the U.S. fail to come to the financial rescue of the Saudi state, the British stood ready in the wings to gobble up American oil concessions. Such a deal could benefit the American Government, the executives stated, in that the Saudis could make oil available at a special price to U.S. Navy ships.

Although the oil executives did not succeed in winning direct U.S. aid to the Saudi regime, the U.S. Government increasingly came to view with favor assistance to Ibn Saud's state, culminating in the decision to make it eligible for Lend-Lease aid. At first blush such a move didn't appear to meet the intent of the 1941 Lend-Lease legislation, for the kingdom was not a war combatant. It had not come under direct attack, like Russia had, from an Axis nation, nor did it host substantial numbers of U.S. servicemen, like Iran, within its borders. The Lend-Lease legislation passed by Congress in March 1941, however, granted wide latitude to the U.S. President in determining which nations he deemed "vital to the defense of the United States." After a year of bureaucratic wrangling, President Roosevelt in early 1943 deemed Saudi Arabia eligible for Lend-Lease aid.[105]

According to Brown, FDR made this Lend-Lease move with an eye largely to prevent the British from stealing the Saudi oil concession to American companies.[106] This granting of wartime aid probably stemmed from a number of other influences, too. As Senator Austin's letter suggested, even before the war there existed an American desire to keep German influence out of the Arabian Peninsula. Plus, diminished British influence in the Middle East coincided with one of FDR's broader goals, as in Iran. Whatever the causes, the granting of Lend-Lease status to Saudi Arabia, along with millions of dollars of other aid that followed after the war, marked the beginning of a long and tight – albeit sometimes dysfunctional – military relationship between the United States and Saudi Arabia, which mirrored in some respects Washington's bond with Tehran.

Lend-Lease brings equipment, trainers, and tension at the upper levels with the British. Tension quickly marked the U.S.–British relationship in

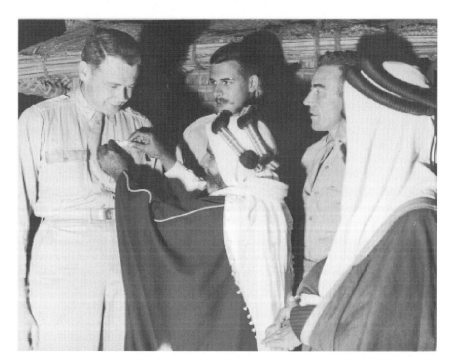

Figure 35 Sheikh of Bahrain presents a pair of aviator wings to American pilot, World War II.

Local Gulf leaders have their first prolonged and intimate contact with American military service members during World War II. Above, the Sheikh of Bahrain presents a pair of hand-carved ivory wings to Major George C. Bieberback, U.S. Army Air Forces. The major led the American Air Transport Command detachment situated on the island.

delivering military aid to the Saudis. After becoming eligible for U.S. Lend-Lease aid on 18 February 1943, the Saudis compiled many requests for armaments and associated equipment and training. The British, however, initially demanded that the Saudis route all requests for Lend-Lease aid through London,[107] reflecting an early attempt to prevent the Americans from nosing into their domain. American officials later rebuffed their Anglo rivals, however, and instructed the Saudis that "the United States would receive requests direct from Saudi Arabia."[108] As one American reported, "competition . . . in implementing the program of supplies to Saudi Arabia was very keen."[109]

British and Americans reluctantly agree to match 50–50 their contributions to Ibn Saud during the war. Both British and American officials recognized the peril of Anglo-American feuding among wartime allies, and attempted to replace competition with cooperation. In one of the hallmarks of U.S.–British policy in the Arabian Peninsula in World War II, the two allies agreed to split evenly their cash subsidy contribution to the Saudis.[110] This tacit agreement marked a conscious American restraint, for the King's granting oil concessions to American companies over the British during the previous decade would otherwise have led the Americans in World War II to play a larger role in the affairs of Ibn Saud's court. In other words, while the American tendency was to increase their influence in Saudi Arabia, the British sought to fend it off, and convinced the Americans to do so, against the strident objections of America's diplomat in Jeddah, William A. Eddy. The British demanded that the spirit of this "50/50" agreement would be extended to military missions, as well. When the U.S. offered to train Saudi officers and soldiers in Taif in modern armaments and first aid, for example, the British demanded an equivalent mission.[111]

The Saudis, for their part, attempted to maximize their benefits by playing off one English-speaking power against another. According to U.S. accounts, Ibn Saud's defense officials submitted overlapping requests for military aid to both Britain and America, cognizant of the fact that both nations were vying for favor in the king's court. Discovering this, British and American officials recognized that they would have to subsume their individual nations' drives for pre-eminence in the kingdom, and jointly work together, for both agreed that Saudi forces should not procure more arms than the "minimum amount required to maintain internal security."[112] U.S. military aid to Saudi Arabia amounted in its first year (1943) to $4.5 million, and comprised mostly trucks, associated automotive equipment, and silver to pay for the construction of an oil refinery approved by the Joint Chiefs of Staff. That aid grew in following years to include medical supplies, agricultural equipment, textiles, radio equipment, and desalination equipment.[113]

Fight over Dhahran. Toward the end of World War II the U.S.–British rivalry also played itself out in a competition over the rights to make improvements at two important airfields in the kingdom, Jeddah and Dhahran. Saudi officials, sensing another opportunity to take advantage of the

Anglo-American rivalry, again played one superpower against the other. According to American accounts, the Saudis approached both the U.S. and the U.K. for funds and assistance in improving "night-lighting, runways, installations for maintenance, and repair of planes." William Eddy, the American minister in Jeddah, who consistently fought against the British making inroads into the kingdom, expressed concern to his superiors that the British would seize this opportunity to trump the Americans should Washington fail to fund these improvements.[114] Of the two airfields, however, one eventually became of paramount importance to the Americans. The oil town of Dhahran, on Saudi Arabia's east coast, lay in the middle of the kingdom's petroleum reserves, the defense of which American decision-makers during the war increasingly believed represented a critical American national interest.

But the original American interest in Dhahran's airfield did not spring only from oil. As the European war wound down, U.S. planners also eyed Dhahran as a transit air base, anticipating the re-deployment of troops and material to the still-raging Pacific war. In spring 1945, therefore, U.S. War Department officials voiced to their State Department counterparts a desire to investigate the establishment of an air route to Asia – via Cairo, Saudi Arabia, and Karachi, India – which would likely require the construction of an air base at Dhahran[115] to relieve the already overloaded and geographically less desirable air base at Abadan, Iran, which lay further from the great-circle route to Asia. Attempting to avert any further deterioration in bilateral relations with its chief ally, U.S. decision-makers decided to first seek British consent, believing it would be forthcoming quickly. Although the British military Chiefs of Staff posed no objection and offered their approval,[116] other London officials tried to quash the construction, citing potential economic losses at the nearby airport in British-controlled Bahrain. By May 1945, however, top British decision-makers overcame lower-level objections, and passed along British blessings, even prompting the embassy to assist in procuring the Saudi king's approval.[117]

The Saudi king approved the construction of the Dhahran airfield that same month, in May 1945,[118] but American efforts to gain a long-term lease on the field ran up against Ibn Saud's demand to retain control over the kingdom's sovereign territory. The king had not fought for three decades to unite the Arab Peninsula only to see a Western power grab a piece of it, as Western powers had done in the Persian Gulf since the Portuguese. Despite the persistent travails of America's able representative in Jeddah, Col. Eddy, the king would not consent to any American possession of the field exceeding three years. As Eddy explained, the king deemed anything longer to be "inconsistent with the independence of his kingdom, especially in the eyes of his subjects who are quick to suspect foreign domination on the slightest pretext."[119]

Due to changing military deployment patterns that transported forces to the Pacific theater via the United States and not through the Gulf, the War

Department by June 1945 believed that it no longer needed to build the airfield. Officials in several other Washington departments, however, recognized that long-term American interests might be served by its continued construction, and urged the President to fund it.[120] By early 1946 the base was essentially complete.[121] Continued use of the U.S. base in Dhahran would become a key strategic aim of U.S. policy in the Gulf throughout the 1950s and early 1960s. (In 1961, however, a beleaguered King Saud, under pressure from Arab nationalists, chose not to renew the base agreement.[122])

Thus, during World War II London and Washington officials found themselves struggling against each other over who played the paramount role in the kingdom. At war's close an event of monumental symbolic importance took place: the meeting between FDR and Ibn Saud. Its occurrence sums up the rivalry on the Arabian Peninsula between the British and the Americans during World War II, and marked a turning point after which the U.S. had become in Saudi Arabia – although not in the rest of the Persian Gulf – the rising power.

Figure 36 King Abdul Aziz Al Saud (Ibn Saud) walks through U.S. Navy honor guard, to confer with FDR, 1945.

The founder of the modern state of Saudi Arabia King Abdul Aziz (Ibn Saud) walks through a U.S. Navy honor guard, to cross onto a U.S. Navy warship in Egyptian waters, to confer with American President Franklin Roosevelt, 14 February 1945. Colonel William Eddy, U.S. Marine Corps, follows.

Figure 37 Ibn Saud and FDR, USS *Quincy*, Great Bitter Lake, Egypt, 1945.

Saudi Arabia's King Ibn Saud meets with American President Franklin Roosevelt onboard the USS *Quincy*, on Great Bitter Lake in the Suez Canal. U.S. Marine Corps Colonel William Eddy served as interpreter.

Roosevelt's secret meeting with Ibn Saud. With European victory impending, the wartime Allied leaders met one last time in Yalta, a Soviet city on the Black Sea, in February 1945. U.S. President Franklin Roosevelt sent word to his minister in Jeddah, Col. William Eddy, to arrange a secret meeting with Ibn Saud following the Yalta conference. The fact that FDR also chose to meet after his Yalta trip with Egypt's King Farouq and Ethiopian Haile Selassie – all without British foreknowledge – suggests that the American president wanted to deliver a stark message to the British: in the post-war era independent nations would become free of British dominance. The fact that FDR met with Ibn Saud on the Suez Canal, right under the nose of the British in the middle of a British-dominated country that served as London's wartime headquarters in the Middle East, speaks volumes to the message that he wished to send.

Roosevelt took great pains to keep the meeting secret. According to Eddy's account, prior to departure only six people in Saudi Arabia knew of the plan: the King, his secretary and de facto foreign minister Sheikh Yusuf Yassin, a coding clerk at the American legation, and Eddy and his wife. Even the Saudi

Figure 38 Ibn Saud's desert tent pitched aboard USS *Murphy*, 1945.

While transiting from Jeddah to meet with FDR, the Saudi king refused the Navy ship captain's offer to sleep in his cabin, preferring to set-up a Bedouin tent on the forecastle of the ship.

attendees, whose number exploded from a desired handful to four dozen, did not divine the King's intentions until minutes before boarding the U.S. Navy ship that would transport them to the Great Bitter Lake on the Suez Canal, in British-dominated Egypt. For his part, FDR also proved able to keep this meeting secret, even from his wartime ally Winston Churchill. When Churchill later discovered FDR's travels, the Prime Minister flew into a rage:

> Churchill was informed of what was afoot and he burned of the wires to all his diplomats in the area, breathing out threatenings and slaughter unless (the same) appointments were made with the same potentates after they had seen FDR. Churchill was wild at the news that the Americans were putting something over on the British by direct approach to these heads of state in an area which the British considered (and today still consider) to be their own preserve. Worst of all, there would be no Britisher to hear what was said, and he was determined to see each of the Kings later to preserve the British position.[123]

The King's journey to meet FDR is a colorful story.[124] The U.S. Navy arranged to have a destroyer, the USS *Murphy*, pull into Jeddah harbor for

Figure 39 Slaughtering Ibn Saud's sheep, USS *Murphy*, 1945.

The king brought with him a coterie of attendants, this one slaughters a lamb on the deck of the ship. Note the other sheep tied-up next to the combat helmet.

the King's pick-up, the first time an American warship had called on the port. After hosting the ship's crew at a banquet on shore on 11 February, the next day the King ordered the tents pulled up from his traveling camp, and to prepare to travel. Members of his group never imagined that they would be heading out of the country. When the King's motor caravan diverted to the pier to board a U.S. warship for his journey northward, it shocked the residents of Jeddah, where "all hell broke loose." Members of the King's harem wept. No one knew the King's destination, or whether or not he would come back. Other than a sojourn as a child in Kuwait and a brief trip to British Mesopotamia,[125] the monarch had never left his realm.

The scene on board the ship proved extremely unusual. The ship's crew set up a tent on the deck, under which rested oriental rugs, for the King and his retinue of 48. After turning away over 90 live sheep, Navy crew members housed seven live animals to be slaughtered for the king, who recoiled at the thought of eating frozen food stored in refrigerators. Despite being given the captain's cabin, the King preferred to sleep on the ship's forecastle, under the tent, reflecting his desert heritage. The ship's crew appeared both bemused and excited at the thought of hosting this exotic group. Ibn Saud hosted the American crew to an Arab-style desert meal, where everyone sat around the deck of the ship cross-legged, while the great desert king amused

Figure 40 Egypt's King Farouk boards U.S. Navy warship to meet with President Roosevelt, 1945.

> FDR desired that after World War II the nations of the Middle East would gain their actual as well as nominal independence from the British, who had maintained a grip on much of the Middle East for decades. In a cutting blow to his wartime ally Prime Minister Winston Churchill, FDR arranged secretly to meet with the heads of three states that the British considered in their area of influence: Egypt, Ethiopia, and Saudi Arabia. By doing so he made clear that the future actions of these states and their leaders would not be subject to British control. Above, Egyptian King Farouk boards a U.S. Navy ship to meet the President, 13 February 1945.

the crew with stories of his exploits of hand-to-hand combat. According to Eddy, the Americans and Saudis "fraternized without words with a success and friendliness which was really astonishing."

FDR and Ibn Saud met on board the USS *Quincy* for over five hours, during which they discussed the ongoing hostilities between Arabs and Jewish refugees in Palestine, the French promises of independence to Syria and Lebanon, and agriculture in the Middle East and other subjects.[126] The subject of their talks, however, may not be as important as the sheer fact that the two met and appeared to get along quite well. They exhibited respect and mutual admiration for one another. Roosevelt took care not to insult the King's Wahhab sensibilities. A chain smoker, FDR neither drank nor smoked in front of the monarch, for example, going so far as to stop his elevator

Figure 41 Ethiopian Emperor Haile Selassie on board U.S. Navy ship, 1945

President Roosevelt met with three regional leaders on board U.S. Navy warships in Egyptian waters. Above, Emperor Haile Selassie of Ethiopia.

between decks for two cigarettes prior to a luncheon so as not to offend. The President even gave Ibn Saud one of his wheelchairs, which the monarch later proudly showed off to guests. As their time together drew to a close, the King invited the President to a sumptuous Arab feast, but due to time constraints, the two enjoyed Arabic coffee instead. In short, the two leaders during their visit established a tight bond. Eddy insightfully explained that the true significance of the meeting between the two rests less in what was discussed than in how they got along. As Eddy explained, "In [Ibn Saud's] simple Arab view such a friendship depends upon good will and good faith. When these cease to exist they cannot be resurrected by producing a scrap of paper."[127]

An enraged Churchill later demanded, and received, a meeting with the Saudi king after Roosevelt's. Those meetings later in the week in an Egyptian hotel proved less cordial. The Prime Minister exhibited insensitivity toward his Muslim guest, drinking and smoking in front of him. The King related to Col. Eddy that the British attempted to impress him by sending him back to Jeddah in a ship larger than the Americans.' The ploy, in Eddy's mind, however, failed to impress:

The King told me later that his return trip was very dull – the food was terrible; there were no demonstrations of armament; no tent was pitched on the deck; the crew did not fraternize with his Arabs, and altogether he preferred the smaller but more friendly U.S. destroyer.[128]

At the time, few saw the Great Bitter Lake meeting as ending British supremacy in the region. The Great Bitter Lake meeting is sometimes described as the defining moment in the Middle East, before which British power held supreme and after which America supplanted it. That exaggerates the strength of the United States in the region as World War II drew to a close, however. It is true that the war marked the arrival of the United States as a central player in Saudi Arabia as well as Iran. And it is true that during the course of the war it became increasingly apparent that Saudi oil reserves might eclipse those of any state in the world. But at the end of the war Britain, by far, remained the dominant power in the region. It possessed military forces and bases throughout the region, including major facilities in Egypt, Palestine, Iraq, Kuwait, Bahrain, the Trucial States, Oman, and Yemen. America possessed there no such strength, and would not for decades. With the shutdown of the Persian Gulf Command, the logistics deliverers, the United States possessed virtually no bases nor military troops in the region, except a handful of advisors in Iran, a small construction crew at Dhahran's nascent air base, and a clutch of naval ships.

The Saudis certainly didn't see America as the future dominant power in the region. Ibn Saud, in fact, continued to believe that the Persian Gulf remained, and would continue, a British sphere of influence. Almost half a year after the meeting, for example, he related to William Eddy in July 1945 that, "Britain continues to dominate . . ." The Saudi acting Foreign Minister, furthermore, told Arab League colleagues in Cairo that, "The Americans are our friends and we like them; but Britain is the power with which to deal." As Eddy succinctly summarized, the Saudis foresaw in the Middle East the continuance of the "British sphere of influence, similar to her past position and similar to our Monroe Doctrine."[129]

World War II, then, ended with the British still the dominant actor in the Persian Gulf. Their forces in the Middle East, drawn largely from India, early in the war had eliminated potentially hostile regimes throughout the region, and had turned back in Egypt the Nazis' eastward advances. With the Allies' victory, His Majesty's Government maintained its control of lands from Egypt through Iraq, as well as all the coastal emirates of the Gulf. FDR's actions and words, however, particularly in Iran and Saudi Arabia, had shown that America desired over the long term to see an end to Britain's monopoly in the Persian Gulf region; in his talk with Ibn Saud, he envisaged, "a decline of spheres of influence in favor of the Open Door . . . with no monopoly by anyone; for only by a free exchange of goods, services and opportunities can prosperity circulate to the advantage of free peoples."[130] Before the end of the war, however, FDR was dead, and his successor proved less desirous of seeing an end to London's hegemony in the region.

Over the next two decades the Persian Gulf region would undergo momentous changes. The independence of India – over which FDR sparred with Churchill – would deprive Britain of the armed forces and resources with which it had maintained order in the Persian Gulf. And the Cold War would bring American aid and advisors in greater numbers to Iran and Saudi Arabia. Despite this, however, throughout the 1940s and 1950s, the Persian Gulf remained a British domain, the subject of the next chapter.

3   The early Cold War, the loss of India, and Nasser's revolt against the British, 1946–58

World War II ended with the allies victorious. During the conflict Iranian and Saudi leaders had invited American military trainers and advisors to assist them in bolstering their defenses; from Saudi Arabia they departed, but in Iran, government leaders asked them to stay. It would be a great mistake, however, to say that World War II marked the beginning of an American march to dominate the Persian Gulf. Great Britain's influence greatly exceeded that of any other power, and those in London wished to keep it that way. They retained paternalistic defense relationships with the emirates on the Gulf, after all, and they possessed military bases throughout the region, including Iraq, Oman, and Aden. They maintained a flotilla of operational warships in Gulf waters. They garrisoned large numbers of troops within striking distance of the region. And perhaps most importantly, London officials felt themselves committed to maintaining order in the region, as they had done for over a century. The British in the first decade-and-a-half after World War II, however, faced one setback after another in the region, forcing London officials – against their wishes – to take the first steps in an unplanned and very drawn out retrenchment from the region, starting with the nation's departure from India. These setbacks played out during the early years of the Cold War, in which America took the lead around the world in facing down an increasingly aggressive Soviet Union. This chapter, then, looks at British challenges and America's growing presence in the Persian Gulf region from 1946–58.

Many accounts of Britain and America's involvement in the Gulf after World War II concentrate on two things. First, the roots of the Cold War in Iran, Greece, and Turkey. And second, the growth of the oil industry and America's growing involvement in Saudi Arabia and Iran. There exist plenty of good reasons for this historical approach. The five-decade long Cold War *did*, one could argue, commence in the Persian Gulf region, as the Soviets immediately after the war delayed their departure from Iran and tested the resolve of Great Britain and the United States to confront them. And America's participation in the Persian Gulf oil industry – particularly in Saudi Arabia – *did* grow exponentially in the years following World War II, which brought the attention of its military leaders, along with its navy, to the region. But accounts that concentrate solely on petroleum and the Cold War present a misshapen chronicle. Such tales miss two enormously important factors that shaped the Gulf: the independence of India, and the nationalist revolt against the British. All of these events, of course, are interrelated, as India's independence in 1947 deprived the British of the army and navy that had maintained order in the Persian Gulf for over a century, as well as dispossessed the British of the treasure to pay for it all. India's independence also fanned the fires of anti-British, anti-colonial drives elsewhere, particularly in the Arab world, movements that the Soviet Union proved ready to assist.

The Cold War starts in Iran, and draws together U.S. and Britain's aims

As discussed in the previous chapter, during World War II American and British aims in the Persian Gulf, particularly in Iran, at times diverged. Franklin Delano Roosevelt, for example, aspired to see in the Middle East a collection of truly independent states where once the British and Russian Empires dominated. Toward that end, Roosevelt pushed for concessions from London and Moscow that aimed to end old colonial excesses.

During the first two years following World War II, however, Roosevelt's successor Harry S. Truman began to view with some favor a strong Britain in the Persian Gulf and Indian Ocean region. Faced with a number of crises around the world involving an increasingly strident Soviet Union, Truman became convinced that Britain must retain its responsibility to maintain order in the greater Middle East. But Britain's post-war financial situation proved bleak, and nationalist sentiments amongst the colonial peoples had increased. In an interesting twist of history, just as Britain appeared bound to grant independence and self-rule to millions around the globe, as FDR had pushed, President Truman increasingly longed for a return to a strong British Empire, particularly in the Middle East. As Russian actions continued to grow more brazen, and Anglo-American antagonisms from World War II concerning the Gulf states faded, the divide between the two English-speaking powers became smaller, and Washington and London's leaders saw their strategic aims coincide. As an important 1947 memorandum prepared in the U.S. Department of State concluded: both nations' interests are furthered if "the British maintain their strong strategic, political and economic position in the Middle East . . . [and that] they and ourselves follow parallel policies in that area."[1]

Growing anxiety with Soviet intentions in Iran. America's and Britain's concerns with Soviet behavior in Iran started during the war itself and increased in the immediate aftermath of the war. The Soviets refused Iran's 1942 demand, for example, to allow Iranian troops into Soviet-occupied Iranian Azerbaijan to put down a Kurdish rebellion. Later, in 1944, the Soviets appeared to give encouragement and funding to members of the anti-regime, pro-Moscow Tudeh communist party.[2] Well aware of the Soviets' poor record of fulfilling wartime promises to Iranian leaders, American officials grew alarmed in the months following the May 1945 Allied victory in Europe, when it appeared that the Soviets dragged their heels in withdrawing their troops from their occupation zone in northern Iran.[3] The British and Americans, for their part, upheld their own wartime commitments – enshrined in the Tripartite Pact – to withdraw military forces from Iran within six months of the termination of the conflict in Europe, but the Soviets did not. The Persian Gulf Command – the U.S. logistics force dedicated to delivering Lend-Lease supplies to Russia through Iran – for example, began to draw down within weeks of the end of the European war.[4] The British planned to follow the Americans, and encouraged the Soviets to withdraw concurrent with London's forces, in equal stages. But the Soviets refused even to respond. In what appeared a stalling tactic, the Russians claimed that they would withdraw six months after the completion of the war in the *Pacific*, not in Europe as stated in the Tripartite agreement of 1942. The Russians' behavior later, however, suggested that they intended all along to violate even that deferred commitment.[5]

By late 1945, thus, it appeared that the Soviet Union had begun to assume the former Russian Empire's quest for empire. Whereas Bolshevik leaders subsequent to the last world war renounced many of the Czar's conquests, following World War II Premier Stalin appeared eager to regain those lands, plus others. The "Great Game" that Britain and Moscow fought during the nineteenth century was being reincarnated in the middle of the twentieth century, with Washington supplanting London as Moscow's chief antagonist in the lands surrounding the Persian Gulf. One of the initial battlegrounds of the subsequent conflict, known as the Cold War, thus took place in Iran.

Installation of Soviet puppet regime in Azerbaijan draws unified U.S.–U.K. response. The event that caused great consternation in London and Washington was the December 1945 Soviet move to set up an autonomous Republic of Azerbaijan in northwest Iran, in the former Soviet zone of occupation, against the wishes of Tehran. In light of this flagrant violation of Iranian independence, Tehran's diplomats pleaded with U.S. leaders to take on the Soviets, claiming that the future effectiveness of the United Nations in the post-war world was at stake. American leaders, including Acting Secretary of State Dean Acheson, increasingly came to see this crisis in Iran as part of an alarming pattern of Soviet behavior, which by all Western accounts violated both the spirit and content of the Atlantic Charter. Some Americans and Britons feared that a Western capitulation in Azerbaijan might lead to further Soviet violations elsewhere. As the U.S. Ambassador in Iran stated in September 1945: "I am strongly of the opinion time has come for us to take a positive stand against the continuance of present Soviet activities."[6] The Iranians echoed these fears, with the Iranian ambassador warning that the Soviet action in Azerbaijan was "only the first move in a series which [will] include Turkey and other countries in the Near East." If the United States failed to respond, the diplomat warned, the "history of Manchuria,

Abyssinia, and Munich [will] be repeated and Azerbaijan [will] prove to [be] the first shot fired in [the] third world war."

International tensions in early 1946 continued to rise over Soviet behavior in Iran. Joseph Stalin gave a bellicose speech on 9 February 1946 that rattled many Westerners, citing the Soviet Union's encirclement by hostile capitalist nations, and calling for an increase in the production of armaments. Justice William Douglas characterized the speech as tantamount to a "Declaration of World War III." The next month Winston Churchill, whose wartime government had fallen the summer before, delivered his famous "Iron Curtain" speech in Fulton, Missouri, drawing inspiration in part from the Soviets' actions in Iran. In yet a further sign of Moscow's ultimate designs, American and British intelligence sources reported that Soviet military forces in early March 1946 had begun to move from their wartime occupation positions in northern Iran toward Tehran, as well as toward the Turkish and Iraqi borders. To American and British decision-makers, this Soviet behavior grew even more menacing, and now threatened not only obscure Azerbaijan, but also all of Iran, Turkey and Iraq.[7]

America and Britain united to face down the Soviets. The United States

Figure 42 Iranian rifleman on the Azerbaijani border, 1946.

Cold War tensions flared shortly after World War II, when Soviet leaders refused to withdraw from Iranian Azerbaijan. In the new United Nations, Iranian diplomats pleaded with the Americans and British to help enforce Soviet wartime commitments to evacuate troops from the entirety of Iran. After a period of rising tensions in early 1946, the Soviets agreed to withdraw. Above, Iranian troops occupy an observation post near the Azerbaijani border in December 1946.

sent a terse message to Moscow on 9 March, delivered by chargé d'affaires George Kennan. The Iranian ambassador to the United Nations, furthermore, brought the issue to the U.N. spotlight. In the face of Anglo-American diplomatic pressure and adverse publicity in the nascent United Nations, however, Moscow blinked. After several months of rising tensions, Stalin capitulated on 4 April 1946, and the Soviets agreed to withdraw the Red Army from Iran within six weeks. Thus, one of the first conflicts of the Cold War had played itself out in the Persian Gulf region. America and Britain – rather than antagonists, as they had sometimes become in World War II over the issue of Iran's future sovereignty – found themselves united in a reincarnation of the Great Game against Russian expansionism. This withdrawal from Azerbaijan did not end Russian antagonism toward the British and Americans in the Gulf, however. The Soviets, throughout the late 1940s and continuing for decades, broadcast "violently anti-British" radio programs into the Gulf states and encouraged circulation throughout the region of anti-British newspapers.[8]

The loss of India sets back the British position in the Persian Gulf

Although victorious in Europe, Great Britain in 1945 proved virtually bankrupt, with its empire, including India, in dire jeopardy. Disillusioned at the enormous financial and human cost of two debilitating world wars in a generation, and facing the daunting prospect of reconstructing their ruined nation, the British electorate in July 1945 – even before the fighting had stopped in the Pacific theater – turned out of office their victorious wartime government, including its charismatic Conservative leader Winston Churchill. The succeeding Labour leadership won in part due to its focus on the home islands, along with a stated desire to curtail the nation's expenses related to the colonies. In a decision that had monumental repercussions for the Persian Gulf, the Labour Government of Prime Minister Clement Attlee presided in August 1947 over the granting of independence to India, which had for over a century served as both the reason for British presence in the Persian Gulf and the source of military forces to keep the region in the British orbit.

British India and the military forces drawn from it had cast a long shadow over the Gulf region. The British Political Residents and Agents reported primarily to British imperial superiors on the subcontinent, not to Whitehall, for example. The British-led armies and navies drawn from the subcontinent, furthermore, had for over a century maintained order in the Persian Gulf area. Indian-crewed ships sailed close ashore to convince locals to submit to British will, blockaded ports, fired rounds from their broadsides, and sent small armed parties ashore. When more force was required, as in Persia during the Great Game, and in Iraq and Persia in World Wars I and II, the bulk of forces hailed once again from India. So the independence of the subcontinent in 1947 literally overturned political and military arrangements in the Persian Gulf dating back decades.

With regard to the day-to-day operations of the British diplomats in the Persian Gulf, the independence of India proved not so disruptive. Rather than working for the Indian Government, the Political Resident and Agents of the Persian Gulf simply turned toward London, and became part of the diplomatic apparatus of the Foreign Office in the capital city's Whitehall district. The Political Resident in the Persian Gulf remained essentially the chief diplomat for the Persian Gulf's littoral states, and the position beginning in 1950 carried the perquisites of ambassadorial rank.[9] Bahrain remained the Resident's headquarters, as it had since the 1940s, when the British vacated their long-established post at Bushire. The Political Resident in October 1948, reporting from Bahrain, summarized the ease of reporting to London instead of to India "In the Residency the conversion to Foreign Office procedure is pursuing an orderly course. . . ."[10]

But the independence of India also gave rise to some deeper, more profound strategic questions for Great Britain's leaders. With India gone, for example, what would happen to Great Britain's presence in, and commitment to, the states and rulers ringing the Indian Ocean? Britain had arrived during the previous century to these environs largely to defend the flanks and approaches to the subcontinent; with respect to the Persian Gulf, the British came to eradicate piracy and prevent disruptions in maritime trade to India. The British had concluded dozens of treaties with local Persian Gulf rulers, and had made formal and informal promises of security to them. Did the independence of India presage an impending pull-back from the Gulf region? In the immediate aftermath of World War II, Whitehall's answer was "no": British policies in the Persian Gulf region remained essentially intact, due in large part to bureaucratic inertia in London following World War II.

"*It was there because it was there.*" British leaders in the immediate aftermath of the war did not conduct a sweeping reassessment of the nation's diplomatic and military goals and objectives in light of their loss of India. That is the thesis of scholar Phillip Darby, who deemed this failure to reconcile the nation's security commitments with its reduced military and financial assets a monumental "failure to reappraise."[11] This resulted in the nation for over two decades stumbling along previously trodden paths despite the fact that the strategic underpinnings for the old policies had substantially changed. Such a fundamental rethinking in the late 1940s and 1950s almost certainly would have involved trimming British involvement in, and commitments to, nations in the Indian Ocean region – "east of Suez" – including the larger Middle East, the Persian Gulf, eastern Asia, and coastal Africa. But inertia ultimately proved difficult to overcome. In Darby's words:

> The survival of the east of Suez role in its broader form for some two decades after Indian independence was possible only because it was never seriously challenged. It is true that at times committees in Whitehall

Figure 43 British Political Resident Burrows with Bahraini Ruler, 1956.

British hegemony over the Persian Gulf continued after World War II. Agreements between the British and the local Arab sheikhs, some them penned as far back as the mid-1800s, essentially traded British military protection for Arab obeisance. Until 1947, British officials in the Gulf reported eastward to India; despite the end of the British-Indian government, some vestiges of its old foreign policy remained, like the unique office of the British Political Residency. The Resident was originally the British-Indian government's chief representative to the Gulf emirates, fulfilling in many ways the role of an ambassador. Unlike ambassadors, who serve as representatives from one sovereign state to another, the Residents fulfilled a more paternal role. Above, British Political Resident Sir Bernard Burrows and Sheikh Sulman bin Hamed al-Khalifah, ruler of Bahrain, in 1956.

made attempts to reappraise the position, and in Parliament there were calls for withdrawal, but they aroused no great debate and generated little rethinking in the cabinet or the Defence Committee. The structure of British defence was too firmly weighted east of Suez and the role was too deeply rooted in Britain's outlook and history to be vulnerable to routine questioning and criticism. At this level it was not difficult to find persuasive reasons why the Indian Ocean role should be maintained. Economic interests, alliance obligations, and considerations of moral responsibility and world influence served at once to reinforce and to rationalize the continuance of a defence system in the East which, to paraphrase the words of one senior official, was there because it was there.[12]

Britain reduces its naval presence in the region as security concerns in the region were growing. The independence of India took from Britain the ability to draw upon the naval might of the subcontinent as it had for over a century. Leaders of the Royal Navy, accordingly, found themselves in the decade after World War II with a shortfall of resources, coming at a time when Britain's security concerns in the region grew. As one Admiralty report explained:

> Up until 1947 the British position in the Persian Gulf rested on the availability of the Indian Army and the Royal Indian Navy to deal with any emergency and the administration of our protected territories in this area was controlled from India. Since that date four developments had radically altered the situation:
>
> (a) we no longer have Indian power to fall back on;
> (b) the development of oil resources has made the Persian Gulf an increasingly desirable region to hold;
> (c) Saudi Arabia has emerged as a leading Arab power with territorial claims (which she is prepared to push) against our protected Sheikhdoms and against our friend the Sultan of Muscat;
> (d) Persia has ceased to be friendly.[13]

The combination of Britain's post-war financial problems and the loss of the Indian Navy forced the British Admiralty to reduce the number of combatant ships in the Gulf, raising objections from Britain's diplomats. Specifically, London's top naval officials proposed deploying to the Gulf only two frigates for six months of the year, and one frigate for the other six months. As one top naval official explained, "It is clear that we have now reached the stage when the manpower situation will not allow even the smallest additional commitment to be accepted without a corresponding reduction elsewhere."[14] This budget-cutting move amounted to more than a 50 percent reduction in naval presence compared to the years prior to the war.[15] The move met fierce resistance from the British Foreign Office, whose officials for several reasons believed that such cuts would ultimately prove short-sighted. It would lead to the impression that Britain's commitment to the Gulf was wavering, as some believed. Furthermore, in a period of rapid political change and de-colonization around the world, such a move would give umbrage to radical forces who wished the British to depart. And finally, a reduced British role would exacerbate conflicting territorial claims amongst the Gulf's leaders. As one Whitehall official explained in 1954:

> In the view of the Foreign Office [we need to] keep up our naval strength in the Persian Gulf at a time when the importance of that area is growing and its problems are becoming more complex. . . . The Foreign Office are therefore strongly opposed to the proposed reduction . . . In general, too many people in the Middle East have the idea that with a little pushing

we shall leave the whole area. The spread of such a belief in the Gulf would seriously undermine our position there which is so important politically, economically and strategically. It rests largely on our naval strength in those waters; and a reduction in that strength would certainly encourage this dangerous idea.[16]

For those who remained, the mission of maintaining order continued. Even with the reduced number of naval vessels in the Gulf, the British diplomats and naval crews were expected to perform roles that they had fulfilled for decades: maintaining peace in the region between perpetually warring parties, and conducting diplomacy with the local leaders. In March 1952, for example, the Political Officer in the Trucial States directed Royal Navy ships to take action against "the well-known Salim bin Salih" who had been "creating a nuisance." In response, a naval contingent from the ship put ashore to quell the disturbance.[17] In another example of the low-level tribal violence that the British continued to manage, several months later in June 1952 an Arab assassinated the ruler of Kalba, a small emirate near Sharjah. The Royal Navy, at the suggestion of the Political Resident, sent a warship to the coast, "in the hope that the appearance of His Majesty's ships off the town will assist in the 'cold war' against the usurper's morale."[18]

Not only did the Royal Navy ships after the independence of India continue to maintain order in the Persian Gulf, but they also carried out diplomacy with the smaller emirates in the region. The Captain of the HMS *Wren* detailed in colorful language his 1952 meeting with the leader of Fujairah, now part of the United Arab Emirates:

> At 0830, the Ruler of Fujairah, Sheik Mohammed bin Hamad al Sharqi, very recently related by treaty, arrived alongside in all his glory in a gaily bedecked 20-manpower canoe. He was greeted with the usual ceremony and paid his respects to His Excellency and myself. His rather bedraggled personal guard which lined the quarterdeck whilst he was being entertained in my cabin looked most apprehensive about the whole business. On the Sheik's departure he was accorded a 3 gun salute. He seemed to like that and to want more, for his canoe loitered around the ship for some little time. He had had his ration, however, so he was persuaded by a certain amount of handwaving to return to shore.[19]

Sometimes British diplomats went ashore. In another rich account, the Captain of the HMS *Wren* explains:

> Later, His Excellency and I, accompanied by the Political Officer Trucial Coast, landed through the surf on the backs of natives and were met by the entire village who were thronging the beach. Embarking in a land Rover we proceeded through the village, which was very gay with colourful pieces of material fluttering from every barasti hut. Driving inland

through locust infested palm groves occasionally broken by open scrub-land we arrived at the Sheik's residence. We were greeted with sword dances and "threatening" chants by his guards and we sat down to break-fast, a sumptuous Arab feast. We wished we had left our bacon and eggs on board for another day. A motor trip round part of the Sheik's terri-tory occupied the rest of the morning and it was tragic to see the desola-tion amongst the crops as a result of the locusts. We were told that a few days previously, two very young infants had been eaten by them, but we treated this gruesome tale with a certain amount of suspicion. On our return to the village about 1230, more food awaited us: this time, mainly assorted fruit, nuts and halwa (Turkish delight). Having forced this down and showing deep appreciation for everything, we tried to get away, but this was not to be. The main feast was scheduled for 1400 so we lingered on. Some carpets, mattresses and pillows were produced and we did not require much persuasion to take an hour's nap in the heat of the day. At 1430 we sat down to the "real thing", regrettably with practically no appetite. It took six men to carry in the main meat dish! Out of respect for our host we of course had to eat and it was quite an ordeal. Feeling weary and burdened with victuals we took our leave about an hour later.[20]

British continue to prevent tribal sheikhs from attacking one another. The British after World War II also remained heavily involved – as they had for a century – in keeping the feuding families in the Gulf from attacking one another. Many Arabs welcomed the "referee" role that the British played in keeping order. One ruler in the Trucial States, for example, asked for British permission prior to attending a luncheon with a rival. Not only did the sheikh desire to stay on good terms with the British, but he also sought protection from a potential foe, and assistance should the foe take action against him. According to the Political Agent in Sharjah:

On 8 March 1947 the Shaikh of Sharjah invited Shaikh Muhammed bin Hamad ash-Sharqi of Fujairah to lunch. Before accepting, the Shaikh of Fujairah consulted the Residency Agent stating that he feared that the Shaikh of Sharjah might be asking him to lunch to arrest him because Fujairah had, years ago, attained its independence by breaking away from its allegiance to the Jawasami Shaikh of Ras al Khaimah. The Residency Agent advised him that it was safe to accept the invitation and he did so; but, before attending the party, Fujairah called at the Agency to say where he was going. His attitude gives a fair indication of the value certain Trucial Shaikhs place on Sharjah's word.[21]

Thus, despite budget and mission cutbacks after World War II, British dip-lomats and sailors largely carried on in the Persian Gulf as they had for over a century: maintaining order between the perpetually warring locals, and courting the support of their leaders.

After India, British military attention shifts to Egypt. In the years following World War II, then, British Government officials retained their commitments throughout the Persian Gulf, forcing defense officials to develop plans to defend the region without benefit of Indian troops or naval assets. Great Britain maintained promises of defense assistance to virtually all of the Arab emirates along the Gulf's southern coast, as well as to the British-installed monarch in Iraq. Additionally, the British needed to defend their interests at their refinery at Abadan. The task of rethinking defense plans in the region was made even more difficult because of the British withdrawal from Palestine in 1948. Palestine, since World War I, had served as a garrison for large numbers of British troops (although during the last decade of Britain's rule those forces spent the majority of their time and attention maintaining order within Palestine's borders).

One of the chief decisions the British needed to face in the late 1940s surrounded where to place troops designated for action in the Persian Gulf, greater Middle East, and Indian Ocean regions. Without the benefit of the enormous manpower reserves of British India, London's leaders needed to maximize the utility of their human resources by making them as geographically versatile as possible. Worldwide British interests made it equally as likely for the nation's armed forces to be called to the Persian Gulf, Europe, Africa, or Asia. Egypt's Suez Canal Zone emerged as the most adaptable replacement for the garrisons formerly based in India and Palestine. In 1949 the British Joint Planning Staff determined that, of the Middle Eastern states, only Egypt had the requisite nearby supplies of skilled and unskilled labor, industries, port facilities, communications, and airfields.[22] (It should be noted that, as a result of India's independence, the British also augmented their forces in the Far East, where Singapore and Malaya's importance grew.) In British defense plans, the importance of the mammoth base at Suez accordingly increased. The word "base," however, does not really reflect the enormity of the expansive facility, nor the integral role that it played in British defense planning. William Roger Louis, historian of postwar Britain in the Middle East, described the strategic significance of Suez:

> The Suez enclave stretched not only from the Mediterranean to the Red Sea but also westwards three-quarters of the way to Cairo. In the west it included the supply ordnance depot at Tel-el-Kabir, the site of the defeat of the Egyptians in 1882 that signaled the beginning of the British occupation. The enclave's physical structure consisted of a network of roads, railways, harbors, ports, military garrisons, airfield, and a flying boat station. There were ammunition dumps and extensive repair facilities that were irreplaceable. In short it was a vast arsenal.[23]

The loss of India, then, coupled with the failure of the British to substantially scale back their diplomatic or military commitments to the Persian Gulf and other spots "east of Suez," led to a growth in importance of Egypt, and the

Suez Canal Zone facilities that lay inside it. Great Britain's ability to stay in Egypt, however, as well as in other parts of the Middle East would come under attack from a number of different directions. Just as a strong and vocal nationalist movement helped to unseat the British from India, so too did anti-British campaigns threaten London's operation in Egypt and other locales in the greater Middle East and Persian Gulf.

U.S. bilateral relationships with Iran and Saudi Arabia tighten after World War II

During the first two years after World War II the United States and Britain continued to tussle with the Soviets in the latter's attempted drive southward. In addition to the diplomatic row over Azerbaijan, the Soviets the following year threatened Greece and Turkey. When the British informed their American counterparts that London could no longer provide to either Mediterranean country substantial financial aid or troops, the U.S. commenced a mammoth aid package. In all three cases – Iran, Greece, and Turkey – the U.S. had essentially drawn a line beyond which Soviet meddling would meet an American response. By 1948 the Joint Chiefs of Staff confirmed this, stating that the number one U.S. defense priority in the Persian Gulf was the "denial of a foothold to any potentially hostile power."[24] One of the front-line states in that battle to contain the Soviet Union was the nation from which the Gulf was named, Persia.

America's involvement in Iran during World War II had long-lasting repercussions, and kept military trainers involved there for decades. As discussed in the previous chapter, the Shah and Majlis members during World War II welcomed U.S. military forces into Iran. As the last of the American logistics transport troops departed their coastal posts at the end of the war, however, the small advisory teams deep inland in Tehran stayed behind; the U.S. training and advisory commands that they founded would remain through the 1970s. As the official U.S. military historian of the Persian Gulf theater astutely noted in 1952, the lasting effect of America's military involvement in Iran in World War II lay less in the superpower's logistics prowess delivering aid to the Soviet Union than in the political and military bonds that formed between Washington and Tehran:

> The true historical significance of [the U.S. military activity in the Persian Corridor during the war years 1941–45] may well prove to be not the success of the aid-to-Russia supply effort – significant as that was to the victory – but the intimate association of the United States with the state of Iran.[25]

As the war in Europe drew to a close, and as Washington and London re-deployed their troops to the still-raging war in the Pacific, U.S. military officials sought to close the advisory missions in Iran, a move that met with strident objections from Iranian leaders. So strong was the Iranian desire to keep the American advisors that they lobbied the U.S. State Department, who successfully overturned the War Department's recommendation to send them home. From the perspective of the U.S. State Department, the continued presence of the U.S. Gendarmerie and military training missions offered a way to influence events in a nation that bordered the Soviet Union.[26] Accordingly, after the war the U.S. and Iranian Governments chose to renew the U.S. training missions in a formal agreement that stated, "The purpose of this mission is to cooperate with the Ministry of War of Iran and with the personnel of the Iranian Army with a view to enhancing the efficiency of the Iranian Army."[27]

In the late 1940s and early 1950s not only did United States officials continue to provide advisors to the Iranian Government and its military, but they also sent military aid, and large amounts of it, with an eye toward strengthening the state against possible Soviet incursions. In the late 1940s Washington sold surplus World War II arms to the Iranians, for example, including tanks and planes.[28] The Mutual Defense Assistance Act of 1949 served as one of the watershed pieces of legislation during Washington's Cold War battle with the Soviet Union. In it, the U.S. promised to provide military assistance to any "nation whose ability to defend itself, or to participate in the defense of the area of which it is a part, is important to the security of the United States."[29] Along with Korea and the Philippines, U.S. officials designated Iran as an early recipient of aid due in large part to her proximity to the Soviet Union, as well as Moscow's decision three years earlier to contest Tehran's sovereignty over Azerbaijani lands. Along with that materiel came the need for even greater numbers of advisors and trainers. (It should be noted, however, that the U.S. did not open operational bases in Iran, nor did they garrison any troops there during the Cold War battle against the Soviets.) Thus, in the years after World War II, the threat of the Soviet Union led the United States to increase its small cadre of trainers in Iran, long the bastion of the British and Russians who had trampled upon the nation in previous centuries.

U.S. post-war relations with Saudi Arabia. Across the Gulf in Saudi Arabia, America's involvement during World War II also turned into a growing post-war military and diplomatic role in the country. Whereas in Iran the involvement arose as a reaction to the Soviet threat, in the kingdom the U.S. presence stemmed equally from Cold War causes as well as growing U.S. oil industry interests.[30] In both states the superpower desired access to local facilities that might dissuade a Soviet attack, or if it came, might serve as a staging area from which to repel it. And in both states the conflicting aims of America and Britain, which became clear in World War II, gradually diminished. There existed some fundamental differences between the U.S. presence in the 1950s in Iran and Saudi Arabia, however. In Iran, the Shah – whose power and control over the state grew throughout that decade – desired an open and conspicuous role for the United States, believing the superpower's

Figure 44 Traditional Iranian nomad with camel, next to U.S.-supplied armored vehicle, 1956.

> U.S. assistance in the decades after World War II modernized Iran and Saudi Arabia's militaries. During World War II Iran invited American advisors into the country to assist in crafting a new military. After the war those bonds endured, and the U.S. advisory teams stayed in this state that shared a long border with the Soviet Union. This photograph includes both the old and the new, as a U.S.-supplied armored vehicle rolls down a dirt road in Iran.

presence served as a counterweight to historic Russian and British designs. The Saudis, on the other hand, particularly patriarch of the state King Abdul Aziz (Ibn Saud), preferred to keep low profile the American connection, fearing the reaction of conservative elements within the kingdom.

Dhahran Air Base. Throughout the 1940s and 1950s American officials struggled to gain as much control as possible over the Dhahran base, while Saudi officials fought to limit it, a battle that the Saudis ultimately won. The Americans originally pushed for jurisdiction over the field for sixty years, which King Abdul Aziz dismissed "out of hand as inconsistent with the independence of his kingdom, especially in the eyes of his subjects who are quick to suspect foreign domination on the slightest pretext."[31] The King considered this proposal tantamount to a "post-war occupation."[32] The U.S. then back-pedaled, and back-pedaled again, and finally got the King to yield, but were never able to gain from the fiercely independent monarch more than a three year concession.[33]

The Saudi refusal to grant to the U.S. long-term access to Dhahran was

Figure 45 U.S. and Saudi personnel at the U.S.-built Dhahran air base, c. 1947.

> The War Department commenced construction of this base in 1945 at the close of World War II with an eye toward using it in the redeployment by air of thousands of troops and tons of war materiel from the European to the Pacific theater. When the War Department wished to terminate construction of the field at the conclusion of the war, the U.S. State Department urged its completion, for political reasons. With no other military facilities nearby, the American diplomats foresaw the advantage of having a toe-hold in the Persian Gulf region. King Ibn Saud, however, steadfastly refused to grant to the United States a permanent military presence in Dhahran, and the bickering over base rights renewals continued for years. Note the Saudi and American flags.

accompanied by other Saudi rebuffs to American military requests toward the end of World War II. Unlike the Iranian monarch, who fought for, and received, a continuation of U.S. military advisory teams, the Saudi monarch refused to consider an American request to replace a wartime Military Training Mission in Taif with a more permanent mission elsewhere in the kingdom. The Saudi monarch also chose not to accept American offers to construct roads and train military pilots. According to the American minister to Jeddah William Eddy, the King declined these American overtures in order to avoid domestic and international condemnation of foreign involvement in his sovereign domains.[34]

The U.S. did not give up in its quest for long-term rights to Dhahran. As the Cold War intensified in the late 1940s and early 1950s, it became increasingly accepted within U.S. diplomatic and military circles that future

Figure 46 Saudi Bedouin inspects B-29 intercontinental bomber at Dhahran, c. 1947.

The old meets the new. Here a Saudi Bedouin inspects the tail gun of the first B-29 intercontinental bomber to land in Saudi Arabia. In addition to serving as a logistics and transportation base, U.S. Strategic Air Command planners anticipated using Dhahran as a staging field from which to strike Soviet targets.

wars would involve bombing runs by opposing air forces,[35] highlighting in U.S. eyes the importance of Dhahran. Unlike the British, who possessed a number of major air facilities in Iraq, Jordan, Suez, and elsewhere in the Middle East, the United States controlled only Dhahran. General Harper, Commanding General of the Air Transport Command, visited Saudi Arabia in April 1948, as Russian bellicosity toward Berlin and elsewhere was increasing. The base would be critical, the General said, should the Soviet Union march southward toward the valuable oil fields of the Persian Gulf:

If war should come tomorrow, fifty, eighty, or perhaps one hundred

B-29's would have to come to Dhahran for the defense of Saudi Arabia. . . . What would save the Saudi Arabian army from destruction if 100,000 Russians should suddenly appear in Saudi Arabia?[36]

Saudis concerned less with Soviets than neighboring Hashemites. Despite America's preoccupation with the Soviet threat, in reality the Saudis' chief post-war security concern proved their neighboring Hashemite rivals. In the late 1940s, as the Saudi monarch found himself surrounded by potentially hostile British-backed regimes, the King reversed some earlier rebuffs to the Americans, and made requests to the United States for military assistance. But the Saudis wanted military assistance less to deter a Soviet invasion than to deter their neighbors. They recognized that while the U.S. would undoubtedly support the Saudi dynasty should the Russians attack, Washington would likely do little in the more likely event that the Hashemites invaded. The Saudi monarch believed that, after he chose America over Britain as the recipient of the Saudi oil concessions, London officials set out to destroy him. The British, after all, had installed on the Iraqi and Trans-Jordanian thrones two sons of his arch-rival the Sharif Hussein of Mecca, whom Ibn Saud defeated in the 1920s as he swept across the Arabian Peninsula. In his eyes, the Hashemite family longed to reclaim the position as custodian of the holy places, and thus viewed Ibn Saud as a foe. To bolster his defenses against the British-supported Hashemites, then, Ibn Saud felt as if he had nowhere else to turn but to America, but America was not fulfilling their portion of the bargain:

> Since [we gave our oil concession to the Americans and not to the British] the British feeling [of friendship toward me] has changed. They have been looking with jealous eyes because they know we [the Saudis and Americans] have established close relations. So they have started to support the Sharifian [Hashemite] Family against me, from the military point of view. . . . I am in a very critical situation. The British themselves will never give me any help. Those Sharifian friends of the British will find an opportunity against me. They have soldiers; they have troops, and they have already sent for military equipment.[37]

In pleading his case, the King argued that America had a moral obligation to help, in return for the oil concessions. Ibn Saud also felt that he had put himself in a very precarious position with respect to his own people, and that only U.S. assistance would help:

> The whole people [are] saying that my country is an American colony. They are plotting against me and saying Ibn Saud has given his country to the United States, even the Holy Places. They are talking against me. I have nothing, and my country and my wealth I have delivered into the hands of America. . . . I want [the Americans] to treat me as the British

are treating the Iraqis, so that I will be strong enough to defend myself in any case. . . .

I used to depend on the British for help. Since I have established relations with the Americans I am weak. I have no soldiers, no mechanized equipment. Since the British are strengthening my enemies I ought to have such military help and mechanized equipment. I have given to the Americans all my wealth. I want two things: I want them to strengthen me and to deal with me as the British are treating my enemies.[38]

What Ibn Saud wanted, in other words, was a promise from Washington to defend the Saudi regime from their British-backed jealous Arab neighbors. As the Saudi Deputy Foreign Minister explained in 1948:

If [an attack on Saudi Arabia] is from Russia then the defense will be a joint effort of the whole world. His Majesty has no doubt that America and Britain will make a joint effort to stop such an attack. There is no need for His Majesty to have assurances of defense by America and Britain in case of attack by Russia, but if Bahrain were to attack Saudi Arabia it would be referred to the United Nations. We want some assurance that if an attack does take place [from] nearby we will have something to defend ourselves with. His Majesty is expecting to receive the help of the United States Government to form four military groups with mechanized equipment and arms. These will defend Saudi Arabia in case of any attack from any neighboring country and these will be at the same time helpful to you.[39]

With this in mind, if the United States sought to use Saudi territory in its battle against the Soviet Union, the Saudis believed, then the superpower ought to stand ready to defend the kingdom from its neighbors. Such a promise the U.S. never delivered, and Washington rebuffed Saudi attempts at such a formal agreement.[40]

Just as the Mutual Defense Assistance Act of 1949 gave the legislative backing to American efforts to assist Iran, so too did that legislation ultimately provide the legal framework for the United States to provide robust quantities of military assistance to Saudi Arabia. In 1951 – after much Saudi prodding – the U.S. government designated the kingdom as authorized to receive military assistance, a mix of outright grants of military equipment, and the cash-sale of the same, to Saudi Arabia. To go along with the new military equipment, the U.S. agreed, with Saudi concurrence, to send to the kingdom a military training team (similar to the one the Saudis terminated at the end of World War II). The U.S. Military Training Mission to Saudi Arabia, a U.S. unit that still exists in the early twenty-first century emerged from this act, and in the words of the U.S. Ambassador to Saudi Arabia, aimed to provide "assistance and advice to the Saudi Arabian Minister of

Defense and Aviation, as well as units of the Saudi Arabian armed forces, with respect to plans, organization, administration principles, training methods, and the conduct of such training as is agreed upon between the Saudi Arabian Minister of Defense and Aviation and the Chief of the Advisory Group. This training will include the use of the various kinds of weapons, tactics, and logistics."[41]

Anglo-American relationship in post-war Saudi Arabia. If the U.S. and Saudi Arabia, then, emerged from World War II with decidedly stronger bilateral ties, how did London officials, who for decades had provided the king with generous cash subsidies, react? Initially, as they had during the war, the British fought the emerging relationship, but later acceded to it, and then finally encouraged it. During World War II, the British and Americans competed for favor with Saudi leaders. The two sides ultimately reached a tacit agreement in which both sides agreed to limit their donations to that of the other. In a reflection of their determination to supplant the British in Saudi Arabia after the war, however, U.S. officials refused to limit their contribution to King Ibn Saud to the £1.25 million that the British had deemed the maximum that their treasury could afford.[42]

By the early 1950s, with American and British attention increasingly devoted to the Cold War against the Soviet Union, Washington leaders reached out to their counterparts in London, to try to calm their rivalry within the kingdom. With regard to a 1951 controversy over British desires to train Saudi officers, for example, U.S. Secretary of State Dean Acheson remarked that, "In general, there would be no objection to British participation in military training of Saudi Arabian forces if there is coordination of U.S. and U.K. programs." Furthermore, after a visit to the Middle East, one top U.S. diplomat voiced to another his displeasure at the lack of U.S.–U.K. strategic agreement in the Middle East, stating that he was "a little perturbed over what he considers to be a lack of complete overall strategic agreement between the U.S. and U.K. in this region. . . . Don't you think that we should get all this cleared up?"[43] Several months later, briefing the first military planning group to travel to the kingdom following the U.S. military assistance agreements of June 1951, State Department officials suggested that the Americans do everything possible to keep the British engaged in the region, and that U.S. interests were furthered by doing so:

> The British have been training Saudi Arabian Army officers and NCOs at Taif since January 1947. A military cadet school has been established there for both basic and specialized training. British experience might be very useful as a guide in planning and in appraising Saudi capacity to absorb military instruction. Friendly coordination with the British training mission to avoid duplication of effort has been agreed upon by both State and Defense. The British Government has been so informed and it concurs. It is possible that the Saudi Arabian Government may wish to terminate British training activities when the U.S. mission becomes

operative. The British are our principal allies, and the defense of the Near East generally is, in the first instance, their responsibility. Those relationships should not be disturbed. We accordingly prefer that the British mission should remain and possible Saudi Arabian suggestions to the contrary should be discouraged.[44]

Thus, by the early 1950s, several years of Russian aggression around the world had pushed American and British officials to see eye-to-eye in Saudi Arabia. American officials had come to value, and wanted to keep, Britain's presence and security involvement in the region.

Notwithstanding this rapprochement, both sides nonetheless continued to rib and compete with one another, and proved reluctant to cede advantages to the other. Acheson himself, although approving the British training of Saudi officers, noted, "It would also be preferable that British training should not be extended on a basis more favorable than that which we may be able to offer."[45] The lingering U.S.–British rivalry also shows up in naval reporting in the region. Although the Royal Navy by most all accounts welcomed their American counterparts to the Gulf after World War II – one British ship's crew in 1948 entertained or met with American officials and businessmen seven times in one month[46] – the Senior Naval Officer in the Persian Gulf's reports to his British seniors include stinging put-downs of the Americans: "The passage was only noteworthy for almost criminally bad navigation by an American tanker,"[47] and, "By a misfortune which seems fated to occur whenever American warships are involved, my only serviceable motor boat broke down between the boom and gangway when coming alongside."[48] Notwithstanding these biting comments, U.S. Navy and Royal Navy officers and sailors, for most of the time, seemingly worked together well, as Washington deployed to the Gulf for the first time a modest naval flotilla to complement its growing oil interests in Saudi Arabia.

U.S. Navy's Middle East Force reflected growing oil interests in Saudi Arabia. Despite a few isolated American merchant voyages and military naval calls in the Persian Gulf over the previous decades,[49] World War II essentially served as the United States' entry into the maritime affairs of the region. Throughout the conflict, furthermore, U.S. oil tankers began to move fuel out of the Gulf for use in the Pacific and other theaters. At the conclusion of the conflict, while the combatant ships largely sailed home, the tankers remained. The U.S. military continued to draw fuel from the refineries in the Gulf; from 1946 to 1950, for example, approximately a third of all petroleum transported by the U.S. Navy originated in the Persian Gulf.[50]

As a result of the growing military dependence on Persian Gulf oil, the U.S. Navy formalized its presence in the region in the late 1940s. On 28 January 1948 the U.S. Navy formally established a task force of oil tankers in the Gulf. The organization went through two name changes before receiving the moniker "Middle East Force" (MEF) on 16 August 1949.[51] For the next several decades MEF crews sailed the region, paying calls on diplomats and heads of state throughout the region. To be sure, the U.S. Navy's flotilla inside the Gulf was small – usually less than a handful of ships through the 1990s – and it did not rival the naval presence in the Gulf of the British. The Navy captains who originally commanded the units were far junior to their British Vice Admiral counterparts.[52] Nor did the U.S. MEF attempt to assume the role of maintaining order in the region, as Britain's forces had been doing for over a century. But the MEF's establishment did reflect a growing interest in the Gulf relating to oil, and to the growing U.S. relationship with both Saudi Arabia and Iran. Of the two, to U.S. Navy officials, the Saudi relationship predominated, due to the Navy's job of transporting oil. Reflecting the growing importance of that country, the MEF's commanding officer in 1949 spent most of his time in Saudi Arabia, not in his homeport of Bahrain. According to British naval reports, he only went on board his ships "three or four days in the last two months. He spends a lot of time ashore at Dhahran."[53] Reflecting the U.S. Navy's growing involvement in the region, the Chief of Naval Operations in 1948 directed the crew of the USS *Rendova*, an aircraft carrier, and a clutch of other escort ships into the Gulf on a short public relations cruise. How much goodwill the U.S. Navy gained from the trip is uncertain, however, for in protest of America's recent recognition of the state of Israel, many Arab dignitaries declined their invitations to tour the mammoth U.S. warship.[54]

If the U.S. interests in the kingdom stemmed primarily from oil concerns, then, why didn't the U.S. Navy operate from Saudi Arabia instead of Bahrain? First, large and existing British facilities existed in Bahrain, only 30 miles from Dhahran, the center of U.S. oil activities in eastern Saudi Arabia. American ships since the war had enjoyed access to Bahrain, and local officials posed no objections to continued operations there. As well, Bahrain itself possessed some American interests; despite being a British-controlled island, the Bahraini Petroleum Company was run chiefly by Americans. Had American naval officials desired to operate from the nearby Saudi coast, gaining permission to do so would have proven difficult. As the struggle over the Dhahran air base suggested, Ibn Saud jealousy guarded the sovereignty of his nation, and any attempt to gain additional U.S. military rights in the kingdom would undoubtedly have proven time-consuming and expensive. In the end, American officials chose to continue operating from the British naval base in Bahrain.

Anti-colonial movements in Iran, Egypt, and Iraq shape British defenses and Anglo-American relations

Throughout the 1950s the British faced one setback after another as anti-colonial movements erupted in the Middle East. By the end of the 1950s the British were in retreat, struggling to figure out where to garrison their troops designated for Persian Gulf defense, and how they would fulfill their commitments to the region.

Figure 47 U.S. Navy's Middle East Force flagship on diplomatic mission to Oman, c. 1956.

The United States by the end of World War II had become a net importer of oil. Although the continental states received the bulk of their imports from the Western hemisphere, America's military forces in Asia and Europe grew increasingly dependent on oil from the Persian Gulf. Reflecting the growing importance of the region to the defenses of the United States, in the late 1940s Washington directed U.S. Navy leaders to stand-up a small flotilla that eventually took the moniker "Middle East Force." Far from a war-fighting unit, the collection of 2–4 small ships spent the majority of their time engaged in diplomatic missions, traveling from port to port in the area. Above, the flagship of the Middle East Force, the USS *Valcour* (AVP-55), in the waters of Oman, with an Omani sailor in the foreground. The ship was originally a seaplane tender, and painted white prior to service in the sun and heat of the Persian Gulf. Circa 1956.

Britain's deteriorating position in Iran. Since the early 1900s Great Britain's primary interest in the Persian Gulf – control of the sea routes and flanks to India – had begun to wane, while the growth of British oil interests grew. Those concerns centered upon southern and western Persia and the refinery complex at Abadan, in the Iranian tributaries to the Persian Gulf. The word "refinery," however, doesn't capture the size and importance of the facility to the British, which historian William Roger Louis has aptly described:

> The refinery at Abadan was the largest in the world. Its importance for the British economy . . . may be conveyed here by the fact that in 1945 Iran produced more oil than all of the Arab countries combined. The British community of 4,500 lived as a separate and self-contained cultural unit. The oil fields in southern Iran and the refinery at Abadan functioned independently from the Iranian economy. The Anglo-Iranian

Oil Company possessed its own fleet, its own hospitals, and its own schools. Members of the Gymkhana Club in Abadan read the airmail edition of *The Times*. The refinery itself was a tribute to British technology. Between 1945 and 1950 the production of Arab and Persian oil increased from 13 to 18 per cent of the world's total. In 1950–52 the world's oil production rose from 535 million tons to 637 million, of which Iran produced 30 million.[55]

Britain's control of this complex, however, along with the riches that came from it, increasingly drew Iranian ire. This is not surprising, given that a prominent theme of modern Iranian history is an attempt to throw off domination by outside powers.

Paralleling the swell of post-war anti-colonial movements that erupted after World War II, in Iran popular resentment grew in the 1950s against the lingering vestiges of British dominance, particularly London's continued control of Abadan and the Anglo-Iranian Oil Company (AIOC), which dated back to 1914.[56] These anti-British feelings increased even further in late 1950 following the announcement from across the Gulf that Americans had capitulated to the Saudis and agreed to a 50/50 split in oil profits. This American deal proved much more generous than the British 16 percent original royalty to the Iranians that dated back to the concession of 1901,[57] or the 30 percent concession of 1949.[58] Presciently sensing the explosive nature of the new American royalty deal, prior to making it public American diplomats approached the British to give them advance notice, to head off a possible crisis.[59] The British, however, did not initially match the American offer. When the terms of the new U.S.–Saudi deal became public, as the Americans predicted, an Iranian uproar ensued. According to U.S. Assistant Secretary of State George McGhee's first-hand account of the crisis, the Iranians demanded from the British more money and greater control of the oil industry within their borders:

> Prime Minister Razmara had demanded four points to sweeten the agreement in order to obtain Majlis ratification: a ten-year Iranianization program, the right of Iran to examine the AIOC books to determine their share of the profits, oil prices in Iran equal to the lowest given to others, and full information as to destination of oil exported.[60]

Responding to McGhee's attempts to help foster an agreement, the AOIC board of directors essentially told him to "mind his own business."[61]

In the end, the British officials at the Anglo-Iranian Oil Company grudgingly proffered concessions, ultimately offering a 50/50 split in profits, but it proved too late: a nationalist revolt against the British had begun. The political situation quickly grew out of hand in Iran. A temperate Iranian prime minister who opposed radical calls for nationalization fell to an assassin's bullet, and popular calls for taking over the British oil concerns grew. The National Front, a left-leaning group whose populist leader Mohammed Mossadegh championed appropriating the British oil giant, grew in stature. The young Shah – before the virtually unlimited powers that he later took for his police state in the 1970s – proved unable to rein in the increasingly uncontrollable forces within the Majlis. Assistant Secretary of State McGhee, who met with the Shah during this turbulent period in 1951, described a dejected monarch, resigned to the parliament's ultimately confiscating the British oil company without his approval:

> I had been with the Shah about a year and a half earlier during his much publicized official visit to Washington. He had been a proud, erect young man, insistent that his requests be taken seriously. As I saw him in the darkened audience chamber in which he received me, lounging on a sofa, he was a dejected, almost broken man. I sensed that he feared he, too, might be assassinated. . . . He looked lost, as if he thought the whole affair hopeless. I left him alone in his darkened room. I will always remember his sad, brooding face. I was greatly influenced in reaching my own conclusion, from the Shah's attitude, that neither he nor anyone else could persuade the Iranians not to nationalize the AOIC. It was not long after this that the Shah fled the country.[62]

Despite the attempts of British and American diplomats to head off such an eventuality, in April 1951 the Shah bowed to pressure from the public and appointed Mohammed Mossadegh as Prime Minister. Three days later, the Shah signed legislation nationalizing the AIOC.

After nationalizing the oil company the Iranians evicted the British in 1951 from the Abadan refinery complex. British warships sailed up the Persian Gulf headwaters to preside over an orderly evacuation, with Royal Navy crews prepared to take the refinery by force if ordered.[63] But those orders never came from Labour Government leaders, and by the end of the year the British were gone from Iran.

Arab leaders on the other side of the Gulf lamented the Labour Government's inaction, believing it incredible that London would allow the Iranians to insult them in such a manner. The ruler of Kuwait believed that the British should have used force, and Bahrain's ruler longed for a return to a strong leader like Churchill.[64]

Iranian production of oil fell drastically, from 30 million tons annually to one million.[65] With the decline in oil production came a corresponding decline in Iranian oil revenues. The deteriorating condition in one of the Soviet Union's border states caused grave concern in Washington and London. CIA documents released in the early twenty-first century reveal that the White House and Whitehall leaders feared that a crumbling economy under Mossadegh would lead to bedlam, anarchy, and the ensuing collapse of the Iranian state, conditions from which the Soviets would assuredly benefit.[66]

Figure 48 Abadan refinery, 1951.

The petrochemical complex in Abadan, above in 1951, remained after World War II one of the largest in the world. British intransigence in renegotiating royalties to the Iranian government in the early 1950s preceded a crisis between the Anglo-Iranian Oil Company and the Iranian government that ended in the company's nationalization. Royal Navy ships stood ready to take over the complex, but the order to do so never came from London. Instead, British residents embarked on navy ships and evacuated the complex, after a half-century of presence there. British Petroleum, a successor to the AIOC, opened a refinery at Aden shortly after the crisis. Oil exports from Kuwait became increasingly important after the British loss of AIOC.

With this in mind, and growing increasingly uncomfortable with the National Front and Mossadegh, American and British officials working through the Central Intelligence Agency and MI6 engineered a 1953 coup,[67] which a U.S. Secretary of State several decades later confirmed.[68] After Mossadegh's ouster, an army general took power as Prime Minister, and the Shah – who had characteristically fled – returned home to face a more compliant Majlis.

After siding for decades with the Iranians in their attempts to break free of British domination, why in 1953 did Washington side with London to overthrow a nationalist leader? In short, because of the danger a disintegrating Iran posed in the larger Cold War battle between the United States and the Soviet Union. Early in the Anglo-Iranian oil row American officials actually proved sympathetic to Iran, supporting Tehran's claims that they should have a larger voice in the affairs of the Anglo-Iranian Oil Company. American

Figure 49 Tehran riots, encouraged by covert Anglo-American campaign to overthrow Prime Minister Mohammed Mossadegh, 1953.

London and Washington feared the economic chaos that followed Iran's nationalization of the Anglo-Iranian Oil Company, viewing it as a potential setback in the Cold
War battle against the Soviet Union. Anglo-American intelligence officers stirred up
anti-Mossadegh protests in Iran.

diplomats, in fact, encouraged the British to concede on some matters, aiming
to defuse the tension.[69] Although U.S. officials hoped to avert an Iranian
nationalization of AIOC, when it came, they recognized the Iranian right
to do so, assuming proper compensation for the rightful shareholders.[70] In the
early stages of the oil nationalization feud, thus, the United States Government often sympathized with the nationalist aspirations of the Iranians, as
FDR had in World War II.[71]

Economic mismanagement that might lead to government collapse, however, was a different matter. Such an outcome in Iran proved a vital national
security risk that Washington officials in the Eisenhower Administration
proved unwilling to take. As long as support for nationalist groups did not
jeopardize Washington's position vis-à-vis the Soviet Union, then Washington
tended to support them. But when such action threatened to set back the U.S.
in its Cold War battle with the Soviets – which is what ultimately Eisenhower
officials envisioned the Mossadegh government would do – then the U.S.
dropped its support of nationalist causes. U.S. leaders in 1953 simply proved
unwilling to take a chance that a critical state on the Soviet Union's southern
border – a principal battleground during previous centuries in Great Britain's

battle to hem in the Russian Empire – might fall. In a state further distant from the Soviets, however, U.S. officials in the 1950s proved more accepting of moves by a nationalist leader to attack British interests, attacks that would adversely affect Great Britain's ability to defend the Persian Gulf.

Egypt and the British Suez base. Although Egypt lays several hundred miles away from the Persian Gulf, its central role in Arab politics in the 1950s and 1960s makes it an integral part of this story. After World War II, when Britain lost India, it lost its strategic garrison with which to maintain order in the Gulf. Egypt, and particularly the military facilities adjacent the Suez Canal, became the new British military garrison for the greater Middle East. The Egyptians, however, as the Indians before them, longed to rid their country of British domination. A nationalist, anti-colonial movement arose that eventually drove the British from that country, too.

The roots of British involvement in Egypt went back eight decades. Beginning in the 1870s the Egyptian Khedive's profligate government turned to British creditors to keep his regime afloat, and thereafter British bankers assumed large roles in affairs of state. The new Suez Canal also attracted London's interest and involvement. Although a French concern originally constructed the Suez Canal, British ships accounted for 80 percent of the waterway's early shipping traffic, plying back and forth from British interests in India and Asia. British leaders concluded that they needed to control the Canal, and in 1875 purchased 44 percent of the Canal Company's shares from the Egyptian leader.

Reflecting the growing British commercial and strategic interests in Egypt, in 1882 British military forces intervened in riots in Alexandria; later, British troops marched on the canal cities of Port Said, Suez, Ismailiyya, Tel-el-Kabir, and finally the capital Cairo, marking the start of a long military occupation of the nation.[72] For the next seven decades, the British dominated the nation. Although Egypt was nominally part of the Ottoman Empire in the late 1800s and early 1900s – like several of the emirates of the Persian Gulf – London more than Istanbul maintained real control over the state. When the British and the Ottomans opposed each other in World War I, the British terminated Cairo's fealty to Istanbul, deposed the Egyptian monarch, replaced him with his uncle, and declared that a British protectorate existed over Egypt.

Throughout the first half of the twentieth century the British presence stoked fierce anti-colonial passions in Egypt. The Egyptians received in 1922 a nominal grant of independence from the British; a 1936 Anglo-Egyptian treaty strengthened the Arab state further. The nation's independence, however, proved chimerical. The enormous British military garrisons in and around Suez served as the ultimate arbiter of politics in Egypt. In 1942, for example, the British viewed with disfavor the German tilt of the Egyptian Government and demanded that the Egyptian king select an anti-fascist party to rule the parliament. When the monarch refused, the British surrounded the palace with troops, and prevailed.[73] Whatever credibility the king had previously enjoyed he lost, and the Egyptian masses increasingly concluded that the monarch served as a stooge to the British occupiers.

Immediately after World War II, however, while granting to India its independence, British leaders refused to consider an evacuation from Egypt. Even Labour leader Clement Attlee – champion of anti-colonial causes – rebuffed Egyptian overtures at the initial United Nations proceedings in San Francisco. Attlee decided to "move cautiously,"[74] and to keep British troops in Egypt.

In July 1952 a group of Egyptian military officers seized power and forced the king to abdicate and flee into exile. No outpouring of grief followed. King Farouq remained in the eyes of Egyptian nationalists, after all, a part of the British establishment. If the Egyptians wanted *true* autonomy, many nationalists believed, they also needed to evict the British military from Suez, a key demand of the new revolutionary regime led by the so-called Free Officers of Egypt.

Egyptian calls for British departure from Suez coincided with a growing recognition within the ruling Conservative Party that Britain's overseas commitments, including those in the Middle East, exceeded their resources. Whitehall officials saw the rising Egyptian agitation – even *before* Farouq's overthrow, Egyptian parliamentary leaders assailed the Anglo-Egyptian treaty[75] – and questioned whether or not it made military sense to stay. The future of that garrison at Suez carried great importance for if it should go, Great Britain's ability to defend the greater Middle East, and of course the Persian Gulf, would go with it.

In the face of financial constraints at home and nationalist agitations in the Middle East, the British in the early 1950s engaged in negotiations with the Egyptians over the future of the Suez Canal Zone. Foreign Secretary (later Prime Minister) Anthony Eden explained in 1953 that whatever benefit Great Britain might derive from staying in Suez would be squandered if the British had to spend inordinate resources quelling local opposition:

> We cannot afford to keep 80,000 men indefinitely in the Canal Zone. Already our overseas current expenditure – mainly military – has risen from £160 million in 1950 to £222 million (provisional estimate) in 1952.
>
> With our limited resources, it is essential that we should concentrate on the points where our vital strategic needs or the necessities of our economic life are at stake and that we should utilize our strength in the most economical way. It is not possible for our present forces in the Canal Zone to support our peace-time interests elsewhere in the Middle East. If we leave them there in defiance of the Egyptians they will be wholly absorbed in coping with the situation which their very presence creates.[76]

The Conservative Government in October 1954, in that vein, concluded with Egypt's revolutionary government an agreement that called for Britain's total military withdrawal from Suez by June 1956. This agreement, however, provided for Britain's use of Egyptian facilities in wartime, if needed, and committed both parties to uphold the 1888 convention guaranteeing the freedom of navigation on the waterway.[77]

This proposed withdrawal from Suez proved important with respect to Britain's defense of the Persian Gulf, for after the independence of India the British had envisioned Egypt as the primary repository of equipment and personnel from which to draw in an emergency. With the military soon to depart from Suez, the British had to figure out how to defend the Gulf. This decision would become critical after the Suez Crisis of 1956, in which Israeli, British, and French forces attacked the Suez Canal.[78] The debacle that ensued proved so egregious that Cold War foes U.S. and U.S.S.R. agreed to condemn it. The British, French, and Israelis later withdrew.

The fiasco in Suez proved equally disastrous to Britain's ability to sustain its security commitments to the Persian Gulf. Not only could Britain after

Figure 50 Aircraft carrier transits Suez Canal, 1948.

The aircraft carrier USS *Rendova* transits the Suez Canal in May 1948 on a trip to the Persian Gulf. The British since the 19th century garrisoned troops near the canal, a vital link in that connected London to its interests in Asia. During the decade following World War II, tensions flared between Egyptian nationalists and British leaders concerning basing rights at Suez. Egyptian President Gamal Abdul Nasser nationalized the canal in 1956, a move that precipitated an attack by Britain, France, and Israel.

1956 not depend on the use of the Suez base in wartime, as promised in the 1954 Anglo-Egyptian agreement, but a huge question emerged as to whether or not Britain in time of war could use the canal to transport materiel and personnel to the scene of a crisis. With British-Indian army forces gone, and with the facilities in Palestine and Suez now gone, too, how would Britain sustain its military commitments in the Indian Ocean area, including the Persian Gulf? The Suez Crisis began a period of profound rethinking of defense decision-making that stretched into the early 1960s.

Arabs use oil as a weapon. One of the notable developments during the Suez Crisis was the use for the first time by the Arabs of their oil supply as a political weapon. During the conflict Egyptian forces scuttled ships in the entrance to the Suez Canal, rendering it impassable. Nasser proclaimed that the critical waterway would remain closed "so long as there is a single foreign soldier left on Egyptian soil."[79] At the same time, several hundred miles away the Syrian Army sabotaged the pumping stations along the pipeline that delivered oil from Hashemite Iraq to Mediterranean ports. Taken together, the Egyptian and Syrian moves had a substantial – although not crippling – effect on the West, particularly Europe. In the mid 1950s approximately 80 percent of Europe's oil supplies came through the Suez Canal,[80] most from the Persian Gulf. (The age of the enormous "supertanker," whose draft and beam often prohibit transit through the canal, had not yet arrived.) Although burdensome and somewhat costly, the Egyptian and Syrian moves did not have a crippling effect on the West. Although the 1956 Suez crisis marked the *first* time that the Arabs used oil as a weapon, it would not be the last. In conjunction with two later conflicts – in 1967 and 1973 – the Arab states would do the same thing.

The Eisenhower Doctrine. President Eisenhower viewed with great concern the British humiliation that stemmed from the Suez Crisis, which seemed likely to spread and hasten Britain's further disengagement from the region. Although he had consistently condemned the British, French, and Israeli invasion of October–November 1956, the President abhorred this growing vacuum in the greater Middle East, which he believed would leave the door wide open to Soviet meddling. Since a 1955 arms deal between Egypt and Czechoslovakia, after all, the Soviets' shadow had grown over the Middle East, and as London's position continued to deteriorate Moscow's appeared likely to strengthen. Such was the thinking behind President Eisenhower's political initiative of early 1957, later called the "Eisenhower Doctrine."[81] In a speech before Congress on 5 January 1957, less than two months following the British capitulation in Suez, the President put forth proposed legislation "designed to deal with the possibility of Communist aggression, direct and indirect" in the Middle East.[82] America's view of the Middle East, one could say, had increasingly come to be seen in terms of the Cold War. In his presentation to Congress Eisenhower attacked Russian designs on the region, stating: "Russia's rulers have long sought to dominate the Middle East. That was true of the Czars and it is true of the Bolsheviks. . . . The reason for Russia's interest in the Middle East is solely that of power politics. Considering her announced purpose of Communizing the world, it is easy to understand her hope of dominating the Middle East."[83]

What did the Eisenhower Doctrine entail? Essentially the President believed that economic and military weakness in the Middle East that would likely follow a British disengagement from the greater region would breed conditions that the Soviets would exploit. To prevent this, the President proposed – and Congress approved in March – that the United States should "cooperate with and assist any nation or group of nations in the general area of the Middle East in the development of economic strength dedicated to the maintenance of national independence." Washington, in other words, aimed to prevent Moscow's further encroachment on the greater Middle East. The legislation also provided for "military assistance and cooperation with any nation or group of nations which desires such aid." Finally, the plan author-ized the U.S. to provide "such assistance and cooperation" necessary, includ-ing the use of American armed force, "to secure and protect the territorial integrity and political independence" of Middle Eastern nations threatened by "overt armed aggression from any nation controlled by International Communism."[84] Within a year of Congress's assent to the Eisenhower Doctrine, the U.S. president would invoke it to send troops to the Middle East region. Why? The unexpected loss of another British lynchpin in the Persian Gulf, Iraq, whose Western-friendly regime fell in an anti-monarchical coup.

British forced out of Iraq. As President Eisenhower had feared, throughout the 1950s Egyptian-inspired anti-colonial fervor spread throughout the Arab world. Nasser's quest for Arab unity took one step forward with the announcement in February 1958 that Syria would join Egypt in a "United Arab Republic." Syria had become a hotbed of anti-Western activism, which spilled into neighboring Iraq. Feeling the heat of Nasserism, the Iraqi regime during the mid 1950s had demanded a lower profile for the British in the country, particularly at Iraq's largest military base outside of Baghdad, Habbaniya. In addition to the military facility at Suez, the large air base at Habbaniya played the next most critical role in the British ability to project power to the Persian Gulf. Habbaniya dated back to the late 1920s and early 1930s when Britain, desiring to free itself of the need to police and administer the nation while still maintaining an air presence in the region, struck a deal with the Iraqi regime to abandon a highly visible Baghdad air base and move its facilities to a much less noticeable location 50 miles outside of town.[85] In the 1950s it became increasingly likely that Britain would lose the use of the mammoth military facility at Suez. The Iraqi air facility for a few years became increasingly important, and London redeployed from Suez to Habbaniya some air units.[86]

But in Iraq, like in Egypt, growing pro-nationalist sentiments forced the British-backed regime to renegotiate the military agreements with London. Iraqi public sentiment would have favored a complete severing of ties with the

British, but the Westward-leaning regent to the young King Faisal II proved able to arrange a deal that turned over to the Iraqis nominal sovereignty of their military bases, but still provided for some British use. From that point on, however, it was the Iraqis, not the British, who possessed ultimate control. In 1955 the British penned with Iraqi leaders a formal agreement. King Faisal himself attended the ceremony at the Habbaniya base on 2 May 1955, where the Royal Air Force flag came down and the Iraq flag raised in its place.[87]

Despite their limited access to Habbaniya and Shaiba, another air base outside Basra, the British understood the magnitude of the loss. According to Air Chief Marshal Sir David Lee:

> The loss to the RAF of the Habbaniya base, which had been built up and magnificently equipped over the years, was clearly to be a major disadvantage. In addition, it would no longer be possible to use Iraq as a base from which to operate either in the Persian Gulf area, or to the west in the Eastern Mediterranean. The acceptance of these disadvantages was, however, inevitable and it was hoped that they would be offset by the advantages which would accrue from the broader based treaty relationships.[88]

Despite these concessions, however, on 14 July 1958, members of a military-led coup murdered and dismembered many members of the Iraqi ruling regime. King Faisal II was killed, along with his uncle Abdul Illah. With the revolution came the loss of what many believed to be the West's most stead-fast ally in the region, the Iraqi monarchy. As Eisenhower lamented, "This was the country that we were counting on heavily as a bulwark of stability and progress in the region."[89]

The strategic implication of the loss of Egypt and Iraq: an air barrier emerges. By 1958, then, the British had suffered twin blows, both of which brought into question how they would uphold security commitments to the Persian Gulf. They had lost the right to operate from Egypt's Suez base, and they had also ceded control of the air bases in Iraq. With none of these bases, and without guaranteed overflight permission of the host nations, the British lost the ability to freely move personnel and material back and forth from the Mediterranean to the Persian Gulf and points east. Nor could they depend on shipborne traffic transiting unmolested through the Suez Canal. These geo-political developments on the southern coast of the Mediterranean created what RAF Air Chief Lee called an "air barrier" between the northern and southern parts of the Middle East:

> The increasing hostility of Egypt to the Canal Zone bases coupled with a gradual withdrawal of the RAF from Iraq created [what] eventually became loosely known as the "air barrier" between the two areas of the Middle East Command. Although this "barrier" never became absolute and could always be circumnavigated, it was a political obstruction

which made communication and reinforcement between the two areas extremely difficult.[90]

By the end of the 1950s, then, at the hands of anti-colonial revolutionaries, British leaders suffered two key blows in their ability to project power and respond to contingencies in the Persian Gulf. By losing military rights in both Egypt and Iraq, Britain had lost the ability to garrison land and air forces in two of the largest states in the Arab world. London had lost unfettered and guaranteed sea transit through the Suez Canal. And it had lost the air corridor to the Persian Gulf, for the loss of Iraq made it impossible to reach the Gulf via Turkey; Saudi approval, which one could never count on, would be required. In short, Great Britain had lost the ability to quickly move forces from the Mediterranean theater to the Persian Gulf, or any site south or east of Suez. The end result was that the British had to look elsewhere for locations in which to base their strategic naval, air, and army reserves. But the

Figure 51 U.S. military aircraft in Beirut, 1958.

President Eisenhower feared that the spread of anti-western regimes in the Middle East would usher in a new period of Soviet dominance. President Nasser's anti-colonial Arab movement gathered steam throughout the 1950s. In 1958, when the British-backed Iraqi monarchy fell and westward-leaning regimes in Lebanon and Jordan appeared ready to follow, President Eisenhower – implementing a doctrine that bore his name – deployed air, sea, and ground forces to Beirut. Above, U.S. airmen unload a Douglas C-124 Globemaster cargo plane in Beirut, 16 July 1958.

Figure 52 U.S. Army troops in Beirut, 1958.

> U.S. Army soldiers operate from the Beirut Airport, Lebanon, 16 July 1958, as part of President Eisenhower's campaign to support the nation's westward-leaning regime. Concurrent with the American move into Lebanon, the British assisted the beleaguered Hashemite monarchy in Jordan, whose continued rule was also threatened by adherents to Egypt's anti-colonial, anti-West President Nasser.

threat to Western-friendly regimes in the region was not over. The fall of the Iraqi regime led quickly to thoughts that two neighboring states would be next.

The immediate reaction to the loss of Iraq was an Anglo-American move to shore up two nations near the Persian Gulf, Lebanon and Jordan, whose regimes came under increasing attack. Jordan's monarch King Hussein, whose Hashemite grandfather Abdullah the British had installed over three decades earlier, turned naturally to the British for assistance.[91] Lebanon, a former French mandate territory, turned to the new power in the Mediterranean, the United States. The dual crises in Lebanon and Jordan that followed the Iraqi Revolution proved the first test of the Eisenhower Doctrine, and reflected the notion that if the U.S. Cold War position vis-à-vis the Soviet Union became threatened, then Washington, and likely Britain, would act. In short, during the second half of 1958, President Eisenhower directed over 5,000 U.S. Marines and 8,500 Army personnel to Lebanon, "to encourage the Lebanese government in defense of Lebanese sovereignty and integrity ... They will demonstrate the concern of the United States for the independence and integrity of Lebanon, which we deem vital to the national interest and world peace."[92]

In neighboring Jordan, the government of Hashemite King Hussein also came under increasing attack from Nasser-sympathetic, pan-Arab, pro-republican forces. The king appealed for military assistance to his historic benefactors in London,[93] who drew upon reserve forces in Cyprus and flew 2,200 paratroopers into the beleaguered country. With the arrival of British forces, the Hashemite monarch survived the 1958 crisis.

Pan-Arab, anti-British agitation begins to lap at the small Gulf states. Although the pan-Arab, anti-British movement struck most visibly in Egypt, Syria, Iraq, Lebanon, and Jordan, similar movements spread into the Persian Gulf's emirates. As early as 1954, for example, British diplomats noted "agitation for constitutional reform in Bahrain."[94] The British feared that these calls would spread further up the coast into Kuwait.[95]

In neighboring Saudi Arabia, Nasser's movement met with particular concern, stoking enough opposition that it reportedly elicited a Saudi attempt on the life of the Egyptian President. As Egyptian radio stations blasted forth invective critical of the Saudis, King Saud conspired with a Syrian government "henchman"[96] to have Nasser killed. Saud, however, one of the eldest sons and successor to Ibn Saud, enjoyed few of his father's traits of strength, drive, popularity, and far-sightedness. Even before inheriting the throne, American diplomats had deemed Saud incompetent. The Syrian government official who was to have arranged Nasser's assassination, however, turned against King Saud, and announced the scheme, magnifying further the republican attacks on the Persian Gulf's largest state.[97]

Anglo-Saudi dispute over Buraimi Oasis. Finally, although it doesn't fit neatly into the category of an "anti-colonial" dispute, a mid-1950s row between Great Britain and Saudi Arabia deserves attention, for in it Americans and Britons once again found themselves at times at odds in the Persian Gulf. The quarrel involved an oasis in the desert lands between the Trucial States and Oman, both controlled by the British, near the current city of Al-Ain in the United Arab Emirates, about 100 miles east of Abu Dhabi. Although the oasis sits far from what is now generally considered Saudi Arabia, the borders then were ambiguous. Although the territory fell inside the 1935 boundary of the Trucial States, the residents had in the past paid *zakat* alms taxes to Ibn Saud, hence Ibn Saud claimed dominion over the region. The region, furthermore, was thought to possess oil reserves, which elicited the interest of the American oil company executives.

A Saudi official and a party of several dozen arrived in Buraimi, presumably to buttress their claim to the territory, a move countered by the British military with a desert blockade of the oasis using RAF aircraft.[98] The British appealed to submit the issue to arbitration, but this proved unsuccessful in prompting the Saudi contingent to leave. The Americans were caught in the middle between two allies. The U.S. State Department conducted a good faith effort to determine who was correct in the matter, seeking guidance from experts knowledgeable in the region's geographic nuances at the Arabian-American oil company.[99] In the end, the U.S. State Department concluded that arbitration served as the best course of action in the dispute, although not in the eyes of the Saudis:

We have supported the British proposal that the dispute be arbitrated, since disputes of this character are generally resolved by this procedure. However, the Saudis, especially the King, have not reacted in favor of this suggestion but contend that the area involved is part of Saudi Arabia's sovereign territory."[100]

The British attempted aircraft intimidation to prompt the Saudis to leave. British planes from Sharjah, Bahrain, Aden, and Habbaniya flew threatening patterns overhead Buraimi, with no effect. Finally, the British mounted an air operation to capture the Saudi interlopers. On 26 October 1955 a group of British forces and local levies operating from Sharjah touched down at the airfield in Buraimi and captured the majority of Saudis. The British force flew the trespassers to Sharjah, transferred them into a waiting Royal Navy ship, moved them to Bahrain, then ultimately repatriated them in aircraft to Dhahran.[101]

Failed designs to defend the Gulf region after the loss of India: mutual defense agreements and the Baghdad Pact

During the first 15 years after World War II, then, Britain remained the primary power in the greater Middle East and Persian Gulf region, and took unilateral action to safeguard its interests in the area. Facing severe financial constraints following the war, however, London officials explored other cost-saving options. One of the ideas that London officials earnestly tried to implement as a cost-saving device in the late 1940s and 1950s was the concept of collective defense of the Middle East, i.e., the pooling of resources amongst independent nations. In this, the British aimed both to defend against the most likely external aggressor, Russia, while retaining influence and control in a region that grew each day more hostile to continued European presence. American leaders, however, remained skeptical of British attempts to forge a Middle East alliance.

The first British moves toward a military alliance with Middle Eastern states came in the late 1940s during the Labour Government of Clement Attlee. Foreign Secretary Ernest Bevin championed such a collective defense plan, with Britain taking the leading role.[102] Problems with Egypt quickly developed, however, with the population there growing increasingly incensed at the continued presence in their country of British troops; plans to revise the Anglo-Egyptian military treaty, a necessity for any arrangement that would involve the Egyptians, however, fell apart, dooming the larger idea of a Suez-based alliance. Washington's leaders, likewise, never gained enthusiasm for the British plan, which concentrated on an "inner ring" of states comprised of Egypt, Jordan, Palestine, and Lebanon, rather than the "outer ring" – Turkey and Iran – bordering the USSR.[103] These early British efforts in the years immediately following World War II to create a Middle East alliance system thus stalled.

The victory of the Conservative Party in 1951 breathed new life into the idea of a British-led Middle Eastern alliance. The new Foreign Secretary Anthony Eden envisioned creating a multilateral organization like NATO that would spread amongst many states – if they could convince the U.S. to join – the cost of defending the region. Such a plan, according to British leaders, would keep their Russian foes at bay, preserve British influence in the region, and relieve Britain's treasury of the burden of solely bankrolling the security of the Middle East. Revealing his desire to hoodwink the U.S. into joining, Eden in 1952 wrote:

> We ought to recognize that the United Kingdom is over-committed, and reduce the commitment. The only practical way of removing this permanent strain would be for the United Kingdom to shed or share the load of . . . major obligations, e.g., the defence of the Middle East, for which we at present bear the responsibility alone . . . our present policy is in fact directed towards the construction of international defence organizations for the Middle East and South East Asia, in which the United States and other Commonwealth countries would participate. Our aim should be to persuade the United States to assume the real burdens in such organizations while retaining for ourselves as much political control – and hence prestige and world influence – as we can. . . .[104]

Eden's attempt in the early 1950s to bind Arab states together in a multi-lateral Arab defense pact called the "Middle East Defense Organization," however, met with a tepid U.S. response. American diplomats in the Middle East called such plans "weak and inept" and "shadowy."[105] No such alliance could get off the ground, they believed, until the British defined with some specificity what such an alliance would entail. Would the United States or Britain, for example, unwaveringly come to the aid of an Arab state should it fall victim of armed aggression, as the members of NATO several years before had pledged to each other? The American diplomats thought not, nor did they believe it in the superpower's interest to make such promises.[106] The U.S. thus refused in the early 1950s to join a British-led Middle Eastern security pact, although it would sign on later as an observer to the organization informally known as the Baghdad Pact.

Origins of the Baghdad Pact. What type of security arrangement did the British finally prove able to construct? Egypt, both under King Farouq and Nasser, steadfastly refused to join anything. In Baghdad in 1955, however, Iraq and Turkey signed a "Pact of Mutual Cooperation" for defense issues, binding the two states to "co-operate for their security and defence."[107] This agreement would ultimately serve as the nucleus of the "Baghdad Pact," a British-led loose collection of states that Iran and Pakistan later joined.

From the beginning, however, the alliance was not a strong one. The British never proved able to expand the group southward to include other Arab nations. The signatories came under scorching criticism by pan-Arab Nasserite forces as lackeys and stooges for the colonial powers, which ironically further increased pressure on the signatories to evict the British. The Soviet Union – ostensibly the power the pact aimed to keep out of the region – entered the Middle East through Czech arms sales to Egypt within months of the Baghdad Pact's signing. Dr. Behcet Yesilbursa, historian of the Baghdad Pact, offered this requiem of the agreement:

> Although the United States and Britain continued to regard the [Baghdad] pact as an anti-Soviet instrument, the fact was that battle lines in the Middle East were drawn between those states favouring the West and those favouring Nasser's pan-Arabism. The reverse of nearly everything that the pact was designed to promote occurred less than twenty months after its formation. The Baghdad Pact failed in its basic objective of preventing the expansion of Soviet influence in the Middle East. The Soviets succeeded in "leaping" the northern tier and expanding their influence in the Middle East. They provided extensive military and economic aid to Egypt and Syria.
>
> Moreover, far from strengthening their external defences and internal stability, the consequence of the pact for the regional members was worsening relations with their neighbors. The pact improved neither the internal stability of the regional members of the pact nor the security of the Middle East.[108]

Following the Iraqi Revolution of 1958, members of the new government not surprisingly pulled out their country from the Baghdad Pact. Thereafter the regime became known as CENTO, the Central Treaty Organization, to which the United States continued to serve as an observer into the 1970s.

The first 15 years after World War II, in conclusion, proved a time of dramatic change for the British in the Persian Gulf. Great Britain's granting of independence to India deprived the nation of the military garrisons that ultimately maintained order in the region, while also cutting off an enormous source of revenue. The British attempted to shift their strategic garrison of military troops to Suez, but nationalist revolts resulted in the British being forced to withdraw from Egypt, too. Shortly thereafter the pro-West Iraqi regime in Iraq fell. By the late 1950s the British struggled to figure out a way to fulfill their commitments to the Gulf nations.

4 The British position in the Gulf under assault, 1958–67

The late 1950s and 1960s proved a period of trial for the British in the Persian Gulf, as London's leaders attempted to reconcile their enduring political and military commitments with their shrinking financial and military resources.[1] This task became even more daunting in the face of expanded anti-colonial attacks against British interests on the Arabian Peninsula. In the eyes of American leaders throughout the 1960s, the Persian Gulf remained the preserve of the British. Growing increasingly weary of their commitment of "bearing any burden and paying any price" to face down the Soviets in the Cold War, Washington leaders aimed to keep London engaged in the region. By the end of 1967, however, Britain had abandoned its strategic base at Aden, bringing into question how long it would remain as the guardian of the Gulf.

Long-term demographic changes stimulate calls for political change, starting in Kuwait

It is beneficial to highlight some of the long-term demographic trends of the Gulf region, and note that the British in the late 1950s and early 1960s recognized that these changes would inevitably give rise to demands by local residents for independence. Contrary to the rhetoric of pan-Arab Nasserites who claimed the British designed forever to keep Arabs subservient everywhere, the British in the late 1950s and early 1960s realized that the Gulf states would one day become free, and began to set them on a trajectory toward independence, a move that U.S. leaders cautiously welcomed.

The first thing to note about the post-World War II Persian Gulf is the region's sparse population. The largest of the emirates in the Gulf, Kuwait, for example, possessed in 1946 just 90,000 Arabs.[2] Down the coast the populations proved even smaller. In Dubai and Abu Dhabi, for example – two boom cities that in the first decade of the twenty-first century boast thriving economies with populations in the millions – residents similarly numbered only in the tens of thousands.[3] One of the Trucial states, Ajman, possessed in 1968 but an estimated 2,000–3,000 residents,[4] and as late as the mid 1970s Um al Qawain, another of the emirates in the UAE, had only 7,000, of whom

2,000 were expatriates. In the years immediately following World War II, then, these emirates remained very small, hardly holding a critical mass of people that might constitute a sovereign state.

The education and sophistication of the Gulf residents proved as modest as their numbers, with the vast majority remaining illiterate. During World War II, for example, one senior U.S. officer who worked in Iran estimated that nation's literacy rate at just 10 percent.[5] Across the Gulf in Saudi Arabia, top U.S. State and Defense Department officials similarly observed in 1951 that, "Illiteracy is the rule rather than the exception."[6]

Beginning in the 1950s, however, the demographic tenor and complexion of the Persian Gulf began to change abruptly, with both the population and levels of education skyrocketing. As oil revenues exploded following World War II, the population climbed along with them. Several states in the Gulf experienced population growth rates in excess of 5 percent, with the area later comprising the UAE topping a jaw-breaking 7 percent,[7] corresponding to a doubling of the population every decade. Kuwait's population by 1965 had increased over 500 percent in the two decades following World War II. The author of one comprehensive international study observed that, "On a country-by-country basis it was mainly the oil exporting nations of Western Asia that had the highest population growth rates over the past 45 years . . . fueled by both very high rates of fertility and immigration."[8]

Commensurate with the increase in oil revenue and the corresponding swelling in fertility and immigration rates, the leaders of the Gulf region directed large chunks of the state revenues to education. In Kuwait, for example, the government in the mid 1950s established primary, middle, and secondary schools throughout the emirate, leading the following decade to compulsory education for all children under age 14.[9] Other Gulf state regimes undertook similar education drives. Down the coast in Qatar, for example, government outlays on education increased 25-fold from 1955–60.[10] The end result was a populace that by the late 1950s was growing in education and sophistication, and also an awareness of the greater world around them.

The rise in education levels did not escape the notice of British diplomats, who increasingly recognized in the late 1950s that the region's residents would sooner or later demand their freedom, and that the British would do well to ensure that they were ready to rule themselves. In the Political Resident's 1959 annual report from the Gulf, for example, a top British diplomat cautioned:

> But as education spreads, and despite the forces of inertia, the need to modify and modernize the paternalistic pattern of Sheikhly rule becomes increasingly urgent. The products of the new schools must be given an outlet for their (admittedly modest) capabilities; it will not be possible to restrict and control all political activity indefinitely. Since our protection is an important element in maintaining the traditional Sheikhly role, we are inevitably criticized for the shortcomings of the present system.

If only for that reason we should not hesitate to press the Rulers to widen progressively the basis of their administration.[11]

Of all the sheikhdoms in the Gulf, Kuwait proved the most advanced, and among the first in their population calling for freedom. The British recognized in the late 1950s that the time had come to think about the future of the Gulf state, whose aspirations of independence were being closely watched by leaders of the region's other emirates:

> Kuwait [has] showed an ever-increasing wish to stand on her own feet and pressed for the speedy surrender of our capitular jurisdiction. We have recognized the need to move with the times and are anxious to concede all reasonable demands. Kuwait's example may well be followed elsewhere in the Gulf and indeed this has already happened in Abu Dhabi.[12]

In Kuwait – the most sophisticated, educated, and populous of Britain's Persian Gulf protectorates – the British in the 1950s began to come under fire

Figure 53 Iranian students in U.S.-funded English class, village near Tehran, 1951.

In the decades following World War II, the population of the nations bordering the Persian Gulf experienced rapid rises in literacy. Some estimates put literacy in the 1940s at just 10%.

from a new generation raised on the fiery rhetoric of Egypt's Nasser. Increasingly, citizens and rulers called for an end to British domination in the region. The modern move to create an independent Kuwait gained momentum in the chaotic year of 1958.[13] In that year Nasser successfully concluded a treaty of union with Syria, creating a United Arab Republic that Egyptian leaders claimed would continue to grow. The move prompted a brief counter-union of the two conservative Hashemite neighbors, Jordan and Iraq.[14] The dominant politician in Iraq, Nuri al-Said, then turned to the south and pressured Kuwait's ruler to join the union.[15] This caused much consternation in Kuwait City, as the ruling Sabah family attempted to reconcile three conflicting needs: the need to fend off Iraqi bullying, which ultimately rested upon British security guarantees; the need to address pan-Arab calls for ejecting Great Britain from the region, wildly popular with the masses; and the increasing public calls to seek independence. In facing the first, the political threat from Iraq, one thing was clear to the Kuwaiti ruler: he couldn't resort to calling in British military forces, for that would evoke strong condemnation from around the Arab world, and from his people as well. As one British diplomat concluded, such a move "would do more harm than good."[16]

The events of 1958 – the UAR's formation and the subsequent Iraqi Revolution – prompted Kuwait's leaders to seek more political distance from Britain. The Sabah ruling family wished to exhibit to the Arab world that the Kuwaitis were more than British minions. In that vein, Kuwaiti leaders in the late 1950s sought British permission to join several international organizations. In 1959, for example, they signed as an independent signatory the International Conventions on the Load-Line and the Safety of Life at Sea, and asked as well for HMG's support in gaining admission to the International Telecommunications Union as a full member.[17] The British looked favorably on both endeavors. The British proved less enthusiastic, however, when the Kuwaiti Ruler voiced his desire to join the Arab League in Cairo, which the British viewed as a mouthpiece for Nasser's radical pan-Arab movement; British leaders saw "little merit and much danger" to the proposal and succeeded in dissuading the Ruler from it. The Kuwaitis, nonetheless, wanted their state to engage in the international arena with other sovereign states, highlighting their ability to act independently.

While desiring to establish his state as an independent entity, however, the Kuwaiti Ruler tried to maintain a security guarantee from Britain. Toward that end, in 1958 he asked that Her Majesty's Government "renew to him the assurances of support given to Shaikh Mubarak in 1899," while at the same time moving toward independence, "recognizing that he should be free to entertain direct relations with other Arab States."[18] The British Government cautiously moved down this path.

For the British, the move to put Kuwait on a road toward independence stemmed less from an altruistic desire to set more people free as much as from a conclusion that, by doing so, long-term British interests would be furthered in the region. With radical Arab regimes sprouting all around the Middle

East, keeping a strong military presence in the Gulf might safeguard British interests. But such a presence there risked a backlash from pan-Arab nationalists. The British finally concluded that the proper path lay somewhere in the middle: they should grant increasing autonomy to the local rulers in the Gulf who were ready and willing to accept it, thus providing relief from the taunts and threats from Nasserites, while keeping British military units nearby for support. The British Resident in 1958 explained London's trade-offs in attempting to craft their Persian Gulf policy:

> I think the time may be coming when we should examine how far the existence of our jurisdiction is a necessary part of our general political influence here, or how far on the other hand it may, by arousing political animosity, hinder the continued existence of that influence. . . .
>
> It is also possible to be fairly sure that the Gulf States will like to continue to have our obligation to protect them as a last resort in their dealings with a turbulent world of powers much larger and more rapacious than themselves, provided that the existence of this protection does not in itself add too greatly to the dangers that beset them. This is what has worried the governments of these States more than anything else in the past few years. When we are in conflict with another Arab state or with powerful forces in the Arab world the strain on the Gulf Rulers is nearly intolerable. However parochial they may often be they feel in moments of stress as Arabs and they are conscious of the growing fervor of their populations for Arab causes. At the same time as Rulers responsible for their country's safety they are conscious of the comfortable feeling induced by having a frigate or two of the Royal Navy at their call over the horizon. The longer that we can avoid presenting them with this conflict in too acute a form, the longer will some elements of our present position remain.[19]

In this vein, in 1959 the British and Kuwaitis commenced a substantive dialog concerning independence.[20]

The long legacy of British rule, and the institutions that emerged during that period, made the transition to independence much smoother. Although the original British agreements with these states in the 1800s and early 1900s stated that Britain would handle only defense and interstate relations of the emirates, over time the British assumed a much larger role in the emirates' domestic affairs. The British supervised trademarks and copyrights in the region, for example, which influenced greatly the nature of trade and commerce in the Gulf. Under British direction, furthermore, the local emirates had developed a corpus of civil codes, which would after 1971 become the foundation for the newly independent nations' civil laws. These included laws governing the medical profession, trade licenses, criminal procedure, civil courts, hunting, antiquities, industrial affairs, as well as a law for the discipline of public officials.[21]

The question of whether Kuwait would survive, however, would quickly face a test when Iraq threatened a military invasion shortly after the state's independence. Britain's military reaction to these Iraqi provocations would shape London's policy toward the Persian Gulf for much of the 1960s, and would confirm in British eyes the importance of possessing a strategic garrison of troops and supplies nearby, for rapid deployment to the emirates.

Britain's 1961 protection of Kuwait shapes London's Persian Gulf defense plans

British leaders granted to Kuwait her independence on 19 June 1961, declaring null and void the 1899 treaty that had under-girded the two nations' relationships for the majority of the twentieth century. A new treaty of friendship took its place. British Government leaders declared the old agreement "inconsistent with the sovereignty and independence of Kuwait," and stated that the new state was "now completely independent," possessing even its own foreign service.[22] London officials made clear, however, that they were not about to run from the Gulf. Desiring to publicize Britain's enduring commitment to the region, when announcing the move toward independence, London officials stated, "Nothing . . . shall affect the readiness of her Majesty's Government to assist the Government of Kuwait if the latter requests such assistance."[23] The British still desired to maintain their influence over the region, in other words, and stood ready to provide military force toward that end. The question of *how* Britain would defend Kuwait was not a new one, and had actually been debated for much of the preceding decade, well before the emirate gained her independence.

Rethinking the defense of Kuwait. Two events during the preceding decade highlighted the importance to the British of defending Kuwait: the Mossadegh crisis in the early 1950s and the fall of the Iraqi monarchy in 1958, both of which jeopardized the free flow of oil to the British home islands. Prior to these two events the British had enjoyed predictable access to the oil fields of the Persian Gulf, especially those in Iran. As the previous chapters have explained, the Anglo-Iranian Oil Company's refinery at Abadan had become the largest in the world, and the home islands had become dependent upon petroleum products from it, as well as from other sites in the region. Prime Minister Mossadegh's nationalization of the company, however, prompted a crisis during which for several years only a few drops of oil flowed to Britain from Iran. The United Kingdom's principal supplier of oil had turned off the spigot and virtually overnight the nation, as well as much of Europe, looked to neighboring Kuwait to absorb much of the shock. When new British Prime Minister Macmillan met in Bermuda with U.S. President Eisenhower after the Suez crisis, Macmillan emphasized the importance to Britain of Kuwait's oil reserves.[24]

As long as the British-backed monarchy in Iraq ruled from Baghdad, however, London officials felt confident that they could restrain the state from acting on irredentist claims to Kuwait. Such claims had periodically arisen since the British fused together from the former provinces of the Ottoman Empire the modern state of Iraq.[25] In short, Iraq's claim to her southern neighbor arose from the control that Basra – one of the three Ottoman provinces that comprised modern Iraq – possessed in the nineteenth century over Kuwait. The British discounted such claims, and relied upon Iraqi goodwill to tend to the security of oil supplies in Kuwait.

In 1958 a crop of Iraqi military officers overthrew the Hashemite monarchy in Iraq, however, raising great concern in London. Specifically, with the murder of Iraq's young king Faisal II and Prime Minister Nouri al-Said, both stalwart allies of Great Britain, fears rose in London about Kuwait, and whether or not the new Iraqi military regime would act upon previous claims against it.[26] It is during this time, 1958–60, then, that serious planning began in Whitehall about how to defend Kuwait, leading to a military blueprint that would essentially guide the British in 1961 in deploying forces to the region to square off against Iraq.[27]

This plan to defend Kuwait featured command and control exercised from Aden, and a short-notice deployment of military forces pulled from Aden and all over the world. Aden, for years a British military coaling station near the mouth of the Red Sea used to refuel ships transiting to India and beyond, had grown in importance after World War II, especially after the British loss of Suez and Iraq, when it became Britain's chief garrison between Cyprus and Singapore. An airstrip allowed Royal Air Force units to operate from there, and communication facilities ensured continuous contact with the fleet. When Egypt evicted British forces from Suez in the 1950s, some operational units repositioned to Aden. But the heart of Aden in the late 1950s and early 1960s was the new administrative authority set up by the British to command military operations in the Persian Gulf and Indian Ocean theater. No longer would forces dedicated to the Persian Gulf be commanded from India, Egypt, Cyprus, or anywhere else. In October 1959 the British formed in Aden the "Headquarters British Forces, Arabian Peninsula," evolving in March 1961 into the "Headquarters, Middle East Command (Aden)."[28] From Aden, top uniformed officers would direct any conflict that arose in the greater Indian Ocean area, including the Persian Gulf.

The plans to defend Kuwait using widely scattered assets came of necessity, and reflected a policy shift late in the 1950s that attempted to reconcile Britain's paucity of funds with its enduring military commitments around the world. Strategic mobility became a key operational concept. No longer could Britain afford to garrison its military forces in small numbers all over the world; they must be centralized at key points, ready to move quickly to anywhere on the globe.[29] Such a policy also brought another benefit: reducing the number of locations where British troops faced hostile Arabs. As the Chairman of the British Chiefs of Staff Committee explained, continued military training in Arab lands was an "embarrassment" to local rulers, and thus undermined long-term British interests in the Arab world. He concluded,

"The retention of a permanent garrison in foreign states is becoming increasingly difficult to justify."[30]

In the absence of India or Suez, which in previous years had housed such strategic garrisons, Aden became Britain's outpost in the Indian Ocean. Despite drastic budget cuts that mandated military drawdowns in other parts of the world, the British in the late 1950s increased the funds and forces earmarked for Aden. According to the British 1957 Defence White Paper, a strategic vision statement:

> In the Arabian peninsula, Britain must at all times be ready to defend Aden colony and Protectorates and the territories on the Persian Gulf for whose defence she is responsible. For this task, land, air and sea forces have to be maintained in the area.[31]

By 1960, in advance of Kuwait's independence, British planners had prepared a lengthy study of the military requirements of defending Kuwait.[32] The war plan posited that the chief threat to Kuwait lay in aggression from its northern neighbor Iraq. It addressed the challenges of defending a state where no British forces were based; Britain had not permanently deployed forces in Kuwait, except in wartime.[33] And it addressed the challenges of deploying a military force thousands of miles from other British garrisons in Singapore and the home islands. With respect to chronology, the plan posited an unambiguous seven-day warning, during which time British troops could reposition themselves from other locations so as to deter, or possibly pre-empt, Iraqi military action. This warning time proved pivotal, for it allowed time for the British to bring in forces from around the globe, making less important the basing in the region of all of the required British troops; this assumption ultimately proved faulty. In its November 1960 incarnation, then, the British war plan to defend Kuwait came to be known as "*Vantage*," a moniker that the British would use for the actual military response to Iraqi provocations that would come less than a week after Kuwait gained its independence the following year.

Iraq threatens Kuwait in 1961, prompting the British to implement Operation Vantage. Less than a week after the residents of Kuwait received from the British their independence, a belligerent Iraqi regime declared the oil-rich emirate as Iraq's nineteenth province, eliciting a British response. On 25 June 1961, Iraq's leader, Abdul Karim Qassim, announced that Kuwait was an "inseparable part of Iraq" and that Iraq would "demand every inch of its territory."[34] Qassim's harsh rhetoric included threats to annex Kuwait, with military might if needed. It appeared as if Kuwait's long-sought freedom from outside rule might be short-lived. With their independence, however, Kuwait's leaders had retained a security guarantee from Great Britain. As Iraqi bellicosity increased in the days after Kuwaiti independence, London officials offered repeatedly their military assistance.[35] Kuwait, after all, remained the largest producer of oil in the Persian Gulf region in the early

1960s, and provided approximately 40 percent of Britain's petroleum needs. Kuwait's emir first resisted these offers of British military assistance. He had worked assiduously to earn independence, after all, and didn't want within the first week to crawl back to London for help. As the Iraqi threats continued, however, he assented to London's recommendation. Prime Minister Macmillan willingly set in motion Operation *Vantage*, and a military build-up of air, naval, and ground forces ensued. Given the Iraqi provocations, few in London denied the need to act; in his response to the Iraqi moves, according to the *Times*, Prime Minister Macmillan enjoyed "overwhelming" bi-partisan support.[36]

Although Operation *Vantage* was planned in advance, it still required a high degree of British improvisation. In previous decades such a military force would have hailed from India, as similar invading forces did in the nineteenth and first half of the twentieth centuries. Had the need for such a force come a decade earlier, British troops would have arrived in Kuwait from the mammoth British base at Suez, where thousands of British troops were garrisoned. In the early 1960s, however, neither India nor Suez remained under British control. As foreseen in the planning that preceded Kuwaiti independence, the British had to draw ships, aircraft, and troops from Aden and all over the globe. To add to the British military challenges, when the Iraqi–Kuwaiti crisis arose the Royal Navy had only one of its assigned three frigates in the Gulf, in Bahrain; the second was in Karachi undergoing maintenance, while the third sailed the waters off the coast of Africa.[37] The small naval contingent, less than half of what it was in pre-World War II years, reflected a drawdown in funds that had befallen the Royal Navy. The Royal Navy turned eastward for augmentation, however. The aircraft carrier *Victorious*, for example, received orders to depart Hong Kong for the Gulf, as did the commando troop ship *Bulwark*, carrying 600 Royal Marines, in Karachi.[38] Royal Air Force units from Nairobi and Aden also responded.[39] In all, over 7,000 British military forces took part in the operation, with an additional 3,000 in auxiliary roles around the world.[40] Early in the crisis, in a reflection of the improvised nature of the operation, British Prime Minister Macmillan confessed that Britain's military and political response to the "tangled" situation came "one step at a time."[41] In the end, the Iraqis backed down, and British and Kuwaiti officials negotiated the replacement of British forces by Arab League units. Iraq in 1961 was not to add a nineteenth province.

British military lessons learned: move the forces closer to the Gulf. An Iraqi invasion of Kuwait remained the chief concern for British military planners in the Persian Gulf in the early 1960s, and as a result of *Vantage*, they moved additional forces closer to Kuwait to provide for a more rapid response. Underlying this move lay the faulty previous assumption of a seven-day warning of impending hostilities. Iraqi provocations after Kuwait's independence had caught the British almost totally off-guard; there existed virtually *no* advance unambiguous warning. Henceforth, the British concluded, they must plan for little or *no* advance warning of any kind, for they realized that the Iraqis could quickly move southward their permanently based armor units toward Kuwait from the southern city of Basra.[42]

As part of these changes designed to increase the speed with which London could respond to a Kuwaiti plea for help, the British increased the size and readiness of their military presence inside the Gulf.[43] War plans that emerged in the aftermath of Operation *Vantage* in the early 1960s foresaw British aerial attacks launching from Bahrain as the initial response to Iraqi aggression against Kuwait; fighters would pound Iraqi ground and air units, and paratroopers would assault the Kuwait International Airport, which would then become a forward air base.[44] In support of this, the British constructed new air facilities in Bahrain, including a low-humidity air-conditioned building especially for rigging and storing parachutes. Whereas the paratroopers for the original planning for *Vantage* were envisioned to come from Cyprus,[45] afterwards Bahrain became the close-aboard home for these fast-reaction units. Bahrain also became the home for detachments of British fighter and reconnaissance squadrons, whose crews rotated in and out of Aden.[46] In preceding years such an increase in British military presence in Bahrain would have proven unthinkable, for the Saudis likely would not have stood for it; the ruling Khalifa family, after all, received substantial funding from Saudi Arabia, whose leaders harbored substantial antipathy toward the British, as reflected in the Buraimi Oasis crises of the 1950s. The prompt British defense of Kuwait, and the Britons' subsequent withdrawal, however, had led to a warming of Anglo-Saudi relations, prompting the Saudi monarchy to give a tacit go-ahead for the Bahrainis to increase Britain's military posture on the island. Operation *Vantage* also led to an increase in further investments in Britain's other Persian Gulf area air bases. At Sharjah the British re-surfaced the gravel runway. And outside the Strait of Hormuz at Masirah, off the southern coast of Oman, the British obtained a 99-year renewal of base rights.[47]

For even quicker response, British military officials would have liked to position air and ground troops within Kuwait itself, but recognized that for political reasons this could not happen. After fighting for her independence for decades, the ruling Sabah family would almost certainly refuse any British overture to base troops in the nation. One senior British military officer, anticipating the response he would receive in proposing to base British troops in Kuwait, correctly concluded, "I realize that a suggestion of this kind has been considered before and rejected as politically unacceptable."[48]

The lessons from the British execution of Operation *Vantage* also prompted further growth of the base in Aden. The British concluded that henceforth the defense of Kuwait – the defining contingency in the Gulf around which the British based their Persian Gulf defense posture in the early 1960s – included a minimum of four battalions of ground troops. One was the parachute battalion in Bahrain. A second would be a commando unit based on a deployed aircraft carrier, or one deployed to the Far East.[49] The other two – half the force required to defend Kuwait – would come from Aden. The base also welcomed new units redeployed there from Kenya, in connection with that nation's independence.[50] As R.J. Gavin, a historian of the colony in Aden observed, Great Britain's eviction from Suez, plus the increased forces required for possible use in Kuwait in the early 1960s, led to an explosion in the early 1960s in the number of personnel based in Aden: "British military forces were rumbling into [Aden] in unprecedented numbers."[51]

Not only did Operation *Vantage* uncover Britain's shortage of Gulf-based land troops, it also highlighted their vulnerability in relying on aircraft from the home islands. In the initial phases of Operation *Vantage*, Turkey and Sudan denied British diplomatic clearance requests for transiting aircraft. According to Air Chief Marshal Sir David Lee, a historian and former leader of British air forces in the Middle East, the British in the early 1960s recognized that they must increase their ability to conduct flight operations in the Persian Gulf without relying on forces from outside of the theater. As described in a previous chapter, the British after Suez recognized that an "air barrier" might cut off British forces in the Mediterranean and the home islands from those in the India Ocean; Operation *Vantage* confirmed their concerns:

> What the overflying ban did prove was not that air transportation was an unsound operational concept, but that . . . the stationing of adequate transport aircraft on the right side of a potential air barrier, or deliberate overflight without permission, is essential if an airlift is to be carried out successfully.[52]

Early lessons from use of pre-position equipment. One program's success in *Vantage* led to its expansion later in the decade: pre-positioning. Prior to Kuwait's independence British forces pre-positioned in the country several pieces of armor, including eight tanks and ammunition, ready to be used by British forces should the need arise. Down the coast in Bahrain British forces also kept armored cars, guns, aircraft supplies, radios, and foods, "in readiness" for the build-up of British military forces there should an invasion of Kuwait take place.[53] Of note, the Americans in the 1980s would adopt this strategy of relying on pre-positioned equipment in the Gulf, although it had been first applied and used successfully three decades before by the British.

After Operation *Vantage*, therefore, the British concluded that they must reduce their dependency on forces and supplies from Europe and other places outside the Persian Gulf theater if they were to respond rapidly and effectively to a threat to Kuwait's independence. The British committed themselves to keeping two aircraft carriers and one troop commando ship "east of Suez" for such contingency operations.[54] The British base at Aden continued to grow in importance. Thousands of new troops moved to Aden, many with their families. The British presence at Aden, however, was built on a shaky foundation. Within two years of Operation *Vantage*, Arab nationalists intent on driving the British from their remaining footholds in the Middle East launched attacks on London's forces in the region. After losing India in the 1940s and then Suez in the 1950s, Britain's ability to project military force to the Persian Gulf in the 1960s became increasingly difficult as Aden – along with other British interests in the southern Arabian Peninsula – came under attack.

Escalating anti-colonial movements in Yemen, Aden, and Oman contribute to the British questioning their commitment to the Persian Gulf

Nasser's triumphs over the British in the 1950s stoked anti-colonial fervor elsewhere in the Middle East, including the southern Arabian Peninsula, where Arab nationalists in the 1960s assailed British military targets, particularly the strategic British garrison at Aden. The assault on Aden became wrapped up in a struggle for succession in neighboring Yemen, as well as an ethnic insurrection in Oman. These problems on the Arabian Peninsula, coupled with London's continuing economic challenges, led many Britons in the 1960s to question why the nation remained in the hostile region.

Yemen. In the 1960s Yemen was one of the most remote and backward nations on earth.[55] Only 5 percent of the population attended school, and of those, almost all studied in Koranic schools. Only 15 doctors existed in the entire nation. Over 50 percent of the population reportedly suffered from untreated venereal diseases.[56]

Not surprisingly, in the 1940s and 1950s a movement grew to replace Yemen's monarchy with a more modern system. Despite their seclusion, Yemenis had heard the voices of Nasser and his ilk, who railed against the conservative monarchies of the Arabian Peninsula and urged Arabs throughout the Middle East to rise up and overthrow their monarchs. Some young Yemenis, including many military officers, even traveled to Cairo, Baghdad, and other foreign cities for education, where such ideas freely circulated.

The monarchy, thus, came under increasing attacks. Members of Yemen's Free Officers Movement in 1961 physically attacked the ruler, Imam Ahmed, and he died later from the wounds.[57] His son Mohammed al Badr ascended the throne, but within a week, a group of army officers deposed him, and he fled into the hills surrounding Sana'a, pledging to fight. The army officers, of whom Colonel Abdullah as-Sallal eventually emerged as the leader, quickly proclaimed the end of the monarchy and announced the birth of a new Yemen Arab Republic. These officers turned to President Nasser for military assistance, who quickly and willingly obliged; Egyptian troops poured into Yemen, whose numbers in the mid 1960s would top 70,000. Whether or not the Egyptians organized or took part in the Yemeni coup remains a subject of conjecture; the author of one recent study concluded that the 1962 overthrow included at least "a measure of Egyptian connivance."[58] Whether or not the

Egyptians staged the coup, one thing is certain: afterward, the Egyptian Government flooded the country with troops, aiming to prevent the return of the hereditary monarch.

The conflict between the Yemeni royalists, who supported the Imam, and the Cairo-funded republicans grew into a civil war, and ultimately drew in not only Egypt, but also Saudi Arabia, Great Britain, and the United States, and threatened to engulf the Middle East in a larger fight.[59] The Saudis viewed with great concern the fight in neighboring Yemen. From the perspective of King Saud and his Crown Prince Faisal, Nasser in the early 1960s seemed practically invincible. He had defeated Great Britain in the 1950s, and he appeared closer each day to achieving his vision of a unified pan-Arab republican state in the Middle East under his leadership. The Saudis quickly began to provide weapons, money, and refuge to royalist forces fighting against the new Egyptian-backed Yemeni republican regime.

Great Britain as well as Saudi Arabia shared a desire to see the republican coup in Yemen overturned and Nasser's armies returned home. London officials concluded in 1962 that the greater threat to Britain's interests lay in Nasser. The British had suffered eviction from Suez and humiliation at the hands of the Egyptian president, after all, and he appeared likely to attempt to drive the British from their new strategic garrison at Aden, too, the key to Britain's defense of her interests in the Persian Gulf region. Eschewing a direct military role, however, the British between 1962 and 1965 "engaged in covert operations in support of Royalist forces."[60]

The Americans, too, found themselves greatly concerned with the civil war in Yemen, as the battle threatened to spread to neighboring Saudi Arabia. Using Egyptian aircraft, Nasser-supported republican forces periodically bombed southern Saudi cities including Najran, through at least 1967.[61] Fearing an eruption of an all-out Egyptian–Saudi conflict in summer 1963, the Americans deployed a squadron of eight F-100 fighter aircraft, two RB-50 electronic surveillance planes, two C-130 cargo craft, several helicopters, and over 500 people to the Kingdom of Saudi Arabia.[62] In a defensive show of force along the Saudi–Yemeni border, U.S. Air Force planes flew from bases in Dhahran and Jeddah. In the words of Secretary of State Rusk, in this deployment, code-named "Hard Surface," the U.S. aimed to, "conduct training exercises and operations with Saudi air forces. . . . [and] To provide a limited air defense capability to Saudi Arabia to deter UAR air operations over Saudi Arabia should such air operations be resumed."[63]

The U.S. policy under President Kennedy toward the war in Yemen proved more complex than a simple deployment of aircraft, however, and parts of it raised the ire of both the British and Saudis. In short, the Americans desired first and foremost to defuse expeditiously the crisis in Yemen before it engulfed Saudi Arabia. Washington officials really did not care whether a republican or a royalist regime controlled the country, they simply did not want the fighting to spread. In this vein, aiming to defuse the tensions, the Americans developed a two-prong strategy: against the desires of Britain and

Figure 54 Operation *Hard Surface* in Saudi Arabia during Yemeni Civil War, 1963.

President Kennedy from June-July 1963 deployed U.S. Air Force aircraft to Dhahran and Jeddah, Saudi Arabia during the Yemeni Civil War, which pitted Egyptian-backed republican forces against Saudi- and British-backed loyalists. The Kennedy administration feared that this conflict might engulf the Arabian Peninsula. Above, F-100 fighters and C-130 cargo aircraft arriving in Saudi Arabia, likely at Jeddah Airport.

Saudi Arabia, Washington extended diplomatic recognition to the Egyptian-backed republican regime in Sana'a, while at the same time using direct diplomacy and the U.N. to encourage all parties to disengage. With this, U.S. diplomats hoped, the Americans could avoid a sharp break with Nasser. Otherwise, the U.S. leaders feared, the fight might devolve into an Egypt vs. Saudi confrontation, with the Soviet Union and United States backing their opposing Middle Eastern allies. Such a conflict might quickly spiral out of control. As ex-American deputy head of mission in the Yemen Arab Republic David Ransom later explained:

> What we were trying to do in the Middle East as a whole was to prevent a split between the conservative Arab countries and the progressive Arab countries, a split between the Soviet Union on one side and us on the other. It was called at that time a pluralization, which means that any dispute could become a broader, very serious, dispute. And in Yemen, we tried . . . to stand with one foot in both camps.[64]

The revolution and ensuing civil war in Yemen continued for several years, with Saudi Arabia and Great Britain – antagonists just a few years before in the disputed Buraimi Oasis – providing aid and support for the loyalists, and Russian-backed Egypt endowing their republican allies in Sana'a with troops and aircraft.

The importance of the conflict in Yemen proved larger than the tug-of-war over who controlled the backward and economically insignificant state. Egyptian entry into Yemen in the 1960s also fueled the fire of anti-colonial and anti-British sentiments in the entire southern Arabian Peninsula, and contributed to labor protests in Aden evolving into an all-out uprising against British control there.

In the early 1960s, as the civil war raged in neighboring Yemen, the Aden protectorate became another battleground in the larger anti-colonial movement against the British. In 1963, two years after the British had prohibited a group of particularly irascible tribes in the mountains surrounding Aden from levying tolls upon passing travelers, a tribal revolt erupted.[65] The conflict could have been one of dozens the British had put down in previous

Figure 55 British soldiers threaten local boy in Aden, 1967.

When Great Britain lost its military base at Suez, Whitehall directed that part of its military garrison move to the former coaling station at Aden, a port on the southern coast of the Arabian Peninsula. A fierce insurgency against British rule erupted in the 1960s, however, inspired in part by Nasser's anti-Western invective. Above, British soldiers threaten a young civilian in Aden. The British abandoned the base in 1967, raising questions about London's commitment to the Persian Gulf.

decades, but in this instance the tribesmen proved receptive to propositions put forth by pan-Arab fighters, working under the moniker "National Liberation Front." Hundreds took flight into Yemen, where they received weapons, funds, and training from the Egyptians. By early 1964 British interests both in Aden and the surrounding protectorate regions had come under attack. Extra numbers of British security forces arrived in Aden, but these proved unable to staunch the fighting. In light of the continuing problems, under Conservative Party leadership, Britain in summer 1964 agreed that the South Arabian Federation, including Aden, would become independent by 1968, with the caveat that British soldiers and airmen could use the base at Aden.[66] Britain's pullback from the Gulf had begun.

Labour Party wins election. Perhaps the most important event affecting the eventual outcome of the British plight in the region, however, took place in London. After over a decade in power the Conservative Party lost a very close election in October 1964, after which the Labour Party under Harold Wilson took the reins of power. The chief issues in the election were domestic – nationalization of the steel industry chief among them – and British policy in Aden proved a sidelight. But the results of the election had weighty consequences for the British presence in the Persian Gulf. Like the Tories whom they succeeded, the Labourites initially announced that they foresaw British forces continuing to play roles in the Indian Ocean area.[67] Labour leaders declared their intent to keep open Aden, proclaiming that Britain would "retain the base, in agreement with the government of the Federation of South Arabia, for so long as it is required to serve the interests which we have in common."[68]

According to Labour Defence Minister Denis Healey, however, the new government's top ministers were inclined from the earliest days to abandon Aden, fully aware that the loss of that strategic garrison base might doom British defense commitments in the Persian Gulf and Indian Ocean. In interviews during his retirement, Healey confessed that Labour's initial pronouncements served as diversions for their true preferences. Healey explained that he personally wanted to rid Britain of Aden "from the word go," and "the sooner we got out of the whole area the better."[69]

British travails in neighboring Oman. Britain's problems in the Persian Gulf and Arabian Peninsula region extended beyond Yemen, Aden, and the protectorate regions, for they faced in Oman throughout the 1960s a rebellion that eventually would gain resources and traction from anti-British, anti-colonial forces operating from Yemen. The so-called Dhofar rebellion would entangle large numbers of British advisors and active duty military personnel, some of whom became "seconded" as officers in the Sultan's armed forces. As the Americans later described it:

> The current situation emerged in 1958 when the Imam (the religious leader in the [Dhofar] area) came out in opposition to the Sultan of Oman. This resistance was taken up by the dissident faction in Dhofar

under the rubric of the Popular Front for the Liberation of the Arabian Gulf (PFLOAG) in 1965. This entity has been recognized by the Arab League, leftist Arab organizations, eastern European communist countries and Communist China. The British sent military forces to bolster the Sultan and put down the rebellion in the interior ... However, the PFLOAG remains active in the Dhofar. Its objectives are (1) an independent "socialist" Dhofar. (2) Eliminate British influence in the Persian Gulf. ... Dhofari rebels, aided and given sanctuary by communists in neighboring Yemen, are attempting to create an independent Dhofar state.[70]

By the mid 1960s, then, anti-British movements and armed rebellion had spread throughout much of the southern part of the Arabian Peninsula.

Wrestling with the "East of Suez" question: Britain's future in the world. Britain's travails in Aden and Dhofar, as well as its continuing battle against Arab nationalism, continued through the 1960s, a period that coincided with deep soul-searching in London concerning the nation's role in the world outside of Europe, specifically in the Persian Gulf and Indian and Pacific Oceans. Should British Labour leaders retain what remained of

Figure 56 Dhofar rebels train with Chinese weapons, c. 1971.

The turmoil in Yemen brought to the Arabian Peninsula funding and weapons from the Soviet Union and China. In Oman, the British-backed sultan in the 1960s and 1970s battled separatists in the Dhofar region. Above, Dhofar rebels train with Chinese weapons.

Figure 57 British seconded troops in Oman, Dhofar rebellion.

> Two types of British soldiers took part in putting-down the Dhofar rebellion in Oman: loan service personnel "seconded" from the British military, and contract service (direct hire) personnel. Above, a British contract non-commissioned officer (left) stands by an Omani service member. Undated photo, likely in 1970s.

their worldwide empire? Or, during a period of constrained budgets, should they concentrate instead on their European back yard, where moves toward a common market had gathered steam? With many top Labour leaders predisposed to jettisoning overseas military and political obligations the Wilson Government nonetheless engaged in several years of deep and penetrating study of their "East of Suez" commitments. By 1966, however, the broad outlines of British disengagement from the region were becoming apparent, although Labour leaders would take pains to make it appear otherwise.

Labour cuts weapons systems deemed critical to the "East of Suez" mission. Labour leaders won the fall 1964 election pledging to reduce defense expenditures. Two very expensive weapons systems – new aircraft carriers and long-range bomber aircraft, deemed essential to Britain's continued presence in the Indian and Pacific Oceans – quickly became flashpoints in the debate over Britain's future role in the world, including the Gulf.[71] In the mid 1960s the British possessed four aircraft carriers, two of which needed replacement by the 1970s. The estimated price tag for those two new ships – dubbed CVA01 and CVA02 – stood at £750 million. Another huge purchase also loomed: a new tactical strike and reconnaissance aircraft to replace the British Canberra, the American-built F-111. While Defence Minister Healey evaluated the purchase of these weapons systems, he also had to figure out, at the direction of Prime Minister Wilson, how to whittle £400 million from his annual budget of £2.4 billion, that is, how to reduce by one-sixth the entire defence budget.[72] Something had to give: one or both of the new weapons systems, the mission East of Suez, or all of them.

In a February 1966 Defence White Paper – the culmination of an intensive evaluation of Britain's worldwide defense posture – the Labour Party announced several key strategic decisions that would put Britain on a path to leave the Persian Gulf region within a decade, although it publicly stated otherwise. First, in light of the continuing anti-British insurgency in the southern Arabian Peninsula, Britain would withdraw its military forces from Aden after independence in 1968.[73] Second, Labour would refuse to fund the CVA01 aircraft carrier (the second carrier had already been cut). Third, the British would purchase fewer than half of the proposed number of F-111 long-range bombers. In short, in a money-saving quest, the Labour Government announced its intention to abandon the military base from which Persian Gulf security commitments were fulfilled, and also to cut weapons systems needed to fulfill the East of Suez role.

Impact of the 1966 White Paper. The announcement to withdraw the military from Aden breathed life into the insurgency in the colony and the surrounding protectorates. Attacks mounted. Casualties increased to 480 during 1966.[74] The Egyptians chose to stay in Yemen, sensing an impending victory in their quest to push the British even further back.

The larger repercussion of the White Paper, however, surrounded the effect that the shutdown of the military base on Aden would have on Britain's ability to project power to the Persian Gulf region: for the third time since World War II, the British garrison that maintained order in the Persian Gulf had lost a home. Despite the 1966 White Paper's announced intent to abandon Aden, British leaders had taken pains to signal their intent to maintain their commitments inside the Persian Gulf. How would they do that? How could they respond to an Iraqi invasion of Kuwait, for example, without Aden's forces? British military leaders discovered in 1961, after all, that they must keep in theater sufficient forces – at least four battalions, or several thousand troops – to respond to a surprise attack on Kuwait. By choosing in 1966 to withdraw all military forces from Aden, British leaders had to make a choice: either augment their forces in other parts of the region or relinquish some security commitments. The Labour Government concluded in 1966 that the first option, to move all 11,000 troops at Aden to other bases in the Persian Gulf region, was "impossible on both political and financial grounds."[75] They approached the Emirs of Bahrain and Sharjah, both of whom agreed to accept additional British forces in their sheikhdoms: the former would receive 600, and the latter 2,000. That still left the British with but a quarter of the forces that they would soon lose in Aden, however. As American diplomats concluded after a briefing from their British counterparts in advance of the 1966 White Paper's unveiling, "The British hope that their troop increases in the Gulf will mitigate in the Arab World the impression of weakness which may be implied in their withdrawal from Aden and will underline their determination not to relinquish their position in the Gulf."[76]

Although the public announcement of troop increases inside the Gulf may have alleviated the *impression* that the British were fleeing Aden in the face of adversity, it did nothing to address the actual *deficiency* in troop levels that the British knew they needed to defend Kuwait. Operation *Vantage* had proven that organic theater troops were needed; relying on forces from outside the theater took too long, and deprived them of the ability to respond on a moment's notice. Accordingly, the British made plans to tell the Kuwaitis in the future that, although they would continue to provide security guarantees, they couldn't do it quickly enough to *forestall* a rapid Iraqi attack.[77]

With the impending withdrawal from Aden and the decision to draw down their numbers, for the first time since World War II the British had abandoned the quest to base a strategic garrison in the Persian Gulf capable of defending the region. In the future, defense of Kuwait – from which one third of the free world's oil production came in the early 1960s, more than from Saudi Arabia – would have to depend on forces from the home islands and Britain's other garrison in the East, Singapore.

The question of exactly when Labour leaders decided to leave the Gulf region – and why it took so long to share those plans with Arab and American allies – has been debated over the years. Did leaders, as Defence Minister Healey intimated earlier in the chapter, enter office in 1964 aiming to complete such a plan? Or did an autumn 1967 financial crisis, on the other hand, prompt Labour leaders as a last resort to reluctantly withdraw?[78] The truth appears somewhere in the middle: that Labour leaders, who exhibited a predisposition to rid the nation of its anachronistic commitments, studied the East of Suez commitments but concluded by 1966 that the nation had to get rid of them. Sensing it inappropriate in 1966 to announce Britain's wholesale departure from the Gulf at the same time that it announced its military departure from Aden, Labour leaders quietly chose instead to publicly proclaim that Britain would stay, while preparing for departure. According to historian Saki Dockrill:

> The abandonment of Kuwait at the same time as Aden was regarded as too drastic and too disruptive a step and one which would destabilize the regional balance of power. Such a move would be seen as a "triumph" for Nasser's anti-British propaganda. The OPD [high-level defense planning staffers] therefore [in mid decade] recommended a two-stage approach: that is, the departure from Aden should be followed, after a decent interval of about seven years (1975/6), by withdrawal from the Gulf. During that period Britain expected to complete negotiations with Kuwait to terminate its existing treaty obligations, promote the "modernization" of

Britain's current relations with the Gulf rulers, encourage the reorganization of the Trucial Coast states into two groups, and increase their contacts with their larger neighbor, Saudi Arabia.[79]

*Local sheikhs also lose confidence in Britain's commitment to stay in the region,
and turn early to Washington for help.* Britain's travails in Aden and South
Arabia, particularly the plan to abandon its military base and grant
independence to the protectorates, caused great consternation amongst the
ruling Arab sheikhs inside the Gulf. London's continuing financial troubles,
coupled with Egypt's growing power, might doom the small emirates should
the British precipitously withdraw, several thought. In 1966, for example, the
brother of the ruler of Bahrain, Shaikh Khalifah bin Salman Al Khalifa,
traveled to Washington to voice his private concerns, and to encourage the
United States to involve itself in the security of the region. Failure to do so,
he warned, could set back Western interests in the region. According to a U.S.
State Department account of his meetings, Sheikh Khalifah said:

> Bahrain and all the other Gulf states are most worried over the antici-
> pated developments in South Arabia following the 1968 [later moved
> forward to late 1967] British departure [from Aden]. They fear the UAR
> [Egyptian-led United Arab Republic] will take over in that region and
> ultimately threaten seizure of the Gulf. The UAR's current activities in
> Yemen foreshadow the nature of its possible future activities elsewhere in
> the Peninsula.
>   Bahrain is most desirous that the British remain as protectors in the
> Gulf and has received strong assurances from HMG that they intend to
> do so. However, Bahrain feels that the same type of internal British
> financial and political pressures which led HMG to evacuate Aden may
> similarly lead it suddenly to leave the Gulf. In this contingency Bahrain
> most strongly hopes that the U.S. will be willing to assume some
> responsibility for Gulf security.[80]

U.S. seeks continued British involvement in Persian Gulf region. With regard
to the overall idea of British leadership in the Gulf, the U.S. position in the
mid 1960s was clear: American interests were furthered by the U.K.'s continuing to serve as security guarantor for the region. The Labour victory
in 1964 received close attention in defense circles in the United States, as
Americans struggled to discern if Britain's foreign policy would turn in a new
direction.[81]

There appeared a consensus in Washington that America should push
Britain to stay engaged in the Middle East. A memo for Lyndon Johnson
under Secretary of State Dean Rusk's name, for example, urged the President
to pressure the Prime Minister to keep British commitments in place:

> Both U.K. and U.S. interests would be damaged were the U.K. to with-
> draw from its long-established positions in Europe, the Far East and the

Middle East. In many areas (e.g. Middle East) the U.K. can perform political security functions that no other nation can take over.[82]

Some foresaw repercussions of a British pull-back. Some in Washington, notably in the mid-level of the enormous bureaucracy, began to look beyond the British statements expressing their commitment to stay, and foresaw the emergence of a military vacuum in the Persian Gulf and Indian Ocean region. The United States, they feared, would have great difficulty in filling such a void. In mid 1966 the Deputy Special Assistant for National Security Affairs remarked:

> The big remaining issue on the UK defense review seems to be the extent of British presence in the Suez–Singapore area. . . . it seems to me that our larger response must be based on the fact that, viewed globally, the new area where the U.S. itself is militarily weakest is the Indian Ocean area. An even greater vacuum here 1968–75, because of gradual drawdown of the modest UK presence, is worrisome.[83]

In the words of the same analyst, keeping the Royal Navy in the region became critical, particularly if the British drawdown of land forces continued:

> The U.S. must "attempt to keep a mobile U.K. carrier force in the Indian Ocean, whether based in Singapore or Australia. . . . If the U.K. doesn't maintain at least a carrier on station, I predict that the pressures on us to set up an Indian Ocean squadron will increase. No matter how we slice the pie, it would be far more expensive if we had to fill the power vacuum in the Indian Ocean area than to keep the U.K. there."[84]

Key U.S. leaders don't recognize Britain's precarious position. But top military and civilian U.S. decision-makers didn't grasp the increasingly precarious British position in the Gulf. Why? First, they believed that the British could still protect U.S. interests there, even without Aden. The nation's top uniformed leaders, the Joint Chiefs of Staff, for example, concluded in 1966 that the loss of Aden would not prove catastrophic, but rather require simply a modest "revision of current plans." It would "hamper but not prevent attainment of objectives," requiring that friendly forces use "alternate and, in some cases, not quite as convenient routes and facilities."[85] Second, they didn't recognize just how deep the financial difficulties of the British were, nor did they fathom the inclination of the Labour Party leadership to jettison their remaining British imperial obligations. Simply applying American pressure, the Secretary of Defense believed, would prove sufficient to keep London engaged. According to Robert McNamara:

> I consider it of cardinal importance that the British continue to shoulder

their responsibilities east of Suez and, consequently, do not favor any U.S. action that would suggest the possibility that we are willing to replace them in this area.[86]

It is this belief – that the U.S. must avoid giving to Britain any excuse to slough off their commitment to the Persian Gulf – that led McNamara to refuse funding in the 1960s for the construction of a joint U.K.–U.S. facility that would have provided Anglo-American leaders with a military base in the region.

Addressing the need for a sovereign base in the Gulf and Indian Ocean region. One of the high points in the Anglo-American defense relationship during the 1960s surrounded bilateral planning for an Indian Ocean military base that both nations could use without having to rely on Arab or Persian consent. The drive stemmed from Britain's continued troubles in Aden, along with the spread through the region of Nasserist, anti-Western movements that threatened to destabilize Western-friendly regimes in Kuwait, Saudi Arabia, Iran, and the other British-protected sheikhdoms in the Gulf. The Joint Chiefs of Staff in the mid 1960s concluded that, notwithstanding all the Western efforts to prevent it, such instability would likely continue. Thus, as the uniformed leaders in Washington concluded, the British and Americans should begin to find ways to project forces into the area using more reliable alternatives than "rights" in Arab lands that one day may be granted and the next denied.[87]

This desire to avoid reliance upon bases in potentially hostile lands led military planners in Washington and London during the mid 1960s to search for sites for constructing alternative military facilities in the Indian Ocean area.[88] The search concentrated on remote islands that the British then owned. According to a Joint Chiefs of Staff paper from 1964:

> We are particularly interested in the potential usefulness of a number of strategically situated Indian Ocean islands under British control. It is not possible to predict, apart from the specific circumstances of a case, how various governments on the Indian Ocean periphery would react to US or UK military operations in the area. . . . This makes it important, in our view, to keep available wherever possible those island locations which could be put to the military service of the West in an emergency without delay, negotiation, or political restraint. . . . It is believed that certain of the Indian Ocean islands under British control might lend themselves to such planned or pre-arranged use.[89]

British and American planners reviewed dozens of possibilities, and looked particularly hard at the Maldives (south of India) and Socotra (south of Yemen), but discarded them in large part due to their existing native populations. During the search it became apparent that the top priority lay in finding a sparsely populated island without an independence movement, whose existing residents could be resettled at minimal financial and political cost.[90] Of the hundreds of islands in Britain's colonial empire, three emerged as finalists: Diego Garcia, 900 miles south of the Indian peninsula; Cocos Island, 1,000 miles northeast of Australia; and Aldabra, off the African coast. Of these, Diego Garcia won the favor of Anglo-American defense officials.

Planning started in the mid 1960s for the construction of an airfield and refueling facilities on Diego Garcia, but the U.S. ultimately refused to fund it. American and British officials had agreed initially to split costs. The Labour

Figure 58 Hut and native on Diego Garcia, prior to Anglo-American defense improvements, c. early 1960s.

> In the 1960s Diego Garcia became a symbol of Britain's troubles in the Persian Gulf, and America's reluctance to assume security duties there. London's growing political and military problems in the Middle East led Anglo-American planners in the 1960s to sift through colonial possessions in the Indian Ocean region, in search of a military base that might be used free of the fetters of local officials. Of the multitude of locations, the archipelago of Diego Garcia in the 1960s became the prime candidate. The island's location in the middle of the Indian Ocean, its proximity to the Persian Gulf (approximately 2,000 miles from the Strait of Hormuz), and its small native population, made it attractive to Anglo-American defense planners. In the mid-1960s the United States and Great Britain appeared close to breaking ground on the construction of a base there. American Secretary of Defense Robert McNamara, however, quashed the plan, believing that if Washington showed any willingness to take-over from the British the costs of defending the Persian Gulf and Indian Ocean, the British would soon depart altogether. Above, an undated photo, likely from the early 1960s, of the few native families who lived on Diego Garcia, most of whom hailed from Mauritian roots. Although the U.S. constructed a small communications facility on the island a few years later, the island sat undeveloped as a large-scale military base until the mid 1970s.

Government, however, refused to provide even minimal expenditures toward that end. When Washington officials discovered the British penny-pinching, the U.S. stopped the project. U.S. Secretary of Defense McNamara proved adamant that the British ought to bear the bulk of the political and financial cost of maintaining a Western military presence there.[91]

So in 1967, in an ultimately unsuccessful attempt to keep the British engaged in the region, the U.S. stopped planning the construction of a major U.K.–U.S. military base at Diego Garcia.[92] The American move did not, of course, have the desired outcome: it did not prevent the British Labour Government from renouncing the next year their defense commitments to the Persian Gulf region.

Washington ponders, but can't afford, other alternatives to British protection of the Gulf. The refusal to fund the construction of a military base on Diego Garcia deprived the U.S. of the ability to conduct sustained military operations in the Persian Gulf. This was not a weighty matter in the 1960s, however, as long as the British upheld their commitment to maintain order in the region, which they repeatedly proclaimed and which the Americans trusted. Despite their announced intent to withdraw from Aden, after all, the British planned to garrison inside the Strait of Hormuz over 2,500 troops, in Bahrain and Sharjah, plus they possessed aircraft carrier battle groups based out of Singapore. Despite Britain's travails, the Americans trusted British resolve.

That trust would prove misguided, however. Within two months of Britain's 1967 pledges to stay in the Gulf region, Britain's Labour Government would renounce those security commitments, and set the nation on a path to withdraw from the Persian Gulf before the end of 1971.

America's military involvement in the Persian Gulf in the 1960s

Although Washington during the majority of the 1960s looked to London to provide order in the Persian Gulf region, the superpower remained engaged – as it had been since World War II – in Iran and Saudi Arabia, the former because of the Shah's key role in the Cold War battle against the Soviet Union and the latter because of America's growing oil industry. America largely limited its military involvement in those two countries, however, to military trainers, along with naval personnel embarked on a handful of Navy ships working from Bahrain. Washington, in other words, depended on the British for maintaining order in the region, despite the substantial and growing U.S. interests.

Iran. The Iranian Government – both the Shah and its assembly members – in World War II turned to the United States for help crafting a military strong enough to hold at bay Britain and Russia, and during the post-war years a tight relationship emerged. Through the 1950s and early 1960s robust arms transfers (later sales) and a training regime grew between the two states. Iran's leaders benefited in that their military grew increasingly stronger, which they thought could prevent the type of subversion that had afflicted Egypt, Syria, Iraq, and others. America benefited because it possessed a close ally on the Soviet Union's southern border, and it provided an example of how a Middle Eastern state could modernize along a Western model, free from the upheaval and violence that had erupted around the region. The U.S.–Iran relationship, then, with some minor exceptions, proved strong throughout the 1960s. According to a U.S. military briefing paper which aptly summarized the U.S. view of the importance of Iran during this time:

> Iran is important to the U.S. because of its position blocking historic Russian southward expansion, its oil and other resources, its potential as a trading partner, its influence in other Islamic areas and among the Emerging Nations, and because of the base and overflight privileges it provides to Western forces. The U.S. has a general interest in supporting a staunch Free World ally which is modernizing itself primarily under Western auspices.[93]

Iran fears the spread of Nasserism. Iran's leadership – which after the Mossadegh affair in the early 1950s grew increasingly to mean Shah Mohammed Reza Pahlevi, who systematically squelched opposition through a heavy-handed secret police force – looked to the United States as a strategic counterweight to the spread of Nasser. Nasser, after all, aimed to rid the Middle East of conservative monarchs who enjoyed the support of the West, and though the Shah was not an Arab, the Iranian monarch nevertheless feared Nasser's message, particularly since the 1958 revolution that toppled the neighboring Hashemite monarchy in Iraq. The Shah feared also the specter of a union of Egypt and Iraq, and pleaded with U.S. defense officials in the mid 1960s to prevent such a potentiality on Iran's border. According to U.S. military documents:

> In discussions with Ambassador Holmes in September 1964, the Shah, in his assessment of the Arab Summit Conference (early September 1964), pointed out that as a result of Nasser-Arif [President of Iraq] conversations there was an agreement to unify the political structure of Iraq and Egypt. The Shah felt that this move confirmed his concern about the likelihood of Nasser's domination of Iraq and expressed the opinion that we should not sit idly by and allow this to happen.[94]

U.S. concern in Iran lay in potential Soviet actions. The United States' leaders proved less concerned with the spread of Nasser's message into Iran, however, than a potential march southward by Russia through Iran toward the Persian Gulf. After almost two decades as the recipient of substantial U.S. military aid and training, Iran's military by the mid 1960s proved the most lethal in the region, and could fend off attacks by its neighbors. According to a Joint Chiefs of Staff brief book, "the Iranian Army could defend successfully against an attack by either Iraq or Afghanistan."[95] What it could not do, however, was "contain or even seriously delay a major Soviet attack."[96]

Noting the Soviet strength in central Asia, the U.S. throughout the 1960s sought to bolster the power and effectiveness of the Iranian armed forces through increases in arms sales, training, and exercises. In the first half of the 1960s, for example, the Americans and Iranians signed two landmark military modernization deals, in which Washington provided to the Shah a mix of loans and grants for military equipment, along with American military expertise needed to re-shape the Shah's forces. According to U.S. accounts, America aimed to:

> provide for the development of a streamlined, mobile force that will insure internal security while at the same time provide sufficient deterrent to external aggression to permit time for the U.S. to come to the assistance of Iran.[97]

Iran was an inviting assignment for U.S. military advisors and their families. The vast increase in arms sales to the Iranians led to an explosion in the number of U.S. military trainers and advisors living in Iran, attached either to the U.S. Military Assistance Advisory Group (MAAG), the training operation that aimed to train principally the Army, or the Army's mission to its Gendarmerie (ARMISH), both of which had roots dating back to World War II. In the mid 1960s U.S. personnel and family members exceeded 2,000, of whom approximately 750 were active duty ranks.[98] The amenities that these American military expatriates enjoyed there would have made many domestic American residents envious, including an Army recreation area on the Caspian Sea, water sports, movies, tennis, volleyball, libraries, an auto craft shop, and U.S. Armed Forces Radio and Television programming in English. According to a U.S. military activities guide from the 1960s, Tehran also boasted of "many" Western-style night clubs, and "more movie theaters per capita than any city in the world."[99]

Although Iran played host in the 1960s to increasing numbers of U.S. military trainers, no operational forces were permanently based in Iran, nor did they deploy there on a regular basis. Unlike Britain, whose operational military forces stretched from Aden to Salalah to Masirah to Sharjah to Bahrain, the U.S. had very few; excepting the handful of U.S. Navy ships at Bahrain and the air transport base at Dhahran – which would be closed for U.S. use by the Saudis in the early 1960s anyway[100] – the Americans depended on the British to keep troops in the region to deter, or respond to, any threats to Western interests. (It should be noted, however, that the United States had a number of CIA listening posts in Iran through the 1970s, directed against the Soviet Union.[101])

Saudi Arabia. In addition to strengthening Iran's ability to slow down a possible Russian attack, the United States' other chief interest in the Gulf remained – as it had since World War II – the protection of American oil interests in Saudi Arabia. But in the 1960s, with petroleum cheap and supplies readily available, few Americans spent time pondering the Persian Gulf.

Just as the U.S. had provided extensive military aid and training assistance to Iran, Washington officials did the same for Saudi Arabia, and a large American population sprouted in the kingdom. The U.S. Military Training Mission (USMTM) did for Saudi Arabia what ARMISH and the MAAG did for Iran: trained local personnel to operate the equipment that the U.S. Government gave or sold to the nation. Aircraft, armored personnel carriers, anti-tank missiles: the U.S. sold to the Kingdom a wide range of military equipment, which Washington officials deemed particularly important in light of Nasser's 60,000 troops in neighboring Yemen. The Americans even joined forces in 1965 with the British in a $400 million arms sale to Jeddah and Riyadh.[102]

The U.S. Army's Corps of Engineers also played a key and growing role in the Kingdom in the 1960s. The Saudi Government, for example, tapped the Corps of Engineers in 1963 to help engineer, contract, install, and initiate television service in the Kingdom.[103] The organization also played a leading role in the design and construction of mammoth defense facilities in the Kingdom. In 1965 the Saudis and Americans penned an agreement that stated that the U.S. Government would "complete engineering and construction management services for design, contracting and construction of certain facilities for the military forces of the Saudi Government." The Corps was tapped to "carry out these duties on behalf of the U.S. Government."[104] Over the next decade enormous U.S.-designed bases would emerge from the desert across the Kingdom, including Taif, King Khalid Military City in Al Bateen, and Khamis Mushait.

As in Iran, although substantial numbers of U.S. trainers and Corps of Engineers advisors lived in the country, the U.S. generally did not deploy or base operational military forces in the Kingdom, and those few it had were forced out in 1962. The only American-controlled base in the Kingdom had been in Dhahran. Although since the end of World War II the U.S. enjoyed access to the air force base in Dhahran, the superpower generally used the facility for non-combatant transport flights. U.S. basing rights at Dhahran, however, had always served as an irritant to the Saudi ruling family, who cancelled them. According to Saudi diplomats in Washington, the furor over the Americans' presence at the base had reached such a level that embattled King Saud felt a need to "quiet his opponents both inside and outside the Saudi Arabia" by terminating the U.S. presence there. American officials commented at the time that the "precipitate action" reflected the "shaky internal position" of the King.[105]

U.S. attempts to court moderates through training at U.S. military bases. Although Washington officials did not post to the Persian Gulf region large numbers of operational military troops – preferring instead to rely on the British for providing order – this did not mean that the superpower did not

Figure 59 U.S. trained Royal Saudi Air Force pilot straps in to jet aircraft, 1963.

The Saudi government after World War II turned to the United States to help build its defenses, while Britain remained the dominant protector of emirates to the south of the kingdom. Above, a U.S. trained Saudi pilot conducts pre-flight checks, June 1963.

want to court favor with military leaders throughout the area. The U.S. developed in the 1960s a long-range strategic plan to train Arab military personnel at American schools, which aimed both to strengthen bilateral relations as well as curtail radical Arab and Soviet inroads into the region. U.S. leaders hoped that by exposing military officials from Saudi Arabia, Iraq, Jordan, Libya, and other Middle East nations to democratic Western institutions, the long-term influence of the radical revolutionaries in Egypt and Syria would wane, and with it, the sway of Moscow. Reaching out to those in the Arab military, American officials believed, would over the long term prove important because large numbers of the new generation of Arab leaders had hailed from lives in uniform. Writing in 1967, one official from the Defense Department's International Security Affairs office explained:

As you know, the military plays a key role in many of the Arab states and it is the largest group of educated men. By training the future military leaders from Arab countries, we have provided exposure of the younger officers to U.S. military doctrine and to the democratic way of life in the

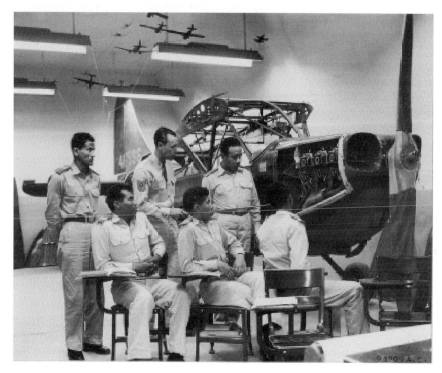

Figure 60 U.S. military trainers teach Saudis about aircraft engines, c. 1957.

> Headquarters of the 2nd U.S. Air Division, Dhahran Airfield, c 1957. One of the missions of the U.S. Air Force personnel in Dhahran in the 1950s was the training of Saudi airmen in the control and maintenance of airfields and aircraft. In the center, a U.S.A.F. Master Sergeant instructor explains the principles of an airplane engine to Saudi cadets. Many graduates proceeded to the U.S. for further training.

United States. We have also given them an opportunity to associate with our own military personnel. We believe these programs, limited though they have been, have served to provide a useful offset to the Soviet influence in the Arab military establishments.[106]

By 1967 this program had grown to include dozens of Arabs from states that Washington officials deemed "moderate," including 154 personnel from Morocco, 65 from Saudi Arabia, 57 from Jordan, 45 from Libya, 12 from Sudan, and 8 from Iraq.[107]

Continued U.S. Navy presence: little military value, but a token of U.S. interests. The U.S. since the late 1940s had deployed to the Persian Gulf a small flotilla of ships, generally three to five, more as a symbol of American interest in the region than a robust show of force. Operating from a rotating group of three seaplane tenders, USS *Valcour*, USS *Duxbury Bay*, and the

USS *Greenwich Bay*, the Commander of the Middle East Force aimed to accomplish a two-part mission:

> The mission of [the Middle East Force] is to plan for and conduct operations within the assigned area to manifest the continuing strong interest of the United States in the Persian Gulf and to visit friendly countries there and in the Arabian and Red Seas and Indian Ocean Areas.[108]

The "assigned" missions were almost never tactical, and the crews of the Middle East Force in the 1960s were scarcely put in harm's way. The seaplane tender, furthermore, was anything but threatening, sporting bright white paint and suffering from a dearth of large guns or missiles, possessing only a 40 mm machine gun on her fan tail. According to the Naval Historical Center, Middle East Force crews conducted mainly "diplomatic and ceremonial" duties, involving "incessant shuttling between numerous ports in this large region."[109] When the two older Middle East Force ships were retired in mid-decade, the British and the Bahraini ruler approved the U.S. request to homeport the *Valcour* in Bahrain.[110] Far from representing a determined effort to increase the superpower's military might in the region, however, the move to homeport stemmed from logistic necessity, as the *Duxbury Bay* and the *Greenwich Bay* headed for the scrap heap.

U.S. Strike Command. If the U.S. Navy's contribution to the defense of the Persian Gulf in the 1960s proved more show than substance, the U.S. Army and Air Force's contribution fell short of even that benchmark. The United States, after all, had always allowed Britain to maintain order in the region, and Washington's leaders in the 1960s took pains to ensure that their London counterparts continued playing the leading role. The U.S. must avoid any overt moves toward increasing their military involvement in the region, according to Secretary of Defense McNamara, lest the British use it as an excuse to flee. Not surprisingly, the U.S. organization tasked with responding to military contingencies in the Persian Gulf region (and elsewhere), the U.S. Strike Command, never possessed the funding, the hardware, or the staff to mount a major sustained operation in the Middle East.

What was the Strike Command, and what did it do? The command, based at MacDill Air Force Base in Tampa Florida, in the 1960s was an Air Force dominated unit tasked with deploying force over long distances to hot spots. As such, the organization did not necessarily concentrate only on Persian Gulf contingencies, but on fast-reaction scenarios elsewhere. In one real-world operational mission named *Bonny Date*, for example, Strike Command personnel received tasking to "assist the government of Mexico in rescue and relief operations by providing helicopter lift of persons from disaster areas in the vicinity of Acapulco."[111] With the growing financial expenditures in Vietnam, not to mention McNamara's prohibition on any actions that might suggest to the British that America stood ready to defend the Persian Gulf, the Strike Command's operations were mainly directed at staging a series of rapid deployment exercises in the continental United States.

The exercises were almost always air-centric, and shunned the participation of the sea services. Although Strike Command planners made a point of calling them "joint" with the other services, they almost never included Navy or Marine Corps forces. The U.S. Air Force dominated the U.S. Strike Command; its logo and senior officers came from the air service, and the administrative headquarters stood on an Air Force base. The U.S. Strike Command admitted this air-centric focus and its failure to integrate their operations with naval forces. In its 1964 Joint Task Force Headquarters Standing Operating Procedures manual, for example, Strike Command leaders confessed that "this SOP is pointed primarily to the Army and Air Force and their operational environments." The authors, sensing the shortcoming, promised "at a later date" to expand the SOP "to include a more detailed appreciation of Naval/Marine operations."[112] That promise, however, was not fulfilled. In subsequent years the Joint Task Force operations manual again stated that the exercises dealt with the "organization of Joint Task Forces utilizing primarily U.S. Army and U.S. Air Force forces."[113] The Strikecom organization, in other words, was hardly prepared to mount a sustained, large multi-service military operation in the Persian Gulf. Strikecom proved challenged to staff, fund, and execute the simple storm relief effort in neighboring Mexico in 1967![114]

U.S. recognizes the need for pre-positioning, but chooses not to do it. The idea of pre-positioning equipment in the Middle East for possible contingency use dates back at least to the mid 1960s, but for a number of reasons the U.S. chose not to pursue it.[115] In 1964, for example, the Joint Chiefs of Staff voiced a need to have such equipment in place. U.S. budgetary constraints, regional political instability, and the lack of a centralized site in the Middle East that could meet all objectives, however, all played a role in the U.S. decision in the mid 1960s to defer the issue. According to the Joint Chiefs of Staff, there existed more pressing budget priorities; should a development in the Persian Gulf or elsewhere in the Middle East necessitate an American response, an Italian pre-position facility, although less than optimal, must in the interim suffice:

> Although a strategic requirement continues to exist for prepositioned supplies to support operations in the Middle East, the political instability in the area, the resulting contribution to an added deficit in the U.S. balance of payments and the detrimental effect on limited manpower, equipment, and financial resources of the Services militate against establishment at this time of additional pre-stockage in the Middle East. To a certain extent, prepositioning of equipment places limitations on its world-wide deployment requirement for active and reserve divisions . . . Camp Darby, Italy, is adequate as an interim location for prestocked unit equipment, accompanying supply and initial resupply for Army forces

deployed in Middle East contingencies. . . . Relocation of certain Army equipment and supplies at Camp Darby to a site east of the Suez may be desirable.[116]

In addition to studying the idea of pre-positioning vital equipment and supplies in the Middle East, the U.S. Joint Chiefs of Staff also investigated the idea of basing them at sea in a group of large cargo ships, or "Forward Floating Depots" (FFDs). Such a concept might prove more flexible, top military officials believed, in that heavy equipment like tanks and artillery pieces could be stored on boats, reducing substantially the need for military personnel living ashore in potentially hostile foreign lands. Such a program would also provide flexibility, in that military leaders could direct the stocks on short notice to different parts of the globe, subject only to a host nation's permission to offload them. Commenting on the expansion of the FFD program from the Pacific to the Middle East region, officers serving in the military command responsible for the Middle East suggested that:

No one site in the Middle East is an optimum location to meet prepositioning requirements for the wide range of contingencies envisaged . . . The additional observation is made concerning the Forward Floating Depot (FFD) established on a trial basis at Subic Bay, P.I. [Philippines] that its mobility characteristics provide the degree of flexibility which is also desirable to meet contingency situations in the Middle East. Conceivably, conditions might permit its use outside the CINCPAC [Pacific] area to meet emergency requirements in the [Middle East].[117]

In the end, in a reflection of more pressing financial commitments in Vietnam and elsewhere, the U.S. would not in the 1960s embark on such pre-positioning initiatives. The need for them, however, would remain, a fact that American leaders would painfully learn in the following decade.

The June 1967 Arab-Israeli War and the November 1967 British financial crisis presage sea changes that would shortly rock the Gulf

In June 1967, after months of increasing tensions, Israel pre-emptively attacked Egypt and Syria, and by the end of the ensuing six day war had captured the Sinai, Golan Heights, the West Bank of the Jordan River, and all of Jerusalem. In every theater the Arab militaries suffered crushing defeats at the hands of the Israelis. It was an Arab disaster. The defeat proved most debilitating to Egypt, and the nation's collective bravado and swagger deteriorated after the 1967 debacle, and with it, the stature and health of its charismatic leader President Gemal Abdul Nasser. The leader of the pan-Arab movement, Nasser had gone too far in taking on Israel. After his string of dramatic political and military victories that stretched over a decade and a half, Nasser's military proved unable to match the intensity of the leader's own vitriol. Nasser would die three years later, a broken man. The 1967 catastrophe would mark the end of Egypt's self-proclaimed leadership in the Arab world, and neutered Nasser's anti-colonial message. Egypt shortly thereafter withdrew from Yemen. The Arab legend who forced Britain to run from Suez and stood behind its departure from Aden would not again threaten Great Britain's interests in the Arabian Peninsula or Persian Gulf.

Radical Arab states impose oil embargo against Britain and United States. London and Washington's support of Israel during the June 1967 war elicited an Arab backlash against the two powers, and in a foreshadowing of a crippling oil embargo six years later, the large Arab oil-producing states curtailed shipments of petroleum products to Britain and the United States. Pan-Arab regimes in Cairo, Damascus, and Baghdad bullied other oil-producing states – including the Saudis, who according to U.S. diplomats never displayed a "very high courage quotient"[118] – to join. On the initial day of the war, 5 June 1967, delegates to a Baghdad conference of Arab oil-producing countries agreed to cut off oil supplies to any nation aiding or abetting Israel.[119] Rumors of U.S. and British involvement in Israel's crushing attacks, furthermore, led to mob riots against Anglo-American oil facilities throughout the region. The United States, Britain, and West Germany eventually emerged as the central targets of the embargo.[120]

In the face of continued expressions of these countries' support for Israel, other Arab regimes felt that they must comply with the oil boycott or be pilloried by radical Arab regimes. One prominent Saudi explained to the U.S. Ambassador that:

> The Saudi government remains under heavy pressure from extremist Arab states for what the latter regard as mild Saudi restrictions on oil exports to U.S. and U.K. users. Iraqi, Syrian and Algerian radios are currently strongly attacking the Saudi government on this score. The Saudi public still accepts many of the charges against us. . . . [Furthermore] the U.S. Government has failed to make public statements that the Saudi government can effectively use to help placate Saudi public feeling. The Saudi government wants to help, but the U.S. government isn't making it any easier to do so.[121]

Several factors diminished the effectiveness of the 1967 Arab oil embargo, however. The Arabs, first and foremost, split. Nasser – predictably – called for a complete shutdown of oil production in the Arab oil-producing states, but Saudi Arabia – possessing the world's largest proven reserves – refused, calling for moderation.[122] Another development that ameliorated the effectiveness of the embargo involved the Russians bringing to market substantial amounts of additional oil.[123] The war also ended quickly, just six days after it began. According to one official at Kuwait Oil speaking in June 1967, "The troubles look as though they could blow over very quickly. . . ."[124] Finally, the war took place at a time when there existed a world "surplus" of crude oil.[125] Taken together, all of these factors prevented the Arab oil embargo of 1967 from impacting the West in a measurable way.

In Washington the oil embargo of 1967 appeared a *European*, but not an American, concern. A Deputy Assistant Secretary of Defense stated as much in October 1967, writing: "Arab oil is not of *paramount* importance in the determination of the Middle East policy of the United States. Arab oil is an important consideration, *one of many* which must be considered in the formulation of U.S. policy."[126]

Envisioning Britain's future in the Gulf after 1967. By the end of 1967, Britain's withdrawal from Aden and South Arabia, not surprisingly, cast doubts in the minds of Persian Gulf Arab rulers about Britain's long-term commitment to the region. The rulers questioned whether or not the British might flee on short notice, just as they had from South Arabia. According to the Political Resident in the Gulf:

> It had been expected that the withdrawal of British forces from South Arabia would cause a severe shock to the Rulers of the Southern Gulf; but when it came, it proved the more severe because of the events leading up to it: the collapse of the South Arabian Federal Government, the flight of the Sultans, the emergence of the National Liberation Front and the discovery that Her Majesty's Government were prepared to treat with its leaders despite their revolutionary political affiliations and the violent methods they had used to seize power. It was inevitable that the suspicion should be propagated that Her Majesty's Government would before long abandon the Gulf Rulers also. . . .[127]

Into this cauldron of Arab uncertainty and apprehension the British sent in November 1967 one of their most distinguished and experienced officials, Minister of State at the Foreign Office Mr. Goronwy Roberts, on a mission to assuage the rulers' fears and instill in them confidence in British plans to stay in the region. His mission was a tough one: convincing Gulf rulers that the British would stay in the Persian Gulf when they had just run away from South Arabia and Aden. According to British diplomatic reports, Mr. Roberts "left the Rulers greatly heartened by his statement to them that the British political and military presence would be retained in the area for so long as it was necessary for the preservation of peace and stability and that no time-limit had been set to this presence."[128] His success, however, would be fleeting, for events in the following months would confirm what many Arabs had feared: that the British would soon be leaving the Gulf.

British financial crisis. Almost immediately after Roberts' trip the British Government announced yet another thorough review of its international security commitments and government expenditures in response to a severe economic crisis. Excessive government spending, coupled with the concomitant demands for foreign currency, had forced the British Government to mandate a wrenching devaluation of the British pound, a process that effectively reduced the wealth of all British citizens. The British Political Resident in the Gulf explained that these crises confirmed the doubt in the mind of the Arab rulers about London's willingness to maintain their commitments in the region:

> It was unfortunate that almost immediately after [Mr. Roberts' trip], as a result of the economic crisis in the United Kingdom which led to the devaluation of sterling, their fears were reawakened by the news that Her Majesty's Government were undertaking a fresh and rigorous review of all fields of expenditure, including overseas spending. Thus, the end of the year left the Rulers once again in a state of great perturbation. Their reactions to these developments took the same form as in 1966 when they were originally told of Her Majesty's Government's plan to withdraw from South Arabia: first, reassurance through the establishment of closer contacts with Saudi Arabia, and second, the strengthening of local security forces.[129]

Within weeks, however, the British would turn upside down the Persian Gulf. Despite over a century of military presence there, and despite promises to stay made just weeks before, Britain in January 1968 would announce plans to grant independence to the Arab emirates there, and withdraw within three years.

5 Britain births a new Gulf order, 1968–71

The period from 1968 to 1971 proved monumental in the Gulf, for not only did it bring to a close over a century of British supremacy in the region, but during this time a new political order in the Persian Gulf emerged. In early 1968 the British announced their intention to shed Britain's paternalistic ties to the Gulf, along with most military commitments "East of Suez." During the subsequent three years Britain's diplomats exhibited determination and perseverance in their efforts to prepare the way for a new Persian Gulf order, attempting to solve unsettled issues that for decades had remained unresolved as long as British power stood nearby. What type of political order would emerge? Would the Arabs in the former protectorates unify into one state, or venture forth as independent entities? In January 1968, no one knew.

In distant Washington, American leaders proved incredulous of Britain's precipitate decision to abandon her role in the Gulf. Labour leaders provided to their counterparts in Washington virtually no warning before the January decision was announced. This is not to say that America's leaders would have offered much military assistance, even if asked. The January 1968 announcement of British withdrawal, after all, came during the same month as the Tet offensive in Vietnam. After the initial surprise, however, an open and frank dialog began between American and British officials. After three years of furious British diplomacy, then, the British pulled out from the Gulf in 1971, but unresolved interstate issues remained. The seeds for some of the subsequent conflicts of the 1970s and 1980s in the Persian Gulf lay in the decisions made between 1968 and 1971, as America stayed away and London presided over the emergence of a new Gulf order.

Britain's leaders decide to abandon the Gulf

> We are recognizing that we are no longer a superpower. Because of our history, this is a most difficult fact for Britain to accept about itself, and for some people outside to accept about Britain.
>
> —Chancellor of the Exchequer Roy Jenkins[1]

The year 1967 proved a tumultuous year in the Persian Gulf region. As the number of attacks on British forces in Aden spiraled upward, the Labour Government moved forward to November the date on which the military base would close, and speeded up the withdrawal of troops.[2] Gulf rulers interpreted this British flight from Aden in the face of adversity as a precursor to a greater British retrenchment from the entire region. To staunch such feelings, in late October 1967 the Minister of State at the Foreign Office Goronwy Roberts traveled to the Gulf. In meetings with the rulers of Kuwait, Bahrain, Qatar, the Trucial States, and Iran, Roberts assured them that the hasty departure from Aden would not lead to the British discarding their other responsibilities inside the Gulf. In London, leading Labour party officials repeated this theme several times over the ensuing weeks.[3]

The very next month after Roberts' visit to reassure the leaders of the Gulf, however, the British faced yet another in a series of financial crises that resulted in further cutbacks in government expenditures.[4] In November 1967, London Treasury officials announced that Great Britain teetered on the brink of bankruptcy. To halt the outflow of remaining foreign currency reserves, which the nation needed to avoid insolvency, the British Treasury resorted on 18 November to devaluing the pound sterling, which curtailed Britons' purchases of imports by making them more expensive. At the same time, the Treasury also approached the International Monetary Fund for an emergency loan. Finally, the Labour Government set in motion further draconian reductions in defense outlays. It is in this crisis atmosphere that the final Labour decision to abandon the Gulf emerged.

As introduced in the previous chapter, over the past several decades scholars have debated the question of exactly when the Labour Party decided to withdraw from the Gulf. It appears that Labour leaders discovered that the East of Suez role, including the stewardship of the Gulf, could not be continued indefinitely, due to financial constraints. They faced an alarming insurgency that chased them from Aden, which after the loss of Suez served as a repository of might for Britain's Gulf forces. At the same time, Labour leaders faced guns-or-butter decisions: buy expensive weapons systems to support Britain's overseas security commitments (like CVOA aircraft carriers and F-111 bombers), or support social programs at home. In the end, they attempted to prolong British influence in the Gulf region for a few years, but without making the financial or military investments needed to fulfill their security obligations there. Labour leaders provided the *illusion* of Britain's continued commitment to the Gulf, but not the substance, by transferring in 1967 a few military units from Aden to locations inside the Gulf, suggesting to their Arab and American allies that they could stay the course for the foreseeable future. When the currency crisis arose in autumn 1967, however, the game was up: the East of Suez obligations simply could not be afforded, and the ability to prolong the illusion of British staying power could not be prolonged. Thus the Gulf would be set free, as part of a larger retrenchment East of Suez.

Whatever the truth concerning the exact date when Labour leaders elected to abandon the Persian Gulf, by the first week of January 1968 the decision had been made. In the days before its public pronouncement, British leaders set off on the unpleasant business of telling their allies of the momentous decision. Less than two months after Goronwy Roberts traveled in October 1967 to the Persian Gulf to assuage doubts about British staying power in the region, the Minister of State at the Foreign Office had to climb back on board a plane to reverse that message.[5] Foreign Minister George Brown departed for the United States and Japan to deliver the same message, while Secretary of State for Commonwealth Relations George Thomson headed for Malaysia, Australia, and New Zealand.[6] After giving Britain's chief allies less than a week's prior notice, Prime Minister Harold Wilson on 16 January 1968 announced the decision in a speech before the House of Commons, and it proved a bombshell. Although in public most international leaders welcomed the moves toward British withdrawal and independence, in private the Americans derided the act, as did the ruling Gulf sheikhs. Even in Saudi Arabia, at times the foe of Britain – the two states, after all, clashed over Saudi expansionism in the mid twentieth century – the move engendered fear. Only in Tehran and Baghdad did the announcement of British withdrawal meet receptive ears.

Britain's harshest critics came from the ruling families in the small emirates, whose future among the local giant powers in the region suddenly became, in the absence of their British protectors, much more perilous. The Emir of Bahrain, for example, was never "so upset."[7] The British move, from the perspective of their Arab clients, seemed all the more treacherous after several years of repeated British promises that the nation's pull-back from Aden would not precipitate a larger withdrawal from the Gulf.[8]

Soon after the January 1968 announcement several Gulf leaders dangled financial incentives in front of the British, in an attempt to get them to stay. How much did the British presence in the Gulf cost anyway? If the Arabs could come up with that amount, some thought, perhaps Britain would stay. A figure of £12 million pounds emerged in the public press as the annual expense to Britain of keeping her military forces in the Gulf (which would later prove but a fraction of the real cost). During a reception at the Libyan Embassy, for example, a Kuwaiti diplomat in London suggested that "he was sure a formula could be worked out whereby Kuwait, Abu Dhabi, Qatar, Bahrain and Dubai would undertake to meet the financial cost of a continuing British military presence in the Gulf area, perhaps by an adjustment in the price [of] oil purchases."[9]

London, for both financial and philosophical reasons, however, rebuffed these offers. In guidance to its diplomats, the Foreign Office suggested the following response:

> We are deeply grateful for their offers and warmly appreciate the spirit of friendship in which they were made. . . . However, the global dispositions which had to be made following the review of Government expenditures

are such that once our forces are redeployed in Europe it will not be practicable to give a military presence in the Gulf the logistics backing it would need, even with financial contributions from the Rulers. . . .

Each battalion in the Gulf requires the backing of two and a half battalions in the United Kingdom . . . an aircraft carrier would also have to be retained east of Suez in case a fighting withdrawal eventually became necessary. The total cost of our military presence is . . . far in excess of the £12–20 million generally quoted.[10]

The British Chief of the Defence Staff offered more insights, explaining that – although prompted by a financial crisis – the decision to abandon the Gulf was primarily a *political*, and not solely an economic or military decision, and pursuing further the idea of the Arabs funding a continued presence would "hinder" a most important principle of the pull-back from East of Suez, "the need to build-up our economic strength [which] is not simply a question of who foots the bill – it is also concerned with the diversion of men and resources into national production so that it can benefit our balance of payments."[11]

The British announcement of military withdrawal within three years set off a wild rush on the part of the states of the region to stake claims to disputed borders. Virtually every state in the region had territorial disagreements with its neighbors. Iran, for example, claimed the entirety of Bahrain, as well as the Gulf islands of Farsi, Sirri, Abu Musa, and the Tunbs, which several of the Trucial States professed as their own. Qatar and Bahrain argued over the coastal town Zubara (on Qatar's west coast), the Hawar Islands, and the sea-bed that underlay the waters between them.[12] Abu Dhabi and Qatar, likewise, couldn't agree on the demarcation line between them. And Saudi Arabia's rulers, who struggled against the British in the 1950s and 1960s to push their borders further into British-dominated Oman and the Trucial States, still refused to demarcate the Kingdom's borders with those states. Despite British-led negotiations that stretched for decades – collections of British documents related to HMG's border dispute mediation during the twentieth century total over 18,000 pages[13] – the British still hadn't resolved most of them by the late 1960s.

The announcement of Britain's pending withdrawal, then, renewed old dynastic rivalries and set in motion a string of competing territorial claims that had largely been held in abeyance as long as British power was present. During the preceding decades of British hegemony, the local parties had grudgingly come to accept the status quo. If one side attempted to change substantially the borders in the region, as the Saudis did in the early 1950s in their claim on Abu Dhabi and Oman's territory in the Buraimi Oasis region, the British interjected appropriate levels of force to compel the offending power to back down. Thus, the British served as a stabilizing force and defended against cross-border aggression. During that time few Gulf leaders dared to challenge the might of the British. London's announced withdrawal, however, substantially changed this. After January 1968 the restraining tendency that accompanied British power dissipated, and local leaders set out to stake their claims. The Iranians proved most assertive, but the Saudis and the leaders of the Trucial States, Qatar, and Bahrain also aggressively pursued their own goals. All sides realized that the rules of the game had changed with the British announcement. Not surprisingly, as political tensions in the region heated, many Gulf leaders sought to bolster their defensive posture, particularly in the smaller states. Kuwait and Bahrain's officials, for example, sought a larger presence for the U.S. Navy's modest naval flotilla in the region, the Middle East Force.[14] The Kuwaitis asked the Americans, furthermore, for the opportunity to purchase advanced weaponry.

Crafting a new political order: Britain prepares for its departure

Once Britain announced the decision in 1968 to withdraw, Her Majesty's Government's diplomats began to tackle the myriad of tasks necessary before granting independence to the region in 1971. First and perhaps most important among them stood the duty of creating a workable and durable political structure for the region. Would the region consist of one unified state or a collection of small independent nations? What type of political structure could fulfill the needs of the people, while at the same time holding at bay the three dominant powers in the region – Iran, Iraq, and Saudi Arabia – all of whom possessed territorial claims on their smaller neighbors? Hand-in-hand with this task of crafting a new political order lay the need to settle the seemingly intractable border disputes that plagued the region, which if left unresolved might give rise to cross-border aggression after British withdrawal. And finally, the British had to address the question of how a superpower "undoes" over a century of paternalistic control of the sheikhdoms on the west side of the Gulf. In that vein, who would assume control of the local courts, of the local security forces, and of the local administration, much of which the British themselves had done? In retrospect, the British diplomats put forth a valiant effort, and given the short period of time the Labour Party afforded them, they perhaps did everything possible to smooth the transition to independence. In the end, however, their diligent travails over 36 months couldn't surmount the weight and enormity of the task, particularly with respect to crafting a durable security arrangement to replace *Pax Britannica*, the "British peace," that enforced order in the Gulf for over a century.

The Labour Party's decision to announce Britain's unilateral withdrawal before the government had put any substantive attention to these questions forced the Foreign Office to conduct its diplomacy under a tight deadline, and in the glare of the spotlight, in both the Western press and also under the eye of Arab nationalists.

The British, however, possessed a talented and resourceful diplomatic corps, whose members sported deep experience in the Persian Gulf region. In a reflection of the breadth of the Foreign Office's understanding of the Gulf, top British officials just weeks after the British announcement of their impending withdrawal proved able to predict the eventual political make-up of the region. Mr. Frank Brenchley, head of the Arabian Department at the British Foreign Office, summed up the possibilities, along with the most likely outcome:

> We might be dealing with one state (the UAE as a unified entity), three states (Bahrain, Qatar, and a Trucial Union), five states (Bahrain, Qatar, Abu Dhabi, Dubai and a union of the five small Trucial States), or all the nine present states. The group of three seemed the most likely. Bahrain would probably go for independent statehood, Qatar would then want to follow, and we would hope that the Trucial States would effectively coalesce. The UAE as a unified entity might be the best solution, but we expected it to fall apart.[15]

There existed some thought within the Foreign Office early in 1968 that London might prove better suited than the Arabs to craft a stable and independent Persian Gulf order, but the British consciously chose to thrust the duty upon the backs of the local rulers. Decisions made by the Arabs themselves, London believed, would prove more enduring than anything the British might propose. In keeping these decisions nominally in Arab hands, the British believed that they could better nudge and shape the eventual outcome from the sidelines, directly intervening only when necessary, all the while making the final outcome more able to endure the pan-Arab onslaught that would likely follow. Furthermore, should the British at the beginning of the move toward independence get too deeply involved in the negotiations between the leaders, the Arab rulers would likely prove less willing to make other difficult decisions that lay ahead of them. As one British official explained in May 1968:

> The Rulers have themselves moved a very long way since the beginning of January towards making a serious effort to group the problems which our continuous presence had allowed to remain unresolved. We shall continue to urge them to co-operate closely with each other, and perhaps gently to steer individual Rulers away from any more dangerous ideas they may have, and leaving it to them to make the running provided they do so in a reasonably sensible direction. In due course the time may come for us to take a more active line in putting forward suggestions, but that point has not yet come.[16]

British diplomats had another reason to steer clear of the debate over the future political face of the Gulf, for they might become compelled by their London overlords to push for democratic reforms, as the British had done in other colonies prior to granting independence, a move that the diplomats believed the Gulf wasn't ready for.[17] In the Gulf there existed no previous tradition of popular participation in government in a Western sense, they pointed out, and such a transformation would prove very difficult to achieve in the short period allotted. It might also prove destabilizing, and lead to the introduction of Arab nationalist sentiment into the Gulf region. This would prove especially unacceptable to Saudi Arabia, whose forces in Yemen had battled the Arab nationalists earlier in the decade. As the British Political Resident in the Persian Gulf Stewart Crawford argued in 1968, "the Rulers might want to damp down any pressure for popular institutions . . . [and] King Faisal would back the Rulers." Any move to push democracy into the Gulf, thus, would ultimately backfire, and erase whatever British goodwill remained in the region.

Thus, the British initially stood on the sidelines in 1968, and pushed the local ruling sheikhs to decide for themselves the political complexion that they wished to craft on the Arab side of the Persian Gulf. The British closely observed the proceedings, however, all the while growing frustrated as the Arabs feuded and bickered. Despite this fighting, two competing political plans initially emerged in early 1968. The first featured an Abu Dhabi–Dubai union, announced on 18 February,[18] with the other states left out. As the British recorded:

> The . . . union . . . between Abu Dhabi and Dubai [came at the] initiative [of] the Ruler of Abu Dhabi. He was acutely conscious of the Saudi claim to his territory and was alarmed by our withdrawal decision. He considered that his best insurance was a close union with the other Trucial States, especially Dubai. The Abu [Dhabi–] Dubai union was announced and the accession of the other Trucial States, and of any other states interested, was invited.[19]

The fierce objections of Qatar's ruler to the Abu Dhabi–Dubai union, however, gave rise to a second plan, which called for a loose unification of all nine of the emirates. Although the British had believed from the start that a tight unification of all of the emirates into a single state would prove the smartest move, this Qatari-led counter-proposal didn't enjoy universal acceptance amongst the Arab leaders. Bahrain, the best-run of the emirates in British eyes, for example, expressed only tepid support, hinting at their inclination to strike out as an independent state. British diplomats recorded these Arab intrigues in spring 1968:

> Agreement on the [larger nine-member Union of Arab Emirates] had not been reached without misgivings. Bahrain was not enthusiastic about the initiative taken by its rival, Qatar, and was in any case intent on independence without too close relations with the other Protected States. It also had links, such as a common currency, with Abu Dhabi which was anxious not to see the smaller union swallowed up. There were thus cross currents between Qatar and Dubai on one hand and Bahrain and Abu

Dhabi on the other, while the smaller Trucial States remained uncertain and confused.[20]

Despite the misgivings, however, rulers of all nine of the emirates met in Dubai, and on 28 February 1968 – in the month following London's announcement of withdrawal – agreed to the second of the two proposals, declaring an impending union amongst their states[21] to take effect at the end of the following month.[22]

This nine-member Union of Arab Emirates may have been doomed from the beginning, however, for it appeared that although all of the leaders signed up for it, few truly wanted it. Bahrain, for example, from the beginning harbored ambitions of sovereign statehood. The five smallest Trucial states, furthermore, appeared more interested in a smaller union amongst themselves, citing their fear of losing valuable trade with Iran should they unite with Bahrain, which Tehran claimed.[23] Several other leaders expressed their fear of Abu Dhabi's dominance in such a union, based upon its leader's "continuing practice of buying over the other Rulers' subjects."[24] Even Qatar itself appeared to have proposed the union more for the corrosive effect that it had on the Abu Dhabi–Dubai relationship than for any true commitment to unity. As the Arabian Desk Officer at the Foreign Office summarized:

> The primary motive of the sponsor of the nine-state union, Qatar, seems to have been the negative one of wrecking the Abu Dhabi/Dubai link-up, which they and doubtless their Saudi friends see as an unwelcome strengthening of Abu Dhabi. Abu Dhabi, Dubai and Bahrain seem to have agreed primarily for the sake of agreement; the first two remain more interested in their own new association and Bahrain in her plans for separate independent statehood.[25]

One month did not provide much time to prepare for a unification of nine states. Exactly what would happen on that date – 31 March 1968 – no one knew. Would there be a new government? Would there emerge a unified set of laws? A unified currency? In meetings with their American counterparts, the British confided that "nothing significant was expected to happen on that date,"[26] and they were correct. Nothing did. Future progress on the specifics of the union would await follow-up meetings scheduled for late April and May in Bahrain. Those subsequent meetings, however, suffered from problems before they got underway, and some of the rulers threatened not to attend, giving rise to further "mutual jealousies."[27] Before long the momentum to unify all nine of the emirates stalled. To add to the difficulties, the high-profile movement had elicited strong, but conflicting, emotions in two of the three largest states in the Gulf: Iran and Saudi Arabia.

The proposed union of the Arab emirates met with very different receptions in Tehran and Riyadh. The Iranians criticized the plan, fearing the growth of a strong rival to their south, a development that they perceived as a challenge to their rightful role as the leader of the region.[28] The Iranians forthrightly condemned the move toward union, blaming it on the "imperialists."[29] One of the causes of Iranian opposition to the proposed union stemmed from Iran's long-standing claim to Bahrain; should the Shah accede to the creation of a union that included Bahrain, he would essentially forfeit his claim to the predominantly Shia island. Of particular concern was the likelihood that Bahrain might become the leading emirate in the group, with its principal city Manama serving as the union's capital, or its leader serving as the collective head of state. In a similar vein, the Shah held with high disregard the incorporation into the proposed union of those emirates that claimed any of the disputed Gulf islands. In short, the Shah had concluded by early 1968 that the union of the Arab emirates was "prejudicial to [Iran's] interests."[30] To combat the momentum of the union, which from Tehran's perspective appeared to be gathering steam, the Shah attempted to forge bilateral ties with each of the member states, a move that the British believed was an attempt to torpedo a strong, centralized state in the emirates.[31]

If the Shah's biggest concerns surrounded the loss of the disputed territories and the threat of a unified collection of Arab emirates to his south, the Saudi king's biggest fear revolved around the potential introduction into the Gulf of radical republicanism that might lead to the downfall of his own regime. Such a possibility seemed real, for in one Arab state after another over the past two decades, as in Egypt and Iraq, traditional monarchies had fallen to socialist-leaning military-led republics. In neighboring Yemen, King Faisal saw what might befall the Gulf emirates after the British departed. The former U.K. Ambassador in Jeddah explained to a group of British and American diplomats that the Saudis welcomed a speedy unification of the emirates as a way to prevent the spread of radical republicanism. According to Mr. K.C.G. Man:

> King Faisal had told the Minister of State in January that he would welcome a union "from Bahrain to Muscat". He already had close ties with Bahrain and Qatar. . . . The King's main concern was the security of his country and dynasty. He would try to stop the rot of revolutionary socialism in the Gulf during the time left before [British] departure and he saw unification as the best method.[32]

Such a unification ought to be quick, the former ambassador warned, lest the rulers "be swept away rather than . . . form a federal union."[33] Saudi support for the idea of a union of the Arab emirates was kept quiet, however, perhaps due to the fact that the Shah opposed it. In the uncertain future the Saudis did not want a fight with the dominant local power in the region; in the mind of Britain's ambassador designate to Jeddah, King Faisal was "anxious to come to terms with the Shah."[34] The Saudis, therefore, found themselves in a difficult position in 1968, caught between potential threats from the growth in the Gulf of an Arab nationalist movement – which a speedy union of Arab emirates might prevent – and possible friction with Iran.

Whereas the British at first stayed out of the battle surrounding the future political structure of the region, Foreign Office officials from the start involved themselves directly in trying to resolve the host of potentially explosive border disputes, "for the sake of stability, as well as the moral obligation."[35] The British feared that armed conflict might erupt at any time with the Shah, whom the British had noted at least since 1959 had wanted to dominate the region.[36] Of particular concern were conflicting claims between the Arabs and the Iranians over the disputed Gulf islands. As the move to unify the Arab emirates to his south initially appeared to gather steam, furthermore, the Shah made increasingly "threatening noises."[37] The British Ambassador to Iran even warned that Iranian-led hostilities in the Gulf were imminent: "Even if we did survive the next three years without a clash with Iran," Sir Denis Wright, the British Ambassador to Iran, suggested, "the Shah would go for the islands as soon as we left."[38]

As the largest of the emirates designated to gain independence, Bahrain stood as one of the potential flashpoints with Iran. Iran had long claimed ownership of Bahrain, a collection of islands lying just off the Saudi mainland. The islands several centuries before had fallen under the Shah's suzerainty, but the Al Khalifa ruling family beginning in the 1700s instituted a long stretch of Arab rule over its population that is overwhelmingly Shia, many of Persian descent. The British presence in the Gulf throughout the 1800s and 1900s, of course, prevented the Persians from acting upon their claims on the island, which the Iranian monarchy repeated over the decades. With the British announcement of their impending withdrawal, however, the Shah felt pressured to resolve the claims over Bahrain, if only to find a face-saving way to back out of them. A popular vote from the people might serve as one such tack, the Shah offered. But the Bahraini rulers proved suspicious of the Iranian idea and refused it. According to Sir Denis Allen of the Foreign Office:

> Our impression was that the Shah saw this primarily as a problem of public relations. He had been discussing various possibilities [of terminating Iranian claims on Bahrain,] including a plebiscite, but the Ruler of Bahrain had confirmed to us that he was not prepared to contemplate a plebiscite. In any case this was not the way the Arab rulers' minds worked. There were also local reasons for avoiding a plebiscite which might stir up feelings between Arabs and Iranians in Bahrain. However people's minds in Bahrain itself, in Kuwait and in Iran were all searching for ideas on possible solutions to the problems.[39]

The British perceived this Iranian claim to Bahrain, in fact, to be so great a threat to future stability that they engaged in some secret diplomacy between the two claimants. The British held secret meetings in Geneva that brought together leaders from Iran, Kuwait, Saudi Arabia, and Bahrain, along with some other unnamed states. Despite the close and frank relationship that the British and the Americans had developed in 1968, however, the British kept news of these secret negotiations away from the Americans, to whom they had confided virtually everything else.[40] The Geneva meetings between Sheikh Khalifa, the brother of the ruler of Bahrain, and the Iranians proved "affable," but inconclusive.[41]

Despite their initial desire to encourage the Arabs to make their own decisions, the British recognized that in the case of the dispute over Bahrain, London needed to get involved. The British pressured both the Bahraini and Iranian leaders to submit to a process akin to binding arbitration under the auspices of the United Nations, and the two sides consented. Shortly thereafter, independent officials directed by Signor Winspeare-Guicciardi conducted an "investigation of popular opinion."[42] In it, U.N. officials looked at the identity and allegiance of the Bahraini populace: did they feel a greater affinity for, and wish to pay obeisance to, the Khalifa family or to the Shah? If a majority supported the Khalifas, which the British believed strongly would prove the case, then the existing ruling family would stay in power. That is what happened. The ruling family welcomed the results:

> Bahraini apprehensions were successively dispelled by their own success in lobbying other Arab Governments and in selling the operation to their people, by Signor Winspeare-Guicciardi's brilliant conduct of the ascertainment, and by its smooth passage through the Security Council.[43]

The Shah subsequently backed down from his claim to Bahrain. British diplomats rightfully complimented themselves on defusing one potential flashpoint in the Gulf. In a bit of self-congratulatory ardor, the Political Resident in Bahrain reported that the Bahrainis "emerged with nothing but gratitude for the role played by Her Majesty's Government, the United Nations, and by the Shah in removing a dark cloud by which they had felt oppressed for generations."[44] Despite their success in defusing Bahraini-Iranian tensions, however, the British had less success in their attempts to resolve the disagreements over the other disputed Gulf islands closer to the Strait of Hormuz.

Disputed islands. In addition to Bahrain's sovereignty issue, there existed another potentially explosive disagreement that the British, during their lengthy stay in the Gulf, had proven largely able to keep under wraps: ownership of several islands in the middle of the Gulf that both Arabs and Iranians claim.[45] The rulers of Sharjah, Ras al Khaimah, and Umm al Quwwain, as well as Iran, asserted conflicting claims on Sirri, Abu Musa, and the Greater and Lesser Tunb Islands. The debates over these islands stretched back at least into the nineteenth century. When at the turn of the twentieth century, in 1905, Persian forces tore down Arab flags and hoisted their own, British-Indian threats to send gun-boats made the Iranians reverse their move.[46] For the remainder of the twentieth century the British stood ready to prevent any precipitous actions by any of the claimants, although they generally supported the Arab ownership claims. Following the 1968 announcement of British withdrawal from the Gulf, however, tensions rose as all parties renewed their claims. As the British Ambassador to Tehran Sir Denis Wright noted:

> The crux of our withdrawal in Iranian eyes was that it brought the skeletons of Bahrain, the Tunbs and Abu Musa from behind the veil of our protection.[47]

Failed British attempts to resolve the Gulf islands dispute. The British investigated many different solutions to the Gulf islands dispute, including United Nations presence on the islands, the sale of the islands to Iran, various "condominium" arrangements, and arbitration,[48] but they deemed only two possible solutions worthy of serious consideration. The first, although the Iranians previously had dismissed it, involved the de-militarizing of the disputed islands. Despite its simplicity, the British believed that it is "worth asking them to reconsider seriously their objections."[49] The second alternative, although more complex, amounted to what the British referred to as a "package deal" whereby negotiators would negotiate a "Median Line" down the center of the Gulf; those islands that fell on the northern side of the line would go to Iran and those on the southern side to the Arabs. In briefing papers prepared prior to a high-level meeting between British envoy Roberts and Eugene Rostow, a Foreign Office staffer described what such a plan might entail:

> A more satisfactory solution, though it would be a more complex one, would be a "package deal" under which a Median Line was negotiated and in which it might in effect be the measuring point for solving other problems. Under this three of the four disputed Islands (Sirri, and the two Tunb Islands) might go to Iran. Abu Musa, which is on the Arab side, would go to Sharjah. The Iranian claim to Bahrain would disappear, as Bahrain is on the Arab side of the Median Line. This might just be "saleable" to the Rulers (though the Ruler of Ras al Khaimah might need an additional "sweetener" for the loss of the two Tunb Islands), but it would need some concessions on the Iranians' part.[50]

Why so important? British and American diplomats struggled to figure out why the Shah appeared so committed to regaining control of the disputed islands. If the issue represented a vital security concern, then the British might help to craft a regime to ameliorate the Iranians' concerns, such as a demilitarization of the islands, or perhaps position a group of independent observers on the island. The Iranians, in any event, could control shipping traffic through the Strait of Hormuz using shore-based weaponry alone, with or without possession of the islands, reducing the military value of the islands. If, on the other hand, the islands issue represented a matter of Iranian national pride more than a case of security – which appears the case, in retrospect – then the issue would surely prove harder to solve. One of the themes of Iranian history in the twentieth century, after all, is a disdain of foreigners meddling in the nation, particularly British and Russian, and later the Americans. British diplomats never agreed why the islands issue proved so important, and unable to resolve it, they concluded that a conflict over these islands would ultimately ensue. According to Mr. Frank Brenchley of the Foreign Office in March 1968:

> [We] doubted whether security was really the main consideration. It was, rather, a rationalization of the "territorial imperative." The Shah had taken no interest in the idea of demilitarization, his reaction had been an emotional assertion that the islands were Iranian. Besides, although the islands were at the entrance to the Gulf, the channel could be dominated just as well from the mainland. . . . Many solutions had been considered and would be considered further but we had so far been driven to the reluctant conclusion that there was no prospect of arranging a reasonable settlement and that a confrontation seemed inevitable.[51]

Regime change in Oman. Another problem that the British aimed to solve prior to their disengagement from the Persian Gulf region surrounded the lackluster leadership in Oman of Sultan Said bin Taimur, in whom the British had lost confidence. The relationship with Oman proved more opaque than that with the Trucial States, Bahrain, or Qatar. Unlike their formal security commitments to those entities, the British did not have explicit defensive obligations to Oman, and their bilateral relationship was defined chiefly by a 1951 Treaty of Friendship and Commerce and a 1958 treaty that traded British access to the Masirah and Salalah air bases in exchange for assistance with the development of the Sultan's Armed Forces.[52] The British clearly felt it in their best interests, however, to stabilize the situation in Oman as the time grew closer for Britain's withdrawal from "East of Suez." The British Government recognized at least three issues that put in great peril Oman's ability to function as a healthy state: the Sultan's failure to prosecute aggressively the Dhofar rebellion, his fiscal profligacy, and his growing unpopularity with his own subjects. The British came increasingly to believe that the only fix for Oman was a change of regime.

The Dhofar region lay far inland from the Omani coasts, and outside the traditional reach of the Sultan's power. Since at least the 1940s the Sultan aimed to bring the interior of the country under his control, however, which in the past had been ruled by a religious cleric, the Imam.[53] Attempts by the Sultan to extend his domain met with opposition from ethnic groups in the center of the country. An uprising in Dhofar became more than just a separatist conflict, however, as socialist forces from Yemen in the 1960s joined in the battle against the British-backed forces of the Sultan.[54] An insurgency ensued, and throughout the 1960s, ethnic separatists supported in part by the Soviets and Chinese challenged the British-backed Omani regime and took control of parts of the Omani hinterland. British soldiers aided the Sultan. But the conflict dragged on, neither side able to impose its will on the other. The British had concluded that the Dhofaris simply could not be allowed to win, for fear of contagion throughout the Gulf region. As the British Political Resident's Persian Gulf Annual Review for 1970 explained: "A setback [in Oman] could give the irreconcilable Marxist cells which still exist, and their foreign backers, a chance to stage a non-white revolution."[55]

A large part of Oman's problem lay in the personage of the Sultan himself. The Sultan rarely left his own palace, he went months or years in between visits to his own capital, nor had he reinvested his nation's considerable oil profits to modernize his state or improve the lot of his people. The deputy to the British Political Resident condemned Said's prosecution of the Dhofar rebels, his fiscal profligacy, his failure to modernize his state, and his inability to conceive of the need for change:

> [The sultan] dismissed all suggestions for political and economic measures to win over the tribes. Worse still, while his bank balances soured . . . he continued on innumerable petty pretexts to procrastinate over development in Oman to which in principle he had been committed for years. The situation appeared explosive to an increasing number of observers, and in May the Political Resident was authorized to conduct a policy review with the sultan in the hope of getting him to change his ways. The sultan was unmoved.[56]

In 1970 the Sultan was deposed. In the words of the deputy to the British Political Resident for the Gulf:

> The turning point came only the following month when an armed gang, the first to appear in Oman for 11 years, shot up a camp of the Sultan's Armed Forces (SAF). They lost five killed, but proved to be part of a conspiracy with ramifications throughout Oman. Faced with the nightmare of a second front in Oman and a growing distaste in SAF for their purely repressive role, and despairing of any change of heart in his father, the sultan's only son, Qaboos, deposed him on 23 July in a palace coup which received the instant support of the armed forces. So swift and bloodless was the coup that it seemed in retrospect extraordinary, as well as regrettable, that the ex-sultan should have remained in power for 33 years. . . . The new sultan . . . had been a prisoner in Salalah for six years and had never seen Oman. . . .[57]

Although the British diplomat in the passage above refers to a "palace coup," it appears that the British Government itself may have had a large hand in Said's overthrow; evidence points to involvement by Britain's Secret Intelligence Service.[58] (British archival records that might prove or disprove this, however, remain classified well beyond the normal 30-year window, thus this issue must await scrutiny from a later generation of historians.) In Washington, the news of Said's overthrow met with cautious optimism: Assistant Secretary of State for Near Eastern Affairs Joseph Sisco, in a message to Secretary of State Rogers, called it a "hopeful development."[59]

Whatever the cause of the palace coup, the new British-backed monarch took immediate action to strengthen Oman's ties with his Saudi neighbors, against whom Oman fought in the Buraimi crises. Sultan Qaboos, Said's son, "buried the hatchet"[60] with his Saudi rivals. The two states established full diplomatic relations in December 1971, another success by the British in their attempt to smooth over potential flashpoints as they withdrew from the Gulf.

British recommendations for regional security. In addition to pushing the Arabs to create a durable political structure, and attempting to de-fuse territorial flashpoints, there existed a third task that the British realized had to be addressed prior to withdrawal: a viable plan to maintain internal security in the states that emerged in the region. With that in mind the British encouraged the local regimes to cultivate and improve their internal security organizations and police forces, so they could identify and ultimately neutralize domestic enemies before they threatened the local regimes. In the 1960s many of the key advisors to the local rulers were British civilians, and some of them – to the delight of British officials in London – stayed on after independence.[61] The British, however, cautioned the rulers that they needed to temper the need for domestic security with the peril of an overzealous internal police force. According to Sir Denis Allen of the Foreign Office, "we were trying to keep them under some form of control."[62]

The British also attempted to convince the local rulers – unsuccessfully, it turned out – to keep in place the Trucial Omani Scouts, a largely British-officered force of local levies used for decades in the Trucial States and Oman. The British went so far as to continue to offer small numbers of British troops to man and lead the units.[63] Most Arab leaders, however, preferred to start building their own military forces from scratch. Bahrain and Qatar, for example, in 1968 had already started to form their own forces. Rather than turn back to the British for leadership – London had proven itself an uncertain ally, after all – the Bahrainis developed a force "officered mainly by Jordanians."[64] As Sir Denis Allen of the Foreign Office explained in March 1968:

> Some of the Rulers, for example Zaid of Abu Dhabi and Rashid of Dubai, were pressing . . . strongly to be allowed to develop their own forces and Zaid in particular had plans for an Abu Dhabi Defence Force twice the size of the present Trucial Omani Scouts. We [the British] had been doing what we could to hold him back. Sheikh Rashid, when last in London, had also been very insistent that he should have his own Dubai defence force. . . .[65]

If progress toward political union amongst the Arab sheikhdoms proved sluggish in 1968 and 1969, it slowed to a virtual standstill in 1970 when the Conservative Party once again regained power. The Conservatives, after all, had steadfastly opposed the Labour Government's plan to withdraw unilaterally from the Persian Gulf region, and during the 1970 campaign many had pledged to reverse it. What would the new British Government do? Would they bolster forces in the Gulf to the approximately 11,000–12,000 needed to defend Kuwait – a number not seen in the Gulf region since the Labour-directed evacuation of Aden – approximately double the number stationed in the late 1960s in Bahrain and Sharjah?[66] Or would the British continue with the plans to withdraw the military forces entirely, as announced in 1968? The climate of uncertainty walloped whatever slow motion existed amongst Arab leaders toward political change in the Gulf, as the local rulers awaited direction from London.

To assist in their decision-making over the future of the Gulf, the Conservative leadership appointed William Luce as the Foreign and Commonwealth Secretary's "Special Representative for Gulf Affairs." Luce, the Governor of Aden in the 1950s and Political Resident of the Persian Gulf in the 1960s, knew very well the politics and personalities of the region. But until he completed his initial work and the new Conservative Government made its intentions known, the Arab moves toward independence became "virtually stagnant."[67]

After months of travel and investigation, however, Luce concluded that the genie had escaped from the bottle and could never be put back in. Even if the Conservative Government wanted to reverse its decision to abandon the region, and renege on promises of independence to the Arab sheikhdoms, there existed virtually no chance that leaders in the greater Arab world would permit this. The only option available to the British, in that vein, was to proceed on a path toward independence; any delay past 1971, the previously announced target, Luce believed, would meet with howls of Arab indignation, and perhaps violence.

Luce suggested, however, that the British Government re-evaluate the decision to completely abandon all military involvement in the region; he recommended that the British consider keeping in Bahrain and Sharjah small numbers of trainers, advisors, and facilitators, both to train the military members of successor states and also to make it easier to re-open the facilities to British military use should a future need arise:

> We should offer to leave a small naval contingent (perhaps up to 50 personnel) at the existing British naval installations in Bahrain. This contingency would provide services for visiting ships of the Royal Navy, although repair facilities would no doubt have to be provided by civilian contractors. This contingent could also act as, and be described as, a training mission or liaison team to assist with the training of the naval forces of Bahrain and the Union. . . . We should offer to leave a small RAF contingent (perhaps up to 150 personnel) at Sharjah, with possibly

a detachment at Abu Dhabi, to assist in servicing staging RAF aircraft and in connection with occasional visits by an RAF squadron.[68]

Once Luce reported to the Conservatives that the decision to abandon the Gulf was effectively irreversible, however, British moves to keep a footprint in the region died.

Even Luce couldn't get the Arabs to unify. Once it became clear in 1970 that Britain could not reverse course, Luce set about attempting to break the logjam surrounding the shape of the Arab polity that would emerge after independence in 1971. No longer could Britain afford to stand on the sidelines and await an Arab-only decision. Luce pushed for the solution that Whitehall had long considered optimal: a union of all nine emirates. Not only would such a state have adequate resources and a large enough population to survive on its own, but it would also prove more formidable in standing up to neighboring Iran and Saudi Arabia, both of whose leaders disputed the borders in the region. Should Iran and Saudi Arabia "treat them individually,"[69] the minor states might cave in to their giant neighbors' demands. Some British accounts report that Luce's "strenuous advocacy" came "within inches"[70] of a new constitution that would have joined all nine emirates. In reality, Luce probably did not come that close. In the end, age-old animosities among the ruling families made it impossible to craft a polity to which all nine rulers could agree. As the deputy to the British Political Resident explained early in 1971:

> The . . . points on which agreement proved impossible were only symbols of more deep-seated antagonisms between Qatar and Bahrain; and it was the latter which caused the breakdown of the Union of Arab Emirates Deputies meeting in October [1970] and the cancellation of the Rulers' meeting. For most people this was the final demonstration that the will to federate does not exist. The only common ground is that no Ruler is prepared to take responsibility to breaking up the Union.[71]

Meanwhile, it appeared that Bahrain was "quietly preparing to go it alone," rather than joining in a union with the other emirates.[72]

American policy toward the Gulf evolves, 1968–71

Although cooperation generally marked the strategic Anglo-American security relationship during the Cold War, the Labour Government's decision to withdraw from the Persian Gulf virtually without prior notice met with fierce condemnation from Washington. In a testy rebuke not seen in the Anglo-American dialog since the Suez Crisis, on 6 January 1968 U.S. Secretary of State Dean Rusk sent a scathing letter to London concerning rumors that London was about to withdraw from the Gulf. If true, this represented a fundamental sea change for the Western alliance, he believed, and should not be undertaken unilaterally. To announce this in a surprise fashion, as rumors suggested, represented a grave breach of faith:

> I am deeply disturbed by information which has just reached me to the effect that HMG may be considering accelerating its withdrawal from the Persian Gulf. As you know, we attach very high importance to the maintenance of the British position in the Persian Gulf for the indefinite future. We welcomed the repositioning of some of your forces there from Aden last year as an earnest of your determination to continue to play the essential stabilizing role in the Gulf which has been so helpful to us all for so long. While economies can no doubt be made, I would earnestly hope that before we meet next week HMG will not have taken any irrevocable decisions. In our view, fixing of specific timetable at this early stage would be likely to feed instability in the region and increase your own problems in arranging eventual orderly departure.[73]

The British confirmed the veracity of the rumors, and Foreign Office officials confided that even they, too, were caught off guard by the Labour Party decision. They explained that the financial crisis that caused the Government to devalue the pound put "intense pressures" on them to reduce government expenditures,[74] especially defense spending overseas.[75] Not only would the British yield their special role in the Persian Gulf, they related to their American counterparts, but also in the greater Far East, for the two theaters proved inextricably intertwined. As the British explained, "The decision to leave the Persian Gulf was dictated primarily by the fact that there would be no [aircraft] carriers or bases available to support or relieve the Persian Gulf after March 1971 when British forces would have been withdrawn from the Far East."[76] The answer essentially amounted to a tacit admission that the decisions in the 1966 White Paper – cancellation of the aircraft carriers and the military departure from Aden – made inevitable the British departure from the Gulf, although Labour leaders for two years had continued to state otherwise.

Arabs from the small emirates immediately began to request from Washington military assistance. Afraid of the designs of their larger neighbors, they wanted American protection. Kuwait and Bahrain, for example, both sought a larger U.S. Navy flotilla in the region.[77] The Kuwaitis and others also asked to purchase arms.[78]

The British announcement of withdrawal forced the Johnson Administration to cobble together on short notice an ad hoc policy toward the Persian Gulf that – although completed without in-depth study – would nevertheless endure for years. This policy formation process took place in a turbulent period, for January–February 1968 also coincided with the Tet Offensive in Vietnam, which increasingly dominated the foreign policy and administrative functions of the U.S. Government. Although the philosophic rationale for U.S. policy toward the Persian Gulf would not become apparent until the

Kissinger stewardship of foreign policy several years later, a half dozen key themes emerged in 1968 concerning the Johnson Administration's approach to the Persian Gulf.

First, the U.S. must not replace the British as security guarantors in the Persian Gulf. This policy became apparent within days of Britain's January 1968 surprise announcement of their impending withdrawal, when a U.S. State Department spokesman announced that, "We have no plans to move in where the British Forces pull out."[79] With the U.S. military stretched thin with Vietnam and other Cold War commitments, the superpower simply could not – and would not – take on any new obligations in the late 1960s.

The second U.S. policy toward the Gulf that emerged in the immediate aftermath of Britain's withdrawal announcement surrounded Washington's desire to keep the British engaged. As notes from a February 1968 U.S. inter-departmental working group stated:

> Our policy should be directed along the lines of encouraging the British to maintain as much of their present special role in the Gulf as they can, as long as possible, including their role as principal arms supplier to various Gulf states.[80]

These two bulwarks of American policy to the region – refusing to enlarge security commitments there, coupled with an attempt to prolong British involvement – reflected less a *break* of American policies as much as a *renewal* of America's long-standing attitude toward the region. In his decision earlier in the decade to refuse funding improvements to the Indian Ocean military base on Diego Garcia, for example, Defense Secretary McNamara cited both of these two policy goals.[81]

Of note, the desire to steer clear of military commitments in the region also led Washington officials early in 1968 to decide to forswear arms-dealing with new clients in the Gulf. American officials correctly predicted that Arabs in the former British-controlled lands would soon turn to the United States for protection; as Assistant Secretary of Defense for International Security Affairs Paul Warnke cautioned Secretary of Defense McNamara in June 1968:

> We can anticipate that the small states and sheikdoms of the Gulf will rather naturally look to us to take the place of the British, and that it is easier to avoid this temptation at the outset than it would be late to attempt to extricate ourselves.[82]

Even the esteemed Paul Nitze, architect of America's blueprint NSC-68 that guided U.S. policy during the Cold War, remarked that the U.S. must steadfastly avoid arms sales to the new Arab emirates: "Even in the event that they turn to non-Western sources for arms, it is preferable that we not become involved in an effort to make the sales ourselves."[83]

As these officials predicted, insecure Arabs soon turned toward America hoping to purchase arms. When the Kuwaitis requested from the Americans the right to purchase 60 troop carrier vehicles, for example, the Johnson Administration reacted strongly against the request: "I believe we should sell no arms to these states," a view echoed in April 1968 by President Johnson's Assistant Secretary of Defense for International Security Affairs Warnke.[84] Although this prohibition on U.S. arms sales in the Gulf would fade away in the early 1970s[85] – in part because of concern the wealthy emirates would turn elsewhere for arms – in early 1968, U.S. officials curtly replied "no" to all requests except those from Washington's tested allies in Tehran and Riyadh.

If American leaders appeared firm in their refusal to replace the British in the region, who would defend Western interests, including continued Western access to oil, and how? In what one might dub the third component of American policy toward the Gulf after the British announced their withdrawal, the superpower expressed an early interest in encouraging the development of mutual security pacts. Within days of Britain's surprise withdrawal announcement, one of the chief idea men in the Johnson State Department, Walt Rostow, envisioned that the U.S. would rely on "security groupings of nations in the region" to fill the vacuum in the Persian Gulf.[86]

Rostow appeared intrigued with a NATO-like concept of collective security for the Persian Gulf, using the shell of the existing CENTO organization, perhaps with some type of an enlarged role for the United States. In a February 1968 meeting with the British Ambassador to Washington he ruminated whether "under an effective secretary-general CENTO could not be of greater value than in the recent past."[87] As time passed Rostow became more intrigued with his idea, which appeared at first blush to solve the American security dilemma of how to maintain order in a region possessing vital American interests, while at the same time doing so in a manner that would not involve U.S. troops. Rostow, however, soon discovered that any move by a major Western power to increase its influence in the region would promote wrath from all over the globe, with the strongest criticism originating from the Gulf itself. In a press interview that garnered wide attention around the world, Rostow discussed his views concerning a multi-national regional security pact, one that might include American leadership, or even the use of American military trainers to assist Arab states. The reaction to it, however, proved condemning, ranging from "naive" according to London officials,[88] to "sinister"[89] from Moscow representatives, to outright condemnation from some nations in the Arab world, whose leaders proclaimed publicly (though some clearly did not believe it privately) that Gulf residents did not wish to evict one colonial occupier only to have a second follow in its footsteps.

If American planners soon realized that they should not expect a NATO or CENTO-like security alliance to maintain order in the Gulf, upon whose shoulders would rest the role of regional security guarantor? In what one might call the fourth component of America's initial defense strategy in the Persian Gulf, the United States deputized two of the region's dominant powers, Iran and Saudi Arabia, as the policemen in the region. The idea of relying on local, indigenous forces to provide security for Uncle Sam at a minimal price, without the need to commit U.S. forces to the region, proved alluring to Washington officials. The policy appeared to rest upon a firm foundation, for American leaders thought they knew well their two primary Gulf allies. As Paul Warnke summed up:

> We already have a fairly high degree of interest in and close relations with Saudi Arabia (i.e., King Faisal and ARAMCO), and with Iran, whom we have just agreed to sell during the next five years $600 million worth of additional arms. Aside from that, we think that the people of the area can manage their lives better without additional interference from us than they can with it.[90]

In essence, United States' leaders – recognizing that they possessed neither the military wherewithal nor the political will to replace the British paternalistic stewardship over the Gulf – had concluded that they had no alternative but to rely on surrogates to accomplish the mission that London had done for over a century. Of the two surrogates, the real enforcer would be the nation with the stronger military, Iran, and its Westward-looking leader the Shah. As Paul Warnke concluded in June 1968:

> In effect, we are placing our money on a modern Persian Emperor to keep open the Persian Gulf. . . . While it is quite possible that Iran's "peacekeeping" in the Persian Gulf may become from time-to-time a rather messy operation, I doubt that a large role by the United States would be any more effective – or less messy.[91]

It is worth noting that the U.S. decision to rely on Iran and Saudi Arabia to tend to U.S. interests in the Persian Gulf began in the immediate aftermath of the January 1968 British announcement of their impending withdrawal. Some historians, however, date this policy to the Nixon Administration.[92] Although it is correct to associate the rise of the *term* "Twin Pillars" with the Nixon Administration, and especially with National Security Adviser and later Secretary of State Henry Kissinger, who fleshed out the Persian Gulf policy and gave to it a philosophic underpinning, the policy itself originated in early 1968 as the Johnson Administration struggled to make quick decisions in a period of rapid political change.

One of the most difficult decisions with which United States defense and diplomatic officials had to grapple in the immediate aftermath of Britain's announcement of impending withdrawal surrounded the future of the U.S. Navy's Middle East Force, a small handful of ships that had sailed from Bahrain since the end of the 1940s; in the fifth component of America's initial policy toward the Gulf that emerged following Britain's announcement of their withdrawal, the superpower chose to keep its naval flotilla intact. Although the force for 20 years had proved a symbol of American resolve with respect to its growing oil interests in the region, particularly in Saudi Arabia, the flotilla had been little more than a diplomatic showpiece with a weak military punch. The flagship of the force, after all, was normally a submarine-tender or a converted amphibious transport ship, sporting white paint (often the color of non-combatants, like hospital ships) and possessing only small guns.[93] The real military force, of course, and the ultimate arbiter of security in the region for almost 150 years, had remained the British. So when the British announced their withdrawal in January 1968, U.S. political and military leaders had to confront the question of what to do with the Middle East Force? Should they expand it, and give it a real military capability, with an eye to shaping Gulf politics in a way that only the British theretofore had done? Should they abandon it, noting that the British protective umbrella under which the U.S. Navy had sailed in the Gulf had disappeared, and that any U.S. force would be vulnerable? The Shah made no secret of his antipathy toward the British and American military presence in Bahrain, an island that the Persian monarch claimed. Or finally, should the United States pursue a middle course between withdrawal and augmentation, and perhaps keep the Middle East Force in the same size and shape as before?

For their part, U.S. Navy officers saw the departure of the British from the Gulf as an opportunity to play an expanded role in a vital part of the world, and they set about on a campaign within Washington to take over the British facilities in Bahrain. Navy leaders proved especially desirous of HMS *Jufair*, the naval base in Bahrain. Less than two months after the British announcement of withdrawal, U.S. Navy officials – cognizant of the fact that neither the Pentagon nor the State Department had assented to the plan – responded affirmatively to the British question of whether or not the U.S. Navy sought HMS *Jufair*. British Embassy officials in Washington documented these conversations, a dialog that reveals both the strength of the Navy's desire to stake a claim on the Gulf facilities, as well their realization that they were probably acting in advance of high-level, civilian political decisions:

> [U.S.] Rear Admiral O'Grady (head of the Politico-Military Policy Division in the Department of the Navy) ... said that the Americans intended ... to ask the Bahraini authorities for permission to take over the facilities at HMS *Jufair*. He went on to state that the U.S. naval authorities foresaw the need for a Naval force in the Persian Gulf in the context of keeping the peace between Iran and the Arab countries of the area; he described Iraq as also a very uncertain factor.
>
> We should prefer these views not to be quoted back to the Americans; there has incidentally been no reflection of them whatsoever at desk level in the State Department, and [U.S. Navy officials were] very concerned to underline that U.S. Navy thinking was not even Department of Defense policy.[94]

Navy officials were correct in their assumption that they were too far ahead of the politicians, because there existed substantial sentiment on Capitol Hill against opening up any new American bases overseas. Senator William Stuart Symington of Missouri chaired an ad hoc subcommittee of the Senate Foreign Relations Committee looking into the U.S. military affairs overseas. His particular goal, as the British surmised, was to prevent the Pentagon from "establishing foreign policy commitments over which the Congress later finds difficulty in imposing control."[95] Such concerns grew in the 1960s as a result of the U.S. entry into the Vietnam War. Some believed that the U.S. stumbled into that conflict after the Gulf of Tonkin incident, based upon tacit agreements that the executive branch in Washington had provided to the South Vietnamese. Symington proved particularly interested in ensuring that the executive branch – and the military, over which the President possessed day-to-day control – did not enter into any type agreement that might ensnare the nation in a future military engagement. The U.S. takeover of the Bahrain base represented just such a scenario. According to the British, the Senator was on the "warpath" against any such extension of U.S. commitments overseas.[96]

Negative feelings toward keeping the U.S. Navy in the Gulf went beyond Capitol Hill all the way to Tehran. Like Senator Symington, the Shah did not want to see the U.S. Navy operating from a U.S. base in Bahrain, but the Persian monarch in the late 1960s went one step further: he did not want the Americans in the Gulf at all. In public pronouncements the Iranian regime proclaimed that when the British departed the region, the era of outside interference in the Persian Gulf region must end. After that, only local powers, . . . which of course Iran dominated, would control the region. Despite the assistance since the early 1950s that the Americans had provided to the Iranians in training and equipping their military, the Shah appeared committed to drive the American military from the region. The London *Times* captured the flavor of Iranian thinking in April 1970:

> The official Iranian attitude is one of outright hostility to the intervention of the great powers in the affairs of the Gulf after 1971 and of insisting that the responsibility for the security of the area must be with the littoral powers.[97]

American diplomats took seriously the Shah's objections to the Navy flotilla, and worked assiduously to court his favor. The U.S., after all, was placing in his hands the protection of American interests, and Washington needed to keep him happy. One Iranian concern that American diplomats played up was the need to keep the Russians out of the Gulf. If the U.S. were to withdraw, the Americans told the Iranians, the Russians might speed up their march into the Gulf, and deepen their growing presence in neighboring Iraq. In one 1970 exchange between an American diplomat and the Shah of Iran:

> American Ambassador MacArthur [said to the Shah] that he quite understood that the Iranians did not want the Soviet Union to take any

U.S. or U.K. action as a pretext for entering the Gulf. But [according to MacArthur] the Russians obviously intend to continue their presence in the Indian Ocean or the Gulf whether we [the Americans and Iranians] like it or not. From 1905 to 1968 no Russian vessel had entered the Gulf; but there had been five ship visits in the last two years. Moreover, there was the Iraqi base now under construction at the head of the Gulf.[98]

Notwithstanding the opposition from Tehran and Capitol Hill, by autumn 1968 the State Department and Pentagon had concluded that U.S. interests would best be served by continuing to keep its naval force intact in Bahrain, with neither a sizeable increase nor decrease. The White House proposed signing a basing agreement with the Bahrainis, with the pledge that they would not expand them. This proposed policy of "non change" – the fifth component of U.S. policy toward the Gulf – got stuck in the U.S. bureaucracy for years, however. Desirous to keep some type of Western presence on the island, the British warned the Americans of the hazards of this delay, mentioning that, "Others had eyes on our facilities in Bahrain, including even the Iranians."[99] The Nixon Administration finally concluded the basing rights agreement with the Bahrainis – with Saudi and Iranian assent – in December 1971, via executive agreement, which did not require Congressional approval.[100]

The Arabs privately welcomed the U.S. decision to keep its naval flotilla in the region. Although subdued in public, in private the Bahraini Ruler, for example, greeted the news "positively."[101] Other Arab leaders along the Gulf coast shared his sentiments. The U.S. Ambassador to Kuwait, for example, wrote that:

> On various occasions when the subject of the future of MIDEASTFOR came up in my discussions with senior Kuwaiti officials they have reacted affirmatively to the idea of a continuing U.S. naval presence in the Gulf. Shaykh Jaber Ali strongly urged that it remain and be marginally strengthened. He claimed that this represents views of both the Governments of Kuwait and Bahrain . . .
>
> However, despite these affirmative private statements, I suspect that Kuwait's public position would be cool to negative. I do not think they could logically maintain a public posture of advocating British departure and American remaining.[102]

Even the Saudis gave a quiet nod to the U.S. decision. American Ambassador Nicholas Thacher in Jeddah explained that Saudi support for keeping the American Middle East Force in the region stemmed from King Faisal's feeling threatened by "communist and radical encirclement."[103] Just as Bahrain and Kuwait's leaders felt constrained against publicly embracing such a plan, the U.S. Ambassador explained, King Faisal would never endorse publicly a move to keep Western military personnel and hardware in the region, fearing a possible future backlash "should radical Arabs at some time in the future zero in on U.S. naval presence as convenient 'imperialistic' political target in post-British era."[104]

With the Arabs quietly welcoming the move, the big concern in Washington over the U.S. idea of keeping its naval force in the Gulf after British withdrawal surrounded the Shah's possible adverse reaction. In the autumn of 1970, U.S. Ambassador to Iran Douglas MacArthur II met with the Shah to break the news. In his presentation, he aimed to disarm the Shah's probable objections, emphasizing that a continued U.S. presence would thwart Russian designs on the region. Also, denying the Shah's notion that the U.S. wanted to become the policeman in the Gulf, the U.S. diplomat reminded the Iranian monarch that the naval force, as it had in decades past, would spend the majority of its time outside the Strait of Hormuz.[105] In the end, the Shah "made no rejoinder"[106] to the American announcement that it would keep its flotilla in the region, suggesting that although he did not necessarily approve of the decision, he would make no effort to fight it. The U.S. Navy's Middle East Force would remain intact after the British withdrew.

The need to keep a watchful eye on the Soviets served as the sixth and final hallmark of the U.S. immediate policy in the Gulf after Great Britain's announcement of withdrawal, a development that marked more of a *continuation* of policies pursued since World War II rather than a shift. Squaring off against the Russians was a role that the British had previously accomplished. Then, for almost a century stretching from the end of the Napoleonic era to World War I, the British sparred against the Russians for influence and control in Iran, as well as the Ottoman Empire and Afghanistan. For the four decades at the beginning of the twentieth century, however, the meteoric rise of Germany temporarily overcame British and Russian antagonisms. Hitler's defeat in World War II put an end to that rapprochement, and Soviet expansionism renewed the tensions, with Washington assuming from London the duty of checking Soviet designs on the Persian Gulf by way of Iran. Two decades of American military and political support for the Shah followed World War II, with Washington leaders assisting the Shah in designing and funding a military machine aimed to dissuade, or at least slow down until outside help arrived, any move by Moscow southward in the direction of Western oil supplies in the Gulf.

When in 1968 Britain announced its departure from the littorals of the Persian Gulf, the U.S. grew concerned over the effect that the forthcoming vacuum might have on the communist world's meddling there. The Americans had good reason to fear this. In Yemen earlier in the decade, after all, Russian-supplied Egypt helped to stir up such opposition to the British that they fled from Aden in 1967. Shortly thereafter both the Chinese and the Russians involved themselves in the People's Democratic Republic of Yemen, the communist state that emerged from the wreckage of south Arabia. Communist South Yemen, furthermore, served as a base for rebel attacks on two stalwart Western allies in the region, Saudi Arabia and Oman, giving rise to concerns in London and Washington about the repercussions of any further communist moves into the Gulf. To the north on the Arabian Peninsula, yet further, the Soviets increasingly courted post-revolutionary Iraq; just a year after the 1958 revolution the new Iraqi regime signed commercial agreements with Moscow.[107] The following year in Iraq the Communist Party gained legal sanction again after being banned for six years.[108] Although the fortunes of the communists in Iraq would ebb and flow throughout the 1960s as they battled against the rival Ba'athists, after the 1968 coup that brought Saddam Hussein to the second most powerful position in the state, Iraq tilted further toward Moscow.[109] The Iraqis that year purchased patrol boats from the Soviets, for example, and began hosting Soviet warships to port calls at Umm Qasr.[110] Observing this growing Russian presence in the Gulf, a London *Times* reporter went so far as to ponder whether *Pax Britannica* in the Gulf might give way to *Pax Sovietica*.[111]

Washington officials clearly did not want to see a *Pax Sovietica* emerge from the vacuum that would follow the British departure, but they possessed few options to prevent it. About the most the Americans could do – the final hallmark of Washington's 1968 policy toward the Gulf – was to keep a watchful eye on the Soviets and what they did in the Gulf region.

The U.S. decision to eschew a substantive political and military role in the Gulf after British withdrawal also reflected some deeper philosophical inclinations that had been largely subsumed by the Cold War. As discussed in previous chapters, several prominent Americans prior to 1945 had held with disdain British dominance of the region. A few noted American financial experts worked with the Iranians prior to World War II, for example, and attempted to free the nation from the yoke of Russian and British control. President Franklin Roosevelt himself insisted that World War II agreements signed by the Russians and British guaranteed post-war independence for the state. But FDR's successor Harry Truman – who shortly after taking office had to confront an expansionist Russia – largely welcomed British power in the Indian Ocean region.[112] But in 1968, as some of these last vestiges of the British Empire disappeared, some in America welcomed the change, seeing it as an opportunity for former British subjects to win their freedom. As Secretary of State Dean Rusk explained in February 1968:

> The United States Government has no intention of replacing the British. We hope that the littoral states themselves will seize the opportunity to resolve differences and to establish relationships mutually acceptable to them which will contribute peace and orderly development of the Gulf region.[113]

Nixon, Kissinger, and the Gulf

President Richard Nixon assumed office in January 1969 with his country at war, its financial condition deteriorating, and the remnants of the British Empire in Asia and the Persian Gulf collapsing. The President inherited a legacy of high expectations passed down from his predecessor once removed, John Kennedy, however, who had pledged to bear any burden and pay any price in the struggle against communism. From Nixon's perspective, along with that of his foreign policy expert Henry Kissinger, those burdens and that price had become too onerous. No longer could America afford – nor fulfill – the role of an international policeman. The U.S. simply had to curtail its defense obligations, and learn to say "no" to assuming new ones. The Johnson Administration had already come to that conclusion when the British announced in January 1968 their upcoming withdrawal from the Persian Gulf; under no circumstances, the Administration quickly concluded, would the U.S. assume the former British guarantees. But it would take Kissinger to flesh out the reasoning behind this decision.

Simply put, the "Nixon Doctrine" held that the U.S. would no longer bear any burden to halt the spread of communism; local powers must take primary responsibility for maintaining order in their own back yards. America must save its military might for instances where U.S. vital national interests became directly jeopardized. Writing during the first year of the Nixon Administration, National Security Adviser Henry Kissinger explained:

> For about 20 years after the end of the war, American foreign policy was conducted with the maxims and the inspiration that guided the Marshall Plan, that is, the notion of a predominant United States, as the only stable country, the richest country, the country without whose leadership and physical contribution nothing was possible, and which had to make all the difference for defense and progress everywhere in the world.
>
> Now whichever Administration had come into office would have had to face the fact, I believe, that we have run out of that particular vision. Conditions have changed enormously . . . You take the Nixon Doctrine for Asia, the basic philosophy of which has really guided our actions elsewhere. This is based on the proposition, not that the United States withdraws from Asia, but that the defense and progress in Asia, as elsewhere, cannot be a primarily American policy, that the United States can participate where it can make a difference, but it cannot, over an historic period, be the American role to make all the plans, to design all the programs, to execute or implement all the decisions and undertake all the defense and be in the posture where both progress and defense of other areas seem more important to the United States than it is for the countries concerned.[114]

As Britain's stewardship over the Gulf came to a close, U.S. officials cited the Nixon Doctrine in explaining that the U.S. would not replace the British, and that local powers must take over security responsibilities. Undersecretary of State Elliot Richardson, for example, following a meeting in Tehran of U.S. ambassadors in the Gulf region and South Asia, specifically invoked the Nixon Doctrine in 1970:

I would not go so far as to say the matter [of increasing U.S. presence in the Persian Gulf] had not been considered at all. But I think it is quite unlikely under our present view of the situation . . . On the contrary, I think it would be more clearly consistent with the purposes and object-ives of the Nixon Doctrine that we should look to countries in the area and to the leadership of Iran in particular to carry out the objectives of maintaining the framework of peace and stability within which the . . . national integrity of the countries of the area can go forward.[115]

By the early 1970s, then, as the British continued their diplomatic efforts to forge a new Persian Gulf, the American policy toward the Gulf was clear. The U.S. would not replace the British in the region, although the U.S. Navy's Middle East Force would remain. American leaders would try to keep the British engaged in the area as long as possible; one way to achieve that was by initially forswearing arms sales to the region, and encouraging the Arabs to turn back to London for their defense needs. The region's strongest local states – Iran and Saudi Arabia – must assume responsibility for their own security, as the Nixon Doctrine dictated. Notwithstanding the power vacuum that would likely follow the British withdrawal, the Americans had neither the stomach nor the ability to shepherd over the Gulf.

The impending British departure leads to rising tension

It is . . . true that the Gulf today is in a mood of uncertainty. Nobody can guess who is going to emerge strongest there in the next ten years. . . . There is a natural feeling that if assumed rights – over oil, territorial waters, naviga-tion, and so on – are not insisted on now they may go by default later.

—London *Times*, 1969

The year 1971 proved a momentous year in the Gulf, as one state after another prepared for independence from Great Britain: Bahrain in August, Qatar in September, and UAE in December.[116] In tandem with London's impending political withdrawal, British troops in Bahrain and Sharjah throughout 1971 readied for withdrawal. As they prepared to relinquish their facilities, they took home with them what they could, and passed to the locals what proved immovable.[117] After several years of travails and frenzied diplomacy, which proceeded right up to the very end, the British withdrawal proceeded roughly in accord with the timetable the Labour Party laid out three years earlier. It became apparent even before the British had departed, however, that tensions were rising in the region, in part from unresolved issues that neither the Arabs nor the British could solve before the end of 1971.

British leave behind what they believed was a dysfunctional UAE. The last few months of 1971 featured a frenetic diplomatic race on the part of the British to resolve some very thorny diplomatic issues. The first among them was the Union of Arab Emirates.[118] The British continued to lament the failure of the Arabs from Bahrain to Fujairah to unify as one large state, but had accepted the political reality that emerged: two small states – Bahrain and Qatar – preferred independence to union, making it necessary to amalgamate the other seven remaining sheikhdoms into a Union of Arab Emirates. All was not lost, the British thought, however, and with some creative diplomacy and inspired leadership on the part of the Arabs, the plan might succeed. As an opinion piece in the London *Times* concluded, "That solution is not ideal, but it has a good chance of working well."[119]

It remained very difficult, however, to effect a functional union of the seven sheikhdoms. The rulers, after all, had a history of petty in-fighting, dynastic squabbling and tribal conflicts. While Kuwait and Bahrain's societies were maturing to the point where the British felt comfortable setting them on a path toward independence, the Trucial States' leaders still mired themselves in petty rows. Such squabbling was well known. In the mid 1960s, for example, negotiations to replace the Indian Persian Gulf rupee with a new currency stalled, in part because the sheikhs in the Trucial States had been "arguing over what it should be called."[120] It was a disappointment but no surprise to the British, then, that substantive negotiations about the future of the Trucial States initially went nowhere. Into the spring of 1971 – after almost three and a half years of debate – unity talks amongst the seven Trucial leaders had not produced a workable plan. As the deputy to the British Political Resident summarized in January 1971, "The problem child is the Trucial States."[121] Special envoy William Luce, however, applied his best efforts to help solve the impasse. Even with Her Majesty's Government's assistance, it wasn't until 18 July, 1971 – just five months before British withdrawal – that the rulers finally agreed on a constitutional structure, and even then Ras Al Khaimah's ruler stubbornly refused to join due to his diminutive state's failure to achieve parity with Abu Dhabi and Dubai.[122]

Even when the majority of the Trucial States' sheikhs agreed to unify, their arrangement lacked a strong central authority with a robust military force. The individual sheikhs proved reluctant from the beginning to cede authority to a central government. The sheikhs essentially remained paramount within their own autonomous states. Only the largesse of Abu Dhabi – whose oil revenues dwarfed the resources of even Dubai, whose more modest fortunes historically had come from trading, not oil – kept the union nominally intact.

The proposed military of the UAE proved as disjoint as the larger political entity, with at least three separate military forces existing within the nation. Members of the Abu Dhabi Defense Force, for example, owed allegiance to their benefactor Sheikh Zayed, the emirate's ruler. A similar situation existed in the UAE's second city, Dubai, where Sheikh Rashid paid for that emirate's stand-alone military force. Only in the Union Defense Force – which consisted in large numbers of Trucial Oman Scouts, the British-officered tribal force – did military loyalties and responsibilities supposedly bridge across all the emirates in the greater UAE state. The London *Times* cautioned in 1972:

The concept of 'divide and rule' is deeply embedded in the Arab character. For centuries the Sultans and Sheikhs have kept themselves in power by playing off family against family, clan against clan, and finally the tribe against other tribes. The temptation to do the same with army against army will have to be resisted if the Union is to survive. Unless the Union Defense Force becomes *one* [original emphasis] force, and not a combination of several forces each with its primary loyalty to the Sheikh of Abu Dhabi, Dubai, and so on, the possibility of future fragmentation must exist.[123]

As the British continued with their withdrawal plans, the Iranians intensified their bellicose claims on the disputed islands. Drawing from investigations that stretched over eight decades, the British long before had concluded that Abu Musa rightfully belonged to the ruler of Sharjah, and the Greater and Lesser Tunbs belonged to Ras Al Khaimah.[124] As long as London's power proved dominant in the Gulf, the Shah grudgingly accepted the British-imposed status quo: the presence of a small Arab population on Abu Musa and a handful of police forces on the Greater Tunb island; the Lesser Tunb remained unoccupied.[125] As British withdrawal grew near, however, London noted a "hardening"[126] of the Shah's claims to these islands. On 30 November 1971 – just two days prior to the British granting to the Union of Arab Emirates their independence on 2 December – Iranian forces marched ashore in the Tunb Islands as well as Abu Musa. In the struggle that ensued, several Persian military personnel and Arab policemen died.[127] Further west, the Iranians also marched onto Abu Musa.

Although the British had hoped that the Iranians would have acted differently, the Shah's actions did not surprise Whitehall.[128] Iran, after all, had repeatedly voiced its intentions to invade if a deal acceptable to Tehran could not be struck. When it happened, Foreign and Commonwealth Office officials knew instinctively that Iran's actions would provoke a firestorm in the Arab world, and that Britain – who repeatedly received blame for many of the Arabs' woes – would likely sit at the center of that storm. Foreign and Commonwealth Office officials in London instructed their diplomats to explain that Iran's actions should have come as no surprise:

> In commenting on these facts you should emphasize that you hope the Abu Musa arrangements will not be criticized in the Arab world since they were the result of long negotiation and were freely accepted by the parties. Neither side has had to give up its claims nor to recognize the sovereignty of the other. As regards the Tunbs, you should say that we naturally regret that it proved impossible to reach an agreed settlement over these islands also. HMG worked hard for this but the ruler of Ras Al Khaimah felt unable to accept such offers as were made to him by the Iranians. We naturally deplore the loss of life which has occurred. It was however public knowledge that the Iranians intended to assume control

of these islands and the ruler himself was well aware that this could happen at any time.[129]

These post-bellum statements, however, did little to assuage the Arab rage that followed the storming of the islands. Rather than directing their anger at the Shah, however, the Arabs poured their invective against the British, citing their failure to do more to support the Arabs during their two days remaining. In a reflection of the contradictions of Arab policies toward Britain, the most virulent attacks against London came from those regimes that historically had called most stridently for the British to leave the Middle East. Rabid anti-British regimes in Tripoli, Baghdad, and Cairo for years had called upon London to depart the region, but during the November 1971 Iranian attack on the islands – when a large percentage of the British military forces had already departed from the region – those same Arab regimes criticized the British for not taking military action in support of the Arabs. The Libyans, for example, lambasted the British, stating that "Britain had formerly handed over Palestine to the Zionists, and was now handing over Arab islands to Iran."[130] The Iraqis went one step further, and derided the agreement on Abu Musa – to which the Arab leaders of Sharjah had agreed – as a British conspiracy against the Arab homeland:

> The agreement on Abu Musa is categorically rejected by Iraq because it effects a part of the Arab Homeland and Arab Sovereignty ... The British government is responsible for preserving the Arab status of the islands until the withdrawal of British forces. ... Britain is therefore responsible internationally for the surrender of territory admitted to be Arab by Britain. ... and for the grave complications resulting. ... The government of Iraq, in strongly condemning this imperialist conspiracy considers the recent measure an extension of the black record of British imperialist policy in this area."[131]

Even the Egyptians – chastised by their military humiliation in the June 1967 Arab-Israeli war, and since 1970 without the persona of the deceased Gamal Abdul Nasser – blamed the Iranian move on the British: "Egypt considers that Britain is responsible for the protection of the Arab islands in the Gulf against any foreign attack, in accordance with the protection agreements which are effective until the islands are handed over to their owners."[132]

From Tehran's perspective, the military action achieved its objectives. Striking just days before Britain would relinquish the islands to the Arabs, the Shah knew well that the British possessed neither the military ability nor the political will to counter Iran's move. As well, by attacking the islands when the British still held nominal control over them, the Shah avoided the appearance of aggression against the *Arabs*. Finally, the Shah attacked knowing full well that the weak and disjoint Arab states to his south – particularly those states that would comprise the UAE – could pose no military risk to his venture.

Although the 1971 Iranian move against the disputed islands proved the most glaring example of Iran's bid for supremacy in the Gulf as the British withdrew, it certainly was not the only one: Iran's decision to re-open its long dispute with Iraq over the contested border between the two states served as another.

The Shatt al Arab – the confluence of the mighty Tigris and Euphrates rivers as it flows into the Persian Gulf – had long served as the border between the two states, but the exact location of the border within that waterway the Shah disputed. Historically, the border's location fell alongside the Persian shore, at the low water mark. This tradition was enshrined in a series of agreements dating back to the 1800s, when the Ottoman Empire dominated the region and Iranian power under the Qajars ebbed. A 1913 agreement between the Ottomans, Persians, British, and Russians – the latter two having effectively partitioned Iran into their own zones of influence in the decade before – confirmed that Iran's territory extended only to the mean low water mark of the eastern side of the Shatt: virtually all of the waterway, in other words, belonged to the Ottomans. Although both states enjoyed use of the waterway, Iranian ships plying the river did so through foreign waters. A 1937 agreement between Iran and Iraq, consummated during a period of British hegemony in the latter, confirmed again this Iraqi-friendly demarcation, although the British demanded and received a substantial concession near their oil interests in Abadan, Iran. In the vicinity of the mammoth British refinery there, Iranian territorial waters extended out to the center of the river's channel, or thalweg. The 1937 agreement remained for over three decades the document that defined the Iran–Iraq border.[133]

The Shah, however – in the middle of the turmoil over who would control the Gulf after the British withdrew – unilaterally abrogated that border agreement in 1969, claiming that the Iraqis had through various acts of aggression over several years made the agreement null and void. The Iraqis, the Iranians claimed, had repeatedly violated the Iranian border on land and in the air during the course of Baghdad's prosecution of Kurdish rebels. The Iraqis retorted that Iranian forces escorted Kurdish insurgents into Iraq.[134] The tensions between the two came to blows in 1969,[135] as both sides made "warlike noises." As the London *Times* concluded:

> It is to be hoped that once again [as they had several times recently, both Iran and Iraq] will hold back, but the setting is more dangerous today since all the countries bordering on the Persian Gulf are staking claims in view of Britain's withdrawal from the area . . . .[136]

With the British withdrawal pending, the Iranians sought to get what they could, evident in the dispute with Iraq over the Shatt, as well as the dispute over the Gulf islands in the eastern Persian Gulf. Of the three large nations in the Gulf, Iran proved the most vocal and active in its drive to supplant the British as the leaders of the region. But they were not the only ones.

The Shah was not the only leader attempting to maximize power and territory in the Persian Gulf as the British pulled out; the impending British withdrawal in the early 1970s emboldened the Saudis, too, who announced plans to build a causeway to Bahrain. Within days of Britain's January 1968 surprise announcement of their intent to withdraw from the Persian Gulf, the Saudis announced their intention to physically connect the Kingdom to Bahrain, an island 16 miles off the Saudi coast, a move that pitted the Kingdom against her Persian neighbor across the Gulf. The British announcement, as many observers noted, had set off an immediate competition for pre-eminence between the states of the region. According to a New York *Times* correspondent, "The implication of the [Saudi causeway] plan is obvious considering Iran's recent claim that Bahrain is part of her territory and Britain's decision to leave the Persian Gulf area within four years."[137]

The announcement of the construction of the Saudi–Bahrain causeway was not the only reflection of Saudi attempts to expand their influence in the Gulf following British withdrawal, for Riyadh officials also vocally renewed their demands for more territory along the disputed border with the soon-to-be Union of Arab Emirates (UAE). According to the British, Saudi King Faisal was "obsessed" with his territorial claims on UAE, particularly Abu Dhabi.[138]

After studying the border issue for decades, the British long before had concluded that the Saudis possessed no legitimate claim against the UAE. But, like the Shah, as British power and influence waned in the Gulf, the Saudi leaders thought they could get away with opportunistic land grabs. These actions proved yet another reflection of a power struggle that the British withdrawal had set off, as the Saudis, Iranians, and to a much lesser degree the Iraqis battled for power in the Persian Gulf.

While the nation's Ba'ath leaders did help to fund anti-British insurgents in Oman in the 1970s,[139] Iraq largely stayed out of the clamor to replace the British in the Persian Gulf littoral states, for several reasons. First, its leaders directed inward enormous energy in the fight over control of the nation.[140] The leader who emerged from the 1958 revolution, General Abdul Karim Qassim, for example, fell in a coup to erstwhile ally Colonel Abdul Salam Arif in 1963, in the first of a series of disruptive political upheavals that marked Iraqi politics in the 1960s. Arif knocked down his fellow government rivals a few months later in a domestic Iraqi putsch, and several other coup attempts followed later in the decade. Arif's death in a helicopter accident led to his brother's installation, who would in turn fall from power when a Ba'athist regime – with Saddam Hussein as its second-in-command – took power by 1968. While all this was happening, throughout the 1960s secular pan-Arab Ba'athists battled Russian-inspired communists for power, with clans from Tikrit gradually assuming control of the Ba'ath Party and the country.[141] With so much domestic turmoil – American diplomats described the nation in the late 1960s as "basically unstable with more military take-overs likely"[142] – it is not surprising that the Iraqis proved reluctant to clamor after the territories that the British were departing.

Another reason why the Iraqi regime proved slow in staking claims on the former British environs in the Persian Gulf is that the Iraqi state was at war with its own Kurdish minority.[143] Throughout the 1960s the central government fought against the rebellious Kurds, who railed against attempts at assimilation into the Iraqi state; the Iraqi Foreign Minister confided to Secretary of State Dean Rusk that the internal conflict with the mountain population "fundamentally dominated the Iraqi scene," and that the state's leaders were "preoccupied with this issue and had little time or energy" with which to face other "pressing" issues.[144]

With whatever political energy remained, the Iraqis started a bid for leadership of the pan-Arab movement, a quest that took their attention westward toward Damascus and Cairo rather than southward into the British-dominated coastal emirates. The Iraqis increasingly sought a leadership role in the wider Arab world, turning against even their Ba'athist brethren in Syria.[145] In short, as Iraq involved itself in the quest to supplant Cairo and Damascus as the chief Israel-basher, its attention and resources got drawn away from the Gulf. Iraq, of course, had learned a lesson a decade before on the perils of attempting to take over with force a British emirate. The Iraqis had been chastised in their attempts to dominate Kuwait in 1961. The Iraqis in the early 1970s no doubt recognized that any attempt to move down to the south would draw a similar hostile Western and Arab reaction; Saudi Arabia's leaders, in fact, publicly announced their readiness to send troops to Kuwait when small-scale skirmishes erupted later along the Iraq–Kuwait border.[146]

The British depart. As Bahrain, Qatar, and the UAE received their independence in 1971, the old system of Residents and Agents that had formed the basis for British rule over the Gulf came to an end. Ambassadors replaced them, marking the close of one era and the opening of another. While the diplomats changed titles, the military officials redeployed entirely out of the area. By the end of November 1971 Britain's Royal Navy had pulled out from the Gulf. Ashore, the Staffordshire Regiment departed its last postings in Bahrain and Sharjah. The RAF, too, flew off from those two sites, leaving behind only a small staging post on Masirah, an island off the coast of Oman.[147] For the first time in nearly 150 years, by the end of 1971 the Gulf was without the presence or the protection of a major Western power. It would be less than 24 months, however, before Anglo-American leaders lamented their decision to abandon the Gulf.

6 The chaotic interregnum: America cries enough, 1972–91

As promised, the British withdrew their military forces from the Persian Gulf at the end of 1971. The United States – mired in Cold War commitments in Vietnam, Europe, and elsewhere – elected not to replace them. Washington officials kept in the Gulf region their very modest naval flotilla based in Bahrain, as well as their cadre of military trainers in Iran and Saudi Arabia. Those sea and land units, however, were political tools, and did not represent war-fighting, operational forces. By early 1972, then, for the first time in almost 150 years, the Persian Gulf lacked a major Western military presence. Though the British prior to their departure managed to solve a hefty share of the political quarrels in the region, as detailed in the last chapter, even before the last British troops departed it became apparent that substantial turmoil and tension remained. The Persian Gulf in the 1970s and 1980s increasingly became an armed camp. Over the next two decades, without Britain to maintain order, the three large states in the region – Iran, Saudi Arabia, and Iraq – squared off against each other and the small states around them. A very turbulent era followed. Although this story up to this point has concentrated on the British in the Persian Gulf, after 1971 it becomes largely an American saga. As Britain's Chancellor of the Exchequer Roy Jenkins explained when his Labour Government announced their withdrawal from the Gulf, the British were "no longer a superpower."[1] This chapter, then, primarily surrounds America's response to the chaotic "interregnum" between Britain's pull-out in 1971 and America's arrival in force two decades later in *Desert Storm*, a conflict after which the Americans never left the Persian Gulf.

Through several different presidential administrations under both political parties during this interregnum, American leaders consistently proved reluctant to involve themselves in the Persian Gulf. The onset of one political and economic disaster after another, however, convinced them that they had no choice. Like the British who arrived in the 1800s, the Americans entered the Gulf not from a conscious desire to expand their influence or establish an empire, but rather from a need to police distant shores in defense of their own economic safety. Without the presence in the Gulf region of a major Western power, leaders in both London and Washington discovered painfully, their economic interests suffered.

America's two-decade march toward assuming responsibility for Persian Gulf stability came in four steps, in response to four traumas, with the super-power reluctantly assuming a greater involvement in the Gulf after each: the 1973 oil embargo, the fall of the Shah, the Iran–Iraq War, and Iraq's 1991 invasion of Kuwait. The post-*Desert Storm* decision to leave behind in the Gulf a large military force – in part fulfilling U.S. military goals to plant a foothold in the region, and in part an unplanned response to Saddam's attacks against his Kurdish and Shia minority populations – marked America's final assumption of security duties in the region. After a tumultuous interregnum, in 1991 *Pax Americana* had arrived, twenty bloody years after *Pax Britannica* had departed.

Figure 61 USS *LaSalle*, flagship for the U.S. Middle East Force.

The British left a vacuum in the wake of their 1971 departure that the tiny U.S. Middle East Force could not possibly fill. Shortly after the 1968 announcement of their impending departure, Washington leaders made it very clear that they had no intention of assuming Britain's defensive commitments to the region. Mired in an unpopular war in Vietnam, there existed no Capitol Hill support whatsoever for any type of military presence elsewhere in Asia. U.S. Navy officials wanted to bolster their presence in this region, but such a move proved politically impossible; Nixon Administration officials had difficulties getting simple approval for continuing the port lease with Bahrain under which the handful of U.S. Navy ships of the Middle East Force operated. Above, the USS *LaSalle*, painted white for duty in the scorch-ing Persian Gulf environment, heads from the United States to assume duties as the Middle East Force's flagship from 1972–1993. A converted amphibious transport ship, the *LaSalle* and her crews continued with the Middle East Force's primary mission of showing the U.S. flag throughout the region, steaming an average of 55,000 miles per year. The onset of the Iranian crisis in the late 1970s saw the Middle East Force take on more operational duties, and the ship's crew assisted in the evacuation of Iran.

An outward calm after Britain's withdrawal

After 1971's flurry of violence connected to the Gulf islands controversy, the first two years of the post-British era featured an outward appearance of interstate tranquility, with the new Arab states consumed with the tasks of ruling themselves for the first time. Other than Iran's storming of the Gulf islands in late 1971, no shots were fired in conjunction with the independence of Bahrain, Qatar, and the new United Arab Emirates (this name superseded "Union of Arab Emirates"). No threatening armies rushed to the borders of the new states the way Iraq's did to Kuwait the decade before. And unlike the independence movement in Algeria, say, where hundreds of thousands perished, the Persian Gulf transition to independent rule proceeded very smoothly, a testament to work done in 1968–71 by Britain's diplomats. (The ruler of Sharjah, it must be said, was gunned down and murdered by his cousin in January 1972, in an attempt to regain the throne that the British took from him in 1965.[2]) Despite the lack of open hostilities, however, the period following British withdrawal featured great uncertainty, prompting the Persian Gulf states to arm themselves, and to turn to larger states for alliances.

Iran. Since the late 1950s the British noted that the Shah longed to become the dominant power in the Gulf. In the words of Britain's Persian Gulf Resident George Middleton in 1959, the Iranian monarch, "looked to the day when [he] might take our place."[3] The 1971 British withdrawal marked a fulfillment of that dream, and the Shah proved determined to show the world why the body of water bore the name "Persian" Gulf. Throughout the 1960s the Shah purchased – or received through outright grants and gifts from the United States – advanced army, air force, and naval equipment. A robust American training staff assisted Iranian military members in integrating the new gear into their swelling ranks. By the early 1970s, the Iranian forces had become the dominant power in the Gulf. As one British military observer remarked in 1973:

> During the past three years we have been able to watch the expansion and changes in the Iranian forces. . . . Iran has come a long way from the internal security army with a negligible naval and air force, which was all she had when the American [training organization] ARMISH MAAG came into being 17 years ago. In general, the Iranian forces are not up to Western standards, but provided her men are staunch (and only a war will enable us to find this out) she is certainly a match for any other Middle Eastern state excluding of course Russia.[4]

The growth of Iranian power – although generally welcomed by Washington and London – also gave rise to growing apprehension amongst Arab neighbors. As the British Ambassador to Iran Peter Ramsbotham pointed out in 1973, "The Iranian armed forces are the most powerful in the area. . . . The increase in Iranian armed power is, however, causing anxiety among Iran's smaller neighbours and others."[5] The Arab state in which the growth of Iranian power raised the most fear was neighboring Iraq, whose ruling Ba'ath regime soon after British withdrawal deepened their relationship with the Soviet Union[6] in a bid to augment the nation's defenses.

An insecure Iraq brings in the Soviets. Since the 1958 revolution that toppled the British-installed Hashemite monarchy in Baghdad, Iraqi leaders had "moved closer"[7] to Moscow. In 1968 – the year that a coup brought Ahmed Hassan al Bakr to power, with Saddam Hussein as his lieutenant – Iraq purchased patrol boats from the Soviets, and began hosting Soviet warships at port Umm Qasr.[8] Despite these developments, however, the Americans and British believed the Baghdad regime to be more friendly to Western interests than the other pan-Arab regimes in Cairo and Damascus. Washington officials, in particular, thought that Baghdad could be salvaged, so to say, leading to efforts to court their top officials, sending even leading military athletic coaches to Iraq to curry favor.[9] After British withdrawal in 1971, however – as tensions between Iraq and Iran continued to build – the Iraqi regime made a concerted move toward the Soviets to bolster the state's defenses.

This did not stem from a love of communism, however. The Ba'aths, in fact, had engaged in a bloody struggle against the Russian-inspired communists throughout the 1960s and there remained great antagonism between the two movements. To the degree that both Baghdad and Moscow desired to see a weakening of London and Washington's position in the Middle East, however, their interests converged. But perhaps the greatest driver of the Iraqi move in 1972 to draw closer to the Soviets surrounded the deteriorating relations with neighboring Iran.

Tensions between Iran and Iraq had been growing for years. An increasingly assertive Shah in 1969, for example, unilaterally abrogated the treaty that had demarcated the contested border between them since 1937. Repeated Iraqi incursions into Iran to counter Kurdish rebels, furthermore, brought the two nations that same year to the brink of war.[10] The November 1971 Iranian military occupation of the disputed Gulf islands worsened further yet the relations between the two states. And only a few months later, the border flared again.[11] Tensions between the two states, in other words, had degraded to the point where an all-out war might erupt at any time. The departure of the British in late 1971 had deprived the Iraqi leaders of perhaps the most effective restraint on bellicose Iranian behavior.

With the American-backed Shah free of his British fetters, and with it well known that Washington desired to have the Shah impose order in the region, the Iraqis understandably turned to Moscow. In April 1972 – just months after Iran's brash military moves on the contested Gulf islands that accompanied Britain's military withdrawal – Iraq and the Soviet Union signed a 15-year treaty of friendship and cooperation. It provided for increased military assistance, and, as observers noted at the time, ushered in a period during which the Soviet fleet was expected to ply the waters of the

Gulf as frequently as they did the Mediterranean.[12] Saddam Hussein – Vice Chairman of the Revolution Command Council, Assistant Secretary-General of the Ba'ath Party, and by that time already dubbed "the real power behind the Ba'athist regime in Iraq" – proved instrumental in the treaty.[13] The fear of growing Iranian power in the vacuum that London had left behind had thus driven Iraq toward Moscow. Tensions in the Gulf were rising.

Saudi Arabia Iran and Iraq were not the only two Gulf nations attempting to maximize their influence in the Gulf after the British withdrawal, for so too did Saudi Arabia. The Saudi kingdom exhibited greater self-confidence in the region, and in their public pronouncements flexed their new muscles. The U.S. Ambassador, for example, observed the new boastful Saudi swagger, reporting in 1972 that the Kingdom "feels it is coming of age militarily in the Arab world, as it is politically," and as such will likely adopt "a higher profile, at least verbally, in the future."[14] Even the normally taciturn Saudi royal family members began to brag of their military capabilities. In an April 1972 commencement speech to non-commissioned officers graduating from the Dhahran Technical Training Institute, for example, the Minister of Defense and Aviation Prince Sultan proclaimed that the nation's defenses were "not less than any other in the Arab world."[15] In short, following British withdrawal the Saudis began to flex their military muscle, as did their large neighbors. The Saudi boasts were not all blather, however, and came at a time when the kingdom was strengthening – with U.S. help – its military capabilities.

In addition to the arms sales and military-to-military training with the Saudis that the U.S. had carried on since the 1940s, the Nixon Administration in the early 1970s also decided to assist the Saudis in crafting their own National Guard. The United States must support its primary ally in the Arab world, Secretary of State William Rogers urged. In a letter to the Secretary of Defense Melvin Laird, Rogers wrote:

> King Faisal of Saudi Arabia has requested that the United States undertake, under a government-to-government agreement, responsibility for implementation of a planned modernization of his country's paramilitary National Guard. The modernization of the Guard has been given high priority by the King. . . . By assuming responsibility for this program, we would provide the King and other important Saudi leaders proof of our continuing interest in Saudi Arabia's stability and security. . . . We would establish for the first time a close working relationship with this key Saudi security element. . . . There are also important commercial advantages. The program eventually will cost several hundreds of millions of dollars. . . . It will help off-set the sharply rising imports of Saudi crude oil into the United States that are threatening to reverse our favorable trade balance with Saudi Arabia.[16]

Not only did the U.S. aim to bolster Saudi Arabia's land forces, but also its sea forces. In keeping with the Nixon Doctrine's reliance on local powers policing their own back yards, Chief of Naval Operations Zumwalt strived to encourage Saudi Arabia to expand its navy. In January 1972 the Saudi Minister of Defense and Aviation Prince Sultan, for example, penned with U.S. officials a memorandum of understanding that comprised a "basic understanding" between the U.S. and the Saudi Governments for a Saudi Arabian naval expansion program. The head of the U.S. European Command, who in the 1960s and early 1970s operationally controlled forces on the Arabian Peninsula, deemed this naval expansion "extremely important" and would "have a significant influence on U.S.–Saudi relations for the next ten years."[17]

Despite their increased desire for armaments, however, the Saudis did not live up to the role as one of the "Twin Pillars" tending to order in the region. Both the British and the Americans believed that the Saudis acted too passively, although the British appeared more severe in their criticism than the Americans. The Saudis, for example, did not financially support the Omani Sultan in his struggles with the communist-backed Dhofar rebels, the British claimed, a development of particular interest to the British due to the historic ties to Oman. Nor did the Saudis provide ample support to the conservative regime next door in North Yemen, the British charged. Throughout this period the Saudis also kept up their bickering over the border with Abu Dhabi, London lamented. In the eyes of the British it was time that the Saudis faced up to their new regional leadership obligations, for if they failed to fulfill some of the security roles that the British had previously filled, the vacuum would surely be filled by the Shah, whose growing and unchecked power in the Gulf the British began to question.[18]

The Americans agreed with the British about the need to have the Saudis play a more assertive role in the region, but the Americans almost always viewed the Saudis in a more positive light than did the British. Highlighting in bilateral Anglo-American talks the Saudis' advances, U.S. diplomat Joseph Sisco explained what the Kingdom's leaders needed to do from the American vantage:

> [We] would like to see more Saudi–Iranian cooperation; the Shah has already moved some way in this direction and the relationship between him and King Faisal was much better than a year or 18 months ago. There were signs of a more confident Saudi posture: the Saudis had in fact given North Yemen $30 million in budgetary support and aid in kind; they had acquiesced in the independence of Bahrain and Qatar. Mr. Sisco thought it important to keep pressing King Faisal to become more actively involved.[19]

Small states struggle to make sense of the new Gulf order. Iran, Iraq, and Saudi Arabia were not the only states in the Persian Gulf seeking to find their way in the aftermath of British withdrawal, as leaders of the smaller emirates attempted to consolidate their rule and maximize their own security in the newly chaotic world.

At the head of the Gulf, as the British revealed to their American counterparts, Kuwaiti leaders had difficulties in figuring out how to respond after British withdrawal. The British in mid 1972 found the confusion and indecision "distinctly worrying,"[20] particularly given the predatory track record of its much larger neighbor Iraq. Britain's pre-eminent defense concern in the Persian Gulf over the previous decade and a half, after all, had revolved around how to dissuade an Iraqi attack on Kuwait. The Kuwaitis, in the minds of British Foreign Office officials, had not developed a cohesive or intelligent set of domestic, foreign, or military policies toward that end: they exhibited "no sense of purpose."[21] Both the British and Americans grew concerned that the emirate's leaders were alienating the principal nation, Iran, whose military might assist in deterring an attack from Baghdad; the ruling Sabah family continued to protest the occupation of the disputed islands at the other end of the Gulf, for example, and refused Iran's requests to open an embassy in Kuwait City.

Down the Gulf in Bahrain, the ruling emir formally granted to Washington in early 1972 the right to take over the British naval facilities at HMS *Jufair*. Although the Bahrainis had made it clear from earliest months of 1968 that they desired the Americans to stay and even expand their presence there,[22] the Bahrainis grew embarrassed and increasingly felt vulnerable over the high visibility on Capitol Hill of the bilateral lease negotiations. The Bahrainis wished the American moves had been kept quiet, for they felt they were suffering Arab criticism for, in the words of the London *Times*, "opening its doors so blandly to the United States."[23]

In neighboring Qatar, the newly independent emirate suffered from leadership problems stemming from a recent coup. The British confided to the Americans that although the emirate proved better served by the new emir, who had introduced some modest modernizing reforms and a "small measure of liberation," there still existed problems from the old ruler who lived in exile in the UAE as the guest of Dubai's ruler. According to the British, so long as Shaikh Ahmed [remained], relations between Qatar and the United Arab Emirates would be strained.[24]

Despite Iranian overtures, the UAE's leaders refused to establish full diplomatic relations with Iran, eliciting British concern. The emirates' leaders cited the Shah's continued occupation of Abu Musa and the Tunb Islands. The British sought American assistance in the effort to diffuse this source of Iranian–Arab tensions:

> Her Majesty's Government had hoped to see the Iranians establish diplomatic relations with the UAE before now, but they had told us that they could not stand another humiliation of the sort they had suffered in Kuwait [where the state's leaders refused Iranian requests for opening a diplomatic post]. The Shah had now told us, however, that he would send

an emissary to Abu Dhabi, probably in September. In the meantime, we had told him that HMG would try to persuade him to mend his fences with Iran. [American diplomat] Mr. Sisco said that he would see what could be done by the Americans to help over the problem of establishing diplomatic relations between the Iranians and the UAE.[25]

In addition to concerns about the UAE's relations with Saudi Arabia and Iran, British and American diplomats also viewed with apprehension the continued long-term ability of the new state's government to maintain order within its borders. The biggest problem that the UAE would face in the future revolved around the coherence of the state and its population. In short, the Westerners believed that the UAE might in the near future fall apart in discord and dissension. The path toward union in the UAE, as the Americans and British witnessed, had proven difficult, and the resulting federation of seven emirates was a very tenuous one. Briton Mr. A.D. Parsons remarked that "it was something of a miracle that there was a Union at all."[26] In a conversation that would highlight not only this UAE internal weakness but also growing Iranian assertiveness, British and American diplomats in 1972 pondered what would happen if the UAE fell apart, that is, if political uncertainty and confusion should lead to chaos. According to Mr. A.D. Parsons at the U.K. Foreign and Commonwealth Office:

> If the UAE were to break up and the Iranians thought that their interests were threatened by this, the Iranians might land on the southern shore of the Gulf to sort things out. This would be bound to lead to Iranian/Arab conflict.[27]

Oman's continuing British-backed confrontation with separatists. Further south in Oman, British and American diplomats viewed with approval Omani success in battling the anti-monarchical, separatist campaign waged by rebels in the Dhofar region. In the early 1970s, then, it appeared as if the Western-backed monarchy might prevail. According to Britain's A.D. Parsons, "If the Sultan kept up the present rate of progress, there would be a good chance of clearing the Jebel of the 'permanent' rebel presence within two years. . . ."[28]

Britain attempts to prolong its influence, and America welcomes it. While from 1971–73 the large states of the Gulf armed themselves and attempted to settle old scores, and as the small states struggled to find their way, Great Britain and America also attempted to adjust to the new environment of the Persian Gulf region. Great Britain – without substantial military forces in the area for the first time in over a century – attempted to prolong whatever influence it still possessed, while America – still consumed by Vietnam and the Cold War – did what it could to keep the British there. Relations between London and Washington – as they had been since shortly after the British announced in 1968 their withdrawal from the Gulf – remained warm and frank.

The British naturally disliked the loss of influence that their nation suffered when it terminated treaty relationships with the states of the Gulf, and they strived in 1972 and 1973 to maximize the power they had remaining. One leading British diplomat stated emphatically to the Americans that, "Britain intended to play as active and prominent a role in Gulf affairs as was possible in existing political circumstances."[29] Their ability to continue to influence the affairs of these newly independent nations stemmed to a large degree from the Gulf rulers' dependence upon British citizens to fulfill critical government positions, particularly related to defense matters. In Kuwait, for example, over 120 British citizens remained in the military or civil service. In Qatar, likewise, 20 contract personnel served in the armed forces, 13 in the police, and 76 in the civil service. In Oman the numbers proved even more striking, where British citizens served as Defense Secretary and Chief Economic Advisor, and another 172 served in "seconded" or contract roles in the Army, 63 in the Air Force, and 3 in the Navy. Large numbers of British citizens served in similar security and military positions in the United Arab Emirates and Bahrain.[30]

Arms sales served as another way that the British aimed to maintain their influence in the region, although Washington sought to reconcile the desire to keep the British engaged in the Gulf with the desire to stimulate American trade overseas. In that vein, America in the early 1970s softened its prior aversion to arms sales to the Gulf region.[31]

To reconcile these two conflicting ends – the U.S. desire to keep the British engaged in the Gulf and the desire to assist U.S. arms firms – the U.S. State Department leaders crafted in early 1972 a policy that diplomats from both nations believed proved a good compromise. In this plan, the key components of U.S. policy toward the Gulf in the early 1970s became apparent: the desire to keep the British engaged, the hope to see the local states assume a greater security role, and the wish on the part of the Americans to eschew entangling local alliances or other defense commitments. As the chief American delegate Mr. Joseph Sisco explained to the British:

> The Americans did not wish to supplant Britain, but had to recognize that many Gulf states were likely to ask for American arms and that private American firms would be keen to do business with these rich countries. . . . Wherever possible, the United States Government should not approve the sale of sophisticated or offensive equipment which might upset the military balance in the area; nor sales which might lead to the establishment of a permanent American military presence in any Gulf state; nor sales which would undermine British rule.

Mr. Sisco continued that the Americans would prefer to devote any U.S. assistance to the Gulf states to civilian projects or technical assistance.[32]

The British, for their part, deemed this American policy "very fair," and recognized that there would arise occasions in which the two nations found themselves in commercial competition. When that case arose, both sides agreed, the parties should simply agree to say, "May the best man win," while agreeing to continue with their discussions and cooperation in the future.[33]

America's policy: a cautious "wait and see." This is not to say that Washington officials ignored the region, but rather, they made a very conscious decision – taking into account their limited political, military, and economic resources during the Vietnam War – to remain aloof, and to watch developments. The U.S. House of Representatives held hearings in July 1971, five months before the final British disengagement from the region, on the proper U.S. military and political posture in the greater Indian Ocean region, which includes of course the Persian Gulf. Key witnesses cautioned that the U.S. possessed no major interests in the region, a fact that should guide U.S. policy. One respected MIT professor of international studies warned that, "The first and most notable point is that the United States has no direct interest in the Indian Ocean area that could be called 'vital' or even 'crucial' in itself. That is, nothing in our trade, the commodities we get there, or any conceivable military threat from there that would warrant a strong U.S. position."[34] From the perspective of the twenty-first century it appears incredible that – given the tumult and U.S. national treasure that has been expended in the Persian Gulf over the past generation – intelligent, educated, well-meaning individuals would have concluded that Washington possessed no interests in the region; these conclusions, of course, came before the first oil crisis convulsions of 1973, which dramatically brought into focus the true depth of the West's interests in the region.

1973 oil crisis elicits America's first step toward the Gulf

On the Jewish holy day of Yom Kippur in October 1973 the combined armies of Egypt and Syria attacked Israel, attempting to reclaim Arab lands lost in the June 1967 war. Strong U.S. support for Israel – which included high-visibility U.S. Air Force supply flights and billions of dollars of emergency aid – prompted many oil-producing states to curtail production of oil and raise its price, in an attempt to erode American support for the Jewish state. An outright boycott against selling oil to the United States followed. Taken together, these moves resulted in a severe economic jolt to the United States and Western Europe, and tilted their economies into recession. Americans waited in their cars for hours at filling stations. Many Americans' first awareness of the Persian Gulf dates from this period. As municipalities invoked emergency measures like reduced speed limits and odd–even driving days based on automobile license plate numbers, Washington officials pondered the wisdom of the decision made several years before to forego a military presence in the Persian Gulf.

Attempted use of oil as a weapon in the past. As discussed in previous chapters, frustrations over perceived inequities prompted the Arabs three

Figure 62 U.S. military aircraft unloads self-propelled howitzer, 1973 Yom Kippur War.

The highly visible U.S. military re-supply of Israel in 1973 elicited Arab and Persian anger. A U.S. Army self-propelled Howitzer is driven out of a C-5A U.S. cargo plane during the Yom Kippur War, October 1973, at the Lod airport in Tel Aviv. Photographs like this appeared in world newspapers during the fighting, inflaming Arab and Iranian sensibilities and contributing to oil producers' price increases and production cutbacks that quadrupled the price of petroleum.

times since World War II to use oil as a political weapon, but with minimal effect.[35]

By the early 1970s, however, the world petroleum market had changed substantially, as rising Western oil consumption coupled with decreased U.S. production tightened world supplies,[36] making the West in 1973 much more vulnerable to the potential use of oil as a weapon. For much of the first half of the twentieth century, the U.S. proved an oil exporter, providing petroleum products to Europe and elsewhere. During World War II, however, the nation first became a net importer of oil; 1943 served as the last year in which U.S. petroleum exports exceeded imports.[37] In the post-war years, American oil consumption grew, leading to increased oil imports. By 1950, the U.S. imported over five times the amount of petroleum that it exported; by 1960 imports had risen to 100 times exports.[38] In subsequent decades that trend continued. America's demand for oil imports skyrocketed in the late 1960s and early 1970s, roughly quadrupling from 1960 to 1973.[39] While consumption increased, however, U.S. production actually decreased, peaking in 1970.[40] The U.S. economy continued to grow, with the fuel for it starting to come from cheap Persian Gulf oil, although it still accounted in 1971 for just 3 percent of total U.S. oil. In short, whereas the ineffectual Arab embargo of 1967 occurred during a period of oversupply, the 1973 Arab–Israeli war coincided with a substantial tightening of the world's oil market.

Although most in Washington were caught off-guard when the oil embargo and its attendant four-fold increase in petroleum prices crippled the West in autumn 1973, it wasn't because there were no warnings. In fact, there existed plenty of cautionary signs in advance of the embargo. A U.S. National Intelligence Estimate in 1971, for example, discussed in detail the world's tightening oil markets, and acknowledged the growing leverage of the Arabs over Western nations.[41] Gulf leaders themselves increasingly made public threats to use oil as a weapon,[42] which contributed to some U.S. congressmen in 1972 warning of an impending "domestic energy crisis."[43] Finally, one former U.S. consul general at the consulate in Dhahran presciently predicted a politically motivated oil crisis in the near future. Speaking before Congress in August 1972, less than a year after the British withdrawal and slightly over a year before the October 1973 oil crisis, Mr. Lee Dinsmore warned:

> In a few years when, for example, Saudi Arabian production of oil will provide more revenue that the country can use internally and give away usefully, the government of Saudi Arabia may find it prudent to limit production in the interest of conservation of its oil reserves. Or, indeed, let us face all possibilities, they may stop production for political reasons. No country, possibly no combination of countries, could make up the loss of oil available internationally as a result. If other oil producing countries followed suit, even by merely limiting production, a world crisis would develop overnight.[44]

Oil company executives, too, warned of such a development. The head of the American-owned Saudi oil company ARAMCO cautioned:

> The most important aspect in the energy outlook of our country is our growing dependence on oil imports, in particular, imports from the Middle East. . . . By 1980 it is expected that 56 percent of our petroleum consumption will have to be imported, with the Middle East and North Africa supplying about 70 percent of that total. Any further increase in U.S. imports . . . will probably have to come largely from the Middle East. . . . The continuing and orderly flow of oil supplies from the Middle East is therefore fast becoming essential in terms of our own national security as well as economic well-being. . . . The ability of the Middle East countries to halt oil exports to one or more of the consuming nations must be viewed against the background of Middle East politics. . . . Oil supply interruptions caused wholly or in part by political considerations have occurred at intervals in the Middle East since 1948.[45]

These warnings, however, did not prompt the U.S. Government to make itself less susceptible to any use of oil as a political weapon. As the 1971 National Intelligence Estimate concluded, "We do not believe, however, that cooperation among the producing states would soon reach a point where they would concert to withhold oil for an extended period."[46]

In subsequent months and years Persian and Arab states chalked up more dramatic victories, starting with further price increases, to ever-increasing demands for greater ownership in the oil companies, to still higher market prices.[47] A few states took even more radical steps. Iraqi leaders, for example, less than six months after British withdrawal in December 1971, nationalized the British-owned Iraqi Petroleum Company that had dominated the country's oil industry for decades.[48] Libya, whose radical pan-Arab leader Muamar Qadaffi had overthrown the traditional monarch in 1969, did much the same. As a New York *Times* reporter noted in 1971, these victories "demonstrated a clear shift of power toward the producing countries."[49] Thus, by 1973 there had been several years of increasing tensions between the petroleum-producing states and the Western-owned companies that extracted and sold the oil, with the oil-producing states generally gaining in power.

When the Arab–Israeli war erupted in October 1973, then, there already existed considerable sentiment among Persian Gulf leaders for using oil as a weapon: the idea had been discussed and threatened for a considerable time, alongside the growth of tensions between the Gulf regimes and the Western oil companies. The outbreak of the war exacerbated these growing tensions, made more palpable by the international publication and broadcast of images of U.S. Air Force cargo jets delivering military aid to the Israelis, a move that made clear in the mind of the Muslim world that the Americans had entered into the war as their antagonists.

The October 1973 war erupted at a time when representatives of the oil-producing states had assembled for a conference, making it possible for their leaders to make quick political decisions. In mid-October, delegates from the Organization of Petroleum Exporting Countries (OPEC) were in Vienna, Austria, where negotiators wrestled with the same subjects that had occupied them for several years: attempting to reconcile oil-producing nations' demands for further price hikes and increased control over the oil industry within their borders with the desire on the part of the Western companies to moderate such calls. Attempts at compromise failed, and the delegates departed Vienna without a comprehensive agreement.

Delegates from several Gulf states, however, reconvened in Kuwait several days later and made a series of decisions that led to the 1973 oil crisis. From the oil companies, they grabbed pricing authority for themselves. They agreed to a 70 percent price increase, up to $5.11 per barrel.[50] When news of America's emergency re-supply of Israel became public, the enraged Gulf Arabs led a drive to curtail further world oil production. Participating countries immediately cut their production by 5 percent, and pledged to continue to do so in subsequent months.[51] Although they did not give in to Iraq's radical demand of nationalizing all U.S. assets in the Middle East, the delegates nonetheless identified the United States for particular punishment. Even the Saudis jumped into the game. Saudi Oil Minister Sheikh Yamani, for example, made it clear to representatives of ARAMCO, the American-owned oil company, that should company officials refuse to implement the total embargo on Saudi shipments back to the United States, nationalization of the company would follow.[52] (The Shah, who previously had led the drive against Western oil companies, actually proved a moderating influence in the October 1973 crisis. He "sat on the sidelines"[53] as one historian noted, and actually increased production that autumn to offset the Arab cutbacks.[54] By December, however, he joined the other oil producers in substantially hiking prices.)

The deliberate and conscious American decision over the previous six years to avoid military commitments and deployments to the Persian Gulf fell apart during the October 1973 War and the crippling oil embargo that emerged during it. U.S. Secretary of Defense James Schlesinger quickly discovered that he possessed very few military tools with which to influence events ashore in the Gulf region.[55] Lacking other options, the immediate response was naval. In October he ordered the aircraft carrier USS *Hancock* from the Pacific Ocean into the Arabian Sea, within striking range of the Arabian Peninsula, where it steamed as a "visible demonstration of U.S. presence and interest."[56] Having chosen in 1968 to forego taking over British military bases in the region, and having refused to garrison there American troops, the U.S. possessed few other operational military capabilities in the region. The nation's large cadre of military trainers in Saudi Arabia and Iran possessed no weaponry, after all, nor were they organized to assume combat roles. The Americans and British since the outbreak of the October war had discussed military responses to the crippling oil embargo, but despite some highly publicized threats,[57] neither the U.S. nor Britain took steps in that direction. The corpus of American military power available on short notice for contingency operations in the Middle East, after all, was small, amounting to an airborne battalion of perhaps 1,000 soldiers and a Marine amphibious unit of approximately 1,800 men. Britain's position proved equally modest, consisting of an infantry battalion, an armored reconnaissance squadron, plus some peace-keepers in the Sinai.[58] Had Britain and the United States chosen to go to war with these marginally sized units, furthermore, they would have enjoyed no infrastructure in the Persian Gulf region from which to work, no logistics bases, no integrated transportation plan, and only scant forethought regarding issues of command and control. In short, neither the U.S. nor Britain had much more than naval power to bring to bear in the Gulf. With few other alternatives, in November 1973, Schlesinger announced that the aircraft carrier USS *Oriskany* would take up station when the *Hancock* departed, and that from that point onward the U.S. Navy would establish a "pattern of regular visits into the Indian Ocean and we expect that our presence there will be more frequent and more regular than in the past."[59] The United States, in other words, had decided to deploy on a regular basis operational, war-fighting units to the waters near the Persian Gulf, a reversal of U.S. policy from previous years.

Although the United States Navy had kept a token Middle East Force in the Gulf since shortly after World War II, it became clear in fall 1973 that if the superpower wished to influence events ashore, it would need to deploy substantial numbers of *combatant* naval vessels, requiring additional logistics support. The Navy's Middle East Force, as Defense Department officials explained, was never a war-fighting unit. Admiral Zumwalt called it "too small to give us any significant military capability."[60] The primary mission of the two-decade-old flagship and its two accompanying destroyers, after all, was not war-fighting, but showing the flag. As James Noyes, a Deputy Assistant Secretary of Defense for International Security Affairs, explained to a Congressional Committee in 1972, the Middle East Force's primary mission had traditionally been to "demonstrate, by visiting friendly countries in this far-away land, the continuing interest of the United States in these countries and the desire of the United States to maintain good relations with them."[61] The sailors on board those ships were more *diplomats*, in other words, than war fighters. Toward that end, in one year in the early 1970s the Navy's MEF ships made 108 port calls in 17 countries in the region, leaving little time for anything else but transit. In their public statements prior to the 1973 crisis, Navy officials took great lengths to emphasize the peaceful nature of the MEF. The flagship USS *Valcour* was "not configured in a combatant role,"[62] one top defense official stated. The ship's crews also performed limited research and rescue missions, according to U.S. officials, and assisted if needed the emergency evacuation of U.S. citizens in the area.[63] Not surprisingly, up through the 1973 October War, few residents of the Gulf objected to the U.S. Navy's Middle East Force, whose crews proved able to re-supply themselves at their principal port, Bahrain, as well as other friendly ports in the region. The Middle East Force, however, was not a war-fighting unit, and offered almost no offensive punch should the U.S. desire to use it in the Persian Gulf.

Projecting offensive naval power to Gulf area required logistics facilities. Compared to keeping the small Middle East Force afloat in the region, re-supplying an operational aircraft carrier battle-group – whose attack planes might be aimed at the port cities of the Persian Gulf – became a much more difficult task. In stark contrast to 1968 when several Arab leaders begged U.S. leaders to expand their military and political footprint in the Persian Gulf, during the 1973 War the U.S. became, in Arab eyes, allied with the Israeli enemy. The welcome mat was removed. The U.S. Navy could not depend on the goodwill of the locals to berth, resupply, and repair the superpower's war-fighting machines. In fact, during the October War, even friendly Bahrain asked the U.S. Navy to "withdraw" its Middle East Force, a situation that the Defense Department officials correctly forecast that they could reverse when "inflamed" tensions subsided.[64] Navy leaders, consequently, had to stretch a logistics bridge from the Pacific Ocean to keep the growing fleet of combatant ships plying the waters outside of the Strait of Hormuz. This supply operation, in the words of the Navy's top admiral, "taxed our logistics support capabilities to the absolute limit" and required the U.S. to "significantly reduce [our] ability to support our forces in other key areas, such as the

Western Pacific."[65] The ultimate answer, Defense Department officials argued, lay in the construction of a military base on the island of Diego Garcia, a project that had been discussed since the 1960s.

When the Navy Department in 1974 forwarded a special, mid-year supplemental funding request for constructing a naval logistics facility on Diego Garcia similar to the one that Congress had railed against in the previous decade, members of Congress raised skeptical eyebrows, believing – correctly – that the move was an Executive Department attempt to create an all-purpose contingency base from which the U.S. might begin to play the region's policeman. The October 1973 oil crisis lay behind the Administration's request, Defense Department officials explained. If the United States wished to project naval power to the Persian Gulf region, they needed to increase the amount of fuel to be stored on the island, deepen its lagoon, and expand the island's runway to 12,000 feet to accommodate long-range logistics aircraft. Such capabilities could be dual use, however, several Congressmen warned, and might one day lead to offensive B-52 bomber aircraft operating from the island. Lee Hamilton, the chairman of the subcommittee conducting the hearings, conceded at the end of the hearings that such facilities were necessary if the Navy wished to deploy force near the Persian Gulf. But the creation of an innocuous logistics facility might infer some larger political commitment in the region. As Hamilton warned one Department of Defense official in 1974:

> [Your language implies that the United States is] very close to adopting the position that we are the policemen in the area. You seem to kind of accept a responsibility that our job in the area is to keep the peace. I am under the impression that most of us don't want the United States to be policemen of the world."[66]

Despite these concerns on Capitol Hill, in the two years following the 1973 oil embargo, the Pentagon would ultimately win its battle over Diego Garcia. After years refusing to fund construction, in summer 1975 Congress dedicated money to improve the island base. During that time, opposition to the matter had "dwindled to a point at which the battle was hardly fought at all."[67] Within two years ground had been broken. Visitors in spring 1977 reported the presence on the island of 1,400 Americans, 25 Britons, bulldozers, graders, and other construction equipment. Oil tanks arose. The runway grew from 8,000 to 12,000 feet.[68] Almost two decades since the first Anglo-American planners identified the need for such a facility, in the aftermath of the oil embargo, Washington and London would procure their base from which they could project force into Persian Gulf reaches. American leaders had begun to take the first steps toward assuming responsibility for security in the Gulf, a role that the British had abdicated at the beginning of the decade.

America still clings to the Twin Pillars. Despite the shock of the 1973 oil crisis, other than the expansion of Diego Garcia, during the balance of the 1970s the nation did little more to improve its capabilities there beyond "more frequent"[69] deployments to the region of Navy warships. A special investigation undertaken by the Congressional Research Service completed in 1975 identified shortcomings in airlift, sealift, and the mobility of combat forces that might defend the oil fields in the Persian Gulf region.[70] The report includes an interview passage with Schlesinger that warns that in a future conflict, the U.S. would be "less likely to be tolerant" of the use of oil as a weapon, and "might not remain entirely passive" as it did in 1973. After the immediate crisis of the oil embargo subsided in the mid 1970s, however, the Defense Department did not work to correct those deficiencies. The Pentagon, rather, essentially returned to its preoccupation with the battle against the Soviet Union. Annual Defense Department Reports throughout the majority of the 1970s made only passing reference to Persian Gulf security matters, and when they did, it was in the context of U.S. support for its proxies in the region, the Twin Pillars of Iran and Saudi Arabia.[71] During the mid 1970s, when the United States received an offer from Sultan Qaboos of Oman to take over the British lease for the military base on Masirah Island, furthermore, the superpower turned it down.[72] One scholar concluded, "The Ford Administration appeared to have adopted the Nixon approach by continuing to depend on the Shah of Iran to maintain regional security and internal stability. Hence, the Sultan's offer of Masirah was never seriously considered. . . ."[73] Nor was a similar offer entertained by Ford's successor, President Jimmy Carter, when the Sultan proffered it again in fall 1977.[74]

Rather than jettisoning the Twin Pillars strategy in light of Saudi Arabia and Iran's support in the early 1970s of oil price hikes, Washington leaders actually did the opposite: they tightened relations with them, and sold to them copious amounts of military armaments. The United States sold to the Shah a huge complement of military weaponry in the 1970s – including high technology jet and surveillance aircraft and naval vessels – amounting to $20 billion between 1971 and 1978, as the state's military ballooned in size from 181,000 at the beginning of that decade to 415,000 before its end.[75] American presidents warmly welcomed the monarch, and the Shah reciprocated the hospitality by entertaining U.S. leaders. Despite the tension engendered by Iranian moves to hike oil prices, U.S.–Iranian relations, in the Shah's mind, "have never been better."[76]

So, too, did U.S. leaders in the mid 1970s embrace the other Twin Pillar, Saudi Arabia, rather than chastise it for its rulers' role in the 1973 oil embargo. America sold to Saudi Arabia $30 billion in military sales between 1971 and 1980.[77] After a thorough review and discussion of U.S. policy in the Middle East in 1974, the Nixon Administration concluded that a central objective of U.S. diplomacy in the Middle East should be to *strengthen* the U.S.–Saudi relationship. Saudi oil, Washington recognized, was essential to the West. As Sidney Sober, a Deputy Assistant Secretary of State and participant in a special Middle East Task Group, concluded:

Saudi Arabia is the only source which can supply the bulk of the increase in oil which will be needed in the coming decade to fuel the economies of the United States and other major industrialized countries.[78]

The dawn of the Carter Administration in January 1977 elicited a flurry of new defense policy reviews, but a Euro-centric view of security issues, coupled with limitations on funding, generally prevented new initiatives that might bolster U.S. readiness to fight in the Persian Gulf. That said, a net assessment prepared under the direction of Assistant National Security Adviser Zbigniew Brzezinski and Harvard Professor Samuel P. Huntington underlay Presidential Directive (PD)/NSC-18. The August 1977 document focused on Soviet challenges, but it also included a recommendation to form a "deployment force of light divisions with strategic mobility independent of overseas bases and logistical support, which includes moderate naval and tactical air forces, and limited land combat forces. These forces will be designed for use against both local forces and forces projected by the USSR based on analysis of requirements in the Middle East, the Persian Gulf, or Korea. . . ."[79] Despite this directive from the White House, however, the U.S. Defense Department "paid scant attention" to the call for developing such a light, rapid deployment force. The initiative was expensive, and it would detract time and attention from rebuilding NATO, a more immediate priority.[80]

America, then, throughout the mid 1970s continued to exhibit a desire to steer clear of direct involvement in the Persian Gulf by using surrogates, in spite of growing Soviet influence in the region. By the mid decade the Soviets had bases in Somalia and access to the port in Aden, and made port calls at the Iraqi port of Umm Qasr. But in Washington there existed little sentiment to counter the Soviets with bolstered U.S. defense capabilities in the Persian Gulf. Although concerned with the Soviet Navy's growing presence in the general region, Washington voices called for arms control discussions with the Soviets, not unilateral calls for more arms. The height of this sentiment took the form of President Jimmy Carter's March 1977 proposal to "demilitarize" the Indian Ocean region.[81]

The fall of the Shah and the Russian invasion of Afghanistan

The demise of the Shah and the Soviet invasion of Afghanistan prompted American leaders to take a second step toward assuming the duties of security arbiter in the Gulf, a role that the British abandoned in 1971. The twin crises prompted Washington to develop for the first time a military capability to project and sustain military force to the Persian Gulf region – an idea first annunciated in NSC-18 in 1977 – and prompted President Carter to announce that the defense of the region represented a vital U.S. national interest. The chaos of the 1970s, in other words, had become too great for the superpower to allow local states to tend to Western interests.

Figure 63 The Imperial Iranian Ships IIS *Babr* and IIS *Palang*, former U.S. Navy ships, in drydock at the Philadelphia Naval Shipyard, c. 1973.

With America's blessing, Iran's Shah built a formidable military arsenal in the 1960s and 1970s, fulfilling his role as America's deputized policeman in the Gulf. The two former destroyers USS *Zellars* and USS *Stormes* were purchased by the Government of Iran, which funded extensive overhaul and modernization before the ships joined the Imperial Iranian Navy. Of note, the World War II flagship of the Iranian Navy bore the same name *Babr,* but was attacked and sunk by the British in 1941. Reflecting the deep influence of the United States and Britain over Iran's post-war military, the first commanding officers of these two ships both graduated from the British Naval Academy and the U.S. Navy's Postgraduate School in Monterey, California.

A chaotic 1979. The year 1979 proved one of turmoil and tumult in the Persian Gulf. In Iran, a restive population stood in revolt against the excesses of the Shah.[82] Demonstrations had wracked the country for months. Mullahs, bazaar merchants, students, and later, ordinary citizens, joined in opposing the monarch, who – terminally ill, it would later turn out – proved unable to staunch the opposition. In January 1979 the Shah fled, never to return. A reactionary Shia cleric, Ayatollah Ruhollah Khomeini, returned from his exile in Paris, eventually presiding over a revolutionary, decidedly anti-American and anti-Western theocratic regime. With the Shah's demise, the West lost its policeman in the region. Concurrently, a thousand miles southwest, further troubles erupted: the People's Democratic Republic of Yemen attacked conservative and Westward-leaning North Yemen. In what threatened to become a repeat of the 1960s Yemeni civil war, the Saudis turned to the United States for assistance. In response, as they did six years before during the 1973 oil crisis, United States' leaders did what they could: they repositioned to the Arabian Sea an aircraft carrier, the USS *Constellation*. Two carriers, and a total of over 30 U.S. Navy ships, would eventually stand watch in the region, around-the-clock.[83] Early the next year the U.S. also sent Airborne Early Warning and Control (AWACS) aircraft to the Persian Gulf region.[84] This extended projection of naval and air power, however, virtually exhausted the arsenal of tools available to the U.S. policy-makers in Washington.

The fall of the Shah and the crumbling of the Twin Pillars in early 1979 forced Washington decision-makers to ponder new military strategies to influence events in the Gulf. Their options were grim. Although in the immediate aftermath of Britain's 1968 withdrawal many local hereditary sheikhs warmly invited the United States to take over the British bases in the Gulf, those invitations had long since expired. The 1973 war, in particular, had poisoned America's reputation in the minds of the region's populace. No Arab leader in the late 1970s would dare risk an open and close relationship with Washington, lest his people rise up in protest. Even Bahrain, whose leaders had hosted the U.S. Middle East Force since just after World War II, had earlier in the 1970s threatened to evict the Americans.[85] What to do in 1979? The month after the Shah's downfall, in February 1979, the U.S. National Security Council recommended the creation of a rapid response force for use in the region,[86] which would ultimately take the acronym RDJTF, or Rapid Deployment Joint Task Force.

Any U.S. military action in a region 7,000 miles from the U.S. realistically had to have some rudimentary access to a local base in the inhospitable Persian Gulf region, and the U.S. in the late 1970s set off with an open wallet on a campaign to find a willing host. In a frenetic flurry of diplomatic activity in the spring of 1979, State Department and Defense Department officials visited many states in the vicinity of the Persian Gulf, and proved able to conclude agreements with Oman, Kenya, and Somalia.[87] Of the three, the Omani deal proved the most critical. Geographically, the nation stood closer to the scene of probable hostilities than the other two; the Musandem Peninsula along the southern shore of the Strait of Hormuz, after all, belongs to Oman. In return for substantial assistance, some accounts detailed $210 million in direct military aid, the U.S. gained access to several military facilities, including the former RAF base at Masirah, and port facilities at Muscat and Salalah.[88] (Ironically, just two years before the U.S. could have obtained the same access from the Omani Sultan for a fraction of the cost, but both the Ford and Carter Administrations turned it down.) The Kenya and Somali deals also proved valuable, in that bases in eastern Africa might serve as staging areas for reinforcements.[89] Finally, President Carter's March 1980 budget supplement request included monies for further improvements on Diego Garcia, the atoll base.[90]

Figure 64 Diego Garcia improvements, 1980.

> The turmoil that accompanied the 1973 oil crisis prompted Congress in mid decade to approve funding for improvements to the island base on Diego Garcia, monies that Congressional leaders during the Vietnam conflict refused to provide. The fall of the Shah later in the decade sped up improvements to the base. Above, a July 1980 photograph of the airstrip. Note the proximity of the water.

Foreign base rights comprised just one part of the solution to America's Persian Gulf security needs, however, with the enlargement of air and sea lift representing another. As the British had discovered in 1961's Operation *Vantage*, the rapid build-up of forces to defend Kuwait from Iraq's threatened invasion, it is easier to transport *people* to the scene of potential hostilities than it is to move heavy equipment like tanks, artillery, and mobile command posts. On 4 November 1979, just over a month after the Secretary of Defense established the Rapid Deployment Joint Task Force on 1 October, a group of Iranian revolutionary students stormed the U.S. embassy in Tehran and held hostage for over 14 months 52 American officials. President Carter learned from the Joint Chiefs of Staff that America's potential military options were still limited, not because of the lack of will or the lack of personnel, but rather because of the lack of sea and air lift.[91] On 12 December 1979, less than a month after the Iranian hostage crisis began, President Carter announced his pledge to acquire such capabilities:

> Our 1981 defense budget and our Five Year Defense Plan will have better

means for rapid deployment of forces . . . a new fleet of Maritime Pre-positioning Ships that can carry heavy equipment and supplies for three Marine brigades . . . (and) a new fleet of large cargo aircraft.[92]

In his next budget request, Carter fleshed out this vision with enormous requests for extra military logistics and transportation, including $317 million for KC-10 air refueling aircraft, almost $300 million to improve and enlarge the fleet of C-5 and C-141 cargo aircraft, and $275 million for Maritime Pre-positioning Ships and duplicate sets of equipment for three Marine Amphibious Brigades.[93]

Heavy sea lift gives the United States the ability to pre-position equipment at sea near the Gulf. The inclusion in President Carter's budget of new pre-position ships and Marine battle gear is important because it forms a critical part of plans for defending the Gulf, plans which – unbeknownst to most American planners at the time – made the American plans resemble very closely those of the British from almost two decades before. Thus, working independently, the Americans had stumbled upon and adopted roughly the same formula for defending the Gulf: fast-reaction troops from outside of theater swooping in when needed and meeting up with pre-positioned gear. The Carter Administration had put in place by autumn, then, the key central elements of a new military policy: foreign base rights, a rapid deployment force – established on 1 October 1979[94] – and new air and sea lift. The date 1 October 1979 is important, because it took place *before* the 24 December 1979 Soviet invasion of Afghanistan. America's abandonment of the Nixon Doctrine, and its replacement by the willingness of the superpower to rapidly deploy its own forces, then, grew out of the collapse of Iran, not as a reaction to Moscow. It would take Soviet misbehavior, however, to elicit from Washington a formal declaration that the Persian Gulf had become a vital national interest, and that the U.S. stood ready with armed might to defend it.

The tumultuous year 1979 – which saw the fall of the Shah, the attack by South Yemen on the North, the resulting deployment of U.S. forces to Saudi Arabia, and the seizure of American hostages in Tehran – ended in late December with yet another dramatic event, the Soviet invasion of Afghanistan, prompting the U.S. President to unveil the so-called "Carter Doctrine." In his 23 January 1980 State of the Union speech to Congress, the President declared that, "an attempt by any outside force to gain control of the Persian Gulf region will be regarded as an assault on the vital interests of the United States and such an assault will be repelled by any means necessary, including military force."[95]

The annunciation of the Carter Doctrine marked a radical break from previous policy, and laid to rest for good the Nixon Doctrine's reliance on outside powers to safeguard the West's interests in the Gulf. Although it remains in the early twenty-first century unclear whether or not the Soviet leadership ultimately intended to move beyond Afghanistan, such a move seemed to Washington officials to fit into a pattern of past Russian behavior.

Earlier in the century, after all, the Russians had moved in and out of Iran virtually at will, and the Soviets' failure to withdraw from Iranian Azerbaijan in 1945 gave rise to one of the first East–West confrontations of the post-war era. The communist-backed South Yemeni regime's attack on the Saudi-aligned North in early 1979, furthermore, made many suspect that the Soviets possessed larger designs on the Persian Gulf region. These moves on land also seemed to fit in with a pattern of increasingly assertive behavior on the seas. Immediately after the British announced in 1968 their impending with-drawal from the Persian Gulf, after all, the Russians initiated naval visits to the region, and started construction of naval facilities in Aden, the horn of Africa, and Iraq.

The Carter Doctrine – the pledge that the United States would use force to protect U.S. interests in the Gulf, particularly those caused by threats from the Soviet Union – remained a critical component of U.S. policy toward the Persian Gulf despite Carter's loss in the subsequent election of 1980. Before the end of that year, yet another calamity erupted in the Gulf, the third in a rapid string that began with British withdrawal less than a decade before. And like the oil embargo of 1973, and the fall of the Shah and Soviet invasion of Iran six years later, the Iran–Iraq War served as another step in America's march to assuming the role of security guarantor in the region that the British had abandoned.

America's third step toward the Gulf: the Iran–Iraq War

Iran's revolution quickly impacted the other states of the Persian Gulf. The mullahs, led by the Grand Ayatollah Ruhollah Khomeini, envisioned them-selves as the new leaders throughout the Gulf, and beyond. They provided inspiration to the oppressed Shia communities in Iraq, Kuwait, Saudi Arabia, Bahrain, and Lebanon; accordingly, anti-regime stirrings arose in each of those nations, fueled by mullahs in Tehran calling for the end to Westward-leaning regimes throughout the Middle East.[96]

The fall of the Pahlevi regime and the rise of an expansionist, revolutionary Shia state elicited a move by Iraqi strongman Saddam Hussein to face down the Iranian terror and strike a claim as the Gulf and the Arab world's new dominant power. While the revolution wracked Iran in 1979, Saddam in July of that year grabbed for himself from Hassan al-Bakr the titular power of Iraq's President, a role al-Bakr had filled since the Ba'aths came back to power in 1968. In 1979 Saddam also made amends with rival Syria, in part for a chance to lead Arab opposition to Egypt's Camp David peace treaty with Israel. Reminiscent of the runaway military spending that marked the Shah's final decade, President Saddam Hussein built up his own arsenal, purchasing from France new fighter aircraft, missiles, radars, and ships.[97] But it was in his quest to vanquish the radical, theocratic, Shia regime to his east where Saddam most clearly exhibited his drive to lead the Arabs. After several months of border skirmishes along the tumultuous Iran–Iraq border,

Saddam in autumn 1980 threw his army against Iran's in a quest to take the rich oil fields of Khuzestan, the same fields north of Abadan where the British first discovered oil early in the twentieth century.

The Iran–Iraq War stretched throughout most of the 1980s, starting in September 1980, as Iraqi jets raided Iranian air bases and several Iraqi divisions crossed the border at many different points.[98] Although the initial thrust proved capable of moving into oil-rich Khuzestan, it failed to deliver a knock-out blow, prompting a surge of patriotism in Iran. Despite their weakened condition resulting from revolutionary purges of the top officer corps and a lack of maintenance of its Western military equipment, Iran's military forces – aided by the creation of the ideologically driven Revolutionary Guards – not only held off the Iraqis, but pushed them back into their own territory. In what has been called the longest conventional war of the twentieth century,[99] the two sides continued hostilities until 1988, alternating control of each other's border lands, engaging in missile attacks on each other's cities, and finally, assaulting each other's shipping. The war impelled U.S. leaders to interject their operational military forces into the region, a third step in the superpower's eventual move to replace the British in their former role as security guarantors in the region.

Initial U.S. diplomatic and military reaction to the war. Despite the antipathy with which Washington officials held the Iranian regime, the initial U.S. diplomatic reaction to Saddam's attack on Iran was one of restraint. The U.S. announced a policy of neutrality, and publicly warned the Iraqis against any move toward the "dismemberment" of Iran, or any attempt to annex its oil fields.[100] In private, however, as time progressed, the U.S. tilted toward Iraq, going so far as sharing classified satellite imagery with Baghdad.[101] Washington also dispatched air and naval power to the region. As they had the previous year when South Yemen's attack on North Yemen threatened to spill-over into Saudi Arabia, Washington officials again in fall 1980 dispatched Airborne Control and Warning System (AWACS) aircraft into Saudi Arabia. They also augmented the naval presence outside of the Strait of Hormuz. The month after the outbreak of the Iran–Iraq War, for example, *two* aircraft carriers steamed the waters of the Arabian Sea, the *Midway* and the *Eisenhower*.[102] The U.S., of course, also retained its Middle East Force consisting of a command ship and approximately three other ships inside the Strait of Hormuz. U.S. leaders hoped that the display of American might would "discourage any further aggression."[103] The Carter Administration, in other words, looked to the presence of U.S. forces in the beginning of the Iran–Iraq War to have a calming effect on the two combatants, to limit the spread of hostilities. This U.S. policy of using naval power to limit the spread of hostilities during the Iran–Iraq War remained for the next six years. According to the Commander of the U.S. Central Command in 1986 – the new moniker given in 1983 to the now Southwest Asia specific Rapid Deployment Joint Task Force:

The United States is not in the business of settling the Iraq–Iran war. It hasn't been our policy to intervene in that affair, nor do our relationships with the two belligerents facilitate such a role at this time. Our policy has been to prevent the war from spreading to other parts of the region.[104]

The tanker war and re-flagging. Despite the loss of tens of thousands of lives on both sides of the Iran–Iraq War, neither Baghdad nor Tehran capitulated. As it became increasingly evident that there would be no lasting break-through for either side on land, the battlefield shifted to the waters of the Gulf. In the sixth year of the conflict, 1986, both sides began to hunt out and destroy seaborne traffic of the other, particularly oil tankers.[105] The Iranians expanded their targets to include Kuwaiti and Saudi ships, as both of those Arab nations had been funneling money to Saddam Hussein, as well as transporting through their territory large amounts of arms destined for the battlefield.[106] As the attacks on naval shipping continued, the members of the U.S. Middle East Force found themselves literally caught in the middle of a war that no one in Washington wanted to get involved in. Chairman of the Joint Chiefs of Staff Admiral William Crowe, a former Commander of the Middle East Force, described how American ship crews got mixed up in the fray, often siding against the Iranians:

> The American Middle East Force was right in the middle of this battle-ground. Its commanders were operating in what was essentially a war zone (though the administration, myself included, tried hard to avoid labeling it as such) without a well-defined role, and as the attacks on merchant shipping exploded around them the frustration level sky-rocketed. Officers and crews hated to stand around and watch, forbidden to intervene as Iranian naval and air units shot up unarmed tankers and freighters. . . . Limited by our rules of engagement to rendering humani-tarian aid, the American warships would steam toward the action, know-ing that once they arrived the Iranians were likely to give it up and disappear. Some of our skippers, I knew, skirted the gray area of their orders and tried to position themselves between Iranian attack craft and unarmed neutrals. . . . Amid the violence the Middle East Force was walking a fine, perilous line.[107]

The long-standing policy of keeping the U.S. Navy in the region as a damp-ener, but keeping its ships out of the direct line of fire, however, came to an end in 1987 when Washington officials adopted a campaign to re-flag and escort under American military protection Kuwaiti oil tankers. The plan grew out of a Kuwaiti December 1986 overture to the American ambassador for assistance in the tanker war, which late in the year had substantially reduced the emirate's oil revenues. The U.S. reticence – originating from the start of the war in 1980 and continuing through two presidential administrations – to involve its military in the hostilities in the region ended when Washington discovered that the Kuwaitis had made a similar proposition to the Soviets, with whom the Kuwaitis also had a relationship based upon arms purchases over the previous decade. It did not take long for the Reagan Administration to agree to the Kuwaiti request. According to Secretary of Defense Caspar Weinberger:

> My immediate reaction, as well as my conclusion after further study, was that we should agree to the Kuwaiti request. It seemed to me that if we failed to do so, and if, as the Kuwaitis feared, Iran's continued attacks could slow or even stop the flow of oil out of the Gulf, we would be accepting Iran's right to close the international waters of the Gulf, and block nonbelligerent and extremely important commerce from moving in those waters. It was also quite clear that if we did not assist in the movement of the oil shipments through the Gulf, the Soviet Union would be more than happy to become the sole guarantor of the security of the small Gulf states.[108]

The plan to re-flag Kuwaiti tankers, dubbed Operation *Earnest Will*,[109] met with substantial opposition, both within Congress and from the Navy itself. Echoing complaints heard since the Vietnam conflict, Congressional leaders feared that the project might ensnare the U.S. in hostilities in the region from which an escape might be difficult. In that vein, some members demanded that the Reagan Administration follow the dictates of the War Powers Act, which limits the president's actions in situations in which U.S. forces might face "imminent hostilities."[110] Following the Act, which every president since its 1973 inception in the Vietnam era has deemed unconstitutional, would have provided Congress with the ability to terminate the program whenever its members wished.

Uniformed and civilian leaders within the Navy also expressed misgivings over the proposed re-flagging and escort program. Top Navy officers, according to the Secretary of Defense, feared that it would tie up large numbers of ships in their fleet, divert funds from other projects, and result in the loss of life. The civilian Secretary of the Navy, James Webb, voiced even stronger concerns, claiming that the open-ended commitment might drag on without end, and that it would become impossible to determine when "we had won." Further opposition arose in May, when an air-to-surface Exocet missile slammed from an Iraqi warplane into the side of one of the Middle East Force's combatants, the frigate USS *Stark*, almost sinking the ship and resulting in the deaths of 37 American sailors. Notwithstanding these complaints from the Navy and elsewhere, the United States responded affirmatively to Kuwait's 13 January 1987 request for American armed escorts, and the first convoy of tankers set sail on 21 July 1987. As Secretary of Defense Weinberger explained to a skeptical James Webb, the U.S. would win every time "a commercial ship with non-belligerent commerce went back and forth in the international waters of the Gulf without being subjected to attack."

The re-flagging operation, although primarily maritime in nature, involved several different services operating from different parts of the Gulf. After complex negotiations, for example, the Saudis agreed to allow additional U.S. Air Force AWACS planes to operate from the Kingdom (some AWACS had been operating in the country since the start of the Iran–Iraq War, but coverage was limited primarily to the Northern Gulf). The Kuwaitis provided several large barges, anchored off the coast of Saudi Arabia, to house Army helicopters as well as Navy SEAL and Marine Corps crews. The waters off Bahrain – the home of the Middle East Force – would serve as an anchorage point. Kuwait, of course, remained a focal point of the operation, the origin or terminus of the escorts. To accomplish the escort mission – one of the largest prolonged convoy operations since World War II – the U.S. Navy also increased the size of its Middle East Force. To the command ship and two or three small combatants – which since World War II had served as the typical complement in the Gulf – the Navy added another half dozen ships, for a total Middle East Force inside the Strait of Hormuz of ten.[111] As it had done since the late 1970s, the Navy also deployed to the Arabian Sea an aircraft carrier, for use, in the words of the Chairman of the Joint Chiefs of Staff, "in case the Iranians did something so formidable we had to retaliate against targets inside Iran."[112]

It is important to note, however, that the Arab states largely kept United States' operational military forces at an arm's distance. Unlike the British – who up until 1971 had garrisoned troops throughout the region – the Arab states made clear to the rest of the world in the late 1980s that the United States' forces were still not welcome ashore in the Gulf. Although the U.S. was free to operate from barges off the coast, they did not enjoy free run of the coastal states. Admiral William Crowe explained that there remained acute sensitivities among the Arab rulers to the charge of neo-colonialism:

> Kuwait would not allow us to go ashore. . . . The fact was that although the constraints were annoying, they were characteristic of military operations with a high political content, as *Earnest Will* was. Our own rationale for undertaking the operation was political, as it was also for the Kuwaitis and Saudis. From their standpoint this was not a life or death situation. While they were willing to spend money and make some sacrifices, they were not willing to forego even the appearance of sovereignty. They had at that point never allowed any foreign forces in their countries, and although *Earnest Will* was important, it was not important enough to change that principle.[113]

The Vice Chief of Naval Operations explained later that the Navy, due to the lack of access to Arab shore facilities, had to adopt a World War II style of replenishment-at-sea. Logistics supply and maintenance craft were directed to the region, where repairs and replenishment occurred at sea, instead of in Arab ports.[114]

Figure 65 Operation *Earnest Will* – USS *Jarrett* escorts re-flagged Kuwaiti tanker, August 1987.

> The Iran–Iraq War brought the U.S. another step closer to assuming the historic security duties that the British had abandoned in 1971. In the seventh year of the conflict, both sides attacked transiting oil tankers through the Persian Gulf. The Reagan Administration viewed the assault on neutral shipping through the vital sea lanes of the region as a direct threat to the security of the United States. In Operation *Earnest Will*, U.S. Navy warships escorted tankers that flew the United States flag. Above, a starboard bow view of the guided missile frigate USS *Jarrett*, and the re-flagged Kuwaiti tanker *Sea Isle City*, August 1987. Following the Iran–Iraq War, however, almost all U.S. forces quickly returned home.

The first naval escort began outside of the Strait of Hormuz, where three U.S. ships – a cruiser, a destroyer, and a frigate – married up with three empty tankers. The ships passed through the strait on 23 July 1987, but the next day the re-flagged tanker *Bridgeton* struck a mine; the U.S. Navy escort ships avoided damage. Congressional concerns flared anew, but the Reagan Administration proved determined to fulfill the missions. In subsequent weeks, as the convoy escorts continued, naval forces caught Iranian ship crews planting mines in the water. The U.S. Navy captured and destroyed mine-laying boats, and repatriated the Iranian crews.[115] The Iranian mine-laying continued, however. On 14 April 1988 the frigate USS *Samuel B. Roberts*, after completing an escort run to Kuwait City, struck a mine and nearly sank, and had to limp back to Dubai.[116]

After heated debate in Washington during which some argued for attacking an Iranian naval vessel in response and others called for more restraint,

U.S. President Reagan authorized U.S. forces to destroy oil platforms that the Iranians used for naval intelligence collection. Four days after the *Roberts* was hit, U.S. forces provided advance warning to the Iranians on board the platforms, then attacked them in what would become known as Operation *Praying Mantis*. Iranian naval boats responded, and U.S. forces sank them. Of note, some of the Iranian patrol boats sortied from Abu Musa, the disputed island that the Iranian military had occupied in the days before the British withdrawal from the region in 1971. The U.S. leadership expected an Iranian response, but one never came.

Nor did an overt Iranian reaction come several months later when a U.S. ship accidentally shot down a civilian airliner. On 3 July 1988 the USS *Vincennes* was supporting convoy operations in the vicinity of the Strait of Hormuz, when it mistook a civilian Iranian airliner for a hostile F-14, and shot it down.[117] The action occurred after U.S. helicopters in the region had come under attack by Iranian patrol boats, and after the ship's crew incorrectly concluded the aircraft was on a hostile profile. The U.S. Administration apologized. In the waning months of the Iran–Iraq War, no further Iranian military reaction occurred. The debilitating war had exhausted both combatants, and a cease-fire between Baghdad and Tehran took effect in August 1988.

Operation *Earnest Will* did not mark the start of a permanent U.S. operational military presence in the Gulf, however. Despite the chaos in the Gulf during the 1970s and 1980s – trauma that had brought forth oil embargoes, a quadrupling of oil prices, the collapse of the Twin Pillars, and long lines at the gasoline pumps – America was still not prepared to serve as the policeman-on-the-beat in this far-off land, a role the British had fulfilled for over a century. The United States, in fact, lost little time in pulling its Navy back from the Gulf after the end of hostilities, a move welcomed by most representatives and Senators on Capitol Hill. The summer of 1988 had been a difficult one in Congress for the Administration's Persian Gulf policy. Senator Brock Adams' criticisms, for example, reflected the sentiments of many elected officials: "We have no strategy in the Gulf . . . We have some objectives, most of which I share, but no plan to achieve them. We go from day to day. We are allowing Iran to set the agenda. That is not a strategy. That is a prescription for disaster."[118] Less than a month after the cease-fire between Iran and Iraq, on 16 September 1988, the U.S. Defense Department announced the end of convoy operations in the Gulf, and the beginning of the naval redeployment from the region.[119] Although the Navy would still stand ready to render assistance if needed, it would no longer escort groups of ships up and down the Persian Gulf. At the end of the 1980s, the nation still had no appetite to stay in the region.

Unheeded warnings to remain engaged in the Gulf. It should be noted, however, that while the majority of elected officials hailed the end of naval escort operations in the Gulf, the speedy withdrawal of U.S. force from the region following *Earnest Will* was by no means unanimously welcomed. A few isolated academics and policy specialists in the late 1980s and early 1990s warned of instability returning to the Persian Gulf theater, and argued for a more robust U.S. military posture there. As one prominent leader of a long-term study of U.S. interests in the Persian Gulf after the Iran–Iraq War warned in 1990:

> [The] probability is pretty high that either Iran or Iraq or both will once again become belligerents, if not directly against each other, then else-where in the region. ... A significant naval presence, despite recent redeployments, to convince any aggressor in the area of whatever origin that war would be totally unprofitable is perhaps the best deterrent to the situation above outlined. Only by convincing all possible belligerents that they will lose before launching a full attack can the stability of the region be assured. Hegemonic behavior in prudent hands is the past method of attempting to guarantee the peace.[120]

In the absence of an immediate crisis grabbing Washington's attention, however, these policy recommendations fell on deaf ears, and America's military retrenchment from the Gulf continued.

By the time the Iran–Iraq War ended in 1988, however, the United States had nonetheless taken another incremental step toward assuming responsibility for maintaining order in the region. The U.S. Central Command had successfully executed its first large-scale military operations in the Persian Gulf region since President Carter proclaimed the Carter Doctrine at the beginning of the decade. Operations *Earnest Will* and *Praying Mantis* represented the first time that the United States had engaged in open hostilities inside the Persian Gulf since World War II. *Earnest Will* also tightened bonds between the U.S. and Arab nations that had previously held the superpower at arm's length. Saudi Arabia's hosting of additional AWACS aircraft, coupled with Kuwait's provisioning of large operations barges, suggested that the nations on the Arab side of the Gulf would quietly support U.S. military operations when it directly affected them. Despite never receiving from Arab states approval to base troops ashore, the close U.S.–Arab cooperation led Washington officials to believe that – in a future crisis – the Americans might enjoy greater access to military facilities in the Gulf. Just several months after cease-fire, for example, Central Command's Commanding General Crist unveiled a new strategy for defending the region. In it, he suggested that a year and a half of U.S. operations in the region had opened "new opportunities" for the U.S. military, and in the future American service members would very likely operate from shore.[121]

That the superpower could reasonably expect the nations of the Gulf, including Saudi Arabia, to host American military might represented a change of the highest order. By the end of 1988, nonetheless, the United States still possessed no land bases inside the Gulf, and America certainly had not yet assumed the day-to-day obligation of maintaining order in the

Persian Gulf. The fourth and final step in assuming those duties, however, would come less than two years later.

The British in the Persian Gulf in the 1970s and 1980s

If the U.S. leaders throughout the 1970s and 1980s took reluctant steps toward assuming a leadership role in the Persian Gulf, what was Britain doing? Throughout those years the British attempted to preserve in the Persian Gulf whatever influence they could, while at the same time generally acceding to America's leadership. London essentially recognized that its period of ascendancy in the region had forever passed, and in a new era of constrained military capabilities, its interests were best preserved by United States' leadership in the Gulf. After several years of very high visibility diplomacy, after Britain departed in 1971 the nation's top diplomatic and military officials stayed clear. Two years passed before a Foreign Secretary visited.[122] London's leaders seemed to have accepted Chancellor of the Exchequer Roy Jenkins' 1968 pronouncement that Britain was "no longer a superpower."[123]

The British attempted to maintain their influence in the Gulf as long as possible in a number of ways: scheduling greater numbers of bilateral exercises with local states, encouraging arms sales to local regimes, and educating foreign officers in British (sometimes joint Anglo-American) professional military schools. These efforts generally enjoyed the blessing of the Americans, who – although occasionally in commercial arms sales competition with their Atlantic allies – recognized the benefit of Britain's continued engagement in the region.

One of the states that the British attempted to court in the 1970s, not surprisingly, was Iran, with whom relations had deteriorated in the years leading up to British withdrawal. After the Iranian islands disputes – settled in Iran's favor when Britain effectively allowed the Shah to occupy them in 1971 – the British successfully lobbied the Shah to increase the size and frequency of bilateral military exercises. On the seas, for example, the *Arya* 1972 naval exercise featured British Nimrod patrol aircraft crews working with Iranian naval personnel. That same year the Royal Air Force in Akrotiri, Cyprus hosted a detachment of four Iranian F-4 Phantoms and several Iranian C-130s, the first time that the Iranians had engaged in such an exercise.[124] The Iranians in the early 1970s also opened up several military airports and military training routes for training by British military air personnel. Royal Air Force Vulcan aircraft crews, for example, used Iranian facilities for low-level training flights, and practiced emergency landings in the southern city of Bandar Abbas.[125] As part of their engagement with Iran, the British continued to work with the Americans under the umbrella of the Central Treaty Organization, or CENTO. In the Midlink annual exercises, for example, British naval forces exercised in the Arabian Sea with ships and crews of Pakistan, Iran, and the United States.

The sale of military gear to Gulf nations proved another way that the British retained influence in the region in the 1970s. As explained earlier, the British withdrawal from the region elicited Arab and Iranian feelings of insecurity, and many Gulf leaders turned to Britain – as well as the United States – to help arm themselves. Iran and Saudi Arabia proved among the first clients, and the most deep-pocketed.[126] These arms sales, of course, gave rise to the need for growing numbers of British trainers and technicians to work and live in the region, the presence of which tended to prolong British influence in the Gulf. By 1973, the British had several training teams permanently stationed in Iran.[127] Additionally, the British also pushed the Persians to send their officers to Britain for service schools, and even teamed with the Americans to create an Anglo-American-Iranian course at Iran's Armed Forces Staff College.[128]

As the region's economies digested their enormous influx of oil-generated revenues in the 1970s, British companies – along with those from the United States – also landed large commercial development contracts in addition to arms sales contracts.[129] Both arms sales and commercial deals proved very lucrative. The continued interaction of British personnel with the locals provided for London officials some degree of influence in the region despite their military and political withdrawal in 1971.

Britain's modest naval presence in the Gulf grew in the late 1970s and early 1980s, as Revolutionary Iran stirred up trouble in the region and the Soviets marched into Afghanistan. In response to those two political upheavals, just as America built up her naval might in the waters surrounding the Persian Gulf, particularly in the Indian Ocean, so too did Great Britain. To augment her forces in the area, Britain accelerated deployments of ships back to the "East of Suez" region, and dispatched other ships to the waters of the eastern Mediterranean,[130] where they might more easily respond if called upon.

The Iran–Iraq War prompted an increase in Britain's naval involvement inside the Gulf as well. In what British Defence Secretary George Younger later called a "non-provocative, low-profile"[131] naval force, beginning in 1980 and continuing for most of the decade, two to three Royal Navy ships patrolled the environs of the Persian Gulf, principally from the Gulf of Oman to Bahrain, escorting U.K.-registered ships through the Iran–Iraq war zone waters.[132] The mission of this so-called "Armilla" force, however, proved more circumscribed than that of the British troops who served in the region before 1971. Rather than fulfilling British security commitments to the leaders of the Persian Gulf region, as they did in former times, the Armilla force's purpose was to defend ships flying the Union Jack. It is worth noting that the British adopted this escort mission seven years in advance of the United States' highly publicized *Earnest Will* campaign in 1987–88.

Figure 66 British Armilla patrol – HMS *Andromeda* accompanies British-flagged tanker during the Iran–Iraq War, 1980s.

HMS *Andromeda* accompanies a British-flagged tanker through the Persian Gulf during the Iran–Iraq War. Shortly after hostilities erupted in September 1980 between two of the Gulf's major powers, the British dedicated two ships to escorting British ships through the war zone, from the Gulf of Oman up to Bahrain. Of note, these so-called "Armilla" patrols started seven years before the more highly publicized U.S. escort of re-flagged tankers in Operation *Earnest Will*. The British later served alongside the Americans in Operation *Desert Storm* and the subsequent Operation *Southern Watch* as well.

Desert Storm – after twenty years, America replaces Britain in the Persian Gulf

The end of the Iran–Iraq War in the late 1980s saw the drawdown of U.S. military forces from the Persian Gulf, virtually to pre-war levels. Washington thereafter disestablished the Joint Task Force Middle East that had managed and directed Operation *Earnest Will*.[133] The Navy's presence in the Gulf fell from approximately 30 at the peak of Operation *Earnest Will*, to 14 ships six months later (including six minesweepers still attempting to clear the Gulf),[134] to just six in the summer of 1990: the U.S. Navy's Middle East Force command ship *La Salle*, a destroyer, and four frigates.[135] There existed no major U.S. garrison of forces in the area, furthermore, and the deployment of American AWACS aircraft deployed to Saudi Arabia since the start of the Iran–Iraq War had ended. After the Iran–Iraq War, in other words, the U.S. military essentially went home.

Saddam's desperate gambit. Saddam emerged from the Iran–Iraq War in deep trouble. After eight straight years of bloodshed his treasury was empty, and in debt in the amount of $80 billion and rising. The Iraqi dinar had slumped in value, and inflation was running at 40 percent annually. Iraq was bankrupt. At the close of the 1980s Saddam sent his diplomats around the Arab world with donation cup in hand. Fellow Arabs should share the burden of Iraq's war against expansionist Shia Iran, Saddam argued, and forgive the nation's war debts. At the very minimum, fellow Arabs must abide by their oil quota limits, so as to keep the world price of oil high enough for Saddam's regime to survive. When his extortion scheme failed, Saddam chose to take by force what he could not convince others to give up.[136]

In the last week of July 1990 – in a move eerily reminiscent of Iraq's threatened invasion almost 30 years before – Saddam began to amass thousands of ground troops along the Kuwaiti border. The military moves accompanied a ratcheting-up of bellicose Iraqi rhetoric against Kuwait and the United Arab Emirates, both of whom the Iraqis complained had violated OPEC quotas. In a resurgence of Iraqi irredentist claims against its southern neighbor, furthermore, Saddam declared Kuwait an integral part of Iraq.

Back in 1961, just days after Kuwait declared its independence from London, Iraq's leaders also threatened invasion. Great Britain's leaders, however, proved able to assemble from the nation's military forces in Bahrain, Sharjah, Aden, the Indian Ocean, and the home islands a formidable defensive force. This rapid build-up, Operation *Vantage*, deterred the Iraqis, who did not march across the border. Most of London's Persian Gulf battle plans in the 1960s surrounded a recurrence of this scenario, which defense planners assumed would provide virtually *no advance warning* of an Iraqi attack.[137] With that in mind, the British in the mid 1960s moved some of their fast-reaction Gulf forces closer to the scene of potential hostilities, in Bahrain and Aden.

Three decades later, however, those lessons from Operation *Vantage* – which hardly ever, if at all, appeared in U.S defense planning documents[138] – had been long forgotten. Even had the U.S. wanted in 1990 to mount such a British-style fast-reaction defensive operation, the U.S. could not have, for Washington a dozen years before had declined Arab offers to take over the British bases that would have made it possible. And despite the creation of the U.S. Central Command, and in spite of the stronger U.S.–Arab relations forged during the Iran–Iraq War, U.S. forces enjoyed no firm, guaranteed right to use Arab lands inside the Strait of Hormuz on short notice to deter such an invasion.

Lacking such agreements, the Bush Administration responded to the Iraqi bellicosity with only minor military preparations, even when top military and intelligence officials warned that an Iraqi attack was probable. In late July 1990, for example, as tensions rose, the Bush Administration made only two very limited military moves. First, it put on alert its small naval Middle East Force, directing its crews to exercise with the diminutive United Arab Emirates' fleet.[139] Second, the U.S. dispatched two aerial refueling planes to the UAE following a request from that nation's leaders. When word later leaked of the deal, UAE leaders became enraged;[140] Arab leaders still feared a backlash if seen cavorting with the Americans.

The modest American military response grew from several causes. The Bush Administration suspected – along with most of the world's leaders, including those in the Arab world – that Saddam's military build-up was a bluff. Friendly Arab leaders reinforced this notion, assuring Washington officials "not to worry;" Arabs, after all, "did not war against each other."[141] Down Pennsylvania Avenue on Capitol Hill some Congressional voices discussed the growing belligerence of Iraq, and some even talked of applying economic sanctions against Saddam, but prior to the invasion no one seriously proposed a possible U.S. military response. Nor did officials in Britain, the Western nation that for over a century had maintained order in the Gulf. The British Ambassador to Saudi Arabia later summarized that Saddam's move "caught the world off balance."[142] In short, few in Washington or London in July 1990 believed that Saddam actually aimed to move across the Kuwaiti border.

With this in mind, the U.S. tarried in deploying critical war materiel to the region that might have dissuaded Saddam, as it had his forbears in 1961. U.S. intelligence leaders in late July 1990 saw many indications of an impending invasion: large collections of troops, estimated at over 100,000, amassing along the border; forward deployment of artillery; laying down of communications; reinforced stocks of fuel and ammunition.[143] The CENTCOM Commander and CIA Deputy Director, furthermore, voiced their belief that an attack was likely, although they thought that when it came, the Iraqis would likely stop at Kuwait's northern oil fields, and not continue southward to occupy the entire country and de-throne the ruling family.[144]

In spite of this mounting evidence, however, Washington officials did not take critical, time-sensitive steps to augment the U.S. military's ability to fight a ground war in the area. One of the key lessons to come from the Gulf disturbances of the 1970s – similar to those that the British had learned in the 1960s – was the value of pre-positioned equipment in the Gulf region. Without it, weeks might pass before fast-reaction troops airlifted into the region would possess real military might. When the Marine Commandant in July 1990 suggested deploying from Diego Garcia the Marine Corps' military supply ships, however, the Chairman of the Joint Chiefs dismissed the idea.[145] This decision to delay the sailing of the pre-position ships violated one of the central tenets of British lessons in the Gulf in the 1960s: once Iraqi troop movements along the border with Kuwait become apparent, the defender must commence immediately wartime logistics preparations. The time required for Iraq's military units to proceed from Basra to Kuwait City was, after all, very small. The U.S. inaction proved to be time squandered.

Nor did the United States send steadfast messages to Iraq that the U.S. planned to defend Kuwait. In late July, after Iraq's bellicose moves toward Kuwait became apparent, the Bush Administration tepidly announced: "We remain strongly committed to supporting the individual and collective self-defense of our friends in the Gulf, with whom we have deep and longstanding ties."[146] This was hardly a ringing threat to counter Iraqi aggression with American military might. Although the Administration intended the earlier Middle East Force naval alert coupled with the deployment of the refueling planes to "show support" for the threatened Gulf states, and that "Washington was prepared to use military force,"[147] the mild statement clearly did not dissuade Saddam. This less-than-forceful military response came as U.S. diplomats sent the same weak message.

U.S. Ambassador to Iraq April Glaspie has received much criticism for her failure to telegraph clear U.S. intentions to Saddam. In retrospect, however, it appears that the central problem lay more in the underlying White House policy than its execution by diplomats: Washington decision-makers simply didn't believe that Saddam would invade, and therefore neither prepared for it nor delivered credible threats to Saddam's regime that might have prevented it. A policeman walking the beat aims to prevent problems before they occur; that summer it became apparent that the U.S. leaders in their own minds had not yet assumed for themselves such a role. Not daunted by the West's reaction to his bellicose threats, Saddam early the next month made his move.

The Iraqi attack. In the early hours of 2 August 1990, three Iraqi Republican Guard divisions moved across the Kuwaiti border.[148] A mechanized infantry division and an armored division thrust south into Kuwait, while special operations forces attacked Kuwait City. Special commando teams made amphibious assaults against the Emir's palace and other government buildings. High-level Kuwaiti officials fled into Saudi Arabia and beyond. By evening the Iraqis had secured Kuwait City and most of the remainder of the tiny nation. Unlike three decades before when a British rapid build-up of forces proved able to dissuade an Iraqi move southward, in 1990 Iraq successfully captured its southern neighbor, and stood capable of marching southward into the world's most prolific oil fields in eastern Saudi Arabia.

U.S. moves quickly.[149] If the United States up until that point had resisted the role of policeman-on-the-beat in the Persian Gulf, it quickly assumed the role of a policeman-responding-to-a-trouble-call. Before 2 August had ended in Washington, President Bush made it clear that the Iraqi move would meet with strong American action. He signed a public pronouncement condemning the invasion, and his advisors drew up emergency executive orders freezing Iraqi funds in U.S. banks and prohibiting any financial transactions with the new regime. A former U.S. Ambassador to the United Nations, President Bush embarked upon a breakneck diplomatic effort to counter the attack. International condemnations and economic sanctions followed; Great Britain proved among the first to support America's actions. But when it came to discussing immediate military options for the United States, they were limited. The U.S. still lacked any forward military presence in the region except its naval flotilla, and its heavy military gear was still distant because U.S. leaders did not order the ships to sail earlier.

Operation Desert Shield. The subsequent U.S. response to the Iraqi invasion of Kuwait is well documented. The Bush Administration concluded early that they must prevent the Iraqis from invading Saudi Arabia. Three days after the invasion, President Bush dispatched his Secretary of Defense Cheney to Riyadh to gain King Fahd's approval for hosting American defensive troops in the Kingdom. The King assented. Cheney made it clear that the United States did not seek a permanent presence in the region:

> The President asked me to assure you that we will stay as long as you want us. We will leave when you no longer need us. We will stay until justice is done but not stay a minute longer. We are not seeking bases. . . .[150]

Over the next several months over 200,000 more American troops deployed to Saudi Arabia. A broad international coalition of naval forces in the Persian Gulf, Red Sea, and Arabian Sea enforced a blockade against Iraq. In October and November 1990 the U.S. Administration concluded that the United States must build up a larger *offensive* military force, to provide for American decision-makers the option to forcibly expel Iraq from Kuwait. Following 1990's mid-term November elections, the Administration announced that it would double the number of troops in the Persian Gulf region. After a flurry of diplomatic activity, including an ultimately unsuccessful Russian initiative to broker a peaceful agreement, in January the United States leaders in conjunction with their allies set out with military might to do what diplomacy had failed to accomplish: reverse Saddam's aggression.

Operation Desert Storm. On 17 January 1991 U.S. warships in the Persian Gulf and Red Sea unleashed a volley of Tomahawk land attack missiles, and B-52 bombers delivered their own salvos of air-launched missiles, representing the first shots in an international air campaign against Iraq that continued for five weeks. On 24 February, with allied amphibious forces feinting a move ashore directly into Kuwait, international land forces – who made no secret in the international press of their position along the Saudi border with Kuwait – quietly repositioned inland, then surprised the Iraqi forces by crossing from Saudi Arabia into Iraq, well northwest of Kuwait, thence southward into the occupied emirate. Within five days – after approximately 100 hours – the Bush Administration chose to terminate the war. The coalition had successfully evicted the Iraqis from Kuwait, suffering in the process surprisingly few allied casualties.

In the closing hours of the conflict, when asked when the American troops would return home, presidential spokesman Marlin Fitzwater replied, "We'll measure it in days, not weeks. Clearly, the President wants to start the withdrawal as soon as possible."[151] In the weeks and months following the war,

Figure 67 In amphibious assault vehicles, U.S. Marines advance toward Kuwait City, Operation *Desert Storm*, February 1991.

Bankrupt after eight years of war with Iran, in July 1990 Iraqi President Saddam Hussein amassed his forces on the Kuwaiti border, reminiscent of Iraq's threatened invasion of the neighboring emirate in 1961. Unlike those moves almost three decades before, which Britain countered with a strong show of force in Operation *Vantage*, the Bush administration in July 1990 offered only modest military responses to Saddam's warlike moves. After Iraqi forces crossed the border into Kuwait, however, the United States and Great Britain led a multi-national coalition that drove Iraqi forces from Kuwait. Above, a 21 February 1991 photograph showing Marine amphibious assault vehicles advancing toward Kuwait City during the third day of the ground offensive. An AH-1 Sea Cobra helicopter is flying in the background.

however, the U.S. did not reduce its forces to those bare-bones pre-war levels. Rather, Washington officials made a play to bolster permanently their military presence in the Gulf region. It was this decision to remain – a stark contrast from the decision to withdraw after Operation *Earnest Will* several years before – that marked America's assumption of security duties in the Persian Gulf.

The decision to keep a permanent military presence in the Gulf actually sprang from two distinct causes: a conscious effort to build up American military capabilities, based upon a new post-*Desert Storm* willingness amongst Arab leaders to host American troops; and an unforeseen need to fight a continuing low-intensity conflict against Saddam's Iraq, whose military remained robust due in large part to the American decision to terminate *Desert Storm* prior to the destruction of Iraq's forces.

As the bulk of American and Allied forces streamed out of the Gulf after fighting to victory, U.S. leaders took advantage of what they believed might be a fleeting opportunity to establish a military foothold in the region, an unrealized goal sought since the downfall of the Shah over a decade earlier. In Bahrain, the Government announced that the emirate had agreed to Washington's request to host a permanent contingent of American officers. "I'm giving you a clear commitment that we will support any decision taken based on the commitment the United States had made to the area," Bahrain's Information Minister explained.[152] Kuwait similarly announced plans to host U.S. forces and equipment, including pre-positioning equipment. The United Arab Emirates and Oman took like steps.[153] Even in reactionary Saudi Arabia, by far the most conservative of the Gulf states whose core desert constituency had long exhibited anti-Western xenophobic proclivities, top royal family members gave serious consideration to American plans for a recurring series of large-scale military exercises in which American troops would regularly rotate through the desert kingdom, akin to existing U.S.–Egyptian exercises.[154] The U.S.-led victory in *Desert Storm* had wrought substantial political change in the Gulf: clearly, Arab leaders no longer feared a domestic backlash when working with the United States.

The post-*Desert Storm* U.S. military presence in the Gulf grew not only from this conscious American drive to earn basing rights, but also from the need to fight a low-intensity conflict with Iraq that arose in large part due to the way that American leaders terminated the war.[155] During the February 1991 ground offensive in *Desert Storm*, the White House and Whitehall debated when to end the conflict. It quickly became apparent that the Allies would succeed in driving the Iraqis from Kuwait; the critical question they then debated became, "how much destruction of the Iraqi army is necessary or desirable?" If the Allies left Saddam's military forces too robust, the Iraqis might emerge as a military threat again. If, on the other hand, the Allies slaughtered too many Iraqi soldiers, there might develop a strong anti-Western backlash, or leave Iraq so weak that it might split apart or fall to Iran. The need to make a prompt decision grew as press reports emerged from Kuwait of American pilots massacring retreating Iraqi forces along the "highway of death"; there developed in the White House a tangible fear of being charged with brutalizing the Iraqis.[156] In the end, President Bush, his senior advisors, and British leaders agreed to end the war after 100 hours, despite the fact that much of the Iraqi army and its armored forces remained. The political mandate to wrest Kuwait from Iraq was fulfilled, they concluded, and any further military action would jeopardize holding together the Alliance.[157]

In hastily arranged post-war negotiations that followed the 100-hour war, furthermore, General Schwarzkopf – acting with little direction from his civilian overlords – concluded with the Iraqis a post-war deal that allowed Saddam to remain in power and, among other things, to use as he saw fit his nation's helicopter fleet, a concession that the Americans would later regret. Some have criticized that these hurried end-of-war decisions reflected a larger

U.S. failure to anticipate and plan for the post-war peace: confessed U.S. foreign service officer Gordon Brown, who served as one of General Schwarzkopf's foreign policy advisors, "We never did have a plan to terminate the war."[158]

Within weeks it became apparent that – far from vanquished – Saddam proved intent to cling to power, and his moves to crush with brute force Iraqis' rebellions led the U.S., Britain, and France to keep air and naval forces in the region. After the war many Iraqis – encouraged by the Americans to move against Saddam – rose in revolt; the U.S. President himself encouraged the Iraqis to "put him aside."[159] The Kurds in northern Iraq and the Shia in southern Iraq proved most anxious to overthrow the Baghdad regime. Exploiting the loophole in the hastily made post-war cease-fire that allowed the Iraqis to use helicopters, however, Saddam's forces ruthlessly suppressed the twin revolts. Sympathetic to their plight, the Bush Administration in March 1991 considered, but then dismissed as too politically risky, the idea of a "de-militarized" zone in the south to protect the Shia.[160] The Kurds in the north faced a similar plight. Their rebellion had also evoked a brutal crackdown.

Saddam's continued suppression of the Kurdish and Shia uprisings spurred U.S. leaders to impose no-fly zones over the northern and southern portions of Iraq, as a way to shield the oppressed. U.S. Air Force and Navy aircraft, joined by the British and French in the south, worked from air bases in Saudi Arabia and other Persian Gulf states, as well as from aircraft carriers in the Gulf. These no-fly zones became semi-permanent fixtures in the Gulf for over a decade.

Unlike the American redeployment back home that followed Operation *Earnest Will* during the Iran–Iraq War, then, the U.S. and its military after *Desert Storm* remained in the Persian Gulf environs. Sensing a new Arab political willingness to host Americans, the superpower's leaders in Washington jumped at the opportunity to plant roots ashore in the Gulf. While top officials negotiated basing rights with now-hospitable Arabs, allied air and naval forces had stayed behind to counter Saddam. In staying, the Americans had become the policemen-on-the-beat, patrolling Iraq's borders, and maintaining interstate order. Two decades had elapsed since the British abdicated their role as the region's arbiter of security. One Western trauma after another had unfolded during that time in the region, however: the oil crises of 1973–74, the fall of the Shah, the Soviet invasion of Afghanistan, the Iran–Iraq War, and finally, Iraq's invasion of Kuwait. Despite American leaders' persisting desires from the 1960s–1980s to avoid getting sucked into the untidy security affairs of the region, the national pain – and the economic losses – had become too acute to endure any more. After a chaotic interregnum of twenty years, America was in the Gulf to stay.

7 *Pax Americana–Bellum Americanum*, 1991–present

Despite pre-*Desert Storm* pledges to depart after evicting Saddam from Kuwait, American military forces after 1991 remained in the Gulf region, fulfilling duties that the British undertook during the previous century and a half: patrolling the waters, protecting the free flow of commerce – beginning in the twentieth century, oil – through the Strait of Hormuz, quelling inter-state tensions, and when politicians at home deemed it essential to their national interests, engaging in hostilities ashore. This final chapter examines how America's military presence became a permanent one in the Gulf, and how in the aftermath of 9/11, America looked away from Saudi Arabia and more toward the littoral states of the Gulf for presence and access as Britain had done earlier.

For the remainder of the 1990s after *Desert Storm*, Washington shep-herded over a decade-long "*Pax Americana*" of relative peace, prosperity, and interstate stability in the Gulf, free of much of the turbulence of the inter-regnum period during the two decades after Britain's departure in 1971. Not everyone welcomed this Western interloping, however, and a conservative backlash erupted. America's high-visibility military presence in the Gulf fueled groups like al-Qaeda, whose September 2001 strike against Washington and New York elicited an Anglo-American military response in Afghanistan and Iraq. The 2003 expedition into Mesopotamia, however, devolved into a bloody civil conflict and insurgency, which only a change of generals and an abrupt shift in military strategy proved able to tame. During these years, Tehran's opposition to Washington and London's continuing military pres-ence in the region remained steady, although Iran had welcomed the U.S. defeat of Saddam and the Taliban. Noting that since *Desert Storm* it has been Washington officials who have largely determined issues of peace and war in the Gulf, the period following 1991 can rightfully be called a period of "*Pax Americana–Bellum Americanum.*"

"Bureaucratizing" America's military presence in the Gulf

For most of the 1990s American, British, and French aircrews enforced the no-fly zones over Iraq. Operation *Southern Watch*, as the program to deny flight by Saddam's air forces in southern Iraq became known, was largely an air-centric operation, and involved flight operations from high-visibility locations in the Gulf region. Naval air forces from U.S. and British aircraft carriers also participated. Many aircraft flew from Saudi Arabian air bases, with Riyadh initially serving as the nerve center and headquarters for the air operations. Clearly marked U.S. and British (and French, before December 1998) aircraft flew from bases near large population centers in the kingdom, like Dhahran and Riyadh; uniformed Western aviators and support personnel frequently drove and walked through these same cities' centers.

Meanwhile American-led naval forces patrolled the waters of the Persian Gulf, aiming to reduce illegal trade into and out of Iraq, and to reduce Saddam's access to foreign currency. These naval actions commenced immediately following the August 1990 Iraqi invasion of Kuwait, as prescribed by the United Nations,[1] and continued for almost 13 years. Western warships' crews boarded ships bound for, or those departing, Iraq, aiming to prevent the import or export of all but humanitarian and medical supplies. In

Figure 68 U.S. Air Force tanker aircraft refuels Navy attack aircraft, Operation *Southern Watch*, over Saudi Arabia, April 1996.

American, British, and French aircraft remained in the Persian Gulf region following *Desert Storm*, to enforce the no-fly zones against Saddam's regime in Iraq. Above, A U.S. Air Force KC-135 tanker refuels a U.S. Navy F/A-18 from the USS *George Washington* in the skies over Saudi Arabia on 24 April 1996. The continued presence of military forces on the Arabian Peninsula throughout the 1990s elicited a hostile backlash amongst conservative elements of the society. Operation *Southern Watch* continued until 2003.

1995, the United National Security Council members passed resolution 986, the "Oil for Food" program, which allowed Iraqi authorities to sell oil on international markets in exchange for medicine and food. In summary, after the conclusion of *Desert Storm,* Western air and naval forces remained in the Persian Gulf region, attempting to prevent Saddam from harming citizens of his own country, and to prevent him from earning remittances that would strengthen his continued grip on power.

Saddam's defiance of the sanctions and inspections proved steadfast, eliciting periodic reprisals from the U.S.-led coalition. Saddam's air defense batteries, for example, periodically opened fire on patrolling allied aircraft.[2] The Iraqi regime, furthermore, encouraged illicit seaborne smuggling, in order to provide cash for Saddam's strapped regime. And time after time during the years following *Desert Storm,* Saddam's regime denied entry to U.N. weapons inspectors, making more difficult the task of ensuring that Saddam did not regenerate his weapons of mass destruction programs. In response to these Iraqi violations, hostilities occasionally broke out between the Allied and the Iraqi forces. In December 1998, for example, U.S. forces led a strike on Iraq called *Desert Fox.*[3]

Figure 69 USS *Fletcher* conducts post-*Desert Storm* Maritime Intercept Operations aboard a container ship en route to Iraq, November 2000.

U.S., British, and other allied navies participated in Maritime Intercept Operations (MIO) in the years following *Desert Storm*. These operations, aimed at enforcing United Nations' sanctions against Iraqi President Saddam Hussein's regime, stretched from 1991–2003.

The decade following *Desert Storm* marked a period of bureaucratization for America's military facilities in the Persian Gulf region.[4] U.S. leaders, who since 1973 had clamored, largely unsuccessfully, for access to bases inside the Strait of Hormuz, took advantage in the 1990s of the new-found willingness of Arab leaders to host American military members in their ports and on their shores. The U.S. military during that decade began to construct the administrative, logistical, and political infrastructure that could support a robust, long-term military presence in the region.

Of the four U.S. military services, the Navy's growing footprint in the Gulf in the decade after *Desert Storm* best reflected this "bureaucratization." Following *Desert Storm* U.S. naval leaders sent for a major overhaul the USS *La Salle*, the lightly armed ship that since the early 1970s had served as the flagship for the Middle East Force. The Bahraini government consented to the U.S. Navy's request to temporarily move ashore several hundred officers and sailors. This transition from a mobile floating base to a permanent presence ashore, however, would become permanent. The "Great White Ghost of the Arabian Coast," as crews of the USS *La Salle* affectionately called the flagship, never returned to Bahrain. Senior naval officers in the mid 1990s had concluded that the administrative task of running the enlarged Middle East Force – whose size would remain in the dozens of ships as opposed to the handful prior to the conflict – would be much more effective if done from ashore. A land-based headquarters could provide for longer officer assignments, for example, bringing officers and sailors to the Middle East Force headquarters for two or possibly three years, with their families, instead of the one-year unaccompanied assignments that had traditionally been offered to those posted to the *LaSalle*. Communications between leaders in Washington and U.S. ships at sea – as well as between ships and crews in the Gulf – would also improve if accompanied by the construction ashore of new communications antennas and relays. Finally, in the minds of senior naval leaders, a permanent move ashore of the staff would convince America's Arab allies that the United States intended to remain engaged in the region.[5]

For all of these reasons, as the 1990s progressed, the U.S. Navy's "Administrative Support Unit"(ASU), located on the grounds of the former Royal Navy base HMS *Jufair*, became more akin to a modern military base. In the 1970s and 1980s, when the small fenced facility adjacent to the Mina Sulman port included a few office buildings and administrative officials, the moniker "ASU" fit. Less than 100 officers and sailors were typically posted there. Throughout the 1990s, however, the number of shore-based officers grew. Within a decade of *Desert Storm*, the number of U.S. personnel had grown to 1,200.[6]

In part because of the benefits that accrued to the small emirate, American requests to Bahrain to increase the number of officers and staff in Bahrain were generally approved. Greater numbers of U.S. land-based military personnel, after all, brought millions of dollars into the local Bahraini economy.[7]

Figure 70 U.S. aircraft carrier during routine port call in United Arab Emirates, 1994.

The decade after *Desert Storm* marked a "routinization" of U.S. military operations in the waters and adjacent shores of the Persian Gulf region. The decision following the 1991 war to remain engaged in the Gulf marked the start of a "Pax Americana": after a two decade period of turmoil, Washington had assumed the security duties that Britain had abdicated in 1971. Above, the USS *Carl Vinson* during a routine port call in the United Arab Emirates' Jebel Ali in 1994.

As well, there existed political benefits for the Bahraini regime. In the 1990s the emirate's ruling family – whose Sunni roots often put them at odds with the 2/3 majority Shia population[8] – came under increasing pressure to open its political system, and riots against the ruling Al Khalifa family broke out. The presence of American military forces on the island provided for the rulers a show of implied strength, although U.S. troops never deployed in such a way as to defend the government against the protests of the people. Finally, other military benefits accrued to the Bahraini state as a result of the growing American presence there. In 1996, for example, the United

States transferred to Bahrain a modern frigate, the USS *Jack Williams*, which became the Bahrain Navy's largest vessel, the BANS *Sabha*. In a number of bilateral U.S.–Bahraini exercises throughout the 1990s, furthermore, the two nations exercised naval, land, and air forces together throughout the 1990s.[9]

In 1995 the U.S. Navy rechristened the "5th Fleet" for its forces in the Gulf,[10] suggesting a permanence to the seaborne service's presence in the region. By the end of the decade, a brand new U.S. Navy physical facility had begun to emerge from the footprint of the small former British base. Its physical size had tripled, from 23 acres to 68 acres. Enormous new operations and billeting structures arose across the new facility. Spaces for U.S. Central Command staff were constructed, for contingency use for officers deployed from headquarters back in Tampa, Florida. Reflecting this new forward, permanent military presence in Bahrain, naval leaders jettisoned the anachronistic "ASU" name in favor of the more descriptive "Naval Support Activity Bahrain." This new enlarged headquarters in Bahrain, accompanied by the new name 5th Fleet, suggested that America's naval presence in the region was becoming a permanent one.

Just as the need to keep Saddam contained, coupled with a long-standing desire on the part of American leaders to plant a foothold in the Gulf region, led to a "bureaucratization" of the U.S. Navy presence in the Gulf, similar developments took place in the other U.S. military services. Like crabs that remain in tidal pools after a receding tide, Air Force refueling aircraft remained at bases in the United Arab Emirates, for example, from where American air crews in the 1990s participated in Operation *Southern Watch*. Supporting the no-fly zones over Iraq also led to the deployment on a rotating basis of air wing size units to locations in Kuwait, Bahrain, Qatar, and the United Arab Emirates. According to U.S. Air Force leaders, the goals of these "air expeditionary forces"[11] (AEFs) were two-fold. First, the deployments supported the continuing need to project air power over Iraq's southern reaches. But there also existed a more long-term goal: acquire repeated access to the military facilities in the Gulf, and strengthen the bilateral ties that join Western and Arab military forces. As U.S. Air Force Brigadier General William R. Looney said, the AEFs provide "an opportunity for us to strengthen and enhance the long-term working relationship with the host country. It allows us to improve the understandings of both of our cultures and improve our coalition war-fighting skills."[12]

There existed particular interest in gaining access to facilities in Qatar, not just for the U.S. Air Force, but for the superpower's Army as well. A post-*Desert Storm* bilateral defense and security agreement in 1992 provided for America's formal access to the facilities on the peninsula nation.[13] U.S. Army pre-positioned equipment, including substantial numbers of battle tanks, began to be stored in Qatar at Camp As Saylilah, whose first phases were completed in 1996; the facility also served as a location for CENTCOM's forward headquarters. Of particular strategic significance is the enormous al-Udeid Air Base, constructed in the 1990s. The base's twin runways, which stretch for over two miles, can accommodate heavy U.S. Air Force cargo aircraft on hot summer Gulf days. (Of note, the Qatari regime after the terror attacks in 2001 permitted the construction there of a Combined Air Operations Center, and in 2006 permitted the U.S. to base B-1 bomber aircraft on the facility.)[14]

From the vantage of the Qatari leadership, extending to the Americans an offer to populate the al-Udeid base with Air Force aircraft and Central Command administrative units brought several political benefits, similar to those that accrued to Bahrain's leaders in granting expanded access to naval forces. First, as in Bahrain, such a move projected strength upon the Qatari leadership. Emir Hamad in 1995, after all, had overthrown his father in a bloodless coup, and rumors throughout the 1990s circulated that his exiled father would return, perhaps with a group of mercenaries, to retake his position as Qatar's leader. What chance would the ex-emir have, however, if he attempted to overthrow a strategic client of the United States?

Inviting U.S. military forces into Qatar also sent a strong message to two of the Gulf's regional powers. As one of the world's largest exporters of natural gas, Qatar's enormous North Dome gas field extended northward along the floor of the Gulf toward Iran. Might Iran one day challenge or threaten Qatar's extraction and shipment of gas? Might one day Iran take aim at Qatari tankers transiting through the Strait of Hormuz, as Tehran's leaders did against Baghdad's shipments during the Iran–Iraq War? Inviting in the Americans would serve as an insurance policy against such potential aggression. Finally, relations between Qatar and Saudi Arabia have not always proven tight and cordial. Demarcating the border between the two states, in fact, had proven contentious in previous decades. In private some Qataris suggest that the physical location of the al-Udeid air base was purposefully sited to place American defenders in between the Saudis and the Qatari population and gas fields.[15]

U.S. Army and Marine Corps leaders, too, attempted to plant deeper roots in the Gulf in the decade following *Desert Storm*. A number of bilateral and multilateral exercises with the Gulf's Arab states began. U.S. Central Command leaders and American diplomats also proved adept at enlarging the U.S. equipment pre-positioning programs in the Arab Gulf states. The Qatari Government, for example, accepted a contingency stockpile of U.S. Bradley Fighting Vehicles and tanks.[16] Finally, the U.S. Government gained approval from Arab Gulf states to regularly bring into Arab ports those large pre-positioned ships that carried billions of dollars worth of tanks, personnel carriers, weapons, and supplies. While in port for several weeks, ship crews would bring ashore vehicles from the belly of the ship, ensuring the battle readiness of the gear while checking to ensure the compatibility of local facilities, ramps, and cranes.

America's growing military and political presence coincided with a period of economic growth and prosperity in the Gulf during *Pax Americana*. For almost a decade after 1991 the region remained free from the turbulence that had followed Britain's departure from the region in 1971. During those two tumultuous decades few businessmen wanted to invest capital inside the Strait of Hormuz. The year 1991, however, marked a turning point in which businesses and capital began to return to the Gulf. Throughout the decade foreign direct investment in these economies grew year after year. In another reflection of the improved business climate that accompanied America's security umbrella, insurance rates on oil shipments through the Strait of Hormuz plummeted during the 1990s, from wartime highs during the Iran–Iraq War and later during *Desert Storm*.[17] Reflecting the fact that the doors to the Gulf region were wide open, several of the Arab emirates even commenced ad campaigns aimed to bring weary winter vacationers to warm waters and beaches.

Despite the fact that the small Arab emirates welcomed the stability and economic growth that accompanied the *Pax Americana*, however, throughout the 1990s a backlash against the U.S., its military, and its allies began to emerge. By mid-decade it became apparent that America's new presence in the region was growing increasingly unpopular in parts of the Gulf, particularly in the region's largest and most conservative nation, Saudi Arabia.

The conservative backlash

As the U.N-approved sanctions against Iraq continued through the 1990s, Arab and world public opinion began to shift against America and Britain. Stories emerged of humanitarian disasters in Mesopotamia, like malnourished Iraqi babies "no bigger than aerosol cans," infant mortality rates that increased 25 percent in one year, and kidney donors lining up outside hospitals to sell their organs.[18] Pressure mounted for relief from the Western sanctions.

Not only did these Washington-led sanctions stoke anti-Western sentiment, but so did the growing U.S. military presence in the region, particularly in Saudi Arabia. A collection of conservative clerics, dubbed the "awakening sheikhs," preached fiery sermons, condemning King Fahd for inviting the infidel armies and air forces into the birthplace of Islam. Saudi authorities initially attempted to rein them in, and when unsuccessful, in 1994 they jailed dozens including the most prominent, Safar al-Hawali and Salman Al-'Auda.[19] With vocal clerical critics in prison, opponents outside the kingdom continued the fight against Saudi Arabia's cavorting with the Western militaries, of whom the son of a wealthy Saudi construction tycoon, Osama bin Laden, became the most prominent.

Two bombings in mid-decade targeted against American military personnel in Saudi Arabia forced the United States to re-evaluate post-*Desert Storm* military operations, and to re-deploy their forces to less exposed reaches. The first physical warning of the growing opposition to America's presence in the Gulf came in 1995, when a bomb exploded at the headquarters of the U.S.

Office of Program Management/Saudi Arabian National Guard (OPM/ SANG). This headquarters building lay in the capital city of Riyadh, in the harsh desert lands of Nejd, the historic stronghold of conservative Wahhabi clerics. But the Americans had exhibited little cultural sensitivity to the potential negative consequences that their presence in these foreign lands might engender. Following *Desert Storm*, U.S. soldiers could be seen driving and walking around downtown Riyadh, sometimes in full battle uniform, complete with prominent American flags on the sleeve.[20] Even those with but a cursory knowledge of Saudi history know of the xenophobic tendencies in the kingdom's desert heartlands. Such visible manifestations of American military power in the "Bible Belt" of Islam were bound to elicit hostile opposition. The November 1995 explosion killed five Americans at the post.

This Riyadh explosion, however, did not elicit a fundamental rethinking of American strategic goals or force structure in the Gulf region. American forces remained positioned and deployed largely as they had been, working from *Desert Storm* bases. American fighter jets participating in Operation *Southern Watch*, for example, continued to fly from downtown Dhahran, and administrators for *Southern Watch* remained in downtown Riyadh. If U.S. leaders after the 1995 bombing still hadn't recognized the growing hostility to American military presence in the region, such opposition became clear on 25 June 1996, when a truck bomb exploded in Dhahran, Saudi Arabia, severely damaging Khobar Towers, a high-rise barracks used by American service members participating in Operation *Southern Watch*. The explosion killed 19 American personnel, most from the U.S. Air Force.[21]

In the months that followed, U.S. political and military leaders engaged in a deep and penetrating rethinking of American strategic aims in the Gulf. U.S. Secretary of Defense William Perry appointed retired four star Army General Wayne Downing, former head of the U.S. Special Operations Command, to investigate force protection in the region. The report was damning.[22] American leaders at both the strategic and operational level had not countered the perils of deploying their forces to high visibility, high population areas, and had failed to provide adequate force protection for them in Saudi Arabia. They had failed to provide proper perimeter defenses at billeting facilities. They had failed to install protective film on barracks' windows; a large number of the deaths at Khobar Towers, after all, came from flying glass shards. Exactly who perpetrated the attack on Khobar Towers remains in the first decade of the twenty-first century an unresolved issue.

Of note, the Downing Commission report did not challenge the fundamental question of whether or not U.S. forces after *Desert Storm* should have been deployed in Saudi Arabia to begin with. As General Downing noted in the report's introductory comments, "The United States has strategic interests in maintaining a force presence in Saudi Arabia and the Gulf region and in conducting coalition military operations to contain regional aggression."

Figure 71 Aftermath of bomb explosion at Khobar Towers military housing complex in Dhahran, June 1996.

> After *Desert Storm*, the American decision to remain for years in Saudi Arabia elicited a hostile backlash amongst conservative elements in the kingdom. Nineteen American service members died in the explosion at the barracks that housed personnel supporting Operation *Southern Watch* in Dhahran. The explosion, whose perpetrators still remain unidentified, prompted Anglo-American defense officials to discontinue high visibility *Southern Watch* flight operations from large population centers like Dhahran and Riyadh.

The generally cordial relations that had emerged between the two countries since the 1930s had blinded the superpower to investigating other strategic options, like redeploying military forces out of Saudi Arabia and moving them into the coastal emirates, whose population was more accepting of the West, and whose leadership in the past had welcomed the stabilizing presence of Western military power.

After the Khobar Towers bombing, American forces throughout the Gulf did what they might have done immediately following *Desert Storm* – they moved to more secluded and more defensible spots. In Saudi Arabia, for example, Operation *Southern Watch* forces moved deep into the desert to Prince Sultan Air Base at Al Kharj, away from Nejdi citizens' prying eyes. As part of that move, British, French, and American aircraft stopped flying from eastern Saudi Arabia's largest city, Dhahran. In Bahrain, directly as a result of the attacks on Khobar Towers, the U.S. ambassador and Fifth Fleet commander sealed a deal with the Emir to vastly enlarge the size of the naval facility at Jufair. More land was needed in Bahrain, the two believed, to house the growing number of post-*Desert Storm* shore-based personnel and equipment. The facility's walls needed to be pushed out, furthermore, so that the intensity of any future bomb explosion would diffuse before causing damage to personnel or facilities.[23]

By the late 1990s, then, the United States and its military leaders had seized the opportunity to plant deeper roots in the Gulf. Two deadly bombings, however, had demonstrated the hostility from some Arab quarters that these deeper roots had instilled. U.S. forces redeployed to more secure environs, around which more defensible perimeters grew. Despite this U.S. move to less visible locales the Arab campaign to rid the Gulf region of the West's military presence continued. As Osama bin Laden proclaimed in August 1996, "The explosions at Riyadh and Al-Khobar are a warning . . ."[24] Throughout the mid 1990s Osama's attacks on the Saudi ruling family and their American allies continued. As he stated in 1996:

> It has been seven years since [the Americans'] arrival, and the regime is not able to move them out of the country. The regime has made no confession about its ineffectiveness and carries on lying to the people, claiming that the Americans will leave. . . . The occupying American

Figure 72 Defending Prince Sultan Air Base in Saudi Arabia, August 1996.

After the June 1996 explosion at Khobar Towers barracks in Dhahran, Saudi Arabia, Anglo-American forces enforcing the no fly zones over Iraq in Operation *Southern Watch* redeployed to more remote and defensible positions. Above, a U.S. Air Force airman stands guard over a new tent city under construction to house the new military arrivals, Prince Sultan Air Base, Al Kharj, Saudi Arabia.

Figure 73 British communications team deploys to Al Kharj in Saudi Arabia, August 1996.

A communications team from Tactical Communications Wing, RAF Brize Norton, United Kingdom, sets up ground communications for British personnel supporting the RAF Tornadoes in Operation *Southern Watch*, at Al Kharj Air Base, deep in the remote desert of Saudi Arabia.

enemy is the principle and main cause of the situation. Therefore, efforts should be concentrated on destroying, fighting, and killing the enemy until, by the grace of God, it is completely defeated.[25]

Opposition to America's military presence in the Gulf, particularly in Saudi Arabia, was deepened by the collapse in the 1990s of oil prices on the world market, which forced draconian cutbacks to the social welfare system to which many Gulf Arabs had grown accustomed. These cutbacks were particularly pronounced in Saudi Arabia, where a government job and free medical care had become an expectation for many young citizens.[26] As the world price of oil collapsed from its peak in 1980 of \$103/bbl to just \$20/bbl in the mid 1990s, the Saudi regime had to curtail expenditures. The average income level dropped by almost two-thirds during that same time.[27] The government came under increasing pressure from the Saudi regime's critics, who drew a close connection between America's military involvement in their country and their own declining prosperity. The United States' demand that the Riyadh regime pay for much of the expense of *Desert Storm* evoked further resentment against the Saudi royal family.[28] Excoriating the Saudi regime while linking it with America, Osama in 1996 complained:

People are fully concerned about their everyday lives. Everybody talks about the deterioration of the economy, inflation, ever-increasing debts, and jails full of prisoners. Government employees with limited incomes talk about debts of tens of thousands and hundreds of thousands of Saudi Riyals. They complain that the value of the Riyal is greatly and continuously deteriorating among most of the major currencies. Great merchants and contractors speak about hundreds and thousands of millions of Riyals owed to them by the government . . . People . . . believe this situation is a curse put on them by God for not objecting to the oppressive and illegitimate behavior and measures of the ruling regime: ignoring divine Islamic law, depriving people of their legitimate rights, allowing the Americans to occupy the Land of the Two Sacred Mosques, and the unjust imprisonment of the sincere scholars.[29]

Thus, by the end of the twentieth century, increasing calls came from the Saudi clerical establishment and from members of opposition groups like al-Qaeda for the eviction of the Americans from their Persian Gulf region bases, from which Operation *Southern Watch* was still being administered. On 11 September 2001, a day that most Americans remember as an unprovoked attack on Washington and New York, a group comprised mainly of Saudi citizens hijacked commercial airliners and crashed them into the Pentagon and the World Trade Center Twin Towers. To those who had been watching developments in the Persian Gulf since *Desert Storm*, however, the terror acts served as yet another in a string of protests against America's post-*Desert Storm* presence in the region.

America and Britain go to war in Iraq

The terror attacks shook the U.S. populace. In an atmosphere of unease and paranoia, American leaders over the next 18 months – in conjunction with allies, of whom Britain would prove the staunchest – began two wars, one in Afghanistan and the second in Iraq. The Afghan campaign commenced in October 2001, aiming to overthrow the Taliban regime whose leaders had harbored members of the terror group al-Qaeda, masterminds of the attacks on New York and Washington. American land and air forces allied themselves with Northern Alliance soldiers in Afghanistan, and in a six-week drive, pushed the Taliban from Kabul by mid November. Approximately three months after al-Qaeda hijackers crashed aircraft into Washington and New York, American soldiers stood guard in central Afghanistan. American political and military leaders soon discovered, however, that their quest to implant in Afghanistan a stable, Westward-leaning regime would prove more difficult than they imagined. Eight years later, in winter 2009, 45,000 American troops still remained in the mountainous country, with U.S. President Barack Obama pledging 17,000 more to quell growing unrest.[30]

The second of the two American-led wars spawned by the September 2001 attacks took place in the Persian Gulf state of Iraq. President George W. Bush argued that Western nations had a duty to remove President Saddam Hussein's bellicose regime, not necessarily because of its involvement in the terror attacks on Washington and New York, although some suggested it.[31] Rather, the Bush Administration argued that a war was necessary against Saddam for several reasons: because of Iraq's continued violation of post-*Desert Storm* sanctions, his refusal to allow an intrusive weapons inspection regime, his past history of bellicose relations with neighbors, and the widely held belief that Saddam's regime possessed weapons of mass destruction (WMD). Director of Central Intelligence George Tenet deemed this last conclusion, that Saddam had WMD, a "slam dunk."[32]

Unlike the American attack on the Taliban regime in Afghanistan, which enjoyed wide public support in the United States, however, the March 2003 assault on Iraq proved much more contentious among the American populace. A fierce debate raged over the issue in the months preceding the attack, with critics pointing out that there existed no direct evidence of Iraqi complicity in the September 2001 attacks. The Bush Administration's case for war largely lay upon the need to pre-empt Iraq prior to its ability to one day threaten the United States with a WMD. The American populace remained split. Unlike the joint Congressional resolution that preceded the U.S. invasion of Afghanistan, which passed both houses of Congress with only one dissenting vote,[33] the October 2002 resolution authorizing war against Iraq proved much closer, passing the House of Representatives 297–133, largely along party lines.[34]

Despite popular opposition to an attack on Iraq on both sides of the Atlantic, British Labour Party Prime Minister Tony Blair steadfastly supported the Bush Administration's 2003 efforts against Saddam.[35] Like Bush, he argued that nations like Iraq that behave in such an irresponsible manner need to be checked, and that in an era of proliferating weapons of mass destruction, Western governments cannot wait for irrefutable evidence of hostile intent before taking up arms in their own self-defense. British intelligence experts, like their American counterparts, had concluded that Iraq maintained a clandestine effort to procure weapons of mass destruction.[36] Under Blair's direction London played a major role in Washington's ultimately unsuccessful political quest to procure U.N. approval for the use of military force against Iraq.

Despite the failure of American and British attempts to procure U.N. approval for using force, American leaders proved able to cobble together an international "Coalition of the Willing" of over 30 nations, the largest of which was Great Britain. Attacking before the summer heats arrived in the Persian Gulf, on 20 March coalition land and air forces crossed into Iraq. In an advance from the south that in some respects resembled the British attack into Mesopotamia almost nine decades before, American-led units stormed up the Tigris and Euphrates valleys, and within three weeks captured

Baghdad. The fall of Saddam, of note, made obsolete the mission of Joint Task Force Southwest Asia, the military organization tasked with enforcing the no-fly zone over Iraq. Before the end of the year U.S. air units had left Prince Sultan Air Base in the desert of Saudi Arabia. The U.S. military defeat of Saddam had provided a victory not only to Washington, but also in an indirect way to Osama and his ilk. For the first time in 13 years, the Kingdom of Saudi Arabia's lands did not include a large contingent of operational American fighters, although American troops continued to operate from other states along the Arab side of the Gulf.

The 2003 Anglo-American occupation of Iraq stumbled from the beginning. Seemingly unaware of the words or the fate of British General Maude, who in 1917 proclaimed that, "Our armies do not come into your cities and lands as conquerors, but as liberators,"[37] Prime Minister Blair told the Iraqis that, "Our forces are friends and liberators of the Iraqi people, not your conquerors." In the same broadcast, beamed into Iraq on 10 April 2003, President Bush promised that, "We will help you build a peaceful and representative government that protects the rights of all citizens. And then our military forces will leave."[38]

President Bush's promise of a speedy withdrawal, however, would prove overly optimistic. Just as the war in Afghanistan continued for years after the speedy 2001 invasion, so too did the war in Iraq.[39] Despite pre-war entreaties from senior uniformed U.S. officers for additional troops, Defense Secretary

Figure 74 U.S. Army troops scan horizon, Al Najaf, Operation *Iraqi Freedom*, March 2003.

For the second time in a dozen years, in March 2003 U.S., British, and allied nations invade Iraq. Above, U.S. Army Special Operations soldiers scan the horizon for potential threats. In succeeding years, a fierce insurgency developed in Iraq.

Donald Rumsfeld insisted on a smaller, lighter invasion and post-war occupation force, with tens of thousands of personnel fewer than the Army Chief of Staff publicly called for. The Bush Administration, furthermore, based its post-war planning on assumptions that American forces would be welcomed; Vice President Cheney shortly before the war said that, "my belief is we will, in fact, be greeted as liberators."[40] The Bush Administration, furthermore, proved slow to quell the ethnic disturbances that arose in the months after their successful removal of Saddam's regime, and also slow to recognize that an insurgency within Iraq had arisen. Understaffed, and unable to conceptualize the type of conflict that they had stumbled into, by 2006 the Americans had become embroiled in a virtual civil war within Iraq.[41] In October of that year alone, the U.S. suffered 99 combat deaths and 783 wounded.[42]

By the end of 2006 America's expedition in Iraq looked bleak.[43] Saddam's weapons of mass destruction program, the termination of which served as a primary war aim, had proven a huge Iraqi bluff. America's subsequent dismantling of the Iraqi army, and the prohibition of former Ba'ath Party members from serving in the new Iraqi government, had turned tens of thousands of prominent Sunnis against the new American-backed regime; some began to side with the al-Qaeda inspired insurgents. Inter-ethnic tensions flared into open hostilities. Under the leadership of U.S. Central Command's General John Abizaid and his top Iraqi Commander General George Casey, the U.S. aimed to train members of a new military and security force, and attempt to leave Iraq as soon as possible; the two argued for a drawdown of personnel from Iraq, not an increase as some voices in the Bush Administration were beginning to suggest. Conceptually, Casey concentrated his forces in large forward operating bases, from which small units emerged for daytime patrols. Exploiting this lack of permanent presence in the villages, al-Qaeda and other anti-Western insurgents moved in, however, terrorizing the residents, and convincing them that the Americans could not protect them.

General Abizaid and Casey's removal, along with a new strategic concept for the war, quickly reversed the direction of America's foray in Iraq. General David Petraeus and Lieutenant General Ray Odierno argued forcefully for changes in military strategy and force structure that came to be known as the "surge" of 2007.[44] This surge, however, involved not only an increase in troop levels, but also a fundamental shift in the way that American troops deployed and fought in Iraq. After Petraeus' assumption of duties in January 2007 as Commanding General of the Multi-National Forces in Iraq, American troops began to disperse in small numbers into Iraqi towns and villages, where they lived and worked, in order to protect the civilian population. This represented an abrupt change from the prior strategy of concentrating American troops in large garrison bases.

These changes reflected profound shifts in military doctrine that General Petraeus had helped to draft just months before. Drawing upon his experience in Iraq as the commander of the 101st Airborne Division during the first year of Operation *Iraqi Freedom*, as well as from his doctoral dissertation research at Princeton on the American military and the lessons of Vietnam, General Petraeus helped to pen FM 3–24, the revised U.S. Army/Marine Corps Counterinsurgency Field Manual.[45] This text provided the philosophical framework upon which the "surge" rested. Protection of the civilian population became the primary focus of the new American strategy in Iraq, and the forward deployment of coalition forces to Iraqi cities and villages – large and small – became the vehicle to achieve this end.

The results of this increase in troop levels and change of strategy proved sharp. By the end of Petraeus' first year as commanding general, Iraqi deaths from civil unrest plummeted over 75 percent, from a peak of approximately 3,700 per month in December 2006 to approximately 800 per month by late 2007.[46] Likewise, fatalities of U.S. troops in Iraq nosedived, from an average

Figure 75 U.S. Navy sailors apprehend suspected pirates in Gulf of Aden, February 2009.

The first decade of the 21st century ends in much the way that the first decade of the 19th did: with the world's dominant superpower engaged in anti-piracy efforts in the waters around the Persian Gulf, ensuring the continued free flow of commerce. Above, visit, board, search and seizure (VBSS) team members from the U.S. guided-missile cruiser USS *Vella Gulf* close in on suspected pirates. Nine suspected pirates were apprehended and brought aboard the ship. The ship was serving as the flagship for Combined Task Force 151, a multi-national task force conducting counter piracy operations to detect and deter piracy in and around the Persian Gulf, Gulf of Aden, Indian Ocean and Red Sea.

of 88 per month in the first half of 2007 to 14 per month by the end of the year.[47]

As order began to return to Iraq in the fifth year of the war, calls mounted in America and Britain for the troops to be called home. President Barack Obama campaigned on a platform of quickly drawing down U.S. force levels from Iraq. On 27 February 2009 the President announced that by the end of August 2010, "our combat mission will end." After that, a transitional force of 35,000–50,000 American troops would remain behind in Iraq for no more than 16 months, "training, equipping, and advising Iraqi Security Forces." By the end of the following year, in accordance with the U.S.–Iraqi Status of Forces agreement approved by the Iraqi parliament in November 2009, President Obama pledged to remove all remaining military forces from Iraq. Obama promised, "We will complete this transition to Iraqi responsibility, and we will bring our troops home with the honor that they have earned."[48]

What is past is prologue

In Spring 2009 ships from the Bahrain-based 5th Fleet patrolled the waters off the east African coast of Somalia, apprehending pirates who threatened ships passing south of the Arabian Peninsula. The naval ships are gas turbine powered instead of sail driven, but the anti-piracy mission seems hauntingly similar to the one that drew the British to the Gulf almost two centuries earlier. In Britain's case, the superpower stayed in the Gulf region for another century and a half, maintaining order, keeping out other Great Powers, and protecting the free flow of shipping. How long will America fulfill those same roles? Based upon Britain's experience, perhaps for a long time.

Conclusion

Although the atlas does not place Great Britain or the United States anywhere near the Persian Gulf, the impact of these two superpowers upon the region has proven enormous. Originally called to safeguard trade and to protect the flanks to India, small numbers of British diplomats and military officers stationed in the Gulf proved able to maintain order in this sparsely populated region known for its disorder and tumult. Beginning in the 1800s they put an end to piracy that threatened trade to India, kept the pearling season from devolving into months of war and retribution, and prevented tribal quarrels from spilling onto the high seas, accomplishing these tasks by drawing upon small numbers of Navy ships and threatening, when needed, the arrival of the enormous Indian Army that lay over the horizon. In the course of fulfilling these missions, London and Bombay in the nineteenth century developed relations with ruling families along the southern Arab Gulf coast, and over time, treaty relationships developed that essentially traded military protection for Arab submission to Britain's will. Without Britain's support for these small emirates, however, the surrounding large powers would likely have gobbled up the small: the Ottomans (and later the Iraqis) would have subsumed Kuwait, the Ottomans would have overrun Bahrain and Qatar, and the Saudis would have engulfed Oman and the Trucial States. British involvement in the Gulf, then, profoundly shaped the map of the region, with decisions in London and India sometimes determining which nations survived and which fell.

In addition to maintaining order in the Persian Gulf, the British in the nineteenth and twentieth centuries saw emerge another principal interest: keeping out other "Great Powers." In Persia and the Ottoman Empire, Britain engaged in a "Great Game" against Russia, with the two European states jockeying for control. Without Britain's presence, Persia may likely have become part of the tsars' growing empire in Asia. At the end of the 1800s, however, as a mighty German state emerged from the mists of Central Europe, Britain's antagonism toward Russia temporarily faded, and a new hostility toward Berlin grew. German businessmen and intelligence agents moved down through the Ottoman Empire into Mesopotamia and Persia, threatening – in London's eyes – the flanks to British India. Over time,

Britain proved just as interested in keeping Germany's influence out of the region as it did that of Russia.

In addition to Britain's desire to maintain order and to keep out other Great Powers, the dawn of the twentieth century saw the rise of another British interest in the Persian Gulf: the growth of the oil industry, particularly in Iran. British entrepreneurs struck oil in the western reaches of Persia. Abadan, at the head of the Gulf, became a key refinery and port. Protecting the headwaters of the Gulf, therefore, became increasingly critical as the British turned from coal to petroleum to power their factories and fleet.

In World War I the British desire to prevent the encroachment of Germany into the Gulf coincided with the nation's new need to protect growing oil interests there; in autumn 1914 British Indian forces moved ashore in Iran and Iraq to safeguard the oil fields. In what would in the twenty-first century be called "mission creep," the British then moved further inland – in a bloody and drawn out military campaign – to take Mesopotamia from the Ottomans.

By the end of the war the British Empire controlled much of the Middle East, giving rise to resentment on both shores of the Gulf. In part reflecting a desire to free themselves of the yoke of British supremacy, in the years before World War II both the Persians and the Saudis turned to Washington as a counterweight to London. They viewed with favor President Wilson's calls for an end to the old habits of colonial rule. The Persians asked for American help in straightening out their finances, and the Saudis chose U.S. companies to develop the nation's oil resources.

World War II marked the first large-scale entry of the United States' military into the region. A team of approximately 60,000 servicemen and civilians set up camp in eastern Iraq and western Iran, in a mammoth logistics delivery operation that transported Lend-Lease aid to the Soviets. During the course of America's wartime involvement in the Gulf, FDR made clear his desire to see the nations of the Indian Ocean emerge from the war as truly independent states. Although Roosevelt did not use the soaring hyperbole of Wilson, his ideas were similar: the era of the colonial empire had ended. FDR made no secret of his desire to see India and Iran become free of British domination.

America's most lasting wartime legacy in the Gulf sprang less from its logistics delivery effort, Herculean as it was, however, as from the involvement of American military advisors with the top leaders of Iran and Saudi Arabia. In both states Washington and London jockeyed for influence, but in both America emerged as the dominant power influencing military decision-making. And in both, enormous U.S. military assistance and training programs followed World War II. It would be a mistake, however, to conclude that the growing number of American trainers and advisors in those two states reflected Washington's taking from the British the responsibility for security affairs in the Gulf. American decision-makers, in fact, desired just the opposite. For decades after World War II they consciously angled to keep the British presiding over Gulf affairs, as that European power had done for over a century.

Although in World War II the Americans and British disagreed over prior colonial practices, over time Washington leaders discovered that their goals and interests largely coincided with those of London, and that the British could best tend to them. Like those of its British ally, America's central interests in the Persian Gulf proved three-fold: maintaining interstate order, keeping the oil flowing, and keeping out its other Great Power rival, the Soviet Union. Of the first two, Washington was happy to see the British continue to do exactly what they had been doing for over a century; America, after all, never professed any interest in maintaining interstate order in the Gulf, nor in preventing the Arabs and Persians from fighting amongst themselves. The second goal – keeping the oil flowing – proved largely intertwined with the first; as the British discovered in the early and mid 1800s, cross-border skirmishing and interstate aggression could threaten the free flow of trade, and neither Britain nor America after World War II could tolerate any interruptions in the flow of Persian Gulf oil. America in the 1940s, after all, had become a net oil importer of petroleum products, and though the majority of her domestic oil supplies came from the Western hemisphere, the U.S. Navy's deployed fleets had become addicted to Persian Gulf oil.

The U.S. military's dependence on Gulf petroleum gave rise to the founding in the late 1940s of the U.S. Navy's Middle East Force. This unit did little to actually defend those U.S. oil interests, however. The small handful of ships was chiefly a diplomatic symbol. Its flagship, after all, was normally painted white (to avoid the desert heat, although white is also the color of non-combatants), and its crews spent the majority of their time conducting show-the-flag missions rather than engaging in naval exercises or war-gaming. Nor were America's other ground forces in the Persian Gulf region organized as war-fighting units capable of engaging in combat operations. Despite the substantial American military aid going to Iran and Saudi Arabia, U.S. soldiers, sailors, and airmen stationed in those countries largely worked as *trainers*. Very few U.S. operational land or air forces prior to the 1970s ever deployed to the Gulf. Washington, in other words, did not have the forces in place to maintain order in the region, or to unilaterally defend its oil interests; it looked to London to achieve those two goals.

With respect to the third shared Anglo-American interest in the Gulf in the decades immediately following World war II – keeping out the Soviets – the Americans took the lead, by building up the Shah as well as the Saudi royal family, for example, and by keeping open the Dhahran air base as an anti-USSR contingency facility. But even in this paramount Cold War task of preventing Soviet encroachment into the Gulf, however, the Americans nonetheless sought out British involvement, including London's leadership of the Central Treaty Organization. In short, from the 1940s through the 1960s, in American eyes, the Persian Gulf remained a British domain and Washington leaders wanted to keep it that way. So long as the British remained in the region, the Americans could enjoy somewhat of a "free ride," and could divert money, arms, materiel, and attention toward the superpower's more pressing Cold War commitments in Asia and Europe.

Britain's ability to safeguard the three enduring Anglo-American interests – maintaining order, safeguarding oil interests and trade, and denying entry to the Soviet Union – however, became more precarious in the decades following World War II, for interrelated financial, military, and political reasons. Financially, Britain emerged from World War II even more devastated than it had from World War I. Its treasury was bankrupt. Many of its cities lay in ruins, victims of the Nazis' bombs. The crown jewel of its empire, India, clamored for independence, which it eventually won.

Britain's penurious financial condition led, naturally, to a paring down of its worldwide security commitments. Shortly after World War II its leaders renounced weighty obligations in Greece and Turkey, for example. With Indian independence, Britain's Indian army disappeared. Its post-war military budget received draconian cuts, leading to the halving from pre-war levels of its naval presence in the Gulf. In the face of these challenges, the British economized, as military leaders attempted to accomplish a bewildering array of tasks with reduced resources. They pulled troops and materiel from distant parts of the shrinking empire and consolidated them at the central base at Suez, for example, for rapid deployment to other locales.

While Britain's deteriorating fiscal condition underlay its military retrenchment, international and domestic political developments reinforced the drawdown. Egyptian President Gamal Abdul Nasser's rabid anti-colonial movement, for example, proved able for the first time in over seven decades to evict the British from their lodgment at Suez. Other anti-Western regimes took power in Syria and Iraq, and threatened Lebanon and Jordan. With their military evicted from Egypt, the British fled to Aden, which became in the 1960s the new font of British military power in the Persian Gulf and Indian Ocean region. But anti-Western agitation effectively chased the British from there, too. Nasser's troops entered the civil war in Yemen, and helped to foment an anti-British insurgency in the neighboring South Arabian Federation and Aden that ultimately led to London's departure from the base in 1967. Taken together, Britain's deteriorating financial condition, the state's military drawdown, and the growth of anti-Western political movements in the region made very difficult London's task of tending to Western security interests in the Persian Gulf.

In addition to adverse international political developments, British domestic politics also played a role in the decline of Britain's stewardship of the Persian Gulf region. The 1964 election of a Labour Government ushered into office a group of leaders who philosophically disliked the nation clinging to the trappings of its former empire. Better to spend resources at home, they believed, than continue to pour money overseas. Some Labour leaders entered office with a pre-disposition to curtail the expenses of Britain's anachronistic overseas empire. Within 18 months of their 1964 victory leaders had concluded that their East of Suez role, including their stewardship of the

Gulf, could not be continued indefinitely. They faced an alarming insurgency that chased them from Aden, which served as the repository of might for Britain's Gulf forces. Labour leaders were forced to make guns-or-butter decisions: buy expensive weapons systems like aircraft carriers to prolong the East of Suez role, or support social programs at home. In the end, they chose a path that would prolong British influence for a few years by transferring a few military units from the soon-to-close base at Aden to locations inside the Gulf, all the while attempting to convince Arab and American allies that they could stay the course for the foreseeable future. When the currency crisis arose in autumn 1967, the game was up: Labour could no longer prolong the illusion of British staying power in the Gulf, and thus the Gulf – along with most of Britain's other Pacific commitments – would go free.

In their abandonment of their commitments East of Suez, however, Labour Party leaders failed to discern the difference between the anachronistic remnants of the nation's former empire and the state's enduring national interests. With regard to the Persian Gulf, those vital national interests included the need to maintain order in the region, to keep the oil supply flowing, and to keep out the Soviet Union.

Several years before Britain's 1968 withdrawal announcement – viewing the deteriorating financial and political conditions in the Middle East and Britain – some officials on both sides of the Atlantic had become increasingly concerned that the British might one day have to withdraw their military from the region. Pondering how the nations of the West would defend their interests in the Gulf, prescient, mid-level planners within both the British and American security establishments identified the island of Diego Garcia as an ideal location to construct a military base, a facility that neither Iranian nor Arab leaders could close at their whim. U.S. Secretary of Defense McNamara, however, quashed plans for America's funding such a facility, believing it would make it too easy for the British to absolve themselves of their security commitments to the region. The top reaches in Washington never realized just how precarious – financially, militarily, and politically – the British ability to continue their leadership of the Persian Gulf had become.

The January 1968 announcement of Britain's withdrawal within three years turned the Gulf upside down, and heralded the impending close of almost a century and a half in which the British oversaw Persian Gulf order. The haste with which the decision was made, and the lack of consultations with allies, infuriated Washington officials. The divide in Anglo-American relations concerning the Gulf grew larger than at any time since the 1956 Suez Crisis. No one in London, Washington, or the Gulf knew what the future of the region would hold. Would the emirates unite? Would they go their separate ways? Would the United States sweep in to fulfill Britain's commitments? Would the Soviets? Anxieties soared.

America's leaders wasted no time in proclaiming that the United States would not, under any circumstances, take over the role of the British. U.S.

involvement in Vietnam in 1968 seemed to be spiraling out of control, and a perception spread throughout Congress that the nation had gotten involved there due to unspoken and informal security pledges made during the years before; Congressional members pledged that no such similar entanglements would emerge as a result of the Americans replacing the British in the Persian Gulf. Opposition to getting involved in the Gulf proved so fierce that the Nixon Administration had troubles gaining Congressional approval for renewing the lease that would allow the Navy's Middle East Force to remain in Bahrain at its modest complement of three or four ships.

Who, then, would tend to America's and the West's interests in the Gulf? Who, in other words, would maintain interstate order in the Gulf, ensure the free flow of oil, and keep out the Soviets, the enduring goals for decades of the British and the Americans? Washington officials had no choice: politically and militarily constrained by the Vietnam War, they had to turn to their two trusted allies in the region, Iran and, to a lesser extent, Saudi Arabia. In accordance with President Nixon's Vietnam-induced proclamation that local powers must assume a larger degree of responsibility for maintaining order in their own back yards – the Nixon Doctrine – the U.S. encouraged Iran and Saudi Arabia to safeguard Western interests; the two states effectively became America's deputized policemen in the region. American interests thus became more deeply intertwined with those of the Shah and the Saudi king.

The British worked assiduously to solve as many political problems as possible from 1968–71, the three-year transition from British rule to independence. They defused several crises, like Iran's claim to Bahrain, but proved unable to solve others, like the case of the disputed islands. After initially standing on the sidelines awaiting Arab moves to craft their own political future, the new Conservative Government in 1970 appointed an experienced diplomat to help smooth the transition, who assisted in getting the seven small emirates to form a union; Bahrain and Qatar opted for independence.

The British pulled out of the Gulf in late 1971, roughly in accord with the schedule set down three years earlier. The first two years of independence proved largely without international incident, although the outward calm belied increasing turmoil under the surface. Iran and Iraq squared off across their contested border, Saudi Arabia continued to squabble with Abu Dhabi, and the Trucial States decried Iranian duplicity in the continuing islands dispute. All this while the Soviets – emboldened by the British withdrawal and the American refusal to replace them – sent their warships to the region. It took only months after Britain's departure, in other words, for two of the West's enduring interests to begin to crumble: maintaining interstate tranquility, and keeping out the Soviets. Within 24 months the final goal – the continued free flow of oil to the West – would likewise suffer.

Beginning in fall 1973, less than two years after the British departed, a series of four traumas afflicted the region that devastated Anglo-American interests in the Gulf, and which brought the United States successively closer to replacing the British in their historic role as security guarantors. First, in the midst of the October 1973 war, Arab states imposed an oil embargo and engaged in production roll-backs that resulted in dramatic petroleum price increases throughout the West. Gas lines followed. Western economies tipped into recession. American defense officials recoiled at the lack of military options available to them. Not only did their Twin Pillars not quell the disruption, they actually contributed to it. Having declined in 1968 Arab offers to take over British military facilities, the Americans possessed no military foothold in the region. They resorted to the only option available to them: the deployment of naval power, which would continue for years.

The second step in America's move toward accepting the role of security guarantor for the region came at the end of the 1970s, as the Shah fell and the Soviet Union attacked Afghanistan. The gas lines formed again, and the public clamored for action. President Jimmy Carter – who earlier in his administration had declined the Sultan of Oman's offer to take over the British military base on Masirah Island, and who had also entertained the idea of designating the Indian Ocean a demilitarized zone – finally concluded that America's lack of military might in the region served as a strategic shortcoming. In response, he set in motion plans for a Rapid Deployment Force. Coupled with his later pronouncement that an attack on the Persian Gulf represented a threat to the vital interests of America and would be met with force – the Carter Doctrine – the nation had made a philosophical leap toward assuming responsibility for the defense of the region.

President Reagan took the third step toward the U.S. assumption of security duties in the Gulf with his decision to defend with naval might U.S.-flagged oil tankers during the Iran–Iraq War. It represented the first time since World War II that large numbers of U.S. combatant forces had engaged in hostilities in the Persian Gulf region. During the operation, however, Arab leaders largely refused to welcome U.S. troops ashore; U.S. servicemen remained, as they had since the 1973 Arab–Israeli war, unwelcome. Coupled with lingering Congressional opposition to the naval escort program, and despite a few isolated but highly qualified voices who argued otherwise, after the Iran–Iraq War ended in 1988 the American naval force reverted essentially back to its pre-war level. The U.S. in the late 1980s, in other words, had no appetite for a permanent military presence in the region.

That situation changed two years later, however, as a result of *Desert Storm*. Iraqi forces vaulted across the Kuwaiti border in August 1990. Drawing upon pre-position stocks and rapidly-deploying forces administered from a command dedicated to Middle Eastern operations – a mirror-image of the British strategy to defend the Gulf in the 1960s – an American-led coalition of forces drove Iraq from Kuwait. The British played a vital role in the operation. Unlike the aftermath of the Iran–Iraq War, when neither Arab nor American voices supported a permanent U.S. presence in the region, however, following *Desert Storm* the Americans – with the Arabs' blessings – stayed. They remained for two reasons. One was a conscious campaign on the part of Washington officials to take advantage of what they considered a fleeting opportunity to plant a foothold ashore in Arab lands. The second, however, was unplanned – the need to combat Saddam in a low-intensity war that continued after *Desert Storm*, a conflict that grew largely from the U.S. wartime decision not to destroy Saddam's forces.

By the end of 1991, then, the U.S. had arrived to stay. Its air forces and naval forces – along with those of the British, in a supporting role – patrolled the Persian Gulf environs, maintaining interstate order as the British had done for over a century. The twenty-year interregnum period of chaos and confusion had proven too much for the Americans to bear. Washington concluded, as London had done earlier, that a moderate dose of forward-deployed military power could ensure tranquility in the region, which in turn would help to keep the oil flowing and help to dissuade other Great Powers from drawing near. America's march toward the Gulf had stretched five decades from World War II to 1991, but by the end of that year America was there to stay.

What lessons does this story offer for the twenty-first century? First and foremost, the United States must prepare for a long political and military commitment to the Persian Gulf. This is perhaps the chief lesson to come from this study: over the past 150 years the forward presence of a moderate dose of Western military power, primarily naval power, has served as the best guarantor of interstate tranquility in the Persian Gulf region. Why should the states of the West care about tranquility there? The reason, of course, arises ultimately from the West's dependence upon oil. Barring some new technological breakthrough that might make petroleum irrelevant – possible, given that coal's importance dimmed at the beginning of the twentieth century – the West will need a dependable supply flowing through the Strait of Hormuz. During the two-decade interregnum between British and American hegemony in the Gulf, 1971–91, the flow of oil at moderate, stable prices was anything but dependable, and the West suffered: witness the oil cutbacks and boycott of 1973–74, the fall-of-the-Shah-induced supply reductions of 1978–79, and the Iran–Iraq War attacks on oil tankers in 1987–88. The economic and political pain of these traumas simply proved untenable to Washington. With China and India industrializing rapidly, world demand for energy will undoubtedly continue to grow, adding to the Gulf's importance. An attempt to allow local powers to control security of the region failed dismally in the 1970s and 1980s, and America and the West would place itself at great jeopardy should their leaders try again a similar tack.

Why does this region appear to need the presence of the West to maintain interstate order? There are several underlying reasons. The presence of a collection of very small, vulnerable, oil-rich states lying in the shadow of several large, powerful ones makes interstate aggression likely; the rewards for a successful land-grab, after all, are immense. The presence of British might since the 1800s largely prevented such land-grabs, however. As we have seen, British power allowed Kuwait, Bahrain, Qatar, the United Arab Emirates, and Oman to emerge in the first place; without London's and Bombay's protective umbrella those states would all have been subsumed by their larger neighbors. Iraq's moves against Kuwait in 1961 and 1990 serve as the two most visible manifestations of the peril under which small Gulf States live every day, but there are more. A glance at wall maps that Saudi Arabian military officers use offers an interesting perspective: Oman and the United Arab Emirates appear as small tidal strips,[1] suggesting that the Saudis believe that they rightfully own most territory of the coastal states. Throughout history, leaders of these small states generally welcomed the presence of British power – upon which their forbears depended to stay in power – and sought American security guarantees in the early 1970s when British power waned. Due to larger anti-Western political currents, however, the emirates' leaders could not always publicly invite in the West. We should expect that this tension will remain: for their survival the local Arab leaders of these small states want – in fact, need – the support of Washington and other Western nations, but they cannot openly beg for it lest they run afoul of Arab sensibilities.

The presence of small states next to large states, and the high returns to aggression that this affords, is not the only reason for the West to stay, for the large states themselves hold gripes and grudges against one another that might at any time devolve into bloodshed, jeopardizing vital exports of oil. Iraq and Iran throughout the past century have shared mutual antagonisms, for example, and fought a bloody eight-year conflict in the 1980s. America's invasion of Iraq in 2003, furthermore, has increased the influence of Iran in Mesopotamian affairs. Saudi Arabia's leaders, staunchly Sunni, might find themselves compelled to counter Iran's increased role there. Iran's revolutionary clerical leaders, furthermore, as they exhibited in the late 1970s, feel an affinity for, and an obligation to, the sizable Shia populations along the west coast of the Gulf, making interstate conflict with those Sunni-led regimes possible.

What might a future Anglo-American security policy toward the Persian Gulf look like? The question is particularly important as Washington and London grapple with the impact of their withdrawal from Iraq following the 2003 invasion and subsequent occupation. A good start is by emulating Great Britain's practices of the nineteenth and twentieth centuries. Broadly speaking, the British proved able to maintain order with the forward deployment of modest amounts of naval power, coupled with capable diplomacy and the ever-present threat of the over-the-horizon garrisons in India. America's unknowing adoption of this broad-brush British formula led to over a decade of *Pax Americana* in the Persian Gulf in the years after *Desert Storm*.

As the British learned, of course, naval or air power alone isn't enough. There must remain a credible ability to bring quickly – very quickly – to the area a robust and substantive land force. That is the chief lesson that the British learned in Operation *Vantage*, the nation's response to the Iraqi provocations against Kuwait in 1961. In that successful undertaking, London learned the importance of fast-reaction forces, pre-position equipment, and the need to respond quickly to good intelligence, lessons that the Americans in the 1970s, 1980s, and 1990s appeared to have forgotten, or never learned. The presence of pre-positioned equipment, which all of the U.S. military services use in the early twenty-first century, remains critical for maintaining Persian Gulf order, as does the immediate availability of sea and air lift.

The United States must also realize that though fast-reaction forces are vital, and some shore support is essential, keeping large numbers of Western military personnel – particularly land-based forces – in the Gulf region can become a liability. One of the enduring themes of Persian Gulf history in the twentieth century is the nationalist revolt against the West. Though the U.S. at times served on the Arab and Persian side of that nationalist fight – railing against London in World War II and in the Suez Crisis over British colonial habits – Washington by the 1970s had supplanted London as the new, resented colonial power.

It may be necessary for short periods of time in the future to deploy a Western land or air force in the Gulf region. For those occasions, Washington and London ought to favor the small Arab emirates that depend on super-power protection for their independence, and not the larger regional powers of Saudi Arabia or Iraq. The coastal emirates, furthermore, have long played host to sailors and traders from other parts of the globe, and the residents there are less prone to xenophobic reactions of the local populace. Washington failed to recognize this in the mid 1990s, choosing to keep in Saudi Arabia a large post-*Desert Storm* military force. American leaders, furthermore, failed to recognize in a timely fashion the perils of this decision, keeping their deployed forces in Saudi Arabia until a vocal and well-funded opposition had arisen.

The U.S. and Britain, then, today face a conundrum. On the one hand, their leaders must deploy to the region enough military might to tend to order, but on the other hand, those forces must not become too visible, or be placed in areas where a hostile reaction is likely. This is a challenge to which Anglo-American leaders will have to rise over the next decades, a task made much more difficult by the continuing turmoil elicited by the 2003 invasion of Iraq.

There exist limits to this naval-centric strategy, however. Although maritime power, accompanied by the threat of a fast-reaction land force, for over a century served as a successful British formula for keeping tranquility within the Gulf, it proved insufficient to counter Great Power designs on the region, which required extensive land campaigning. During British involve-ment in the Great Game in the 1800s, for example, the British had to fight in Iran on at least two occasions to keep Russian-backed Persia from moving closer to India. Countering Russian designs required, in other words, an operational land force.

Again in the twentieth century, Britain had to engage in land battles to counter new Great Power foes. In World War I London chose to move northward into Mesopotamia and Iran in large part to prevent the spread of German influence. Two decades later in World War II Great Britain battled the German-backed Vichy regime in Syria, the German-sympathetic leadership of Iraq, and the Germans themselves as they marched into Egypt on their way to the Gulf. These fights were in addition to battling the Italians on the Red Sea coast of Africa. American leaders need to keep in mind that although naval power will likely prove the most efficacious way to maintain interstate order in the Gulf, the rise of another Great Power threat would likely require more robust land forces.

Is another Great Power threat to the Gulf looming? Although the Russians do not appear in the early twenty-first century to harbor ambitions in the Gulf, two other giants have substantial growing petroleum interests there, China and India. Both have a vested interest in a continued supply of oil coming through the Strait of Hormuz. On the surface, both nations' interests in a stable Gulf appear to converge with those of the United States. Whether those two Asian nations will move into the region and threaten American interests, as Russia and Germany did to the British at times during the past two centuries, remains to be seen. American leaders must watch carefully the Gulf States, along with their petroleum customers.

In summary, the Persian Gulf was, and remains, a politically fragile place, a patchwork of small and large states whose leaders possess conflicting interests. If not for the presence of the British and the Americans, left to their own, these states would likely fight. First London, and then Washington's leaders, however, discovered that they couldn't afford to let them battle. The economic and political costs were just too high. Accordingly, the Gulf has seen British and American forces patrolling the region for over a century and a half, maintaining order, ensuring the free flow of oil, and preventing the entry of other Great Powers. For the foreseeable future, it is likely that Anglo-American forces will remain there.

Notes

Chapter 1

1 See C.R. Boxer, *The Portuguese Seaborne Empire, 1415–1825* (New York: A.A. Knopf, 1969); Sanjay Subrahmanyam, *The Portuguese Empire in Asia, 1500–1700: A Political and Economic History* (London: Longman, 1993); and David Birmingham, *A Concise History of Portugal* (Cambridge, England: Cambridge University Press, 2003). For a bibliographical treatment of the early Portuguese empire in the Persian Gulf region, see Willem Floor and Farhad Hakimzadeh, *The Hispano-Portuguese Empire and Its Contacts with Safavid Persia, the Kingdom of Hormuz and Yarubid Oman from 1489 to 1720* (Leuven, Belgium: Peeters Publishers, 2007).
2 Salih Ozbaran, *The Ottoman Response to European Expansion: Studies on Ottoman-Portuguese Relations in the Indian Ocean and Ottoman Administration in the Arab Lands During the Sixteenth Century* (Istanbul: Isis Press, 1994).
3 There exists extensive academic and trade literature on the East India Companies and their militaries. See Om Prakash, *The Dutch East India Company and the Economy of Bengal, 1630–1720* (Princeton, NJ: Princeton University Press, 1985); Brian Gardner, *The East India Company: A History* (New York: McCall Publishing Company, 1972); Daniel P. Marston and Chandar Sundaram, eds., *A Military History of India and South Asia: From the East India Company to the Nuclear Era* (Westport, CT: Praeger Security International, 2007); and Jean Sutton, *Lords of the East: The East India Company and Its Ships, 1600–1874* (London: Conway Maritime Press, 2000).
4 Denis Judd, *The Lion and the Tiger: The Rise and Fall of the British Raj, 1600–1947* (Oxford: Oxford University Press, 2004).
5 Diary of the Persian Gulf Political Residency for the week ending 20 May 1906, in Michael Armstrong, ed., *Political Diaries of the Persian Gulf*, Vol. I (London: Archive Editions, 1990), p. 359. (Hereafter cited as *PDPG*). For a full treatment of the Pirate Coast in the early 1800s, see Charles Belgrave, *The Pirate Coast* (London: G. Bell & Sons, 1966).
6 For more on British and Indian naval forces in the Gulf, see D.J. Hastings, *The Royal Indian Navy, 1612–1950* (Jefferson, North Carolina and London: McFarland & Company, 1988); Charles Rathbone Low, *History of the Indian Navy 1613–1863*, 2 vols. (London: Richard Bentley and Son, 1877); and Nigel Robert Dalziel, "British Maritime Contacts with the Persian Gulf" (PhD Dissertation, University of Lancaster, UK, 1989).
7 Hammell, Letter from the Residency in the Persian Gulf Bushire to W.S. Collinson, Commodore Indian Navy, Persian Gulf, Bassadore, 6 September 1831, in Anita L.P. Burdett, ed., *Persian Gulf and Red Sea Naval Reports 1820–1960*, Vol. 1 (London: Archive Editions, 1993), p. 443. (Hereafter cited as *PGRSNR*).
8 Letter from the Residency in the Persian Gulf Bushire to H. Wyndham,

Commodore of the Squadron of the Indian Navy Persian Gulf, 27 September 1832, in *PGRSNR*, Vol. I, pp. 465–7.

9 Ibid.

10 Honorable Henry Meritor, Letter from Superintendent of Marine, Bombay, to the Honorable P.M. Elphinstone, President and Governor in Council, 27 July 1820, in *PGRSNR*, Vol. 1, p. 19.

11 Wyndham, 27 September 1832.

12 Editor's Comments, Anita L.P. Burdett, ed., *PGRSNR*, Vol. I, p. 7.

13 For an in-depth review of the British Political Residency and Native Agency in the region, including an extensive bibliography, see James Onley, *The Arabian Frontier of the British Raj: Merchants, Rulers, and the British in the Nineteenth-Century Gulf* (New York: Oxford University Press, 2007).

14 Editor's Introductory Comments, *PDPG*, p. xi.

15 For more on Britain and Aden, see F.M. Hunter, *An Account of the British Settlement of Aden in Arabia* (London: Frank Cass, 1968); Spencer Mawby, *British Policy in Aden and the Protectorates 1955–67: Last Outpost of a Middle East Empire* (London: Routledge, 2005); and R.J. Gavin, *Aden under British Rule, 1839–1967* (New York: Harper and Row, 1975).

16 Rosemarie Said Zahlan, *The Making of the Modern Gulf States* (London: Unwin Hyman, 1989), pp. 7–8.

17 First Maritime Truce, 21 May 1835, signed by S. Hennell, Assistant in Charge of the Residency Persian Gulf, in Appendix II, J.B. Kelly, *Britain and the Persian Gulf, 1795–1880* (Oxford: Clarendon Press, 1968), p. 840.

18 J.B. Kelly, *Britain and the Persian Gulf, 1795–1880*, p. 365.

19 Zahlan, *The Making of the Modern Gulf States*, pp. 9–10.

20 *Lord Curzon in India: Being a Selection from his Speeches as Viceroy and Governor-General of India 1898–1905* (New York: MacMillan, 1905), pp. 500–507.

21 Lord George Curzon, *Persia and the Persian Question* (London: Longmans, Green, and Co., 1892), Vol. 1, p. 3.

22 See Firuz Kazemzadeh, *Russia and Britain in Persia, 1864–1914* (New Haven: Yale University Press, 1968).

23 Kelly, *Britain and the Persian Gulf, 1795–1880*, p. 295.

24 James Outram, *Lieutenant General Sir James Outram's Persian Campaign in 1857: Comprising General Orders and Despatches Relating to the Military Operations in Persia, from the Landing at Bushire to the Treaty of Peace* (London: Smith, Elder, and Co., Printed for Prive Circulation Only, available at British Library, 1860).

25 Kelly, *Britain and the Persian Gulf, 1795–1880*, pp. 465–6.

26 Ibid., p. 481.

27 Information in this chapter on the Ottoman presence in the Gulf in the nineteenth century drawn from Frederick F. Anscombe, *The Ottoman Gulf: The Creation of Kuwait, Saudi Arabia, and Qatar* (New York: Columbia University Press, 1997).

28 See Philip L. Cottrell, ed., *East Meets West: Banking, Commerce and Investment in the Ottoman Empire* (Surrey, UK: Ashgate, 2008); Chapter 5, Firuz Kazemzadeh, *Russia and Britain in Persia, 1864–1914* (New Haven: Yale University Press, 1968); and Edwin Black, *Banking on Baghdad* (Hoboken, NJ: John Wiley & Sons, 2004).

29 For a discussion of Power Cycle Theory in International Relations, see Charles Doran, *Systems in Crisis: New Imperatives of High Politics at Century's End* (New York: Cambridge University Press, 1991).

30 See Jonathan S. McMurray, *Distant Ties: Germany, the Ottoman Empire, and the Construction of the Baghdad Railway* (Westport CT: Praeger, 2001); Morris Jastrow, *The War and the Bagdad Railway* (Philadelphia: J.B. Lippincott, 1918).

31 Anscombe, p. 121.

32 For the Iranian Constitutional Revolution, see Janet Afary, *The Iranian Constitutional Revolution, 1906–1911* (New York: Columbia University Press, 1996);

Mangol Bayat, *Iran's First Revolution: Shi'ism and the Constitutional Revolt of 1905–1909* (New York: Oxford University Press USA, 1991); and Mansour Bonakdarian, *Britain and the Iranian Constitutional Revolution of 1906–1911: Foreign Policy, Imperialism, and Dissent* (Syracuse: Syracuse University Press, 2006).

33 Sir Percy Sykes, *A History of Persia*, 3rd edn. (London: Macmillan and Company, 1930), p. 403.

34 Diary of the Persian Gulf Political Residency for the week ending 8 July 1906, *PDPG*, Vol. I.

35 See map in David Fromkin, *The Peace to End All Peace: The Fall of the Ottoman Empire and the Creation of the Modern Middle East* (New York: Henry Holt, 2001), p. 21.

36 W. Morgan Shuster, *The Strangling of Persia: A Personal Narrative* (New York: Century, 1920).

37 Geoffrey Kemp and Robert Harkavy, *Strategic Geography and the Changing Middle East* (Washington, D.C.: Brookings Press, 1997).

38 For more on the British Mesopotamian campaign, see Ron Wilcox, *Battles on the Tigris: The Mesopotamian Campaign of the First World War* (South Yorkshire: Pen and Sword, 2006); Paul K. Davis, *Ends and Means: The British Mesopotamian Campaign and Commission* (Madison, New Jersey: Fairleigh Dickinson University Press, 1994); and A.J. Barker, *The First Iraq War 1914–1918: Britain's Mesopotamian Campaign* (New York: Enigma Books, 2009).

39 See David Omissi, "The Indian Army in the First World War, 1914–18," in Marston and Sundaram, eds., *A Military History of India and South Asia: From the East India Company to the Nuclear Era* (Westport, CT: Praeger International, 2007).

40 Stephen Hemsley Longrigg, *Oil in the Middle East* (London: Oxford University Press, 1954), ch. 3.

41 Major R. Evans, *A Brief Outline of the Campaign in Mesopotamia* (London: Sifton Praed and Company, 1926), p. 17.

42 Ibid., p. 14.

43 London *Times*, 18 December 1930, Literary Supplement, "Mesopotamia, 1914–17."

44 For more on British involvement in the Middle East in this period, see John Fisher, *Curzon and British Imperialism in the Middle East 1916–1919* (London: Frank Cass, 1999); Elie Kedourie, *England and the Middle East: The Destruction of the Ottoman Empire, 1914–1921* (London: Bowes and Bowes, 1956); and Fromkin, *The Peace to End All Peace*.

45 See Daniel Silverfarb, *Britain's Informal Empire in the Middle East: A Case Study of Iraq, 1929–1941* (New York: Oxford University Press, 1986); Michael A. Longoria, *A Historical View of Air Policing Doctrine: Lessons from the British Experience between the Wars, 1919–1939*, Thesis, School of Advanced Airpower Studies, Air University, Maxwell Air Force Base, Alabama, 1992; and Major General Charles Gwynn, *Imperial Policing* (London: Macmillan, 1936).

46 Treaty between the British Government and 'Abdul 'Aziz bin 'Abdur Rahman bin Faisal Al-Saud, Ruler of Najd, El Hasa, Qatif, Etc, Dated 26 December 1915, in Lt. Col. Sir Arnold T. Wilson, *Loyalties Mesopotamia: A Personal and Historical Record* (London: Oxford University Press, 1930), p. 314.

47 For more on Iran in World War I, see Touraj Atabaki, *Iran and the First World War: Battleground of the Great Powers* (London: I.B. Tauris, 2006); Mohammad Gholi Majd, *Persia in World War I and Its Conquest by Great Britain* (Lanham, Maryland: University Press of America, 2003); and William J. Olson, *Anglo-Iranian Relations During World War I* (Abingdon, Oxford, UK: Routledge, 1984).

48 Sykes, *A History of Persia*, 3rd edn.

49 For more on these conferences, see Fromkin, *The Peace to End All Peace*; and Aaron S. Klieman, *Foundations of British Policy in the Arab World: The Cairo Conference of 1921* (Baltimore: Johns Hopkins University Press, 1970).

50 Fromkin, *The Peace to End All Peace*, chapter 51.

51 J. Morton Howell, Clipping from Egyptian Gazette, "Hussein in Exile: Story of How He Left Akaba; on Board the *Delhi*," in Transmission # 654, Legation of the United States of America, Cairo Egypt, to Secretary of State, Washington, 24 June 1925, in Ibrahim al-Rashid, ed., *Documents on the History of Saudi Arabia*, Vol. 1 (Salisbury, North Carolina: Documentary Publications, 1976), pp. 228–33.

52 Mohammad Gholi Majd, *The Great Famine and Genocide in Persia, 1917–1919* (Lanham, Maryland: University Press of America, 2003).

53 Fromkin, *The Peace to End All Peace*, chapter 52.

54 Sykes, *A History of Persia*, 3rd edn., p. 521.

55 Fromkin, *The Peace to End All Peace*.

56 R.G., Memorandum on Current Events in Persia, 11 December 1905, in David Gillard, ed., *British Documents on Foreign Affairs: Reports and Papers from the Foreign Office Confidential Print. Part I: From the Mid-Nineteenth Century to the First World War. Series B: The Near and Middle East, 1856–1914*, Vol. 13: Persia, Britain, and Russia (Frederick, Maryland: University Publications of America, 1984), p. 310.

57 For a discussion of Reza Shah's rise in the Cossacks and his participation in the coup, see Steven R. Ward, *Immortal: A Military History of Iran and its Armed Forces* (Washington: Georgetown University Press, 2009), chapter 25; and Fromkin, *The Peace to End All Peace*, p. 460.

58 For the reforms of Reza Shah, see Cyrus Ghani, *Iran and the Rise of Reza Shah: From Qajar Collapse to Pahlavi Power* (London: I.B. Tauris, 2001); and Touraj Atabaki and Erik J. Zurcher, *Men of Order: Authoritarian Modernization under Ataturk and Reza Shah* (London: I.B. Tauris, 2004).

59 Shuster, *The Strangling of Persia: A Personal Narrative*, p. 3.

60 Arthur C. Millspaugh, *The American Task in Persia* (New York: Century Company, 1925), p. 18.

61 Arthur C. Millspaugh, *Americans in Persia* (Washington, D.C.: Brookings Institution, 1946).

62 John L. Caldwell, American Minister to Persia, Dispatch 15 November 1918, in Majd, *Persia in World War I and Its Conquest by Great Britain*, p. 279.

63 Information on the oil industry from this section from Daniel Yergin, *The Prize: The Epic Quest for Oil, Money, and Power* (New York: Free Press, 1991).

Chapter 2

1 See Daniel Marston, "A Force Transformed: the Indian Army and the Second World War," in Daniel P. Marston and Chandar Sundaram, eds., *A Military History of India and South Asia: From the East India Company to the Nuclear Era* (Westport CT: Praeger Security International, 2007).

2 Winston Churchill, *Their Finest Hour: The Second World War*, 2 vols. (Boston: Houghton Mifflin Company, 1949), p. 417.

3 William E. Mulligan, "Air Raid! A Sequel," *Saudi Aramco World*, July/August 1976, pp. 2–3.

4 Peter Calvocoressi and Guy Wint, *Total War: The Story of World War II* (New York: Pantheon Books, 1972), p. 154.

5 J. M. A. Gwyer and J. R. M. Butler, eds., *Grand Strategy III, Part II*, Vol. III, *History of the Second World War: United Kingdom Military Series* (London: Her Majesty's Stationery Office, 1964), Appendix IX, Timeline for War, pp. 695–710.

6 Matthew Elliott, *Independent Iraq: The Monarchy and British Influence, 1941–1958* (London: Tauris Academic Studies, 1996), p. 8.

7 Ibid., p. 12.

8 For a detailed look at the military campaign, see Robert Lyman, *Iraq 1941: The Battles for Basra, Habbaniya, Fallujah and Baghdad* (Colchester, Essex, UK: Osprey Publishing, 2006). For the role of the British-Indian maritime services in the Red Sea and Persian Gulf campaigns in World War II, see D.J.E. Collins, *The Royal Indian Navy, 1939–1945* (Combined Inter-services Historical Section, part of the Official History of the Indian Armed Forces in the Second World War 1939–45), chapters 4–5.

9 Stephen Hemsley Longrigg, *Iraq, 1900–1950: A Political, Social, and Economic History* (London: Oxford University Press, 1953), pp. 276–87.

10 Commodore, Senior Naval Officer Persian Gulf Report No. 15/587 [Dispatch], – Persian Gulf War Diary – April 1941, 27 May 1941, in Anita Burdett, ed., *Persian Gulf and Red Sea Naval Reports*, Vol. 15 (London: Archive Editions, 1993), p. 8. (Hereafter cited as *PGRSNR*).

11 Ibid.

12 Enclosure to Senior Naval Officer Persian Gulf's No. 20/587, 20 June 1941, War Diary, *PGRSNR*, Vol. 15, p.16.

13 Gwyer and Butler, *Grand Strategy III, Part I*, Vol. III, p. 185.

14 Ibid., p. 188.

15 Ibid.

16 Senior Naval Officer Persian Gulf Dispatch #196/655, Operation "Countenance," 26 September 1941, *PGRSNR*, Vol. 15, p. 59.

17 Gwyer and Butler, *Grand Strategy III, Part I*, p. 188.

18 Senior Naval Officer Persian Gulf Dispatch #196/655, Operation "Countenance," 26 September 1941, *PGRSNR*, Vol. 15, p. 59.

19 Gwyer and Butler, *Grand Strategy III, Part I*, p. 188.

20 Joel Sayre, *Persian Gulf Command* (New York: Random House, 1945), p. 139.

21 Gwyer and Butler, *Grand Strategy III, Part I*, p. 191.

22 Alexei Vassiliev, *The History of Saudi Arabia* (London: Saqi Books, 1998), p. 321.

23 Winston Churchill, *The Second World War: The Hinge of Fate*, Vol. 4 (Boston: Houghton Mifflin Company, 1950), p. 563.

24 Daniel Silverfarb, *The Twilight of British Ascendancy in the Middle East: A Case Study of Iraq, 1941–1950* (New York: St. Martin's Press, 1994). See also Air Chief Marshal Sir David Lee, *Flight from the Middle East: A History of the Royal Air Force in the Arabian Peninsula and Adjacent Territories 1945–1972* (London: Ministry of Defence: Air Historical Branch (RAF), Her Majesty's Stationery Office, 1980).

25 East Indies Station Commander in Chief, Persian Gulf 11 June 1940 to 31 December 1940, *PGRSNR*, Vol. 14, p. 679.

26 Vice Admiral Cheatham, Record of Naval Activities on East Indies Station from Beginning of War up to End of February 1940, from Commander in Chief, East Indies Station. No. 361/E.I. 3203, 20 March 1940, *PGRSNR*, Vol. 14, pp. 607–12.

27 Aden Naval Officer in Charge War Diary, June 1940, *PGRSNR*, Vol. 14, pp. 634–5.

28 War Diary – May 1944, *PGRSNR*, Vol. 15, p. 262.

29 Enclosure to Persian Gulf Letter No. 566/P.G. 587, 13 October 1944, *PGRSNR*, Vol. 15, p. 299.

30 Aden Naval Officer in Charge War Diary, June 1940, *PGRSNR*, Vol. 14, pp. 634–5.

31 Ibid.

32 Ibid.

33 For a discussion of the alternate Murmansk route, see Samuel Eliot Morison, *History of the United States Naval Operations in World War II* (Boston: Little, Brown & Company, 1984), Vol. I, p. 158, and John Bunker, *Heroes in Dungarees:*

The Story of the American Merchant Marine in World War II (Annapolis MD: Naval Institute Press, 1995), chapter 6.

34 Statistics on the Persian Gulf Command drawn from T.H. Vail Motter, *United States Army in World War II – the Middle East Theater: The Persian Corridor and Aid to Russia*, Kent Roberts Greenfield ed. (Washington, D.C.: Office of the Chief of Military History, Department of the Army, 1952).

35 Instructions to U.S. military members serving in the Persian Gulf in World War II found in *U.S. Army Instructions for American Servicemen in Iraq During World War II*, foreword by John Nagl (Chicago: University of Chicago Press, 2007 reprint).

36 For a description of Bandar Shahpur, see Robert Carse, *The Long Haul: The U.S. Merchant Service in World War II* (New York: W.W. Norton, 1965), pp. 186–7.

37 For more on railway construction in Iran, see Don DeNevi and Bob Hall, *United States Military Railway Service: America's Soldier-Railroaders in World War II* (Toronto: Stoddart Publishing Co., 1992), chapter 3.

38 Motter, p 125.

39 Ibid., p. 135.

40 Ibid., p. 291.

41 Vassiliev, p. 327.

42 For more on the Liberty ships in the Gulf, see Bunker, *Heroes in Dungarees: The Story of the American Merchant Marine in World War II,* chapter 19, "The Indian Ocean War." For more on the life of personnel assigned to the Persian Gulf Command, see Sayre, *Persian Gulf Command*, p. 99.

43 Persian Gulf Senior Naval Officer, No. 1228/849 30 October 1943, Report of U-Boat Activity in the Gulf of Oman, *PGRSNR,* Vol. 15, p. 240. See Carse and Bunker for reports of merchant shipping in the India Ocean sunk by German and Japanese submarines.

44 Winston Churchill, *The Second World War: The Grand Alliance*, Vol. 3 (Boston: Houghton Mifflin Company, 1950), p. 673.

45 William Roger Louis, *Imperialism at Bay: The United States and the Decolonization of the British Empire, 1941–1945* (New York: Oxford University Press, 1978), p. 8.

46 Ibid., p. 4.

47 In the chapter devoted to the Argentia meeting and the drafting of the Atlantic Charter, for example, a well-respected author of a 2005 biography of Churchill makes no mention of any Anglo-American discord with respect to India or Britain's other colonies. See Martin Gilbert, *Churchill and America* (New York: Free Press, 2005), chapter 23.

48 Elliott Roosevelt, *As He Saw It* (New York: Duell, Sloan and Pearce, 1946), p. 39.

49 Louis, *Imperialism at Bay: The United States and the Decolonization of the British Empire, 1941–1945*, pp.8–9.

50 Ibid., p. 7.

51 Bruce Robellet Kuniholm, *The Origins of the Cold War in the Near East: Great Power Conflict and Diplomacy in Iran, Turkey, and Greece* (Princeton, New Jersey: Princeton University Press, 1980), p. 142. See also *FRUS 1941*, Vol. III, pp. 406–7, 431–3, 435, 446.

52 Ibid.

53 Ibid., p. 144.

54 *FRUS 1942*, Vol. 4, p. 268. Shahanshah of Iran Mohammed Reza Shah Pahlavi to President Franklin Roosevelt, 31 January 1942.

55 *FRUS 1942*, Vol. 4, pp. 238–62; also see Arthur C. Millspaugh, *Americans in Persia* (Washington, D.C.: Brookings Institution, 1946).

56 *FRUS 1941*, Vol. III, p. 446, 2 September 1941, President Roosevelt to the Shah of Iran.

57 *FRUS 1943*, Vol. 4, p. 331. John D. Jernegan, U.S. State Department Division of Near Eastern Affairs, 23 January 1943.

58 *FRUS 1943*, Vol. IV, p. 289. FDR to Lend-Lease Administrator Stettinius, Extension of Lend-Lease aid to Iran, 10 March 1942.

59 For more on Lend-Lease in the Middle East, see A. Jacqueline Swansinger, "*The Magic Carpet: Lend-Lease in the Middle East, 1940–44*," (PhD Dissertation, Rutgers University, 1988).

60 Sayre, *Persian Gulf Command*, p. 101.

61 Motter, p. 461.

62 U.S. diplomats in Iran in World War II grew increasingly concerned about heavy-handed British practices and tactics in Iran in World War II. See Sec State Hull to Ambassador in the U.K. Winant, 11 Dec 1942, *FRUS 1942*, Vol. 4, p. 215.

63 Roosevelt, *As He Saw It*, p. 192.

64 *FRUS 1943*, Vol. 4, p. 419. Patrick Hurley, Letter from the Personal Representative of President Roosevelt in Iran to the U.S. Secretary of State, 21 December 1943.

65 Avalon Project at Yale Law School, *Tehran Conference: Declaration of the Three Powers Regarding Iran, December 1, 1943*. Internet, Accessed 15 June 2006; www.yale.edu/lawweb/avalon/wwii/tehran.htm

66 *FRUS 1943*, Vol. 4, p. 414. U.S. Minister in Iran Louis G. Dreyfus to Secretary of State, 10 December 1943, concerning the signing of the American-British-Soviet declaration regarding Iran and the initial Iranian reaction to its publication.

67 Kuniholm, *The Origins of the Cold War in the Near East*, p. 143.

68 RG 334, Box 1, File "General Administrative Files 1942." C.S. Ridley, Preliminary Report [from Iran], to Chief of Operations and Plans Division, General Staff, War Department, 10 December 1942, USNA2.

69 *FRUS 1942*, Vol. 4, p. 222. Iranian Minister Schayesteh to U.S. Secretary of State Hull, Request for Assistance by the United States in Security for the Iranian Government American Advisers (Military, Financial, Police, Gendarmerie, Etc), 6 January 1942.

70 C.S. Ridley, 10 December 1942.

71 RG 334, Box 2, File "General Administrative Files 1944." C.S. Ridley, Memorandum Detailing Milestones Accomplished by Military Mission to Iranian Army, 21 March 1944, USNA2.

72 RG 334, Box 2, File "General Administrative File 1944." Major General C.S. Ridley, quoting a 26 October 1944 State Department telegram, in Ridley, Letter from U.S. Military Mission with Iranian Army to U.S. War Department General Staff, Concerning Proposed Termination of Mission, 8 November 1944, USNA2.

73 Ibid.

74 Ibid.

75 RG 334, Accession 73-A-3353, Treaties in Force – Iran, Agreement between the Government of the United States of America and the Imperial Government of Iran relating to a Military Mission. U.N. Treaty Series 1949, Number 176, Signed at Tehran 27 November 1943, USNA2.

76 RG 334, Accession 73-A-3353, Treaties in Force – Iran, Agreement between the Government of the United States of America and the Government of Iran relating to a military mission to Iran, U.N. Treaty Series 1947, Number 171, p. 304.

77 RG 334, Box 2, File "General Administrative Files 1944." Arthur Smith, Letter from British General Headquarters, Persia Iraq Force Baghdad, to Major General C.S. Ridley, Commanding Officer U.S. Military Mission with the Iranian Army, 18 March 1944, USNA2.

78 RG 334, Box 2, File "General Administrative Files 1944." C.S. Ridley to Chief War Plans Division, War Department, Concerning British Proposals on Iranian Army, 27 March 1944, Emphasis added, USNA2.

79 Millspaugh, *Americans in Persia*, p. 36.
80 RG 334, Box 1, File "General Administrative Files 1942." C.S. Ridley, Preliminary Report [from Iran], to Chief of Operations and Plans Division, General Staff, War Department, 10 December 1942, USNA2.
81 RG 334, Box 2, File "General Administrative Files 1945." C.S. Ridley to U.S. Ambassador to Tehran, Mr. Wallace Murray, 9 September 1945, USNA2.
82 Susan B. Carter, ed., *Historical Statistics of the United States* (Cambridge: Cambridge University Press, 2006), p. 4–298.
83 Bert Fish, Remarks of Mr. St. John Philby at Jedda; Dispatch No. 2019 from Legation of the United States of America to the Secretary of State, Washington, D.C., 9 March 1940, in Ibrahim al-Rashid, *Documents on the History of Saudi Arabia* (Salisbury, North Carolina: Documentary Publications, 1976), Vol. 4, pp. 32–3. (Hereafter cited as al-Rashid, *Documents*).
84 Ibid.
85 Ibid.
86 U.S. Navy theorist Alfred Thayer Mahan reportedly coined the term "Middle East" in the first years of the twentieth century. See Bernard Lewis, *The Shaping of the Modern Middle East* (New York: Oxford University Press, 1994), p. 3.
87 Ibid.
88 Max W. Thornburg, Memorandum from Vice President of Bahrein Petroleum Company, Ltd., "Notes on Certain Aspects of the Current Situation in the Middle East (Arab Countries)." Place of Origin: New York, New York, 30 October 1940, in al-Rashid, *Documents,* Vol. 4, pp. 50–60.
89 Fish, Remarks of Mr. St. John Philby at Jedda; Dispatch No. 2019, 9 March 1940.
90 Ibid.
91 Ibid.
92 K.S. Twitchell, Letter to Honorable Wallace Murray, Chief of Division of near East, Department of State, Washington D.C., 14 May 1941, in al-Rashid, *Documents*, Vol. 4, pp. 69–72.
93 Bert Fish, Strictly Confidential Message No. 1726, from Legation of the United States of America, Alexandria Egypt, to the Honorable Secretary of State, Washington. Subject: King of Saudi Arabia and Bank Misr in Egypt, 11 July 1939, in al-Rashid, *Documents,* Vol. 4, pp. 22–4.
94 Robert Lacey, *The Kingdom* (New York: Harcourt Brace Jovanovich, 1981), p. 258.
95 Raymond H. Hare, Enclosure No. 1 to Despatch No. 110, 12 September 1941. General Situation in Saudi Arabia, in al-Rashid, *Documents,* Vol. 4, pp. 82–6.
96 Ibid.
97 Ibid.
98 Alexander Kirk, No. 3 Saudi Arabian Series Dispatch from Legation of the United States of America Cairo, to Secretary of State Washington, D.C. Subject: Attitude of King Ibn Saud in Respect of the War, 12 January 1942, in al-Rashid, *Documents,* Vol. 4, p. 106.
99 *U.S. Department of State Background Note: Saudi Arabia.* Internet, Accessed 27 June 2006; http://www.state.gov/r/pa/ei/bgn/3584.htm
100 Thornburg.
101 George D. Henderson, American Consul Dhahran Letter to Secretary of State, Marked Secret, 2 March 1948, in K.E. Evans, ed., *U.S. Records on Saudi Affairs 1945–1959,* Vol. I (London: Archive Editions and University Publications of America, 1997), p. 622. (Hereafter cited as Evans, *U.S. Records on Saudi Affairs*).
102 Senator Warren R. Austin, Letter to Secretary of State Cordell Hull, Endorsing Recommendations from Mr. K.D. Twitchell Concerning the Importance of

a Strong, Independent Saudi Arabia, 15 May 1941, in al-Rashid, *Documents,* Vol. 4, pp. 73–6.

103 Unless otherwise noted, this section based upon Anthony Cave Brown, *Oil, God, and Gold: The Story of Aramco and the Saudi Kings* (Boston: Houghton-Mifflin Co., 1999), chapters 4–5.

104 Ibid., p. 87.

105 See U.S. diplomatic correspondence: "Extension of Lend-Lease assistance to Saudi Arabia; organization of a program for financial and military aid," in *FRUS 1943*, Vol. 4, pp. 854–920.

106 Brown, p. 113.

107 Colonel Carl F. Tischbein, U.S. Army, Chief, Supply Control Branch, Service, Supply and Procurement Division, to Mr. Fred Awalt, near Eastern Affairs Division, Department of State, Concerning Saudi Requests for Remaining Lend-Lease Equipment Deliveries, 10 July 1947, in K.E. Evans, *U.S. Records on Saudi Affairs,* Vol. I, pp. 455–71.

108 Ibid.

109 Ibid.

110 Memorandum from British Embassy Washington to U.S. State Department, 17 April 1945, in Evans, *U.S. Records on Saudi Affairs,* Vol. I, p. 324.

111 Mansour, Letter from Saudi Minister of Defense to the Minister Plenipotentiary of the United States of America in Jeddah, Number 730/1, 6 May 1945, in Evans, *U.S. Records on Saudi Affairs,* Vol. I, p. 48.

112 Tischbein.

113 Wallace Murray, Memorandum from State Department Division of Near East Affairs to Mr. Dean Acheson, 15 February 1945, in Evans, *U.S. Records on Saudi Affairs,* Vol. I, p. 303.

114 William A. Eddy, Telegram Mfd-412 from U.S. Minister in Jeddah to Secretary of State in Washington, Top Secret, Concerning Possible Saudi Requests to Americans and British on Improvements at Jeddah and Dhahran Airfields, 17 April 1945, in Evans, *U.S. Records on Saudi Affairs 1945–1959,* Vol. I, p. 43.

115 Acting Secretary of State, Top Secret Letter from U.S. Acting Assistant Secretary of State to Honorable Henry L. Stimson, Secretary of War, Concerning War Department Requests to Establish an Air Route from Cairo through Saudi Arabia to India, and the Need to Construct an Airfield in Dhahran to Support Such a Route, 25 April 1945, in Evans, *U.S. Records on Saudi Affairs 1945–1959,* Vol. I, p. 87.

116 H. Freeman Matthews, Top Secret Letter from Acting Chairman of the State-War-Navy Coordinating Committee to the U.S. Secretary of State. Subject: Acquisition and Construction of a United States Military Airfield at Dhahran, Saudi Arabia, 25 April 1945, in Evans, *U.S. Records on Saudi Affairs,* Vol. I, p. 88.

117 L.B. Grafetey-Smith, Secret Letter from British Legation Jeddah to Sheikh Yusuf Yassin, Acting Minister for Foreign Affairs, Mecca, Recommending Approval of U.S. Proposal to Construct an Airfield at Dhahran, 6 May 1945, in Evans, *U.S. Records on Saudi Affairs,* Vol. I, p. 102.

118 William A. Eddy, Top Secret Telegram to Secretary of State #Ncb-1077, Concerning Saudi Approval for U.S. To Construct Airfield at Dhahran, 13 May 1945, in Evans, *U.S. Records on Saudi Affairs,* Vol. I, p. 106.

119 Eddy, 13 May 1945.

120 Department of State, Secret Telegram from U.S. Department of State Washington to American Legation Jeddah, Concerning U.S. War Department's Diminished Need for Air Base at Dhahran, 19 June 1949, in Evans, *U.S. Records on Saudi Affairs,* Vol. I, p. 132.

121 U.S. State Department Memorandum of Conversation. Subject: Preparation for

Congressional Hearing on Dhahran Airport. Participants: Mr. Henderson, NEA. . . . Major General George G. Richards, Chief, Budget Division, War Department General Staff, 7 November 1945, in Evans, *U.S. Records on Saudi Affairs,* Vol. I, p. 200.

122 *FRUS, 1961–1963*, Vol. XVII, Near East, p. 51. W.J. Stoessel, Memorandum from the Department of State Executive Secretary (Battle) to the President's Special Assistant (Dungan), 21 March 1961.

123 William A. Eddy, Eddy's Account of Ibn Saud-Roosevelt Meeting on 14 February 1945, in Evans, *U.S. Records on Saudi Affairs,* Vol. 2, p. 255.

124 Unless otherwise noted, this account based on Eddy, "Eddy's Account of Ibn Saud-Roosevelt Meeting," cited directly above.

125 Aaron David Miller, *Search for Security: Saudi Arabian Oil and American Foreign Policy, 1939–1949* (Chapel Hill: University of North Carolina Press, 1980), p. xii.

126 *FRUS 1945,* Vol. VIII, p. 11. William Eddy, Memorandum of Conversation between the King of Saudi Arabia and President Roosevelt, Aboard the USS *Quincy*, 14 February 1945.

127 Eddy, Eddy's Account of Ibn Saud-Roosevelt Meeting on 14 February 1945, in Evans, *U.S. Records on Saudi Affairs*, Vol.2, p. 255.

128 Ibid.

129 William A. Eddy, Letter U.S. Minister in Jeddah to Secretary of State in Washington, Concerning King Abdul Aziz's Decision to Decline a U.S. Army Military Mission in Saudi Arabia, in Evans, *U.S. Records on Saudi Affairs,* Vol. I, p. 54.

130 *FRUS 1945*, Vol. VIII, p. 11. William Eddy, The Meeting of the President and the King, 14 February 1945.

Chapter 3

1 *FRUS 1947*, Vol. 5, p. 576. The American Paper, Top Secret, Memorandum Prepared in the Department of State, Washington, undated (*FRUS 1948*, Vol. VI, p. 39 states that the Anglo-American meetings that preceded this paper took place in October 1947).

2 *FRUS 1943*, Vol. 4, pp. 331–6. John D. Jernegan, American Policy in Iran: Memorandum from the Division of near Eastern Affairs, 23 January 1943.

3 U.S. and British reaction to the Soviets' refusal to withdraw from Azerbaijan is detailed in the section "Concern of the United States for Effecting Fulfillment of Assurances Contained in the Declaration Regarding Iran of 1 December 1943," *FRUS 1945*, Vol. VIII, pp. 359–528.

4 *FRUS 1945*, Vol. VIII, p. 412. Murray, "Events in the Evacuation of Tehran Area by Allied Forces," Ambassador in Iran to Secretary of State, 19 September 1945.

5 Unless otherwise noted, information in the next four paragraphs on the Anglo-American response to the Soviet delay in withdrawal from Azerbaijan, is from Bruce Robellet Kuniholm, *The Origins of the Cold War in the Near East: Great Power Conflict and Diplomacy in Iran, Turkey, and Greece* (Princeton, New Jersey: Princeton University Press, 1980), pp. 272–321.

6 *FRUS 1945*, Vol. VIII, p. 417. Ambassador in Iran telegram 891.00/9-2545 to Secretary of State, 25 September 1945.

7 Kuniholm, pp. 309–19.

8 Persian Gulf Residency Report, Number 97/4/48, 9 December 1948, in Robert L. Jarman, ed., *Political Diaries of the Arab World: The Persian Gulf,* Vol. 21: 1947–68 (London: Archive Editions, 1998), p. 110. (Hereafter cited as *PDAWPG*).

9 Captain R. H. Courage, Royal Navy, "HMS *Flamingo*'s Report of Proceedings

to Senior Navy Officer Persian Gulf," 9 December 1950, in Anita Burdett, ed., *Persian Gulf and Red Sea Naval Reports,* Vol. 15 (London: Archive Editions, 1993), p. 450. (Hereafter cited as *PGRSNR*).

10 Persian Gulf Resident's Report, Bahrain, 29 October 1948, in *PDAWPG,* Vol. 21, p. 106.

11 Phillip Darby, *British Defence Policy East of Suez, 1947–1968* (London: Oxford University Press, 1973), pp. 10–31.

12 Ibid., p. 330.

13 Admiralty Paper O.D. 1057/53, Entitled "Frigates in the Persian Gulf," July 1953, in *PGRSNR*, Vol. 15, p. 634.

14 Ibid.

15 The British had four combatant ships in the Gulf in November 1937, representative of their pre-war presence there. See Allan Polland, Report of Proceedings – November 1937, from Captain, Royal Navy, Senior Naval Officer Persian Gulf on Board HMS *Shorham* at Bahrain; to Commander in Chief, East Indies Station, in *PGRSNR,* Vol. 14, p. 317.

16 Unsigned 1954 Paper, "Draft: Naval Strength in the Persian Gulf," in *PGRSNR,* Vol. 15, p. 820.

17 R. Walters, Office of the Senior Naval Officer Persian Gulf. No. P.G. 205/5, to the Commander in Chief, East Indies. Subject: Rams Incident 13th – 14th July 1952, 23 March 1952, in *PGRSNR,* Vol. 15, p. 552.

18 N.W. Fisher, Office of the Senior Naval Officer Persian Gulf. No. P.G. 205/3, to the Commander in Chief, East Indies. "The Assassination of the Ruler of Kalba," 23 March 1952, in *PGRSNR,* Vol. 15, p. 545.

19 Report of HMS *Wren* 5 June 1952, No. 55/127, in *PGRSNR,* Vol. 15, p. 585.

20 Ibid.

21 Periodic Report from Political Officer, Trucial Coast, Sharjah, "Trucial Coast News Report No. 5," 24th February to 8th March 1947, in *PDAWPG,* Vol. 21, p. 13.

22 Behcet Kemal Yesilbursa, *The Baghdad Pact: Anglo-American Defence Policies in the Middle East, 1950–1959* (London: Frank Cass, 2005), p. 3.

23 William Roger Louis, *The British Empire in the Middle East 1945–1951: Arab Nationalism, the United States, and Postwar Imperialism* (Oxford: Clarendon Press, 1984), p. 8.

24 Top Secret State Department Analysis Paper: "Political and Strategic Importance of United States Oil Operations in Saudi Arabia." Mr. Funkhouser and Mr. Wilkins Listed as Addressees, with No Signature Block., 8 March 1950, in K.E. Evans, ed., *U.S. Records on Saudi Affairs 1945–1959,* Vol. 3 (London: Archive Editions and University Publications of America, 1997), p. 2. (Hereafter cited as Evans, *U.S. Records on Saudi Affairs*).

25 T.H. Vail Motter, *United States Army in World War II – the Middle East Theater: The Persian Corridor and Aid to Russia,* Kent Roberts Greenfield, ed. (Washington, D.C.: Office of the Chief of Military History, Department of the Army, 1952), p. xi.

26 See "U.S. Documents Concerning Interest of the United States in Continuation of the American Military Missions to the Iranian Army and the Iranian Gendarmerie," *FRUS 1945*, Vol. VIII, pp. 526–38.

27 RG 334, Accession 73-A-3353, United Nations Treaty Series 1947 Number 171 p. 304. Agreement between the Government of the United States of America and the Government of Iran relating to a military mission to Iran, in "Treaties in Force – Iran," USNA2.

28 "Iran Renews Plan to Buy U.S. Arms," New York *Times*, p. 15, and "Iran Backs U.S. Aid after Hot Debate: Parliament Agrees to Accept $10,000,000 Credit for Arms, 79–6, with 10 Abstaining," New York *Times*, p. 8.

29 RG 334, Accession 73-A-3353, File 205–6 P27–2 67, "Treaties in Force: Saudi Arabia, United States Strike Command," Pamphlet, 30 November 1967, USNA2.

30 For book-length treatments of the subject of oil in the evolution of U.S.-Saudi relations, see Rachel Bronson, *Thicker Than Oil: America's Uneasy Partnership with Saudi Arabia* (New York: Oxford University Press, 2006); Aaron David Miller, *Search for Security: Saudi Arabian Oil and American Foreign Policy, 1939–1949* (Chapel Hill: University of North Carolina Press, 1980); and Robert Vitalis, *America's Kingdom: Mythmaking on the Saudi Oil Frontier* (Stanford: Stanford University Press, 2007).

31 William A. Eddy, Secret Letter from Legation of the United States of America Jeddah to the Secretary of State, 13 May 1945, in Evans, *U.S. Records on Saudi Affairs*, Vol. I, p. 107.

32 Ibid.

33 William A. Eddy, Top Secret Telegram to Secretary of State #NCB-1077, Concerning Saudi Approval for U.S. To Construct Airfield at Dhahran, 13 May 1945, in Evans, *U.S. Records on Saudi Affairs*, Vol. I, p. 106.

34 William A. Eddy, Telegram DCG 1055 from U.S. Minister in Jeddah to Secretary of State in Washington, Secret, Concerning King Abdul Aziz's Decision to Decline a U.S. Army Military Mission in Saudi Arabia, 4 July 1945, in Evans, *U.S. Records on Saudi Affairs 1945–1959*, Vol. I, p. 53.

35 J. Rives Childs, Enclosure 4 to Dispatch No. 113, 29 April 1948, Concerning Saudi Demands for U.S. Aid, in Evans, *U.S. Records on Saudi Affairs*, Vol. I, p. 584. For a detailed discussion of U.S. military strategy in the region, including the "northern tier" of states – Iraq, Iran, Pakistan and Turkey – see Michael J. Cohen, *Strategy and Politics in the Middle East 1954–1960: Defending the Northern Tier* (London: Frank Cass, 2005), and B.H. Ried, "The Northern Tier and the Baghdad Pact," in J.W. Young, ed., *The Foreign Policy of Churchill's Peacetime Administration, 1951– 1955* (Leicester: Leicester University Press, 1988).

36 J. Rives Childs, Dispatch No. 113 from Jeddah to Secretary of State, Detailing Visit of Major General Robert Harper, and Discussions of Military Aid to Saudi Arabia, 29 April 1948, in Evans, *U.S. Records on Saudi Affairs*, Vol. I, pp. 561–97.

37 J. Rives (American Minister to Jeddah) Childs, Enclosure 3 to Dispatch No. 113, from Jiddah, Saudi Arabia. Transcript of Meeting between His Majesty King Abdul Aziz Ibn Saud; the Honorable J. Rives Childs, American Minister; Major General Robert Harper, Commanding General Air Transport Command; and Others, 22 April 1948, in Evans, *U.S. Records on Saudi Affairs*, Vol. I, p. 577.

38 Ibid.

39 J. Rives Childs, 29 April 1948, Saudi Demands for U.S. Aid. Memorandum of Conversation between Shaikh Yusuf Yassin, Deputy Minister of Foreign Affairs; Honorable J. Rives Childs, American Minister to Jeddah; Major General Robert Harper, Commanding General, ATC; Mr. Richard Sanger, Division of Near Eastern Affairs, Department of State; Colonel R.J. O'Keefe, Commanding Officer, Dhahran; Colonel Harry R. Snyder, Dhahran Air Base; and Others, 29 April 1948, in Evans, *U.S. Records on Saudi Affairs*, Vol. I, p. 585.

40 U.S. State Department Briefing Session with the Joint U.S. Military Group for Saudi Arabia, 9 July 1951, in Evans, *U.S. Records on Saudi Affairs*, Vol. 3, pp. 340–2.

41 RG 334, Accession 73-A-3353, File 205-06 P27–2, U.N. Treaty Series Vol. 141, p. 67, 1955, Number 1906, Exchange of Notes constituting an agreement between the United States of America and Saudi Arabia relating to Mutual Defense Assistance, Jidda and Mecca, 18 June 1951. Letter from the American Ambassador to the Saudi Arabian Minister of Defense and Aviation, in Strikecom Treaties in Force Saudi Arabia – 30 November 1967, USNA2.

42 Memorandum from British Embassy Washington to U.S. State Department, 17 April 1945, in Evans, *U.S. Records on Saudi Affairs*, Vol. I, p. 324.

43 Dean Acheson, State Department cable a-1262, 27 January 1951, in Evans, *U.S. Records on Saudi Affairs*, Vol. 3, p. 63; Caffery, Department of State Telegram # 928, from American Embassy Cairo to Secretary of State, 9 March 1951, in Evans, *U.S. Records on Saudi Affairs*, Vol. 2, p. 245.

44 U.S. State Department Briefing Session with the Joint U.S. Military Group for Saudi Arabia, 9 July 1951, in Evans, *U.S. Records on Saudi Affairs*, Vol. 3, pp. 340–42.

45 Dean Acheson, State Department Cable a-1262, 27 January 1951, in Evans, *U.S. Records on Saudi Affairs*, Vol. 3, p. 63.

46 Martin, Report of Proceedings of HMS *Wren*, 1 September 1948, in *PGRSNR*, Vol. 15, pp. 423–9.

47 Ibid.

48 Ibid.

49 See Michael Palmer, *On Course to Desert Storm* (Washington: Naval Historical Center, 1992), and Michael A. Palmer, *Guardians of the Gulf: A History of America's Expanding Role in the Persian Gulf, 1833–1992* (New York: Free Press, 1992).

50 Palmer, *Guardians of the Gulf*, p. 45.

51 Ibid., p. 46.

52 Ibid.

53 Captain Senior Naval Officer Persian Gulf, Report of Senior Naval Officer Persian Gulf # P.G. 235/100/49, 4 November 1949, in *PGRSNR*, Vol. 15, p. 435.

54 Trucial Coast News Report for the Period from the 9th to the 23rd July, 1948, in *PDAWPG*, Vol. 21, p. 174.

55 Louis, *The British Empire in the Middle East 1945–1951: Arab Nationalism, the United States, and Postwar Imperialism*, p. 8.

56 James Bill and William Roger Louis, eds., *Musaddiq, Iranian Nationalism, and Oil* (Austin: University of Texas Press, 1988), p. 4.

57 Ibid.

58 Ibid., p. 6.

59 George McGhee, *Envoy to the Middle World: Adventures in Diplomacy* (New York: Harper and Row, 1983), p. 320.

60 Ibid.

61 Ibid.

62 Ibid., p. 326.

63 *PGRSNR*, 25 Sept 1951, Vol. 15, p. 486.

64 RN Commodore A. Wallis, citing an earlier discussion, in Report of Proceedings, Senior Naval Officer Persian Gulf, 20 November 1951, to the Commander-in-Chief East Indies Station, in *PGRSNR*, Vol. 15, p. 500.

65 Louis, *The British Empire in the Middle East 1945–1951: Arab Nationalism, the United States, and Postwar Imperialism*, p. 8.

66 Maziar Behrooz, "The 1953 Coup in Iran and the Legacy of the Tudeh," in Malcolm Byrne and Mark J. Gasiorowski, eds., *Mohammad Mosaddeq and the 1953 Coup in Iran* (Syracuse, N.Y.: Syracuse University Press, 2004), p. 102.

67 See Stephen Kinzer, *All the Shah's Men: An American Coup and the Roots of Middle East Terror* (New York: Wiley, 2003); and Bill and Louis, p. 8.

68 Madeleine K. Albright, Secretary of State's Remarks before the American-Iranian Council March 17, 2000, Washington, D.C. Released by the Office of the Spokesman U.S. Department of State.

69 McGhee, chapter 27.

70 Bill and Louis, *Musaddiq, Iranian Nationalism, and Oil*, p. 8.

71 See *FRUS 1952–54*, Vol X, pp. 1–1077.

72 Information on Egypt in the succeeding four paragraphs drawn from M.W. Daly,

ed., *The Cambridge History of Egypt* (Cambridge: Cambridge University Press, 1998), pp. 236–338.

73 Ibid., p. 299.

74 Ibid., p. 304.

75 Air Chief Marshal Sir David Lee, *Flight from the Middle East: A History of the Royal Air Force in the Arabian Peninsula and Adjacent Territories 1945–1972* (London: Ministry of Defence: Air Historical Branch, RAF, Her Majesty's Stationery Office, 1980), p. 92.

76 Memorandum by the Secretary of State for Foreign Affairs Anthony Eden, 16 February 1953, Public Records Office CAB 129/59, in Anthony Gorst and Lewis Johnman, *The Suez Crisis* (London: Routledge, 1997), Document 31.33.32, p. 31.

77 The Suez Canal Base Agreement, 19 October 1954, Parliamentary Papers, Cmd. 9586, 1954, in Gorst and Johnman, *The Suez Crisis*, Document 31.33.33, p. 33.

78 For book-length treatments of the Suez Crisis, see Donald Cameron Watt, ed., *Documents on the Suez Crisis, 26 July to 6 November 1956* (London: Royal Institute of International Affairs, 1957); Anthony Eden, *The Suez Crisis of 1956* (Boston: Beacon Press, 1968); William Roger Louis and Roger Owen, eds., *Suez 1956: The Crisis and Its Consequences* (New York: Clarendon Press, 1989); and Simon Smith, ed., *Reassessing Suez 1956: New Perspectives on the Crisis and Its Aftermath* (Burlington VT: Ashgate, 2008).

79 Egyptian President Gamal Abdul Nasser, quoted in "Canal Warning by Col Nasser: No Clearing before Troops Leave," London *Times*, 10 November 1956, p. 5.

80 Robert Jones, "Major Oil Crisis around the Corner?" London *Times*, 6 June 1967, p. 25.

81 For a detailed study of the Eisenhower Doctrine, see Ray Takeyh, *The Origins of the Eisenhower Doctrine: The U.S., Britain and Nasser's Egypt, 1953–57* (London: Macmillan Press, 2000); and Salim Yaqub, *Containing Arab Nationalism: the Eisenhower Doctrine and the Middle East* (Chapel Hill: University of North Carolina Press, 2004).

82 Dwight D. Eisenhower, *The Eisenhower Doctrine on the Middle East, a Message to Congress, January 5, 1957*. Internet, Fordham University, Accessed 24 July 2006; www.fordham.edu/halsall/mod/1957eisenhowerdoctrine.html

83 Ibid.

84 Ibid.

85 Daniel Silverfarb, *Britain's Informal Empire in the Middle East: A Case Study of Iraq, 1929–1941* (New York: Oxford University Press, 1986), p. 30.

86 Lee, *Flight from the Middle East*, p. 92.

87 Ibid., p. 103.

88 Ibid., p. 102.

89 Dwight D. Eisenhower, *Waging Peace 1956–1961* (Garden City, New York: Doubleday & Company, 1965), p. 269.

90 Lee, *Flight from the Middle East*, p. 148.

91 See Stephen Blackwell, *British Military Intervention and the Struggle for Jordan: King Hussein, Nasser, and the Middle East Crisis, 1955–1958* (New York: Routledge, 2008).

92 Eisenhower, *Waging Peace 1956–1961*, p. 274.

93 Ibid., p. 273.

94 Unsigned 1954 Paper, in *PGRSNR*, Vol. 15, p. 820.

95 Ibid.

96 George Lenczowski, *American Presidents and the Middle East* (Durham: Duke University Press, 1990), p. 58.

97 Ibid.

98 Lee, *Flight from the Middle East*, pp. 110–20.

99 George Rentz, The Areas in Dispute between Saudi Arabia and Abu Dhabi, 11 July 1954, in Evans, *U.S. Records on Saudi Affairs*, Vol. 2, p. 472.

100 Mr. Byroade, Top Secret Memorandum from Assistant Secretary of State to the Secretary of State. Subject Prince Faisal's Call, in Evans, *U.S. Records on Saudi Affairs*, Vol. 2, p. 489.

101 Lee, *Flight from the Middle East*, p. 121.

102 Yesilbursa, *The Baghdad Pact: Anglo-American Defence Policies in the Middle East, 1950–1959*, p. 3.

103 Ibid., pp. 5–6.

104 Sir Anthony Eden, Secretary of State for Foreign Affairs, 18 June 1952. Public Records Office CAB 129/53, in Gorst and Johnman, eds., *The Suez Crisis*, p. 28, Document 21.23.21.

105 Hare, Department of State Telegram No. 268 from Jiddah to Secretary of State, 23 October 1952, in Evans, *U.S. Records on Saudi Affairs*, Vol. 3, p. 484.

106 Ibid.

107 "Pact of Mutual Cooperation between Iraq and Turkey (the Baghdad Pact), Baghdad, 24 February 1955," in Yesilbursa, *The Baghdad Pact: Anglo-American Defence Policies in the Middle East, 1950–1959*, p. 225.

108 Ibid., pp. 221–2.

Chapter 4

1 Substantial academic attention has recently been devoted toward Britain's military retrenchment in the 1960s. See Saki Dockrill, *Britain's Retreat from East of Suez: The Choice between Europe and the World?* (Basingstoke: Palgrave-Macmillan, 2002); Simon Smith, *Britain's Revival and Fall in the Gulf: Kuwait, Bahrain, Qatar, and the Trucial States, 1950–1971* (London: RoutledgeCurzon, 2004); and Tore T. Petersen, *The Decline of the Anglo-American Middle East 1961–1969: A Willing Retreat* (Brighton, England: Sussex Academic Press, 2006).

2 Rosemarie Said Zahlan, *The Making of the Modern Gulf States* (London: Unwin Hyman, 1989), p. 40.

3 *United Arab Emirates Census*. Internet, United Arab Emirates Ministry of Economy, Accessed 12 December 2005; http://www.tedad.ae/english/about_census/background.html

4 Nicholas Herbert, "Trucial States Ignore Withdrawal Symptoms," London *Times*, 9 February 1968, p. 8.

5 RG 334, Box 1, File "General Administrative Files 1942." C.S. Ridley, Preliminary Report [from Iran], to Chief of Operations and Plans Division, General Staff, War Department, 10 December 1942, USNA2.

6 U.S. State Department Briefing Session with the Joint U.S. Military Group for Saudi Arabia, 9 July 1951, in K.E. Evans, ed., *U.S. Records on Saudi Affairs 1945–1959*, Vol. 3 (London: Archive Editions and University Publications of America, 1997), pp. 340–42. (Hereafter cited as Evans, *U.S. Records on Saudi Affairs*).

7 Gerhard K. Heilig, *World Population Prospects: Analyzing the 1996 UN Population Projections*. Internet, International Institute for Applied Systems Analysis; http://www.iiasa.ac.at/Research/LUC/Papers/gkh1/chap1.htm Accessed 19 March 2009.

8 Ibid.

9 *Library of Congress Country Study: Kuwait* (Washington, D.C.: Library of Congress); and Heilig, *World Population Prospects: Analyzing the 1996 UN Population Projections.*

10 *Library of Congress Country Study: Qatar – Education and Welfare* (Washington, D.C.: Library of Congress).

11 FO 371, Box 148896, File No. BA 1011/1, George Middleton, Cover Page to Annual Review of Events in Persian Gulf for 1959, 27 January 1960, BNA.
12 Ibid.
13 For a history of the drive to create a representative government in Kuwait, see Rosemarie Said Zahlan, *The Making of the Modern Gulf States: Kuwait, Bahrain, Qatar, the United Arab Emirates, and Oman* (London: Unwin Hyman, 1989), pp. 24–45; Miriam Joyce, *Kuwait 1945–1996: An Anglo-American Perspective* (London: Frank Cass, 1998), chapter 3; Simon Smith, *Kuwait, 1950–1965: Britain, the Al-Sabah, and Oil* (London: British Academy, 2000); and Simon Smith, *Britain's Revival and Fall in the Gulf: Kuwait, Bahrain, Qatar, and the Trucial States, 1950–1971* (London: RoutledgeCurzon, 2004).
14 For an authoritative treatment of Iraq in the 1950s and 1960s, including its relationship with Kuwait and Jordan, see Hanna Batatu, *The Old Social Classes and the Revolutionary Movements of Iraq* (London: Saqi Books, 1978).
15 Waldermar J. Gallman, *Iraq under General Nuri: My Recollections of Nuri Al-Said, 1954–1958* (Baltimore: Johns Hopkins University Press, 1964), pp. 147–50.
16 A.S. Halford, H.M. Political Agent in Kuwait Annual Review for 1958, 6 January 1959, in Robert L. Jarman, ed., *Political Diaries of the Arab World: The Persian Gulf*, Vol. 21: 1947–58 (London: Archive Editions, 1998), pp. 297–321. (Hereafter cited as *PDAWPG*).
17 Persian Gulf Monthly Summary for the Period January 5 to February 1, 1959, from British Residency, Bahrain, 2 February 1959, in *PDAWPG*, Vol. 22, p. 3.
18 Halford, Annual Review for 1958, 6 January 1959, in *PDAWPG*, Vol. 21, pp. 297–321.
19 B.A.B. Burrows, Letter to Selwyn Lloyd, Foreign Office, from British Residency in Bahrain, 25 October 1958, in *PDAWPG*, Vol. 21, p. 269.
20 Joyce, *Kuwait 1945–1996: An Anglo-American Perspective,* chapter 3.
21 See *Persian Gulf Gazette*, January 1972 (London: Archive Editions), p. 7.
22 "New Agreement with Kuwait," London *Times*, 20 June 1961, p. 12.
23 Ibid.
24 Mustafa M. Alani, *Operation Vantage: British Military Intervention in Kuwait 1961* (Surrey, England: LAAM, 1990), p. 34.
25 For details on Iraq's claim to Kuwait, see David Finnie, *Shifting Lines in the Sand: Kuwait's Elusive Frontier with Iraq* (Cambridge, Mass.: Harvard University Press, 1992).
26 Alani, *Operation Vantage*, p. 80.
27 See Ian Speller, *"Naval Diplomacy: Operation Vantage, 1961,"* in Ian Speller, ed, *The Royal Navy and Maritime Power in the Twentieth Century* (London: Frank Cass, 2005); and Alani, *Operation Vantage*.
28 Air Chief Marshal Sir David Lee, *Flight from the Middle East: A History of the Royal Air Force in the Arabian Peninsula and Adjacent Territories 1945–1972* (London: Ministry of Defence: Air Historical Branch (RAF), Her Majesty's Stationery Office, 1980), p. 31.
29 Alani, *Operation Vantage*, p. 40.
30 DEFE 11, Box 545, File No. D/COS/48/C/2 Vol. 17, File "Planning for Kuwait and the Arabian Peninsula," p. 22. J.K. Watkins, Secretary, Chiefs of Staff Committee (Top Secret), 10 October 1963, BNA.
31 See Cmnd. 124, in Alani, *Operation Vantage*, p. 40.
32 Lee, *Flight from the Middle East*, p. 166.
33 Alani, *Operation Vantage*, p. 34.
34 "General Kassim Claims Kuwait Inseparable Part of Iraq," London *Times*, 26 June 1961, p. 10.
35 For a detailed treatment of the response to the Iraqi provocations of 1961, see

chapter 4, Joyce, *Kuwait 1946–1996*. For the Arab reaction, see Elie Podeh, "Suez in Reverse": The Arab Response to the Iraqi Bid for Kuwait, 1961–63," *Diplomacy and Statecraft*, March 2003, Vol. 14, Issue 1, pp. 103–30.

36 "Mr. Macmillan Explains British Purpose: Withdrawal as Soon as Danger Removed," London *Times*, 4 July 1961, p. 10.

37 Lee, *Flight from the Middle East*, p. 170.

38 "Naval Plans Changed by Kuwait Crisis: Ships Reported on Way from Far East, Commando Carrier Could Be in Area in 48 Hours," London *Times*, 30 June 1961, p. 12.

39 Lee, *Flight from the Middle East*, pp. 170–71.

40 Alani, *Operation Vantage*, p. 248.

41 "Mr. Macmillan Explains British Purpose: Withdrawal as Soon as Danger Removed," London *Times*, 4 Jul 1961, p. 10.

42 DEFE 11, Box 545, File No. D/COS/48/C/2 Vol. 17, File "Planning for Kuwait and the Arabian Peninsula," Top Secret. J.K. Watkins, Secretary, Chiefs of Staff Committee, Overseas Forces: Libya, Middle East, and Hong Kong, Study, 10 October 1963, BNA.

43 Ibid.

44 Ibid.

45 Lee, *Flight from the Middle East*, p. 171.

46 Ibid.

47 Ibid., pp. 258–60.

48 DEFE 11, Box 545, File No. D/COS/48/C/2 Vol. 17, File "Planning for Kuwait and the Arabian Peninsula," Top Secret. J.K. Watkins, Secretary, Chiefs of Staff Committee, Overseas Forces: Libya, Middle East, and Hong Kong, Study, 10 October 1963, BNA.

49 Ibid.

50 Ibid.

51 R.J. Gavin, *Aden under British Rule, 1839–1967* (New York: Harper and Row, 1975), p. 344.

52 Lee, *Flight from the Middle East*, p.186.

53 Ibid., p. 171.

54 Statement on Defense, HMSO, Cmnd 1963, Feb 1963, in Karl Pieragostini, *Britain, Aden and South Arabia: Abandoning Empire* (New York: St. Martin's Press, 1991), p. 48.

55 This section draws upon a 2004 study of British involvement in the Yemeni civil war: Clive Jones, *Britain and the Yemen Civil War, 1962–1965: Ministers, Mercenaries and Mandarins: Foreign Policy and the Limits of Covert Action* (Brighton, Sussex: Academic Press, 2004).

56 Ibid., p. 21.

57 Ahmed Noman Kassim Almadhagi, *Yemen and the United States: A Study of a Small Power and the Super-State Relationship 1962–1994* (London: Tauris Academic Studies, 1996), p. 28.

58 Jones, *Britain and the Yemen Civil War*, p. 26.

59 For a full treatment of British policies in Aden and the Protectorates during this time, see Spencer Mawby, *British Policy in Aden and the Protectorates 1955–67: Last Outpost of a Middle East Empire* (London: Routledge, 2005).

60 Jones, *Britain and the Yemen Civil War*.

61 RG 59, Box 1619, 1967–69, File Name: "DEF-Defense Affairs SAUD." American Embassy Jidda Telegram to Secretary of State, Repeating USMTM Dhahran Ch01160 May 1967 Sent Action, CINCSTRIKE/MEAFSA, USNA2.

62 *FRUS 1961–1963*, Vol. XVII, p. 675. Memorandum on the Substance of Discussion at a Department of State–Joint Chiefs of Staff Meeting, 16 August 1963.

63 *FRUS 1961–1963,* Vol. XVII, p. 577. Memorandum from Secretary of State Rusk to President Kennedy, 12 June 1963.

64 David Ransom, in Almadhagi, *Yemen and the United States: A Study of a Small Power and the Super-State Relationship 1962–1994,* p. 56.

65 J.B. Kelly, *Arabia, the Gulf, and the West: A Critical View of the Arabs and Their Oil Policy* (New York: Basic Books, 1980), pp. 18–20.

66 CAB 148/1; Trend to Prime Minister, 12/11/63, PREM 11/4930, Defence Committee on the Cabinet 30th Mtg, 3 July 1964, cited in Dockrill, *Britain's Retreat from East of Suez,* p. 34.

67 Pieragostini, *Britain, Aden and South Arabia: Abandoning Empire,* p. 106.

68 Ibid.

69 Ibid., p. 192.

70 RG 218, Box 20, File "091 – Oman," Accession 92–0028, "Insurgency in Oman". Background Paper for the Director, Plans and Policy Directorate, 6 August 1973, USNA2.

71 For a detailed presentation of the debate over the CVA01 and the F-111 aircraft, and how the debate over these weapons systems paralleled Britain's larger debate over its role in the Indian Ocean and the Pacific, see Dockrill, *Britain's Retreat from East of Suez.*

72 Ibid., p. 76.

73 For a detailed discussion of the decision-making surrounding the British withdrawal from Aden, see Mawby, *British Policy in Aden and the Protectorates 1955–1967*; Gavin, *Aden under British Rule, 1839–1967*; and Pieragostini, *Britain, Aden and South Arabia: Abandoning Empire.*

74 Lee, *Flight from the Middle East,* p. 228.

75 *FRUS 1964–1968,* Vol. XXI, p. 162. Memorandum of Conversation: U.S.-British Staff Talks. Principal Participants. U.K. – Sir Roger Allen, Deputy Undersecretary, Foreign Office; Frank Brenchley, Head, Arabian Department; U.S. – Ambassador Hare, 4 February 1966.

76 Ibid.

77 Ibid.

78 See David Reynolds, *Britannia Overruled: British Policy and World Power in the 20th Century* (London: Longman, 1991); and Jeffrey Pickering, *Britain's Withdrawal from East of Suez: The Politics of Retrenchment* (London: Macmillan, 1998).

79 Dockrill, *Britain's Retreat from East of Suez,* p. 126.

80 *FRUS 1964–1968,* Vol. XXI, p. 189. Dean Rusk, Airgram from the Department of State to the Consulate General in Saudi Arabia, Bahraini Views on Gulf Security and Request for Help from U.S., 22 November 1966.

81 RG 218, Box 42, Accession 92–0015. George W. Ball signing for Dean Rusk, Memorandum for the President, Subject: Visit of Prime Minister Wilson, 13 December 1965, USNA2.

82 Ibid.

83 *FRUS 1964–1968,* Vol. XXI, Document 41, p. 99. Memorandum from President's Deputy Special Assistant for National Security Affairs (Komer) to the President's Special Assistant for National Security Affairs (Bundy) and Francis Bator of the National Security Council Staff, 26 January 1966.

84 *FRUS 1964–1968,* Vol. XXI, p. 99. Memorandum from President's Deputy Special Assistant for National Security Affairs (Komer) to President's Special Assistant for National Security Affairs (Bundy), 26 January 1966.

85 *FRUS 1964–1968,* Vol. XXI, p. 175. Paper Prepared by Joint Chiefs of Staff, "U.S. Military Interests in South Arabia and Yemen," 9 August, 1966.

86 *FRUS 1964–1968,* Vol. XXI, p. 97. Memorandum from Secretary of Defense McNamara to the Secretary of the Air Force (Zuckert), Request for Approval of Facilities to Support Contingency Planning, 14 June 1965.

87 *FRUS 1964–1968*, Vol. XXI, p. 176. Joint Chiefs of Staff, "U.S. Military Interests in South Arabia and Yemen," 9 August 1966.
88 *FRUS 1964–1968*, Vol. XXI, p. 175. Joint Chiefs of Staff, "U.S. Military Interests in South Arabia and Yemen," 9 August 1966.
89 *FRUS 1964–1968*, Vol. XXI, p. 85. Airgram from the Department of State to the Embassy in the United Kingdom, Indian Ocean Talks with British, 21 January 1964.
90 *FRUS 1964–1968*, Vol. XXI, p. 84. Airgram from the Department of State to the Embassy in the United Kingdom, Indian Ocean Talks with British, 21 January 1964.
91 *FRUS 1964–1968*, Vol. XXI, p. 97. Memorandum from Secretary of Defense McNamara to the Secretary of the Air Force (Zuckert), Request for Approval of Facilities to Support Contingency Planning, 14 June 1965.
92 *FRUS 1964–1968*, Vol. XXI, p. 108. Memorandum from Secretary of Defense McNamara to the Secretary of the Navy (Ignatius), "Austere Support Facility on Diego Garcia," 27 October 1967.
93 RG 218, Box 27, Accession #92–0015, File "091 – Iran (Visits)," "Information Book General Bahram Aryana," Secret, "U.S. Policy toward Iran." Brief Book, 14 October 1966, USNA2.
94 RG 218, Box 27, Accession #92–0015, File "091 – Iran (Visits)," Discussion Paper – "Combined/Joint Planning with Iran." "Visit of General Abdol Hossein Hedjazi, Chief, Supreme Commander's Staff, Iran December 1964-January 1965, Lt. General Goodpaster." Top Secret, 16 December 1964, USNA2.
95 RG 218, Box 27, Accession #92–0015, File "091 – Iran (Visits)," "Visit of General Abdol Hossein Hedjazi, Chief, Supreme Commander's Staff, Iran December 1964-January 1965, Lt. General Goodpaster." Top Secret, 19 December 1964, USNA2.
96 Ibid.
97 RG 330, Box 34, Accession 70-A-3717, File No. 334, File "Iran: MAAG 28 July 1965 I-10732/65," p. 1–2. Major General U.S. Army Eckhart, A Report of Stewardship by Chief, ARMISH MAAG FY 1963–66, Teheran Iran, Report, 29 July 1965, USNA2.
98 RG 334, Box 2, Accession 71-A-0366, File No. 205–6, File "Publications Background," U.S. Strike Command Pamphlet: Administrative and Logistic Support MAAG/Missions MEAFSA Area – Iran, 1 August 1966, USNA2.
99 Ibid.
100 Despite the closure of the U.S. base at Dhahran, U.S. military aircraft would continue to enjoy Saudi overflight and landing privileges there, averaging 520 per year in 1969. *FRUS 1969–1976*, Vol. XXIV, p. 408.
101 Henry Precht, "The Iranian Revolution: An Oral History with Henry Precht, then State Department Desk Officer," in *Oral History Project* (Arlington, Virginia: Association for Diplomatic Studies and Training).
102 "U.S. Sells Saudis Trucks for Army: Personnel Carriers Included in $100 Million Deal," New York *Times*, 28 September 1966, p. 12.
103 RG 334, Accession 73-A-3353, File Name: "205–6 P27–2 67," Letter from the American Ambassador to the Saudi Arabian Deputy Minister of Foreign Affairs, Jidda, 9 December 1963, reprinted in Treaties in Force: Saudi Arabia, United States Strike Command Pamphlet, 30 November 1967, USNA2.
104 Saudi Arabian Deputy Minister of Foreign Affairs to the American Ambassador, 24 May 1965, 5 June 1965, in Ibid.
105 *FRUS, 1961–1963*, Vol. XVII, p. 51. W.J. Stoessel, Memorandum from the Department of State Executive Secretary (Battle) to the President's Special Assistant (Dungan), 21 March 1961.
106 RG 330, Box 32, Accession 71-A-4546, File 353, "Middle East Jan-July 1967,"

Townsend Hoopes to Honorable Lester Wolff, U.S. House of Representatives, Concerning Training of Military Personnel from the Arab Nations, 28 July 1967, USNA2.

107 RG 330, Box 32, Accession 71-A-4546, File 353 "Middle East Jan-July 1967," P.C. Hough, Memorandum for the Chief, Foreign Military Training Division, Directorate of Operations and Others, Concerning Information on Foreign Military Trainees from the Middle East, 21 July 1967, USNA2.

108 Middle East Force Command History, 1973, 30 April 1974, in Michael A. Palmer, *On Course to Desert Storm: The United States Navy and the Persian Gulf* (Washington: Naval Historical Center, 1992).

109 Naval Historical Center, *Descriptions of* USS *Duxbury Bay*, USS *Greenwich Bay*, USS *Valcour*, USS *LaSalle*. Internet, Accessed December 2006; http://www.history.navy.mil/photos/sh-usn/usnsh-d/avp38.htm

110 RG 330, Box 27, Accession 70A6648, File "Bahrain 000.1 1966," Kitchen to Hoopes, 14 April 1966, USNA2.

111 RG 334, Accession 70-A-0360, Paul P. Blackburn, Letter of Instructions, Joint Task Force *Bonny Date*, 28 September 1967, USNA2.

112 RG 334, Box 4, Accession 69-A-5621, File No. 201–46, "CINCSTRIKE Joint Task Force Standing Operating Procedure (1965)," 28 March 1964, USNA2.

113 RG 334, Accession 69-A-5621, Box 5, File No. M525–3 (65), U.S. Strike Command Joint Task Force Headquarters SOP, 31 August 1965, USNA2.

114 RG 334, Accession 70-A-0360, Paul P. Blackburn, Letter of Instructions, Joint Task Force *Bonny Date*, 28 September 1967, USNA2.

115 See discussion in Maxwell Orme Johnson, *The Military as an Instrument of U.S. Policy in Southwest Asia: The Rapid Deployment Joint Task Force, 1979–1982* (Boulder, Colorado: Westview Press, 1983), pp. 59–60.

116 RG 218, Box 27, Accession #92–0015, File "091 – Iran (Visits)," Paper – "Stock-piling/Prepositioning Military Supplies in the Middle East," USNA2.

117 Ibid.

118 RG 59, Box 1620, File "DEF – Defense Affairs SAUD-US 1/1/67," Eilts, American Embassy Jidda Telegram to Department of State, Account of Meeting between U.S. Ambassador and Dr. Rashad Pharaon, 30 June 1967 1115Z, USNA2.

119 "Arab Threat to Stop Oil," London *Times*, 6 June 1967, p. 10.

120 Nicholas Herbert, "Arabs to Continue Oil Embargo: Total Shutdown Rejected," London *Times*, 19 June 1967.

121 RG 59, Box 1620, File "DEF – Defense Affairs SAUD-US 1/1/67," Eilts, American Embassy Jidda Telegram to Department of State, Subject: U.S. Navy Bunkering in Jidda. Account of Meeting between U.S. Ambassador and Dr. Rashad Pharaon, 01 July 1967 1140Z, USNA2.

122 Herbert.

123 "Exports by Russia, Arab Disunity Ease Threat by Nasser to Use Oil as Hostage," *Wall Street Journal*, 16 June 1967, p. 6.

124 "Mideast Oil Production May Resume Soon in Key Nations of Saudi Arabia and Libya," *Wall Street Journal*, 9 June 1967, p. 7.

125 Robert Jones, "Major Oil Crisis around the Corner?" London *Times*, 6 June 1967, p. 25.

126 RG 330, Accession 71-A-4546, Box 32, File No. 353 "Middle East Jan-July 1967," Harry H. Schwartz to Honorable Richard L. Ottinger, U.S. House of Representatives, 8 October 1967, USNA2.

127 FCO 8, Box 3, File B 1/2 "Persian Gulf: Political Affairs Annual Reviews 1967," p. 2. Annual Report from Mr. Crawford, British Political Resident in Bahrain, to Mr. Brown, Foreign Secretary, 17 January 1968, BNA.

128 Ibid.
129 Ibid.

Chapter 5

1 "Excerpts from Text of TV Speech by Chancellor of the Exchequer Roy Jenkins," New York *Times*, 17 January 1968, p. 14.
2 For a detailed study of the British military and political situation in Aden in the late 1950s and 1960s including its withdrawal, see Spencer Mawby, *British Policy in Aden and the Protectorates 1955–67: Last Outpost of a Middle East Empire* (London: Routledge, 2005).
3 For a discussion of this period, see Simon Smith, *Britain's Revival and Fall in the Gulf: Kuwait, Bahrain, Qatar, and the Trucial States, 1950–1971* (London: RoutledgeCurzon, 2004); Saki Dockrill, *Britain's Retreat from East of Suez: The Choice between Europe and the World?* (Basingstoke: Palgrave-Macmillan, 2002); and J.B. Kelly, *Arabia, the Gulf, and the West: A Critical View of the Arabs and Their Oil Policy* (New York: Basic Books, 1980).
4 For a review of Britain's economic plight in this period, see chapter 13, "The Overstrained Economy 1961–67," in T.O. Lloyd, ed., *Empire to Welfare State: English History 1906–1985* (Oxford: Oxford University Press, 1986).
5 Smith, p. 72.
6 Kelly, p. 49.
7 *FRUS 1964–1968,* Vol. XXI, p. 264. Memorandum of Conversation. Washington, 25 January 1968. Subject: U.S.–Bahrain Relations.
8 *FRUS 1964–1968*, Vol. XXI, p. 189. Airgram from the Department of State to the Consulate General in Saudi Arabia, 22 November 1966, Bahraini Views on Gulf Security and Request for Help from U.S.
9 DEFE 11/549, File C/COS/48/C/2, Vol 30. MP Tapsell to the PM Wilson, 11 January 1968, BNA.
10 DEFE 11/549, Box 340 5872. Foreign Office Confidential Telegram to Bahrain Residency, Undated; appears to be January 1968, BNA.
11 DEFE 11, Box 549, File No. C/COS/48/C/2, Vol. 30, File: "Planning for Kuwait and the Arabian Peninsula," Chief of the Defence Staff Gulf Offset Order, 31 January 1968 1510Z, BNA.
12 Persian Gulf: Political Resident Bahrain's Annual Review for 1961, 4 January 1962, in Robert L. Jarman, ed., *Political Diaries of the Arab World: The Persian Gulf*, Vol. 23: 1961–62 (London: Archive Editions, 1998), p. 29. (Hereafter cited as *Political Diaries of the Arab World*).
13 See the published document collection Richard Schofield, ed., *Arabian Boundary Disputes* (London: Archive Editions, 1992).
14 *FRUS 1964–1968*, Vol. XXI, p. 282. Information Memorandum from the Assistant Secretary of State for Near East (Battle) to Secretary of State Rusk, 22 February 1968. Subject: Outlook in the Persian Gulf States.
15 FCO 8, Box 37, File No. B 3/7, Discussions with United States Officials at the Foreign Office on Wednesday 27 March 1968, BNA.
16 FCO 8, Box 37, File No. B 3/7, D.J. McCarthy for Mr. Roberts in Advance of His Visit to the United States for Talks with Eugene Rostow, Foreign Office Briefing Papers, 9 May 1968, BNA.
17 FCO 8, Box 37, File No. B 3/7, Discussions with United States Officials at the Foreign Office on Wednesday 27 March 1968, BNA.
18 FCO 8 Box 37, File No. B 3/7, Discussions with United States Officials at the Foreign Office, 27 March 1968. FCO 8, Box 36, File No. 3/7, Weir, Letter from Arabian Desk Officer to Mr. Brenchley, Foreign Office, 5 March 1968, BNA.

19 FCO 8, Box 37, File No. B 3/7, p. 102. Discussions with United States Officials at the Foreign Office on Wednesday 27 March 1968, BNA.
20 Ibid.
21 FCO 8, Box 36, File No. 3/7. Weir, Letter from Arabian Desk Officer to Mr. Brenchley, Foreign Office, 5 March 1968, BNA.
22 FCO 8, Box 37, File No. B 3/7, p. 102. Discussions with United States Officials at the Foreign Office on Wednesday 27 March 1968, BNA.
23 Ibid., p. 102.
24 Ibid., p. 103.
25 FCO 8, Box 36, File No. 3/7. Weir, Letter from Arabian Desk Officer to Mr. Brenchley, Foreign Office, 5 March 1968, BNA.
26 FCO 8, Box 37, File No. B 3/7, p. 102. Discussions with United States Officials at the Foreign Office on Wednesday 27 March 1968, BNA.
27 Ibid.
28 FCO 8, Box 34, File B3/7. Anglo-American Talks on the Middle East in the U.S. State Department, 13 September 1968, BNA.
29 Ibid.
30 FCO 8, Box 37, File No. B 3/7, p. 103. Opinion of Sir Stewart Crawford, Political Resident Persian Gulf, as recorded in Discussions with United States Officials at the Foreign Office on Wednesday 27 March 1968, BNA.
31 FCO 8, Box 34, File B3/7. Anglo-American Talks on the Middle East in the U.S. State Department, 13 September 1968, BNA.
32 FCO 8, Box 37, File No. B 3/7, p. 103. Mr. K.C.G. Man, former UK ambassador to Jeddah, in Discussions with United States Officials at the Foreign Office on Wednesday 27 March 1968, BNA.
33 Mr. K.C.G. Man, ibid., p. 104.
34 FCO 8, Box 37, File B37. Discussions with U.S. Officials at the Foreign Office 27 March 1968. Mr. H. Phillips, Ambassador Designate to Jeddah.
35 FCO 8, Box 1570, File No. NB 1/2. M.S. Weir, British Political Resident to the Secretary of State for Foreign and Commonwealth Affairs, Prepared by the Deputy Political Resident to the Persian Gulf, 1970 Annual Report, 1 January 1971, BNA. (Hereafter cited as Political Resident Persian Gulf 1970 Annual Report).
36 FO 371, Box 148896, File No. BA 1011/1. George Middleton, Cover Page to Annual Review of Events in Persian Gulf for 1959, from British Resident in Bahrain to Foreign Office, 27 January 1960, BNA.
37 FCO 8, Box 37, File No. B 3/7, p. 103. Discussions with United States Officials at the Foreign Office on Wednesday 27 March 1968, BNA.
38 Sir Denis Wright, U.K. Ambassador to Iran, ibid.
39 FCO 8, Box 34, File B3/7. Anglo-American Talks on the Middle East in the U.S. State Department, 13 September 1968. Sir Denis Allen, Foreign Office.
40 FCO 8, Box 37, File No. B 3/7. Letter from D.J. McCarthy, Foreign Office, to A.B. Urwick at British Embassy in Washington, "Information for the Americans on Gulf Affairs," 4 October 1968, BNA.
41 Ibid.
42 Political Resident Persian Gulf 1970 Annual Report, p. 2.
43 Ibid., p. 3.
44 Ibid.
45 For a detailed look at the Gulf islands issue, see Hooshang Amirahmadi, *Small Islands, Big Politics: The Tonbs and Abu Musa in the Persian Gulf* (Basingstoke, UK: Palgrave Macmillan, 1996); Kourosh Ahmadi, *Islands and International Politics in the Persian Gulf: Abu Musa and the Tunbs in Strategic Perspective* (London: Routledge, 2008); and Lawrence Potter and Gary Sick, eds., *Security in the Persian Gulf* (Basingtoke: Palgrave Macmillan, 2002), which includes the following essays:

Jalil Roshandel, "On the Persian Gulf Islands: An Iranian Perspective"; Hassan Al-Alkim, "The Islands Question: An Arabian Perspective"; and Richard Schofield, "Anything but Black and White: A Commentary on the Lower Gulf Islands Dispute."

46 1905 Memorandum on Current Events in Persia: British and Russian Loans to Persia & Gulf Islands Disputes, 11 December 1905, in David Gillard, ed., *British Documents on Foreign Affairs: Reports and Papers from the Foreign Office Confidential Print. Part I: From the Mid-Nineteenth Century to the First World War. Series B: The Near and Middle East, 1856–1914,* Vol. 13: Persia, Britain, and Russia (Frederick, Maryland: University Publications of America, 1984), p. 310.

47 FCO 8, Box 37, File No. B 3/7. Discussions with United States Officials at the Foreign Office on Wednesday 27 March 1968, Sir Denis Wright, HM Ambassador to Tehran, BNA.

48 FCO 8, Box 37, File B 3/7, p. 7. Foreign Office Briefing Papers dated 9 May 1968, for Mr. Roberts in advance of his visit to the United States for talks with Eugene Rostow, BNA.

49 Ibid.

50 Ibid., pp. 6–7.

51 FCO 8, Box 37, File No. B 3/7, p. 105. Discussions with United States Officials at the Foreign Office on Wednesday 27 March 1968, BNA.

52 Prof. Clive Jones, University of Leeds, UK, "A Guiding Hand or Controlling Grasp? Britain, Intelligence and the War in Oman, 1970–76," Academic paper delivered at the Gulf and the Globe 2009 Conference, Annapolis, Maryland, January 2009.

53 Persian Gulf Political Resident's Report of 9 December 1948, in Robert L. Jarman, ed., *Political Diaries of the Arab World: The Persian Gulf,* Vol. 21: 1947–68 (London: Archive Editions, 1998), p. 113.

54 Thirty years have passed since the end of the Dhofar rebellion in the mid 1970s, and the opening of the British archives has stimulated new academic and literary interest in Oman. See John Peterson, *Oman's Insurgencies: The Sultanate's Struggle for Supremacy* (London: Saqi Books, 2007); Calvin Allen, *Oman under Qaboos: From Coup to Constitution, 1970–1996* (London: Frank Cass, 2000); Ian Gardiner, *In the Service of the Sultan: A First-hand Account of the Dhofar Insurgency* (South Yorkshire, U.K.:Pen & Sword Press, 2007); Major General Tony Jeapes,*SAS: Operation Storm: Secret War in the Middle East* (London Greenhill, 2005). For a look at Soviet involvement in both Yemen and Oman, see Aryeh Y. Yodfat, *The Soviet Union and the Arabian Peninsula* (London: Croom Helm, 1983), chapter. 1.

55 Persian Gulf Political Resident's Annual Review for 1970, p. 6, BNA.

56 Persian Gulf Political Resident's Annual Review for 1970, p. 5, BNA.

57 Ibid.

58 Jones.

59 *FRUS 1969–1976*, Vol. XXIV. Memorandum from Assistant Secretary of State for Near Eastern Affairs Joseph Sisco to Secretary of State Rogers, 29 July 1970, p. 275.

60 Paul Martin, "Saudi Arabia and Oman End Feud," London *Times*, 16 December 1971.

61 FCO 8, Box 1806, File NB2/5. Record of Anglo/United States Talks on the Persian Gulf and Arabian Peninsula Held in the State Department, 26 June 1972, BNA.

62 FCO 8, Box 34, File B3/7. Anglo-American Talks on the Middle East in the U.S. State Department, 13 September 1968, Sir Denis Allen, BNA.

63 FCO 8, Box 37, File No. B 3/7, p. 102. Discussions with United States Officials at the Foreign Office on Wednesday 27 March 1968, BNA. In some places, British

officers stayed with the Trucial Omani Scouts at least through 1972. See "British Cameleers Are Still Patrolling Villages and Dunes of Persian Gulf," New York *Times*, 9 July 1972, p. 16.

64 FCO 8, Box 37, File No. B 3/7, p. 102. Discussions with United States Officials at the Foreign Office on Wednesday 27 March 1968, BNA.

65 Ibid.

66 FCO 8, Box 78, File No. B 10/2. J.W.D. Gray, Force Levels in Bahrain and Sharjah; Letter from J.W.D. Gray to D.A.J. West (Ministry of Defence), 8 January 1968, BNA.

67 Weir, Persian Gulf Political Resident's Annual Review for 1970, p. 2, BNA.

68 FCO 8, Box 1618, File No. NB 10/6. William Luce, excerpts from his final report on the Persian Gulf. Disposal of Military Assets in Persian Gulf, Letters, 1971, BNA.

69 Persian Gulf Political Resident's Annual Review for 1970, BNA.

70 Ibid.

71 Ibid, p. 3.

72 Ibid.

73 FCO 8, Box 36, File No. B 3/7. Letter from U.S. Secretary of State Dean Rusk to British Secretary of State for Foreign Affairs George Brown, 6 January 1968, BNA.

74 *FRUS 1964–1968*, Vol. XXI, p. 256. Briefing Memorandum From Assistant Secretary of State for Near Eastern Affairs (Battle) to Rusk, 9 January 1968. British Plans to Accelerate Withdrawal of Military Presence from Persian Gulf: Your Meeting with Foreign Secretary Brown.

75 *FRUS 1964–1968*, Vol. XXI, p. 258. Briefing Memorandum From Assistant Secretary of State for Near Eastern Affairs (Battle) to Rusk, 9 January 1968. British Plans to Accelerate Withdrawal of Military Presence from Persian Gulf: Your Meeting with Foreign Secretary Brown.

76 Ibid.

77 *FRUS 1964–1968*, Vol. XXI, p. 282. Information Memorandum from the Assistant Secretary of State for Near Eastern and South Asian Affairs (Battle) to Secretary of State Rusk, 22 February 1968, Subject: Outlook in the Persian Gulf States.

78 *FRUS 1964–1968*, Vol. XXI, p. 292. Memorandum from Deputy Assistant Secretary of Defense for International Security Affairs (Schwartz) to Assistant Secretary of Defense for International Security Affairs (Warnke), 22 April 1968. "U.S. Arms Sales in the Persian Gulf."

79 Carl E. Bartch, U.S. State Department, Washington, 16 January 1968, in "U.S. Won't Fill Vacuum," New York *Times*, 17 January 1968.

80 *FRUS, 1964–1968*, Vol. XXI, p. 272. Record of Meeting. IRG/NEA [Interdepartmental Regional Group/Office of Near Eastern Affairs], Washington 1, February 1968. Interdepartmental Regional Group for Near East and South Asia. Record of IRG Meeting – February 1, 1968.

81 In Fiscal Year 1971, however, Congress would authorize on Diego Garcia the construction of a small communications facility, without the lengthened runway, petroleum storage facilities, and dredged harbor that Department of Defense officials sought. See "Diego Garcia Base Finally Approved," *Aviation Week and Space Technology*, 4 August 1975, p. 24.

82 *FRUS 1964–1968*, Vol. XXI, p. 297. Memorandum from Assistant Secretary of Defense for International Security Affairs (Warnke) to Secretary of Defense McNamara, 12 June 1968. The Soviets and the Persian Gulf.

83 *FRUS 1964–1968*, Vol. XXI, p. 304. Memorandum from Deputy Secretary of Defense (Nitze) to the Chairman of the Joint Chiefs of Staff (Wheeler), 2 August 1968. Persian Gulf Study.

84 *FRUS 1964–1968*, Vol. XXI, p. 292. Memorandum from Deputy Assistant Secretary of Defense for International Security Affairs (Schwartz) to Assistant Secretary of Defense for International Security Affairs (Warnke), 22 April 1968. Subject "U.S. Arms Sales in the Persian Gulf."

85 *FRUS* 1969–76, Vol. XXIV, pp. 256–64. Paper Prepared by the National Security Council Staff, 4 June 1970. Persian Gulf: Analytical Summary of IG Response to NSSM 66.

86 Hedrick Smith, "U.S. Putting Hope in New Asia Blocs: Rostow Thinks Void Left by British Will Be Filled," New York *Times*, 20 January 1968, p. 3.

87 FCO 8, Box 36, File No. 3/7. P. Dean, British Embassy Washington Telegram No. 725, 28 February 1968, BNA.

88 FCO 8, Box 37, File No. B 3/7, p. 106. Discussions with United States Officials at the Foreign Office on Wednesday 27 March 1968, Sir Denis Wright, BNA.

89 Ibid.

90 *FRUS 1964–1968*, Vol. XXI, p. 297. Memorandum from Assistant Secretary of Defense for International Security Affairs (Warnke) to Secretary of Defense McNamara, 12 June 1968. Subject: The Soviets and the Persian Gulf.

91 Ibid.

92 See Malcolm C. Peck, *Historical Dictionary of the Gulf Arab States* (Lanham MD: Scarecrow Press, 2008), p. xxix; and Howard Teicher and Gayle Radley Teicher, *Twin Pillars to Desert Storm: America's Flawed Vision in the Middle East from Nixon to Bush* (New York: William Morrow & Company, 1993).

93 U.S. Navy Historical Center, cited 9 October 2006; http://www.history.navy.mil/photos/sh-usn/usnsh-v/avp55.htm

94 FCO 8, Box 36, File No. B 3/7. A.B. Urwick, Letter from British Embassy to British Foreign Office, Arabian Desk Officer, 9 March 1968, BNA.

95 FCO 8, Box 935, File No. BN 3/304/2. Letter from A.B. Urwick (British Embassy Washington) to A.A. Acland (Arabian Department, London), "The Future of COMIDEASTFOR," 12 February 1969, BNA.

96 Ibid.

97 "U.S. Future Role in Persian Gulf," London *Times*, 23 April 1970.

98 FCO 8, Box 1304, File: "United States Interest in Persian Gulf." D.F. Murray, Letter to Mr. Breeze, House of Commons, Titled "MIDEASTFOR," 12 December 1970, BNA.

99 FCO 8, Box 34, File B3/7, p. 11. Anglo-American Talks on the Middle East in the U.S. State Department, 13 September 1968, BNA.

100 *FRUS 1969–1976*, Vol. XXIV, p. 357. Kissinger to Nixon, "U.S. Presence in Persian Gulf – Summary of Developments," 13 March 1972.

101 FCO 8, Box 1304, File: "United States Interest in Persian Gulf." R.A. Jones, Note for the Record, 31 December 1970, BNA.

102 RG 218, Accession 92–0028, Box 106, File: "B-7: Middle East – General." Walsh, Telegram, 18 November 1970 1105z from American Embassy Kuwait to Secstate Washington DC, Subject: "Future Arrangements for MIDEASTFOR," USNA2.

103 RG 218, Accession 92–0028, Box 106, File: "Folder 1 Labeled "B-7: Middle East – General." Thacher, Telegram from Amembassy Jidda to Secstate Washington DC, Subject: "Future Arrangements for COMIDEASTFOR," 18 November 1970 1235Z, USNA2.

104 Ibid.

105 FCO 8, Box 1304, File: "U.S. Interest in Persian Gulf." Recounting of U.S. Ambassador MacArthur's meeting with the Shah, December 1970, BNA.

106 Ibid.

107 For discussion of Iraq's tilt toward the Socialist bloc in the years following the 1958 revolution, see Peter Sluglett and Marion Farouk Sluglett, *Iraq Since*

1958: From Revolution to Dictatorship (London: I.B. Tauris, 2001), p. 50; and Tareq Y. Ismael and Jacqueline S. Ismael, *Politics and Government in the Middle East and North Africa* (Gainesville: University Press of Florida, 1991), p. 174.

108 "Parties Reappear in Iraq: Communists One of First Three," London *Times*, 10 February 1960, p. 8.

109 See Phebe Marr, *The Modern History of Iraq*, 2nd edn. (Boulder, Colorado: Westview Press, 2004), pp. 147–8.

110 Nicholas Herbert, "Visit to Gulf by Soviet Navy," London *Times*, 13 May 1968, p. 5. For a broader discussion of Soviet naval policy in the Indian Ocean region in the late 1960s and 1970s, see Geoffrey Jukes, "Soviet Naval Policy in the Indian Ocean," chapter 9 in Larry W. Bowman and Ian Clark, eds., *The Indian Ocean in Global Politics* (Boulder: Westview Press, 1981).

111 Herbert.

112 *FRUS 1947*, Vol. V, p. 575. The American Paper, October 1947.

113 *FRUS 1964–1968*, Vol. XXI, p. 277. Telegram From Department of State to U.S. Embassy in Southern Yemen, 3 February 1968, Signed Rusk.

114 *FRUS 1969–76*, Vol. I, Document 47. Henry Kissinger, Assistant for National Security Affairs, Subject File, Background Briefings, 18 December 1969.

115 "U.S. Future Role in Persian Gulf," London *Times*, 23 April 1970.

116 Peck, p. xxix.

117 Henry Stanhope, "More British Troops Abandon Bahrain," London *Times*, 17 August 1971, p. 8.

118 For a detailed history of the Trucial States and the UAE, see Rosemarine Said Zahlan's *The Origins of the United Arab Emirates: A Political and Social History of the Trucial States* (New York: St. Martin's Press, 1978).

119 Editorial, "Bahrain's Turn for Independence," London *Times*, 16 August 1971, p. 11.

120 "Anxiety in Trucial States on Future of the Rupee: Britain May Be Asked to Seek Guarantee from India," London *Times*, 21 February 1966. For a short discussion of the evolution of currencies in the Gulf during the twentieth century, see Peck, *Historical Dictionary of the Gulf Arab States*, 2nd edn., p. 69.

121 Weir, Persian Gulf Political Resident's Annual Review for 1970, BNA.

122 A.M. Rendel, "Two Flags Will Fly over Gulf Island under Shaikh's Accord with Iran," London *Times*, 30 November 1971, p. 6.

123 "Fragile Foundation for Union of Arab Emirates in the Persian Gulf," London *Times*, 18 February 1972, p. 12. Emphasis in original.

124 FCO 8, Box 1573, File No. NB 3/304/1. William Luce's opinion, stated to American diplomats, in Letter from S.L. Egerton, Arabian Department Foreign & Commonwealth Office to J.C. Moberly, British Embassy Washington, Titled "U.S. Interest in Our Gulf Policy," 11 March 1971, BNA.

125 Rendel.

126 Egerton to Moberly, 11 March 1971.

127 FCO 8, Box 1776, File No. NBT 4/10. 02 December 1971 1615Z From Cairo, signed Beaumont; and 30 November 1971 1915Z From Foreign and Commonwealth Office, BNA.

128 FCO 8, Box 1776, File No. NBT 4/10. 30 November 1971 1652Z Cable from British Embassy Cairo.

129 FCO 8, Box 1776, File No. NBT 4/10. 30 November 1971 1915Z From Foreign and Commonwealth Office.

130 FCO 8, Box 1776, File No. NBT 4/10. 30 November 1971 1610 Z From British Embassy Tripoli.

131 FCO 8, Box 1776, File No. NBT 4/10. 01 November 1971 0635Z From British Embassy Baghdad.

132 FCO 8, Box 1776, File No. NBT 4/10. 02 December 1971 1200Z From Cairo.

133 "Iran–Iraq Boundary," Bureau of Intelligence and Research Office of the Geographer (U.S. State Department, 1978).

134 "Kurds Create Tension between Iran and Iraq," London *Times*, 28 December 1965, p. 5.

135 Phebe Marr, *The Modern History of Iraq*, 1st edn. (1985), p. 222.

136 "Storm in the Gulf," London *Times*, 29 April 1969, p. 9.

137 "Saudis Agree to Bahrein Causeway," New York *Times*, 18 January 1968, p. 2.

138 Weir, Persian Gulf Political Resident's Annual Review for 1970, p. 2, BNA.

139 Marr, *The Modern History of Iraq*, 1st edn., p. 221.

140 For Iraq's domestic history in the turbulent 1960s, see Peter Sluglett and Marion Farouk-Sluglett, *Iraq Since 1958: From Revolution to Dictatorship* (London: I.B. Tauris, 2001), chapters 2–4; and Marr, *The Modern History of Iraq*, 2nd edn., chapters 5–7.

141 FCO 8, Box 34, File B3/7. Anglo-American Talks on the Middle East in the U.S. State Department, 13 September 1968, BNA.

142 FCO 8, Box 34, File B3/7. Anglo-American Talks on the Middle East in the U.S. State Department, 13 September 1968, BNA.

143 For a discussion of the Iraqi regime's conflict with its Kurdish population, see Ismael and Ismael, *Politics and Government in the Middle East and North Africa*, p. 181.

144 *FRUS 1964–1968*, Vol. XXI, p. 343. Memorandum of Conversation, 10 December 1964, Secretary of State Dean Rusk and Iraqi Foreign Minister Naji Talib.

145 FCO 8, Box 34, File B3/7. Anglo-American Talks on the Middle East in the U.S. State Department, 13 September 1968, BNA.

146 "The Iraq Kuwait Border Incident," London *Times*, 21 March 1973, p. 15. Saudi readiness to send troops comes in subsequent articles in the *Times*.

147 Henry Stanhope, "U.S. Navy Takes over from Britain in Bahrain," London *Times*, 7 January 1972, p. 1.

Chapter 6

1 "Excerpts from Text of TV Speech by Chancellor of the Exchequer Roy Jenkins," New York *Times*, 17 January 1968, p. 14.

2 See *FRUS 1969–1976*, Vol. XXIV, p. 358, Kissinger to Nixon, 13 March 1972; Rosemarie Said Zahlan, *The Making of the Modern Gulf State*s (London: Unwin-Hyman, 1998), p. 115; and "Ruler of Persian Gulf Emirate Shot to Death in Attempted Coup," New York *Times*, 25 January 1972, p. 10.

3 FO 371, Box 148896, File No. BA 1011/1. George Middleton, Cover Page to Annual Review of Events in Persian Gulf for 1959, BNA.

4 FCO 8, Box 1970, File No. NBP 10/11, File "Reports by Service Attaches on Iran." Peter Ramsbotham, Letter from British Ambassador in Iran, to Sir Alec Douglas Home, 17 January 1973, BNA.

5 Ramsbotham to Home.

6 For an overview of Iraqi foreign policy during this time, see Tareq Y. Ismael and Jacqueline S. Ismael, *Politics and Government in the Middle East and North Africa* (Gainesville: University Press of Florida, 1991), pp. 176–8.

7 Aryeh Yodfat and Mordechai Abir, *In the Direction of the Gulf: The Soviet Union and the Persian Gulf* (London: Routledge, 1977), p. 52.

8 Nicholas Herbert, "Visit to Gulf by Soviet Navy," London *Times*, 13 May 1968, p. 5.

9 RG 330, Box 35, Accession 70-A-3717, File "Iraq 091.4 I-14687/65 1965," Arthur Sylvester, After Action Report on Iraq Youth Project, 19 October 1965, USNA2.

10 Phebe Marr, *The Modern History of Iraq, 1st Edn.* (1985), p. 222.
11 "Iraq Says Her Troops Fought Iranians at Border for 4 Days," New York *Times*, p. 3.
12 See Marr, p. 225; Charles Tripp, *A History of Iraq* (Cambridge: Cambridge University Press, 2007), p. 208; and "Soviet and Iraq in 15-Year Pact," New York *Times*, 10 April 1972, p. 3.
13 Paul Martin, "Mr. Kosygin in Iraq to Secure Soviet Foothold," London *Times*, 7 April 1972.
14 RG 59, Box 1792, File "DEF – 1/1/70 SAUD." Thacher, Department of State Airgram, "Saudi Minister of Defense and Aviation Flexes His New Muscles," 25 April 1972, USNA2.
15 Thacher.
16 RG 218, Accession 92–0028, Box 21, File "Folder labeled "091 – Saudi Arabia," Letter from Secretary of State William Rogers to Secretary of Defense Melvin Laird, 28 November 1972, USNA2.
17 RG 218, Accession 92–0028, Box 21, General Burchinal,Visit of Sullivan and Chesarek to Saudi Arabia, 29 January 1972 1120Z, USNA2.
18 FCO 8, Box 1806, File No. NB2/5, Record of Anglo/United States Talks on the Persian Gulf and Arabian Peninsula Held in the State Department (Washington) 26 June 1972, BNA. (Hereafter cited as "Anglo-American Talks 26 June 1972").
19 Anglo-American Talks 26 June 1972.
20 Anglo-American Talks 26 June 1972.
21 Anglo-American Talks 26 June 1972.
22 Such sentiments appear in many pieces of British and American diplomatic correspondence of the period. See, for example, A.D. Parsons, Letter Titled "U.S. Policy in the Gulf," from Political Agent in Bahrain to H.G. Balfour Paul, British Political Resident in Bahrain, Letter, 14 March 1968, FCO 8, Box 36, File No. B 3/7 "Persian Gulf: Political Affairs: Bilateral: U.S. Interest In," BNA.
23 Henry Stanhope, "U.S. Navy Takes over from Britain in Bahrain," London *Times*, 7 January 1972, p. 1.
24 Anglo-American Talks 26 June 1972.
25 Anglo-American Talks 26 June 1972.
26 Anglo-American Talks 26 June 1972.
27 Anglo-American Talks 26 June 1972.
28 Anglo-American Talks 26 June 1972.
29 Mr. A.D. Parsons, in Anglo-American Talks 26 June 1972.
30 Anglo-American Talks 26 June 1972.
31 *FRUS 1969–76*, Vol. XXIV, p. 287. Smith (NSC Staff) to Kissinger, "Eligibility of Kuwait for Foreign Military Sales," 3 January 1971.
32 Anglo-American Talks 26 June 1972.
33 Anglo-American Talks 26 June 1972.
34 Statement of Honorable William P. Bundy, Center for International Studies, Massachusetts Institute of Technology, in *The Indian Ocean: Political and Strategic Future*, U.S. House of Representatives Hearings Before the Subcommittee on National Security Policy and Scientific Developments of the Committee on Foreign Affairs, Ninety-Second Congress, First Session. 20, 22, 27, and 28 July 1971 (Washington: GPO, 1971), p. 4.
35 For a full discussion, see Abdulaziz al-Sowayegh, *Arab Petropolitics* (New York: St. Martin's Press, 1984), chapter 10, "Previous attempts to use oil as a political weapon."
36 Joel Darmstadter and Hans H. Landsberg, "The Economic Background," in "The Oil Crisis: In Perspective," *Deaedalus* 104, no. 4 (1975), pp. 15–37.
37 Susan B. Carter, ed., *Historical Statistics of the United States* (Cambridge: Cambridge University Press, 2006), p. 4–298.

38 *Historical Statistics of the United States,* pp. 4–294 to 4–299.
39 Petroleum imports minus exports grew from approximately 3,670 trillion BTUs in 1960, to 12,980 in 1973. See *Historical Statistics of the United States*, p. 4–341.
40 *Energy Balances of OECD Countries* (Paris: International Energy Agency, Organization for Economic Co-operation and Development, 1987), pp. 524–41; and *International Petroleum Encyclopedia 2006* (Tulsa, Oklahoma: Penwell Corporation, 2006), p. 445.
41 *FRUS 1969–1976*, Vol. XXIV, pp. 306–9. National Intelligence Estimate, NIE 30-1-71, "The Persian Gulf After the British Departure," 1 April 1971.
42 Eric Pace, "Shah of Iran Warns West That Oil May Be Shut Off," New York *Times*, 25 January 1971, p. 1.
43 Congressman Lee Hamilton, in "U.S. Interests in and Policy toward the Persian Gulf," Hearings Before the Subcommittee on the Near East of the Committee on Foreign Affairs House of Representatives: Ninety-Second Congress, Second Session, 2 February; 7 June; 8, 15 August 1972 (Washington: GPO, 1972), p. vi.
44 Lee F. Dinsmore, Hearings Before the Subcommittee on the Near East of the Committee on Foreign Affairs House of Representatives, 15 August 1972.
45 Statement of Robert I. Brougham, Former Chairman of the Board and Executive Officer, ARAMCO, Hearings Before the Subcommittee on the Near East of the Committee on Foreign Affairs House of Representatives, p. 50.
46 NIE 30–1–71.
47 Thomas J. Hamilton, "Arab Lands Win Oil Price Raise," New York *Times*, 21 January 1972, p. 9; "Persian Gulf Nations Set Deadline in Drive to Buy 20% Shares in Oil Companies," New York *Times*, 23 January 1972, p. 14; and Juan de Onis, "Saudi Displeased with Her Oil Pact," New York *Times*, 11 September 1973, p. 63.
48 Paul Martin, "Baghdad Nationalizes Fields of London-Based Iraq Petroleum Company," London *Times*, 2 June 1972, p. 1. For a detailed look at the history of the IPC's nationalization, see Samir Saul, "Masterly Inactivity as Brinkmanship: The Iraq Petroleum Company's Route to Nationalization, 1958–72," *International History Review* 29, no. 4 (2007).
49 John M. Lee, "5-Year Oil Accord Is Reached in Iran by 23 Companies," New York *Times*, 15 February 1971, p. 1.
50 Daniel Yergin, *The Prize: The Epic Quest for Oil, Money, and Power* (New York: Free Press, 1991), p. 606.
51 Yergin, p. 605.
52 Yergin, p. 611.
53 Francisco Parra, *Oil Politics: A Modern History of Petroleum* (London: I.B. Tauris, 2004), p. 183.
54 Manucher Farmanfarmaian and Roxane Farmanfarmaian, *Blood and Oil: A Prince's Memoir of Iran, from the Shah to the Ayatollah* (New York: Random House, 2005), p. 409.
55 For a treatment of the evolving U.S. strategic policy toward the Gulf in the 1970s, see Elizabeth Gamlen, "U.S. Strategic Policy toward the Middle East: Central Command and the Reflagging of Kuwait's Tankers," in Hooshang Amirahmadi, *The United States and the Middle East: A Search for New Perspectives* (Albany NY: State University of New York Press, 1993), pp. 213–49; and Amitav Acharya, *U.S. Military Strategy in the Gulf* (London: Routledge, 1989).
56 Admiral Elmo Zumwalt, Jr., Chief of Naval Operations, in "Proposed Expansion of U.S. Military Facilities in the Indian Ocean," Hearings Before the Subcommittee on the Near East and South Asia of the Committee on Foreign Affairs House of Representatives: Ninety-Third Congress, 21 February 1974; 6, 12, 14, and 20 March 1974 (Washington: GPO, 1974), p. 156.
57 Secretary of State Schlesinger voiced his concern that there existed a "risk" that

military force might be used if the Arab-led oil cuts further crippled the West: see Drew Middleton, "A Word to the Arabs – 'Risk' Is Kicking up a Storm," New York *Times*, 12 January 1974, p. 4. Kissinger would later suggest that economic "strangulation" would prompt a U.S. military response, a view confirmed by President Ford and Schlesinger; see interviews reprinted in "Oil Fields as Military Objectives: A Feasibility Study," Committee on International Relations, Special Subcommittee on Investigations of the Committee on International Relations by the Congressional Research Service (Washington: GPO, 1975), pp. 77–82.

58 Middleton.
59 U.S. Secretary of Defense James Schlesinger, quoted in Richard J. Levine, "The Debate over Diego Garcia," *Wall Street Journal*, 4 April 1974.
60 Zumwalt, p. 131.
61 Prepared statement of James H. Noyes, Deputy Assistant Secretary of Defense, International Security Affairs, for Near Eastern, African, and South Asian Affairs, in "U.S. Interests in and Policy toward the Persian Gulf," Hearings Before the Subcommittee on the Near East of the Committee on Foreign Affairs House of Representatives: Ninety-Second Congress, Second Session, 2 February; 7 June; 8, 15 August 1972 (Washington: GPO, 1972), p. 11–12.
62 Noyes, p. 4.
63 Noyes, pp. 11–12.
64 Seymour Weiss, Director, Bureau Of Politico-Military Affairs, Department Of State, in "Proposed Expansion of U.S. Military Facilities in the Indian Ocean," Hearings Before the Subcommittee on the Near East and South Asia of the Committee on Foreign Affairs House of Representatives: Ninety-Third Congress, Second Session, 21 February 1974; 6, 12, 14, and 20 March 1974 (Washington: GPO, 1974), p. 43.
65 Zumwalt, p. 131.
66 Lee Hamilton, Ibid., p. 44.
67 "Diego Garcia," *Economist*, 20 September 1975, p. 74.
68 "Tiny Atoll Is Keystone of U.S. Policy in Indian Ocean," *Washington Post*, 7 April 1977, p. A14.
69 Secretary of Defense James Schlesinger, "Annual Defense Department Report FY 1975" (Washington: GPO, 1974).
70 "Oil Fields as Military Objectives," pp. 58–74.
71 Secretary of Defense Donald Rumsfeld, "Annual Defense Department Report FY 1977" (Washington: GPO, 1976), p. 10.
72 Maxwell Orme Johnson, *The Military as an Instrument of U.S. Policy in Southwest Asia: The Rapid Deployment Joint Task Force, 1979–1982* (Boulder, Colorado: Westview Press, 1983), p. 21.
73 M.O. Johnson, p. 21.
74 Don Oberdorfer, "Evolution of a Decision," *Washington Post*, 24 January 1980, p. A-1; Thomas W. Lippman, "Base Report Heightens Oman–S. Yemen Tensions," *Washington Post*, 24 January 1977, p. A9.
75 Amitav Acharya, *U.S. Military Strategy in the Gulf* (London: Routledge, 1989), p. 27.
76 C.L. Sulzberger, "The Biggest Deal of All," New York *Times*, 15 March 1975, p. 27.
77 Acharya, p. 30.
78 RG 218, Accession 92–0028, Box 21, File "091 – Saudi Arabia." Sidney Sober, Deputy Assistant Secretary of State/NEA, "Cooperation with Saudi Arabia," "Operation of the Middle East Task Group," to Secretaries of the Military Departments, JCS, 4 April 1974, USNA2.
79 President Jimmy Carter, "PD/NSC-18 U.S. National Strategy," Jimmy Carter Presidential Library.
80 Frank L. Jones, "In Brzezinski's Forge: Fashioning the Carter Doctrine's Military

Instrument," Paper delivered at the Gulf and the Globe 2009 Conference, Annapolis, January 2009.

81 For a discussion of this demilitarization proposal see Gary Sick, "The Evolution of U.S. Strategy Toward the Indian Ocean and Persian Gulf Regions," in Alvin Z. Rubinstein, ed., *The Great Game: Rivalry in the Persian Gulf and South Asia* (New York: Praeger, 1983); Walter K. Andersen, "Soviets in the Indian Ocean: Much Ado about Something – But What?" *Asian Survey*, 1984, 24, pp. 910–30; Ashok Kapur, "Carter's diplomacy and the Indian Ocean Region," in Larry W. Bowman and Ian Clark, eds., *The Indian Ocean in Global Politics* (Boulder CO: Westview Press, 1981). For broader treatments of the superpowers in the Indian Ocean in the 1960s–1980s, see Ferenc A. Vali, *Politics of the Indian Ocean Region: The Balances of Power* (New York: Free Press, 1976); and Rasul Bux Rais, *The Indian Ocean and the Superpowers* (Lanham MD: Rowman & Littlefield, 1987).

82 The fall of the Shah and the Iranian Revolution has elicited extensive academic attention. See Nikki R. Keddie, *Modern Iran: Roots and Results of Revolution* (New Haven CT: Yale University Press, 2006); Said Amir Arjomand, *The Turban for the Crown: The Islamic Revolution in Iran* (New York: Oxford University Press, 1988).

83 Don Oberdorfer, "Evolution of a Decision," *Washington Post*, 24 January 1980, p. A-1.

84 Richard Halloran, "U.S. Flying Electronic Planes over Persian Gulf," New York *Times*, 10 March 1980, p. A13.

85 Admiral William J. Crowe, *The Line of Fire: From Washington to the Gulf, the Politics and Battles of the New Military* (New York: Simon & Schuster, 1993), p. 162.

86 M.O. Johnson, p. 15.

87 Unless otherwise noted, this section based on chapter 2, M.O. Johnson.

88 M.O. Johnson, pp. 20–21.

89 M.O. Johnson, pp. 20–21.

90 "Program Cuts to Offset Indian Ocean Costs," *Aviation Week and Space Technology*, 24 March 1980, p. 18.

91 M.O. Johnson, p. 64.

92 President Jimmy Carter, "Business Council Speech," *Public Papers of the President of the United States, Jimmy Carter, 1979*, Book 2 (1 July to 31 December 1979) (Washington: GPO, 1980), p. 2235.

93 M.O. Johnson, p. 66.

94 M.O. Johnson, pp. 71, xiii.

95 President Jimmy Carter, "State of the Union Address," January 1980.

96 For a discussion of the impact of the Iranian Revolution on the surrounding states, see Rouhollah K. Ramazani, *Revolutionary Iran: Challenge and Response in the Middle East* (Baltimore: Johns Hopkins University Press, 1986); John L. Esposito, ed., *The Iranian Revolution: Its Global Impact* (Gainesville: University Press of Florida, 1990).

97 Flora Lewis, "Reports from Iraq Indicate Crisis in Its Leadership," New York *Times*, 28 July 1979, p. 3.

98 These sections on the Iran–Iraq War from Dilip Hiro, *The Longest War: The Iran–Iraq Military Conflict* (New York: Routledge, 1991); Efraim Karsh, *The Iran–Iraq War* (Oxford, UK: Osprey Publishing, 2002); and Steven R. Ward, *Immortal: A Military History of Iran and Its Armed Forces* (Washington: Georgetown University Press, 2009), chapter 9.

99 Dilip Hiro, p. xxii.

100 Warren Christopher, Deputy Secretary of State, in Bernard Gwertzman, "U.S. Warns Iraq on Seizing Oil Region," New York *Times*, 29 September 1980, p. 14.

101 Bob Woodward, *The Commanders* (New York: Simon & Schuster, 1991), p. 203.

102 Drew Middleton, "Aid for Saudis: A Risk for U.S.; Move to Deploy Planes Enlarges Mideast Role," New York *Times*, 1 October 1980, p. A1. For the broader issue of the U.S. response, see Michael A. Palmer, *Guardians of the Gulf: A History of America's Expanding Role in the Persian Gulf, 1833–1992* (New York: Free Press, 1992), p. 106.

103 Drew Middleton, "Aid for Saudis."

104 "Interview with Gen. George B. Crist, Commander in Chief, U.S. Central Command," *Marine Corps Gazette*, December 1986.

105 See Nadia El-Sayed El-Shazly, *The Gulf Tanker War: Iran and Iraq's Maritime Swordplay* (New York: St. Martin's Press, 1998).

106 Admiral William J. Crowe, *The Line of Fire: From Washington to the Gulf, the Politics and Battles of the New Military* (New York: Simon & Schuster, 1993), p. 173.

107 Crowe, p. 173.

108 Caspar Weinberger, *Fighting for Peace: Seven Critical Years in the Pentagon* (New York: Warner Books, 1990), p. 388.

109 For more details on Operations *Earnest Will* and *Praying Mantis*, see Harold Lee Wise, *Inside the Danger Zone: The U.S. Military in the Persian Gulf, 1987–1988* (Annapolis: Naval Institute Press, 2007); Craig Symonds, *Decision at Sea: Five Naval Battles That Shaped American History* (New York: Oxford University Press, 2005), p. 263; and Edward J. Marolda and Robert J. Schneller, Jr., *Shield and Sword: The United States Navy and the Persian Gulf War* (Annapolis: Naval Institute Press, 2001), pp. 32–40.

110 Caspar Weinberger, *Fighting for Peace: Seven Critical Years in the Pentagon* (New York: Warner Books, 1990), p. 400. Unless otherwise noted, information in the next five paragraphs from this source, chapter 13, "The Persian Gulf Success Story," pp. 387–413.

111 Crowe, p. 413.

112 Crowe, p. 413.

113 Crowe, p. 196.

114 Bernard E. Trainor, "Navy Sees Gulf Activity as Portent of New Era," New York *Times*, 25 November 1988, p. B10.

115 Crowe, p. 198.

116 For a detailed study, see Bradley Peniston, *No Higher Honor: Saving the USS* Samuel B. Roberts *in the Persian Gulf* (Annapolis: Naval Institute Press, 2006).

117 For a first-hand account of the tragedy from the perspective of the U.S. ship captain, see Sharon Rogers and Will Rogers, *Storm Center: The USS* Vincennes *and Iran Air Flight 655: A Personal Account of Tragedy and Terrorism* (Annapolis: Naval Institute Press, 1992).

118 Senator Brock Adams, in Robert Pear, "U.S. Seen as Entangled in Persian Gulf without an Orderly Policy," New York *Times*, 5 July 1988, p. A10.

119 John Cushman, "Navy to End Convoys in Gulf but It Will Still Protect Ships," New York *Times*, 17 September 1988, p. 1.

120 Charles F. Doran, "Gulf Security in Perspective," in Charles F. Doran and Stephen W. Buck, eds., *The Gulf, Energy, and Global Security: Political and Economic Issues* (Boulder, Colorado: L. Rienner Publishers, 1991), pp. 198–201.

121 General George Crist, paraphrased in Richard Halloran, "U.S. Altering Strategy for Defense of Arabian Oilfields," New York *Times*, 4 December 1988, p. 32.

122 "British Minister Holds Talks on Persian Gulf," London *Times*, 14 January 1974, p. 4.

123 "Excerpts from Text of TV Speech by Chancellor of the Exchequer Roy Jenkins," New York *Times*, 17 January 1968, p. 14.

124 FCO 8, Box 1970, File No. NBP 10/11, File "Reports by Service Attaches on

Iran," p. 5. Peter Ramsbotham, Letter from British Ambassador in Iran, to Sir Alec Douglas Home, 17 January 1973, BNA.

125 Ramsbotham to Home.

126 Arthur Reed, "BAC Is Awarded 250 Million Pound Defence Service Contract by Saudi Arabia," London *Times*, 11 May 1973, p. 26.

127 Ramsbotham to Home.

128 Ramsbotham to Home.

129 "Britain and Iran Sign 430 Million Pound Economic Cooperation Agreement," London *Times*, 30 January 1975, p. 1.

130 Henry Stanhope, "Crisis May Put Pressure on Navy," London *Times*, 21 January 1980, p. 5.

131 Paul Koring, "British Show U.S. How to Flex Muscles without a 'Fuss'," Canada *Globe and Mail*, 1 August 1987.

132 For an examination of Britain's Gulf Armilla Patrols, see Warren Chin, "Operations in a War Zone: The Royal Navy in the Persian Gulf in the 1980s," in Ian Speller, ed., *The Royal Navy and Maritime Power in the Twentieth Century* (London: Frank Cass, 2005), pp. 181–96.

133 Palmer, *Guardians of the Gulf* (New York: Free Press, 1992), p. 150.

134 Alan Cowell, "Moscow Urging a U.S.–Soviet Pullout in Gulf," New York *Times*, 26 February 1989, p. 17.

135 Michael R. Gordon, "U.S. Deploys Air and Sea Forces after Iraq Threatens 2 Neighbors," New York *Times*, 25 July 1990, p. A1.

136 See Efraim Karsh and Inari Rautsi, *Saddam Hussein: A Political Biography* (New York: Free Press, 1991), pp. 201–5; and Laurie Mylroie, "Saddam Was in Desperate Trouble," *Wall Street Journal*, 10 August 1990, p. A1.

137 DEFE 11, Box 163, File C/COS/48/G/4/Vol 1. "U.K. Armed Forces – Middle East," Dispositions of United Kingdom Forces in the Middle East Area, 1963–64, BNA.

138 After two years of exhaustive academic research, plus three years of operational military service in the Persian Gulf, the author has never seen in any U.S. diplomatic or military files discussion of any lessons learned from Britain's 1961 defense of Kuwait. The U.S. Naval Institute's magazine *Proceedings* however, included in its January 1974 issue a story entitled "The Kuwait Confrontation of 1961."

139 Michael R. Gordon, "U.S. Deploys Air and Sea Forces after Iraq Threatens 2 Neighbors," New York *Times*, 25 July 1990, p. A1.

140 Michael R. Gordon and Bernard E. Trainor, *The Generals' War: The Inside Story of the Conflict in the Gulf* (Boston: Little Brown and Company, 1995), p. 19.

141 Colin Powell, *My American Journey* (New York: Random House, 1995), p. 460.

142 Alan Munro, *An Embassy at War: Politics and Diplomacy Behind the Gulf War* (London: Brassey's, 1996), p. 1.

143 Powell, p. 461; and Woodward, chapter 17.

144 Central Command General Norman Schwarzkopf and Deputy Director of the CIA Dick Kerr, in Powell, *My American Journey,* p. 461; and Norman Schwarzkopf, *It Doesn't Take a Hero: The Autobiography of Norman Schwarzkopf* (New York: Bantam Books, 1992), p. 295. See also Walter D. "Pat" Lang, Jr., DIA's national intelligence officer for the Middle East and South Asia, in Bob Woodward, *The Commanders* (New York: Simon & Schuster, 1991), chapter 17.

145 Powell, *My American Journey*, p. 462.

146 Michael R. Gordon, "Iraq Army Invades Capital of Kuwait in Fierce Fighting," New York *Times*, p. A1.

147 Michael R. Gordon, "U.S. Deploys Air and Sea Forces after Iraq Threatens 2 Neighbors," New York *Times*, 25 July 1990, p. A1.

148 Unless otherwise noted, material in this paragraph drawn from: "Conduct of the Persian Gulf War: Final Report to Congress, April 1992," U.S. Department of Defense (1992), chapter one.

149 Information in this paragraph drawn chiefly from Bob Woodward, *The Commanders* (New York: Simon & Schuster, 1991), chapter 17.

150 Woodward, *The Commanders*, p. 269.

151 Woodward, *The Commanders*, p. 269.

152 Bahraini Information Minister Tareq al-Moayed, in Patrick E. Tyler, "U.S. and Bahrain near Pact on Permanent Military Base," New York *Times*, 25 March 1991, p. A9.

153 Youssef M. Ibrahim, "Gulf Nations Said to Be Committed to U.S. Alliance," New York *Times*, 25 October 1991, p. A9.

154 Ibrahim, "Gulf Nations Said to Be Committed to U.S. Alliance"; and Michael R. Gordon, "U.S. Plans a Bigger Presence in the Gulf," New York *Times*, 3 March 1991, pp. 2, 19.

155 See extensive debate over the war's inconclusive termination in Gordon & Trainor, chapters 19–20.

156 Gordon & Trainor, p. 416.

157 For a discussion of the decision to end the war as they did, see former President George Bush and National Security Adviser Brent Scowcroft's "Why We Didn't Go to Baghdad," in Micah Sifry and Christopher Cerf, eds., *The Iraq War Reader* (New York: Simon and Schuster, 2003), pp. 101–2.

158 Gordon Brown, quoted in Gordon & Trainor, p. 461.

159 President George H.W. Bush, in Gordon & Trainor, p. 443.

160 Gordon & Trainor, pp. 450–2.

Chapter 7

1 U.N. Security Council Resolution 661, 6 August 1991.

2 Press Conference with Secretary of Defense William S. Cohen in Manama, Bahrain, 10 April 2000. U.S. Department of Defense Transcript, Office of the Assistant Secretary of Defense (Public Affairs).

3 See James McKay, "Fear of the Unknown: The Coalition from Operation *Desert Fox* to Operation *Iraqi Freedom*," *Defense and Security Analysis* Vol. 21, No. 2, 2005, pp. 143–58; Anthony H. Cordesman, "The Lessons of Desert Fox: A Preliminary Analysis" (Washington: CSIS, 1999); "Desert Fox" section in Jay E. Hines, "From Desert One to Southern Watch: The Evolution of U.S. Central Command," *JFQ: Joint Force Quarterly*, No. 24, Spring 2000.

4 Jeffrey R. Macris, "Between the Storms: How *Desert Storm* Shaped the U.S. Navy of Operation *Iraqi Freedom*," *Journal of White House Studies* Vol. 4, No. 2, 2004.

5 Macris, "Between the Storms."

6 Robert John Schneller, *Anchor of Resolve: A History of U.S. Naval Forces Central Command/Fifth Fleet* (Washington, 2007), p. 44.

7 Schneller, p. 44.

8 *U.S. State Department Fact Sheet, Bahrain.*

9 Guy Toremans, "U.S. Navy Hosts Gulf MCM [Mine Countermeasure] Exercise," *Jane's Navy International*, 1 June 2001.

10 Schneller.

11 For an overview of the projected missions of these AEFs, from the vantage of

an Air Force leader, see William R. Looney, "The Air Expeditionary Force," *Airpower Journal* 10, no. 4.

12 Pat McKenna, "Air Jordan: Slammin and Jammin over the No-Fly Zone," *Airman, Magazine of the Air Force*," August 1996.

13 Information in this section from *Jane's Sentinel Security Assessment* – "The Gulf States: Security and Foreign Forces – Qatar; Al-Udeid Air Base." Accessed 4 March 2009.

14 *Jane's,* "The Gulf States."

15 Author's private conversations with Qataris.

16 Gerry Gilmore, "Cohen Visits, Reaffirms UAE, Qatar Ties," U.S. Department of Defense – American Forces Press Service 18 November 2000.

17 "Assessing Threats to Energy Security in the Persian Gulf: Information on Insurance through the Strait of Hormuz." Robert S. Strauss Center for International Security and Law, Accessed 5 March 2009; http://hormuz/robertsstrausscenter.org/insurance#history

18 Jonathan Rugman, "Sanctions Push Iraq to Disaster: Child Malnutrition in Some Areas Is Worse Than in Sudan," London *Guardian*, 18 October 1995, p. 15.

19 Jarret Brachman, *Global Jihadism: Theory and Practice* (London: Taylor and Francis, 2008), pp. 53–5.

20 Eyewitness account of the author.

21 See "Bomb Attack in Saudi Arabia: Hearings before the Committee on Armed Services, United States Senate, One Hundred Fourth Congress, Second Session, July 9 and September 18, 1996" (GPO, 1996); House Committee on National Security, Terrorist Attack against United States Military Forces in Dhahran, Saudi Arabia: Hearing Held, September 18, 1996 (GPO, 1996); and Perry D. Jamieson, *Khobar Towers: Tragedy and Response* (Washington: Air Force History and Museums Program, GPO, 2008).

22 Wayne Downing, *Assessment Task Force – Report of the Assessment of the Khobar Towers Bombing*, 30 August 1996 (Washington: GPO).

23 Observations of the author, who observed the negotiations.

24 Osama bin Laden, quoted in Brad K. Berner, *Jihad: Bin Laden in His Own Words* (Temecula, California: Peacock Books, 2007), p. 33.

25 Osama in Berner, p. 45.

26 For a look at the younger Saudi generation during this era of declining oil revenues, see Mai Yamani, *Changed Identities: The Challenge of the New Generation in Saudi Arabia* (London: Royal Institute of International Affairs, 2000).

27 Douglas Jehl, "In Saudis' Heartland, Unrest Is Aimed at Rulers and U.S.," New York *Times*, 5 November 1996, p. A1.

28 See Rachel Bronson, *Thicker Than Oil: America's Uneasy Partnership with Saudi Arabia* (New York: Oxford University Press, 2006), chapter 10.

29 Osama bin Laden, "Declaration of Jihad Against the Americans Occupying the Land of the Two Sacred Mosques: Expel the Heretics from the Arabian Peninsula," 23 August 1996, in Berner, p. 33.

30 Gerry Gilmore, "Trainers Critical to Obama's New Afghan–Pakistan Plan, Mullen Says," *American Forces Press Service News Articles*, 27 March 2009.

31 Eric Schmitt, "Rumsfeld Says U.S. Has 'Bulletproof' Evidence of Iraq's Links to Al Qaeda," New York *Times*, 28 September 2002.

32 Bob Woodward, *Plan of Attack* (New York: Simon & Schuster, 2004), p. 249.

33 *Authorization for Use of Military Force against Terrorists*, Public Law 107–40, Enacted 18 September 2001.

34 *Authorization for the Use of Military Force against Iraq Resolution of 2002*, Passed House of Representatives 297–133 (Republican 215–16; Democrats 82–126); Passed Senate 77–23 (Republican 48–1; Democrats 29–21), signed by President G.W. Bush 16 Oct 2002.

35 For a discussion of Blair's desire to serve as a "bridge" between Europe and America concerning defense issues, and how this impacted Britain's support of the 2003 war, see Steven Philip Kramer, "Blair's Britain after Iraq," *Foreign Affairs* Vol. 82, No. 4, 2003.

36 "Iraq's Weapons of Mass Destruction: The Assessment of the British Government" (London: HMSO, 2002).

37 Proclamation of Lieutenant-General Sir Stanley Maude at Baghdad, 19 March 1917, Appendix 2 in John Fisher, *Curzon and British Imperialism in the Middle East 1916–1919* (London: Frank Cass, 1999).

38 Tony Blair and George Bush, Video Addresses to the People of Iraq, Delivered 10 April 2003 (American Rhetoric Online Speech Bank, 2003), Internet, Cited 17 April 2009; www.americanrhetoric.com/speeches/wariniraq/gwbushiraq 41003.htm

39 For a collection of essays detailing the performance of America's military involvement in Iraq, see Thomas G. Mahnken and Thomas A. Keaney, eds., *War in Iraq: Planning and Execution* (London: Routledge, 2007).

40 Vice President Richard Cheney, *Meet the Press*, 16 March 2003, quoted by Nora Bensahel, "Mission Not Accomplished," in Thomas G. Mahnken and Thomas A. Keaney, eds., *War in Iraq: Planning and Execution* (London: Routledge, 2007), p. 131.

41 Gwynne Dyer, *After Iraq: Anarchy and Renewal in the Middle East* (New York: Thomas Dunne Books/St. Martins Press, 2008); Nathan Gonzalez, *Sunni–Shia Conflict and the Iraq War: Understanding Sectarian Violence in the Middle East* (Dulles, Virginia: Potomac Books, 2009); Eric Herring and Glen Rangwala, *Iraq in Fragments: The Occupation and Its Legacy* (Ithaca: Cornell University Press, 2006); Nicolas Pelham, *A New Muslim Order: The Shia and the Middle East Sectarian Crisis* (London: I.B. Tauris, 2008).

42 Defense Manpower Data Center; Data Analysis and Programs Division, "Casualty – Operation Iraqi Freedom – Total by Month – Personnel and Procurement Statistics" (Washington: U.S. Department of Defense, 2009).

43 For critiques of the post-war occupation of Iraq, see Thomas E. Ricks, *Fiasco: The American Military Adventure in Iraq* (New York: Penguin Press, 2006); David L. Phillips, *Losing Iraq: Inside the Postwar Reconstruction Fiasco* (New York: Basic Books, 2006); and Ali A. Allawi, *The Occupation of Iraq: Winning the War, Losing the Peace* (New Haven: Yale University Press, 2007).

44 For book-length treatments of this subject, see Bing West, *The Strongest Tribe: War, Politics, and the Endgame in Iraq* (New York: Random House, 2008); and Thomas E. Ricks, *The Gamble: General David Petraeus and the American Military Adventure in Iraq, 2006–2008* (New York: Penguin Press, 2009).

45 *U.S. Army/U.S. Marine Corps Counterinsurgency Field Manual* (Chicago: University of Chicago Press, 2007).

46 Hannah Fischer, "Iraqi Civilian Deaths Estimates" (Washington: Congressional Research Service, U.S. Library of Congress, 2008); and "Measuring Stability and Security in Iraq: A Report to Congress" (Washington: 2008).

47 Defense Manpower Data Center; Data Analysis and Programs Division, "Casualty – Operation Iraqi Freedom – Total by Month – Personnel and Procurement Statistics: Personnel and Procurement Reports and Data Files" (Washington: U.S. Department of Defense, 2009).

48 President Barack Obama, Speech at Camp Lejeune, North Carolina, 27 February 2009.

Conclusion

1 Viewed by the author, serving in a military capacity in the 1990s.

Bibliography

Archival sources

U.S. National Archives II – College Park Maryland (cited as USNA2)

Modern military records

Record Group (RG) 218 – Joint Chiefs of Staff Chairman Files.
RG 330 – Office of the Secretary of Defense – International Security Affairs.
RG 333 – International Military Agencies.
RG 334 – Inter-service Agencies.

State Department records

RG 59 – Central Files Subject-Numeric Files.

Foreign Affairs Oral History – drawn from Foreign Service Institute Arlington

Photograph collections

RG 111, 111SC – U.S. Army (Signal Corps).
RG 306 PS, 306 PD – U.S. Information Agency.
RG 306 NT – New York *Times* Paris Bureau.
RG 330 – Photographs of the Office of Secretary of Defense, post 1982.
RG 342 – U.S. Air Force.

Other U.S. photographic archives

Library of Congress.
U.S. Naval Institute.
U.S. Naval Academy Nimitz Library Special Collections.

British National Archives (formerly Public Records Office) – Kew, England

Foreign and Commonwealth Office.
FCO-8 Foreign Arabian Department and Middle East Department.
FO-371 Foreign Office Political Departments – General Corresp.

Ministry of Defence

DEFE-11 Ministry of Defence: Chiefs of Staff Committee Files.

Other British photographic archives

British Library – Indian Office Collection.
Imperial War Museum.
British National Maritime Museum.

Published primary document collections

al-Rashid, Ibrahim, ed. *Documents on the History of Saudi Arabia*. Salisbury, North Carolina: Documentary Publications, 1967.

al-Rashid, Ibrahim, ed. *Yemen Enters the Modern World: Secret U.S. Documents on the Rise of the Second Power on the Arabian Peninsula*. Chapel Hill, North Carolina: Documentary Publications, 1984.

Armstrong, Michael, ed. *Political Diaries of the Persian Gulf, 1904–1958*. London: Archive Editions, 1990.

Burdett, Anita L.P., ed. *Persian Gulf and Red Sea Naval Reports 1820–1960*. London: Archive Editions, 1993.

Evans, K.E., ed. *U.S. Records on Saudi Affairs 1945–1959*. London: Archive Editions and University Publications of America, 1997.

Gillard, David, ed. *British Documents on Foreign Affairs: Reports and Papers from the Foreign Office. Part I: From the Mid-Nineteenth Century to the First World War. Series B: The Near and Middle East, 1856–1914*. Frederick, Maryland: University Publications of America, 1984.

Jarman, Robert L., ed. *Political Diaries of the Arab World: The Persian Gulf*. London: Archive Editions, 1990.

Foreign Relations of the United States. Washington: United States Government Printing Office.

Books and articles

Acharya, Amitav. *U.S. Military Strategy in the Gulf*. London: Routledge, 1989.

Afar, Janet. *The Iranian Constitutional Revolution, 1906–1911*. New York: Columbia University Press, 1996.

Ahmadi, Kourosh. *Islands and International Politics in the Persian Gulf: Abu Musa and the Tunbs in Strategic Perspective*. London: Routledge, 2008.

Al-Alkim, Hassan. "The Islands Question: An Arabian Perspective," in Potter, Lawrence and Sick, Gary, eds. *Security in the Persian Gulf*. Basingstoke: Palgrave Macmillan, 2002.

al-Sowayegh, Abdulaziz. *Arab Petropolitics*. New York: St. Martin's Press, 1984.

Alani, Mustafa M. *Operation Vantage: British Military Intervention in Kuwait 1961*. Surrey, England: LAAM, 1990.

Allawi, Ali A. *The Occupation of Iraq: Winning the War, Losing the Peace*. New Haven: Yale University Press, 2007.

Almadhagi, Ahmed Noman Kassim. *Yemen and the United States: A Study of a Small Power and the Super-State Relationship 1962–1994*. London: Tauris Academic Studies, 1996.

Alvin, Calvin. *Oman Under Qaboos: From Coup to Constitution, 1970–1996*. London: Frank Cass, 2000.

Amirahmadi, Hooshang. *The United States and the Middle East: A Search for New Perspectives*. Albany NY: State University of New York Press, 1993.

Amirahmadi, Hooshang. *Small Islands, Big Politics: The Tonbs and Abu Musa in the Persian Gulf*. Basingstoke: Palgrave Macmillan, 1996.

Anderson, Walter K. "Soviets in the Indian Ocean: Much Ado about Something – But What?" *Asian Survey*, 24, 1984.

Anscombe, Frederick F. *The Ottoman Gulf: The Creation of Kuwait, Saudi Arabia, and Qatar*. New York: Columbia University Press, 1997.

Arjomand, Said Amir. *The Turban for the Crown: The Islamic Revolution in Iran*. New York: Oxford University Press, 1988.

Atabaki, Touraj. *Iran and the First World War: Battleground of the Great Powers*. London: I.B. Tauris, 2006.

Atabaki, Touraj and Zurcher, Erik J. *Men of Order: Authoritarian Modernization under Ataturk and Reza Shah*. London: I.B. Tauris, 2004.

Badeeb, Saeed M. *The Saudi-Egyptian Conflict over North Yemen, 1962–1970*. Boulder CO: Westview Press, 1986.

Balfour-Paul, Glen. *The End of Empire in the Middle East*. Cambridge: Cambridge University Press, 1994.

Barker, A.J. *The First Iraq War 1914–1918: Britain's Mesopotamian Campaign*. New York: Enigma Books, 2009.

Batatu, Hanna. *The Old Social Classes and the Revolutionary Movements of Iraq*. London: Saqi Books, 1978.

Bayat, Mangol. *Iran's First Revolution: Shi'ism and the Constitutional Revolution of 1905–1909*. New York: Oxford University Press USA, 1991.

Behrooz, Maziar. "The 1953 Coup in Iran and the Legacy of the Tudeh," in Byrne, Malcom and Gasiorowski, Mark J. eds. *Mohammad Mosaddeq and the 1953 Coup in Iran*. Syracuse: Syracuse University Press, 2004.

Belgrave, Charles. *The Pirate Coast*. London: G. Bell & Sons, 1966.

Bensahel, Nora. "Mission Not Accomplished," in Mahnken, Thomas G. and Keaney, Thomas A., eds. *War in Iraq: Planning and Execution*. London: Routledge, 2007.

Berner, Brad K. *Jihad: Bin Laden in His Own Words*. Temecula CA: Peacock Books, 2007.

Bill, James and Louis, William Roger, eds. *Musaddiq, Iranian Nationalism, and Oil*. Austin: University of Texas Press, 1988.

Birmingham, David. *A Concise History of Portugal*. Cambridge: Cambridge University Press, 2003.

Black, Edwin. *Banking on Baghdad*. Hoboken NJ: John Wiley & Sons, 2004.

Blackwell, Stephen. *British Military Intervention and the Struggle for Jordan: King Hussein, Nasser, and the Middle East Crisis, 1955–1958*. New York: Routledge, 2008.

Bonakdarian, Mansour. *Britain and the Iranian Constitutional Revolution of 1906–1911: Foreign Policy, Imperialism, and Dissent*. Syracuse: Syracuse University Press, 2006.

Bowman, Larry W. and Clark, Ian, eds. *The Indian Ocean in Global Politics*. Boulder CO: Westview Press, 1981.

Boxer, C.R. *The Portuguese Seaborne Empire, 1415–1825*. New York: A.A. Knopf, 1969.

Brachman, Jarret. *Global Jihadism: Theory and Practice*. London: Taylor and Francis, 2008.

Brenchley, Frank. *Britain and the Middle East: An Economic History 1945–87*. London: Lester Crook, 1989.

Brinton, Crane. *The Anatomy of Revolution*. New York: Vintage Books, 1957.

Bronson, Rachel. *Thicker Than Oil: America's Uneasy Partnership with Saudi Arabia*. New York: Oxford University Press, 2006.

Brown, Anthony Cave. *Oil, God, and Gold: The Story of Aramco and the Saudi Kings*. Boston: Houghton-Mifflin Co., 1999.

Brown, R.A. *United States Naval Forces in Desert Shield and Desert Storm: A Select Bibliography*. Washington, D.C.: Naval Historical Center, 1993.

Bunker, John. *Heroes in Dungarees: The Story of the American Merchant Marine in World War II*. Annapolis: Naval Institute Press, 1995.

Burke, S.M. and Quraishi, Salim Al-Din. *The British Raj in India: An Historical Review*. Oxford and Karachi: Oxford University Press, 1995.

Bush, George H.W. and Scowcroft, George. "Why We Didn't Go to Baghdad," in Sifry, Micah and Cerf, Christopher, eds. *The Iraq War Reader*. New York: Simon and Schuster, 2003.

Butler, J.R.M. and Gwyer, J.M.A. *Grand Strategy III, Part I. History of the Second World War: United Kingdom Military Series*. London: Her Majesty's Stationery Office, 1964.

Calvocoressi, Peter and Wint, Guy. *Total War: The Story of World War II*. New York: Pantheon Books, 1972.

Carse, Robert. *The Long Haul: The U.S. Merchant Service in World War II*. New York: W.W. Norton, 1965.

Carter, Susan B., ed. *Historical Statistics of the United States*. Cambridge: Cambridge University Press, 2006.

Chin, Warren. "Operations in a War Zone: The Royal Navy in the Persian Gulf in the 1980s," in Speller, Ian, ed. *The Royal Navy and Maritime Power in the Twentieth Century*. London: Frank Cass, 2005.

Churchill, Winston. *Their Finest Hour: The Second World War*. Boston: Houghton-Mifflin Co., 1949.

Churchill, Winston. *The Second World War*. Boston: Houghton-Mifflin Co., 1950.

Cohen, Michael J. *Strategy and Politics in the Middle East 1954–1960: Defending the Northern Tier*. London: Frank Cass, 2005.

Collins, D.J.E. *The Royal Indian Navy, 1939–1945*. Combined Inter-services Historical Section, part of the Official History of the Indian Armed Forces in the Second World War 1939–45.

"Conduct of the Persian Gulf War: Final Report to Congress, April 1992." Washington: U.S. Department of Defense, 1992.

Cordesman, Anthony H. "The Lessons of *Desert Fox*: A Preliminary Analysis." Washington: CSIS, 1999.

Cottrell, Philip L., ed. *East Meets West: Banking, Commerce and Investment in the Ottoman Empire*. Surrey, England: Ashgate, 2008.

Crist, George B., General, Commander in Chief, U.S. Central Command. Interview. *Marine Corps Gazette*, December 1986.

Crowe, William J. Jr., Admiral. *The Line of Fire: From Washington to the Gulf, the Politics and Battles of the New Military*. New York: Simon & Schuster, 1993.

Curzon, Lord George. *Persia and the Persian Question*. London: Longmans, Green, and Co., 1892.

Daly, M.W., ed. *The Cambridge History of Egypt*. Cambridge: Cambridge University Press, 1998.

Dalziel, Nigel Robert. *British Maritime Contacts with the Persian Gulf.* PhD Dissertation, University of Lancaster, UK, 1989.

Darby, Phillip. *British Defence Policy East of Suez, 1947–1968.* London: Oxford University Press, 1973.

Darmstadter, Joel and Landsberg, Hans H. "The Economic Background," in "The Oil Crisis: In Perspective," *Daedalus* 104, No. 4, 1975.

Davis, Paul K. *Ends and Means: The British Mesopotamian Campaign and Commission.* Madison NJ: Fairleigh Dickinson University Press, 1994.

DeNevi, Don and Hall, Bob. *United States Military Railway Service: America's Soldier-Railroaders in World War II.* Toronto: Stoddart Publishing Co., 1992.

"*Desert Shield* and *Desert Storm* Reports and Testimonies, 1991–93." Washington, D.C.: General Accounting Office, National Security and International Affairs Division, 1994.

Dockrill, Saki. *Britain's Retreat from East of Suez: The Choice between Europe and the World?* Basingstoke: Palgrave Macmillan, 2002.

Doran, Charles F. *Myth, Oil, and Politics: Introduction to the Political Economy of Petroleum.* New York: Free Press, 1977.

Doran, Charles. *Systems in Crisis: New Imperatives of High Politics at Century's End.* New York: Cambridge University Press, 1991.

Doran, Charles F. and Buck, Stephen W., eds. *The Gulf, Energy, and Global Security: Political and Economic Issues.* Boulder Co: L. Rienner Publishers, 1991.

Downing, Wayne. Downing Assessment Task Force: Report of the Assessment of the Khobar Towers Bombing, 30 August 1996. Washington: U.S. Department of Defense, 1996.

Dyer, Gwynne. *After Iraq: Anarchy and Renewal in the Middle East.* New York: Thomas Dunne Books/St. Martins Press, 2008.

Eisenhower, Dwight D. *Waging Peace 1956–1961.* Garden City, New York: Doubleday & Company, 1965.

El-Shazley, Nadio El-Sayed. *The Gulf Tanker War: Iran and Iraq's Maritime Swordplay.* New York: St. Martin's Press, 1998.

Elliott, Matthew. *Independent Iraq: The Monarchy and British Influence, 1941–1958.* London: Tauris Academic Studies, 1996.

Energy Balances of OECD Countries. Paris: International Energy Agency, Organization for Economic Co-operation and Development, 1987.

Esposito, John L., ed. *The Iranian Revolution: Its Global Impact.* Gainesville: University Press of Florida, 1990.

Evans, Major R. *A Brief Outline of the Campaign in Mesopotamia.* London: Sifton Praed and Company, 1926.

Fain, W. Taylor. *American Ascendance and British Retreat in the Persian Gulf Region.* London: Palgrave Macmillan, 2008.

Farmanfarmaian, Manucher and Farmanfarmaian, Roxane. *Blood and Oil: A Prince's Memoir of Iran, from the Shah to the Ayatollah.* New York: Random House, 2005.

Finnie, David. *Shifting Lines in the Sand: Kuwait's Elusive Frontier with Iraq.* Cambridge: Harvard University Press, 1992.

Fishel, John T. *Liberation, Occupation, and Rescue: War Termination and Desert Storm.* Carlisle Barracks PA: Strategic Studies Institute, U.S. Army War College, 1992.

Fisher, John. *Curzon and British Imperialism in the Middle East 1916–1919.* London: Frank Cass, 1999.

Floor, Willem and Hakimzadeh, Farhad. *The Hispano-Portuguese Empire and Its Contacts with Safavid Persia, the Kingdom of Hormuz and Yarubid Oman from 1489 to 1720*. Leuven, Belgium: Peeters Publishers, 2007.

Foster, Henry A. *The Making of Modern Iraq: A Product of World Forces*. New York: Russell and Russell, 1935.

Freedman, Robert O., ed. *The Middle East after Iraq's Invasion of Kuwait*. Gainesville: University of Florida Press, 1993.

Fromkin, David. *The Peace to End All Peace: The Fall of the Ottoman Empire and the Creation of the Modern Middle East*. New York: Henry Holt, 2001.

Gallman, Waldermar. *Iraq under General Nuri: My Recollections of Nuri Al-Said, 1954–1958*. Baltimore: Johns Hopkins University Press, 1964.

Gamlen, Elizabeth. "U.S. Strategic Policy toward the Middle East: Central Command and the Reflagging of Kuwait's Tankers," in Amirahmadi, Hooshang, *The United States and the Middle East: A Search for New Perspectives*. Albany NY: State University of New York Press, 1993.

Gardiner, Ian. *In the Service of the Sultan: A First-hand Account of the Dhofar Insurgency*. South Yorkshire, UK: Pen and Sword Press, 2007.

Gardner, Brian. *The East India Company: A History*. New York: McCall Publishing Company, 1972.

Gasiorowski, Mark J. and Byrne, Malcolm, eds. *Mohammad Mosaddeq and the 1953 Coup in Iran*. Syracuse, N.Y.: Syracuse University Press, 2004.

Gause III, F. Gregory. *Oil Monarchies*. New York: Council on Foreign Relations, 1994.

Gavin, R.J. *Aden under British Rule, 1839–1967*. New York: Harper and Row, 1975.

Ghani, Cyrus. *Iran and the Rise of Reza Shah: From Qajar Collapse to Pahlavi Power*. London: I.B. Tauris, 2001.

Gilbert, Martin. *Churchill and America*. New York: Free Press, 2005.

Gonzalez, Nathan. *Sunni-Shia Conflict and the Iraq War: Understanding Sectarian Violence in the Middle East*. Dulles, Virginia: Potomac Books, 2009.

Gordon, Michael R. and Trainor, Bernard E. *The General's War: The Inside Story of the Conflict in the Gulf*. Boston: Little Brown and Company, 1995.

Gorst, Anthony and Johnman, Lewis. *The Suez Crisis*. London: Routledge, 1997.

Gorst, Anthony and Lucas, W. Scott. "Suez 1956: Strategy and the Diplomatic Process," *Journal of Strategic Studies* 11, No. 4, 1988.

Gwyer, J.M.A. and Butler, J.R.M., eds. *Grand Strategy, History of the Second World War: United Kingdom Military Series*. London: Her Majesty's Stationery Office, 1964.

Gwynn, Major General Charles. *Imperial Policing*. London: Macmillan, 1936.

Hashim, Ahmed. *Insurgency and Counter-insurgency in Iraq*. Ithaca: Cornell University Press, 2006.

Hastings, D.J. *The Royal Indian Navy, 1612–1950*. Jefferson NC and London: McFarland & Company, 1988.

Heilig, Gerhard K. World Population Prospects: Analyzing the 1996 U.N. Population Projections, in International Institute for Applied Systems Analysis, http://www.iiasa.ac.at/Research/LUC/Papers/gkh1/chap1.htm

Herring, Eric and Rangwala, Glen. *Iraq in Fragments: The Occupation and Its Legacy*. Ithaca: Cornell University Press, 2006.

Hines, Jay E. "From Desert One to Southern Watch: The Evolution of U.S. Central Command," *JFQ: Joint Forces Quarterly*," No. 24, Spring 2000.

Hiro, Dilip. *The Longest War: The Iran–Iraq Military Conflict*. New York: Routledge, 1991.

Hiro, Dilip. *Desert Shield to Desert Storm: the Second Gulf War*. New York: Routledge, 1992.

Hunter, F.M. *An Account of the British Settlement of Aden in Arabia*. London: Frank Cass, 1968.

Hutchison, Kevin Don. *Operation Desert Shield/Desert Storm: Chronology and Fact Book*. Westport CT: Greenwood Press, 1995.

The Indian Ocean: Political and Strategic Future, U.S. House of Representatives Hearings Before the Subcommittee on National Security Policy and Scientific Developments of the Committee on Foreign Affairs, Ninety-Second Congress, First Session. July 20, 22, 27, and 28 1971: U.S. Government Printing Office, 1971.

International Petroleum Encyclopedia 2006. Tulsa, Oklahoma: Penwell Corporation, 2006.

"Iran–Iraq Boundary," edited by Bureau of Intelligence and Research Office of the Geographer: U.S. State Department, 1978.

"Iraq's Weapons of Mass Destruction: The Assessment of the British Government." London: HMSO, 2002.

Ismael, Tareq Y. and Ismael, Jacqueline S. *Politics and Government in the Middle East and North Africa*. Gainesville: University Press of Florida, 1991.

Jamieson, Perry D. *Khobar Towers: Tragedy and Response*. Washington, D.C.: Air Force History and Museums Program, GPO, 2008.

Jastrow, Morris. *The War and the Bagdad Railway*. Philadelphia: J.B. Lippincott, 1918.

Jeapes, Tony. *SAS: Operation Storm: Secret War in the Middle East*. London: Greenhill, 2005.

Johnson, Maxwell Orme. *The Military as an Instrument of U.S. Policy in Southwest Asia: The Rapid Deployment Joint Task Force, 1979–1982*. Boulder CO: Westview Press, 1983.

Jones, Clive. *Britain and the Yemen Civil War, 1962–1965: Ministers, Mercenaries and Mandarins; Foreign Policy and the Limits of Covert Action*. Brighton: Sussex Academic Press, 2004.

Jones, Clive. "A Guiding Hand or Controlling Grasp? Britain, Intelligence and the War in Oman, 1970–76," Paper delivered at the Gulf and the Globe 2009 conference, Annapolis MD, January 2009.

Jones, Frank L. "In Brzezinski's Forge: Fashioning the Carter Doctrine's Military Instrument," Paper delivered at the Gulf and the Globe 2009 conference, Annapolis MD, January 2009.

Joyce, Miriam. *Kuwait, 1945–1996: An Anglo-American Perspective*. London: Frank Cass, 1998.

Judd, Denis. *The Lion and the Tiger: The Rise and Fall of the British Raj, 1600–1947*. Oxford: Oxford University Press, 2004.

Jukes, Geoffrey. "Soviet Naval Policy in the Indian Ocean," chapter 9 in Potter, Lawrence and Sick, Gary, eds. *Security in the Persian Gulf*. Basingstoke: Palgrave Macmillan, 2002.

Kapur, Ashok. "Carter's diplomacy and the Indian Ocean Region," in Bowman, Larry W. and Clark, Ian, eds. *The Indian Ocean in Global Politics*. Boulder CO: Westview Press, 1981.

Karsh, Efraim. *The Iran–Iraq War*. Oxford: Osprey Publishing, 2002.

Karsh, Efraim and Rautsi, Inari. *Saddam Hussein: A Political Biography*. New York: Free Press, 1991.

Kazemzadeh, Firuz. *Russia and Britain in Persia, 1864–1914*. New Haven CT: Yale University Press, 1968.

Keddie, Nikki R. *Modern Iran: Roots and Results of Revolution*. New Haven CT: Yale University Press, 2006.

Kelly, J.B. *Britain and the Persian Gulf, 1795–1880*. Oxford: Clarendon Press, 1968.

Kelly, J.B. *Arabia, the Gulf, and the West: A Critical View of the Arabs and Their Oil Policy*. New York: Basic Books, 1980.

Kemp, Geoffrey and Harkavy, Robert. *Strategic Geography and the Changing Middle East*. Washington, D.C.: Brookings Press, 1997.

Khedouri, Elie. *England and the Middle East: The Destruction of the Ottoman Empire, 1914–1921*. London: Bowes and Bowes, 1956.

King, Henry Churchill and Crane, Charles. The King-Crane Commission Report, August 28, 1919: Report of [the] American Section of Inter-Allied Commission of Mandates in Turkey. An Official United States Government Report by the Inter-Allied Commission on Mandates in Turkey. American Section. Brigham Young University, http://www.lib.byu.edu/~rdh/wwi/1918p/kncr.html (accessed 15 June 2006).

Kinzer, Stephen. *All the Shah's Men: An American Coup and the Roots of Middle East Terror*. New York: Wiley, 2003.

Klieman, Aaron S. *Foundations of British Policy in the Arab World: The Cairo Conference of 1921*. Baltimore: Johns Hopkins University Press, 1970.

Knights, Michael. *Cradle of Conflict: Iraq and the Birth of Modern U.S. Military Power*. Annapolis MD: Naval Institute Press, 2005.

Kramer, Steven Philip. "Blair's Britain after Iraq," *Foreign Affairs*, Vol. 82, No. 4, 2003.

Kuniholm, Bruce Robellet. *The Origins of the Cold War in the Near East: Great Power Conflict and Diplomacy in Iran, Turkey, and Greece*. Princeton, New Jersey: Princeton University Press, 1980.

Lacey, Robert. *The Kingdom*. New York: Harcourt Brace Jovanovich, 1981.

Lee, Air Chief Marshal Sir David. *Flight from the Middle East: A History of the Royal Air Force in the Arabian Peninsula and Adjacent Territories, 1945–1972*. London: Ministry of Defence: Air Historical Branch (RAF), Her Majesty's Stationery Office, 1980.

Lenczowski, George. *American Presidents and the Middle East*. Durham: Duke University Press, 1990.

Lewis, Bernard. *The Shaping of the Modern Middle East*. New York: Oxford University Press, 1994.

Lloyd, T.O., ed. *Empire to Welfare State: English History, 1906–1985*. Oxford: Oxford University Press, 1986.

Longoria, Michael A. *A Historical View of Air Policing Doctrine: Lessons from the British Experience between the Wars, 1919–1939*. Dissertation, School of Advanced Airpower Studies, Maxwell Air Force Base, Alabama, 1992.

Longrigg, Stephen Hemsley. *Iraq, 1900–1950: A Political, Social, and Economic History*. London: Oxford University Press, 1953.

Longrigg, Stephen Hemsley. *Oil in the Middle East: Its Discovery and Development*. London: Oxford University Press, 1954.

Longrigg, Stephen Hemsley. *Syria and Lebanon under French Mandate*. London: Oxford University Press, 1958.

Looney, William R. "The Air Expeditionary Force," *Airpower Journal* 10, No. 4, Winter 1996.

Lord Curzon in India: Being a Selection from his Speeches as Viceroy and Governor-General of India 1898–1905. New York: Macmillan, 1905.

Louis, William Roger. *Imperialism at Bay: The United States and the Decolonization of the British Empire, 1941–1945*. New York: Oxford University Press, 1978.

Louis, William Roger. *The British Empire in the Middle East, 1945–1951: Arab Nationalism, the United States, and Postwar Imperialism*. Oxford: Clarendon Press, 1984.

Louis, William Roger and Owen, Roger, eds. *Suez 1956: The Crisis and Its Consequences*. New York: Clarendon Press, 1989.

Low, Charles Rathbone. *History of the Indian Navy 1613–1863,* 2 vols. London: Richard Bentley and Son, 1877.

Lyman, Robert. *Iraq 1941: The Battles for Basra, Habbaniya, Fallujah and Baghdad*. Colchester, Essex: Osprey Publishing, 2006.

Macris, Jeffrey R. "Between the Storms: How *Desert Storm* Shaped the U.S. Navy of Operation *Iraqi Freedom*," *Journal of White House Studies*, Vol. 4, No. 2, 2004.

Mahnken, Thomas G. and Keaney, Thomas A., eds. *War in Iraq: Planning and Execution*. London: Routledge, 2007.

Majd, Mohammad Gholi. *The Great Famine and Genocide in Persia, 1917–1919*. Lanham, Maryland: University Press of America, 2003.

Majd, Mohammad Gholi. *Persia in World War I and Its Conquest by Great Britain*. Lanham, Maryland: University Press of America, 2003.

Marolda, Edward J. and Schneller, Jr., Robert J. *Shield and Sword: the United States Navy and the Persian Gulf War*. Annapolis: Naval Institute Press, 2001.

Marr, Phebe. *The Modern History of Iraq*, 2nd edn. Boulder CO: Westview Press, 2004.

Marston, Daniel P. and Sundaram, Chandar, eds. *A Military History of India and South Asia: From the East India Company to the Nuclear Era*. Westport CT: Praeger Security International, 2007.

Mawby, Spencer. *British Policy in Aden and the Protectorates, 1955–67: Last Outpost of a Middle East Empire*. London: Routledge, 2005.

McGhee, George. *Envoy to the Middle World: Adventures in Diplomacy*. New York: Harper and Row, 1983.

McKay, James. "Fear of the Unknown: The Coalition from Operation *Desert Fox* to Operation *Iraqi Freedom*." *Defense and Security Analysis,* Vol. 21, No. 2, 2005.

McKenna, Pat. "Air Jordan: Slammin and Jammin over the No-Fly Zone," *Airman, Magazine of the Air Force,* August 1996.

McMurray, Jonathan S. *Distant Ties: Germany, the Ottoman Empire, and the Construction of the Baghdad Railway*. Westport CT: Praeger, 2001.

Menarchik, Douglas. *Powerlift – Getting to Desert Storm: Strategic Transportation and Strategy in the New World Order*. Westport, CT: Praeger, 1993.

Mercogliano, Salvatore R. "Military Sealift Command: Ships That Wait," in U.S. Maritime Service Veterans, http://www.usmm.org/msts/wait/html (accessed 16 Dec 2005).

Miller, Aaron David. *Search for Security: Saudi Arabian Oil and American Foreign Policy, 1939–1949*. Chapel Hill: University of North Carolina Press, 1980.

Millspaugh, Arthur C. *The American Task in Persia*. New York: Century Company, 1925.

Millspaugh, Arthur C. *Americans in Persia*. Washington, D.C.: Brookings Institution, 1946.

Moberly, F.J. *The Campaign in Mesopotamia, 1914–1918*. London: HMSO, 1923, reprinted 1987.

Monroe, Elizabeth. *Britain's Moment in the Middle East: 1914–1956*. Baltimore: Johns Hopkins University Press, 1963.

Morison, Samuel Eliot. *History of the United States Naval Operations in World War II*. Boston: Little, Brown & Company, 1947.

Motter, T.H. Vail. *United States Army in World War II – the Middle East Theater: The Persian Corridor and Aid to Russia*. Edited by Kent Roberts Greenfield. Washington, D.C.: Office of the Chief of Military History, Department of the Army, 1952.

Mulligan, William E. "Air Raid! A Sequel," *Saudi Aramco World*, July/August 1976.

Munro, Alan. *An Embassy at War: Politics and Diplomacy Behind the Gulf War*. London: Brassey's, 1996.

Nagl, John. *U.S. Army Instructions for American Servicemen in Iraq During World War II*. Chicago: University of Chicago Press, 2007 reprint.

Netton, Ian Richard, ed. *Arabia and the Gulf: From Traditional Society to Modern States*. Totowa NJ: Barnes & Noble, 1986.

"Oil Fields as Military Objectives: A Feasibility Study." U.S. Congress, Committee on International Relations, Special Subcommittee on Investigations, Congressional Research Service. Washington: GPO, 1975.

Olson, William J. *Anglo-Iranian Relations During World War I*. London: Routledge, 1984.

Omissi, David. "The Indian Army in the First World War, 1914–18," in Marston and Sundaram, eds. *A Military History of India and South Asia: From the East India Company to the Nuclear Era*. Westport CT: Praeger International, 2007.

Onley, James. *The Arabian Frontier of the British Raj: Merchants, Rulers, and the British in the Nineteenth-Century Gulf*. New York: Oxford University Press, 2007.

Outram, James. *Lieutenant General Sir James Outram's Persian Campaign in 1857: Comprising General Orders and Despatches Relating to the Military Operations in Persia, from the Landing at Bushire to the Treaty of Peace*. London: Smith, Elder, and Co., Printed for Prive Circulation Only, 1860. (Available at the British Library).

Ovendale, Ritchie. *Britain, the United States, and the Transfer of Power in the Middle East, 1945–1962*. New York: Leicester University Press, 1996.

Ozbaran, Salih. *The Ottoman Response to European Expansion: Studies on Ottoman–Portuguese Relations in the Indian Ocean and Ottoman Administration in the Arab Lands During the Sixteenth Century*. Istanbul: Isis Press, 1994.

Palmer, Michael A. *Guardians of the Gulf: A History of America's Expanding Role in the Persian Gulf, 1833–1992*. New York: Free Press, 1992.

Palmer, Michael A. *On Course to Desert Storm: The United States Navy and the Persian Gulf*. Washington: Naval Historical Center, 1992.

Parra, Francisco. *Oil Politics: A Modern History of Petroleum*. London: I.B. Tauris, 2004.

Parsons, Anthony. *They Say the Lion: Britain's Legacy to the Arabs. A Personal Memoir*. London: Jonathan Cape, 1986.

Peck, Malcolm. *Historical Dictionary of the Gulf Arab States*, 2nd edn. Lanham MD: Scarecrow Press, 2008.

Pelham, Nicolas. *A New Muslim Order: The Shia and the Middle East Sectarian Crisis.* London: I.B. Tauris, 2008.

Peniston, Bradley. *No Higher Honor: Saving the USS Samuel B. Roberts in the Persian Gulf.* Annapolis: Naval Institute Press, 2006.

Petersen, Tore. *The Decline of the Anglo-American Middle East, 1961–1969: A Willing Retreat.* Brighton, England: Sussex Academic Press, 2006.

Peterson, John. *Yemen: The Search for a Modern State.* Baltimore: Johns Hopkins University Press, 1982.

Peterson, John. *Defending Arabia.* New York: St. Martin's Press, 1986.

Peterson, John. *Oman's Insurgencies: The Sultanate's Struggle for Supremacy.* London: Saqi Books, 2007.

Phillips, David L. *Losing Iraq: Inside the Postwar Reconstruction Fiasco.* New York: Basic Books, 2006.

Pickering, Jeffrey. *Britain's Withdrawal from East of Suez: The Politics of Retrenchment.* London: Macmillan, 1998.

Pieragostini, Karl. *Britain, Aden and South Arabia: Abandoning Empire.* New York: St. Martin's Press, 1991.

Podeh, Elie. "Suez in Reverse: The Arab Response to the Iraqi Bid for Kuwait, 1961–63," *Diplomacy and Statecraft*, March 2003, Vol. 14, Issue 1.

Pokrant, Marvin. *Desert Storm at Sea: What the Navy Really Did.* Westport CT: Greenwood Press, 1999.

Potter, Lawrence G. *The Persian Gulf in History.* New York: Palgrave Macmillan, 2009.

Potter, Lawrence and Sick, Gary, eds. *Security in the Persian Gulf.* Basingstoke: Palgrave Macmillan, 2002.

Powell, Colin. *My American Journey.* New York: Random House, 1995.

Prakash, Om. *The Dutch East India Company and the Economy of Bengal, 1630–1720.* Princeton NJ: Princeton University Press, 1985.

Precht, Henry. "The Iranian Revolution: An Oral History with Henry Precht, then State Department Desk Officer," in *Oral History Project*. Arlington, Virginia: Association for Diplomatic Studies and Training.

"Proposed Expansion of U.S. Military Facilities in the Indian Ocean," 21 February; 6 March Hearings Before the Subcommittee on the Near East and South Asia of the Committee on Foreign Affairs: House of Representatives. Ninety-Third Congress, Second Session: U.S. Government Printing Office, 1974.

Rados, Antonia. *Saddam's Revenge.* (Film) New York: Filmakers Library, 2004.

Rais, Rasul Bux. *The Indian Ocean and the Superpowers.* Lanham MD: Rowman & Littlefield, 1987.

Ramazani, Rouhollah K. *Revolutionary Iran: Challenge and Response in the Middle East.* Baltimore: Johns Hopkins University Press, 1986.

Ramerini, Marco. "Dutch Portuguese Colonial History: Portuguese Colonial Remains, Asia 1498–1800." http://www.colonialvoyage.com/remainPasia.html (accessed 22 May 2006).

Reid, B.H. "The Northern Tier and the Baghdad Pact," in Young, J.W., ed. *The Foreign Policy of Churchill's Peacetime Administration, 1951–1955.* Leicester: Leicester University Press, 1988.

Reynolds, David. *Britannia Overruled: British Policy and World Power in the 20th Century.* London: Longman, 1991.

Ricks, Thomas E. *Fiasco: The American Military Adventure in Iraq*. New York: Penguin Press, 2006.

Ricks, Thomas E. *The Gamble: General David Petraeus and the American Military Adventure in Iraq, 2006–2008*. New York: Penguin, 2009.

Rogers, Sharon and Rogers, Will. *Storm Center: The USS* Vincennes *and Iran Air Flight 655: A Personal Account of Tragedy and Terrorism*. Annapolis: Naval Institute Press, 1992.

Roosevelt, Elliott. *As He Saw It*. New York: Duell, Sloan and Pearce, 1946.

Roshandel, Jalil. "On the Persian Gulf Islands: An Iranian Perspective," in Potter, Lawrence and Sick, Gary, eds. *Security in the Persian Gulf*. Basingstoke: Palgrave Macmillan, 2002.

Rubinstein, Alvin, ed. *The Great Game: Rivalry in the Persian Gulf and South Asia*. New York: Praeger, 1983.

Rumsfeld, Donald, Secretary of Defense. "Annual Defense Department Report FY 1977." Washington, D.C.; U.S. Government Printing Office, 1976.

Saul, Samir. "Masterly Inactivity as Brinkmanship: The Iraq Petroleum Company's Route to Nationalization, 1958–72," *International History Review* 29, No. 4, 2007.

Sayre, Joel. *Persian Gulf Command*. New York: Random House, 1945.

Schlesinger, James, Secretary of Defense. "Annual Defense Department Report FY 1975." Washington, D.C.; U.S. Government Printing Office, 1974.

Schneller, Robert John. *Anchor of Resolve: A History of U.S. Naval Forces Central Command/Fifth Fleet*. Washington, D.C.: Naval Historical Center, 2007.

Schofield, Richard. "Anything but Black and White: A Commentary on the Lower Gulf Islands Dispute," in Potter, Lawrence and Sick, Gary, eds. *Security in the Persian Gulf*. Basingstoke: Palgrave Macmillan, 2002.

Schofield, Richard, ed. *Arabian Boundary Disputes*. London: Archive Editions, 1992. (18,000 pp).

Schwarzkopf, Norman. *It Doesn't Take a Hero: The Autobiography of Norman Schwarzkopf*. New York: Bantam Books, 1992.

Shuckburgh, Evelyn. *Descent to Suez*. New York: Norton, 1987.

Shuster, W. Morgan. *The Strangling of Persia: A Personal Narrative*. New York: Century, 1920.

Sick, Gary. "The Evolution of U.S. Strategy Toward the Indian Ocean and Persian Gulf Regions," in Rubinstein, Alvin, ed. *The Great Game: Rivalry in the Persian Gulf and South Asia*. New York: Praeger, 1983.

Sifry, Micah and Cerf, Christopher, eds. *The Iraq War Reader*. New York: Simon and Schuster, 2003.

Silverfarb, Daniel. *Britain's Informal Empire in the Middle East: A Case Study of Iraq, 1929–1941*. New York: Oxford University Press, 1986.

Silverfarb, Daniel. *The Twilight of British Ascendancy in the Middle East: A Case Study of Iraq, 1941–1950*. New York: St. Martin's Press, 1994.

Sluglett, Peter and Sluglett, Marion Farouk. *Iraq Since 1958: From Revolution to Dictatorship*. London: I.B. Tauris, 2001.

Smith, Simon. *Kuwait, 1950–1965: Britain, the Al-Sabah, and Oil*. London: British Academy, 2000.

Smith, Simon. *Britain's Revival and Fall in the Gulf: Kuwait, Bahrain, Qatar, and the Trucial States, 1950–1971*. London: RoutledgeCurzon, 2004.

Smith, Simon, ed. *Reassessing Suez 1956: New Perspectives on the Crisis and Its Aftermath*. Burlington VT: Ashgate, 2008.

Speller, Ian. "Naval Diplomacy: Operation *Vantage*, 1961," in Speller, Ian, ed. *The Royal Navy and Maritime Power in the Twentieth Century*. London: Frank Cass, 2005.

Subrahmanyam, Sanjay. *The Portuguese Empire in Asia, 1500–1700: A Political and Economic History*. London: Longman, 1993.

Sutton, Jean. *Lords of the East: The East India Company and Its Ships, 1600–1874*. London: Conway Maritime Press, 2000.

Swansinger, A. Jacqueline. *The Magic Carpet: Lend-Lease in the Middle East, 1940–1944*. PhD Dissertation, Rutgers University, 1988.

Sykes, Sir Percy. *A History of Persia, 3rd Edition*. London: Macmillan and Company, 1930.

Symonds, Craig. *Decision at Sea: Five Naval Battles That Shaped American History*. New York: Oxford University Press, 2005.

Takeyh, Ray. *The Origins of the Eisenhower Doctrine: The U.S., Britain and Nasser's Egypt, 1953–57*. London: Macmillan Press, 2000.

Teicher, Howard and Teicher, Gayle Radley. *Twin Pillars to Desert Storm: America's Flawed Vision in the Middle East from Nixon to Bush*. New York: William Morrow & Company, 1993.

U.S. Army/U.S. Marine Corps Counterinsurgency Field Manual. Chicago: University of Chicago Press, 2007 reprint.

"U.S. Interests in and Policy toward the Persian Gulf." 2 February; 7 June; 8 and 15 August, 1972 Hearings Before the Subcommittee on the Near East of the Committee on Foreign Affairs House of Representatives: Ninety-Second Congress: U.S. Government Printing Office, 1972.

Vali, Ferenc A. *Politics of the Indian Ocean Region: The Balances of Power*. New York: Free Press, 1976.

Vassiliev, Alexei. *The History of Saudi Arabia*. London: Saqi Books, 1998.

Vitalis, Robert. *America's Kingdom: Mythmaking on the Saudi Oil Frontier*. Stanford: Stanford University Press, 2007.

Ward, Steven R. *Immortal: A Military History of Iran and Its Armed Forces*. Washington, D.C.: Georgetown University Press, 2009.

Watt, Donald Cameron, ed. *Documents on the Suez Crisis, 26 July to 6 November, 1956*. London: Royal Institute of International Affairs, 1957.

Weinberger, Caspar. *Fighting for Peace: Seven Critical Years in the Pentagon*. New York: Warner Books, 1990.

West, Bing. *The Strongest Tribe: War, Politics, and the Endgame in Iraq*. New York: Random House, 2008.

The Whirlwind War: the United States Army in Operations Desert Shield *and* Desert Storm. Washington, D.C.: Center of Military History, U.S. Army, 1995.

Wilcox, Ron. *Battles on the Tigris: The Mesopotamian Campaign of the First World War*. South Yorkshire, UK: Pen and Sword, 2006.

Wilson, Lt. Col. Sir Arnold T. *Loyalties Mesopotamia: A Personal and Historical Record*. London: Oxford University Press, 1930.

Winkler, David F. *Amirs, Admirals & Desert Sailors: Bahrain, the U.S. Navy, and the Arabian Gulf*. Annapolis MD: Naval Institute Press, 2007.

Wise, Harold Lee. *Inside the Danger Zone: The U.S. Military in the Persian Gulf, 1987–1988*. Annapolis: Naval Institute Press, 2007.

Woodward, Bob. *The Commanders*. New York: Simon & Schuster, 1991.

Woodward, Bob. *Plan of Attack*. New York: Simon & Schuster, 2004.

Yamani, Mai. *Changed Identities: The Challenge of the New Generation in Saudi Arabia*. London: Royal Institute of International Affairs, 2000.

Yaqub, Salim. *Containing Arab Nationalism: The Eisenhower Doctrine and the Middle East*. Chapel Hill: University of North Carolina Press, 2004.

Yergin, Daniel. *The Prize: The Epic Quest for Oil, Money, and Power*. New York: Free Press, 1991.

Yesilbursa, Behcet Kemal. *The Baghdad Pact: Anglo-American Defence Policies in the Middle East, 1950–1959*. London: Frank Cass, 2005.

Yodfat, Aryeh Y. *The Soviet Union and the Arabian Peninsula*. London: Croom Helm, 1983.

Yodfat, Aryeh and Abir, Mordechai. *In the Direction of the Gulf: The Soviet Union and the Persian Gulf*. London: Routledge, 1977.

Zahlan, Rosemarie Said. *The Making of the Modern Gulf States*. London: Unwin Hyman, 1989.

Map credits

1 Arabian Peninsula and vicinity (U.S. Government Map, Courtesy of the University of Texas Libraries, The University of Texas at Austin).
2 Persian Gulf 1973 – with disputed borders (U.S. Government Map, Courtesy of the University of Texas Libraries, The University of Texas at Austin).
3 Strait of Hormuz and disputed islands (U.S. Government Map, Courtesy of the University of Texas Libraries, The University of Texas at Austin).

Photograph credits

Cover photo: Bahraini palace guard renders a rifle salute, 1956 (Official U.S. Navy Photo, courtesy of the U.S. Naval Institute).

1 Portuguese castle on Hormuz Island, Iran (Fariborz).
2 British military punitive raid against Arabian pirates, Ras al Khaima, 1809 (R. Temple, *Sixteen Views of Places in the Persian Gulf*. London: W. Haines, 1813. Courtesy of Brown University Library).
3 Entrance to British Persian Gulf Residency at Bushire, Iran, c. 1870 (© The British Library Board. All Rights Reserved June 2009, 355/1(34)).
4 Lord Curzon's party arrives ashore in Kuwait, 1903 (© The British Library Board. All Rights Reserved June 2009, 49/1(2)).
5 Arab sheikhs assemble to hear Lord Curzon, on board Royal Indian Marine Ship (RIMS) *Argonaut*, in Sharjah, 1903 (© The British Library Board. All Rights Reserved June 2009, 49/1(7)).
6 Knocking off time at Abadan refinery, Iran, c. 1910–1930 (Reproduced from the BP Archive).
7 British-Indian troops in Mesopotamia man World War I anti-aircraft gun (Imperial War Museum Q 24781).
8 Royal Navy ship in Persian Gulf or Red Sea, 1920s (Imperial War Museum Q 93334).
9 RAF biplanes from No. 55 (Bomber) Squadron exercise with RAF armored cars, Iraq, 1934. (U.S. National Archives RG 306NT).
10 His Majesty's Armoured Cars (HMAC) and British biplane on maneuvers in Iraqi desert, 1934 (U.S. National Archives RG 306NT).
11 Senior Naval Officer Persian Gulf, between Sheikh of Dubai and Sheikh of Henjam, c. 1920s (© National Maritime Museum, Greenwich, London P39729 B)
12 British troops looking at Baghdad, 1941 (Imperial War Museum E 3464).

13   British and Free French troops invade Syria, 1941 (Imperial War Museum E 3839).

14   British-Indian guard watches over wrecked flagship of Iranian Navy, 1941 (Library of Congress LC G8/BO-349).

15   Indian rifleman guards oil pipeline in Iran, 1941 (Library of Congress LC G8/BO-343).

16   British and American forces defend Abadan complex, World War II (U.S. National Archives RG 111-SC/New Box 715/SC-339421).

17   Unloading U.S. supply ship in Kermanshah port, Iran, World War II (U.S. National Archives RG 342 FH/Box 5, Official U.S. Government Photo).

18   Lend-Lease tanks on their way through Iran to Russia, World War II (U.S. Library of Congress LC-USW3-028357-E DLC, Official U.S. Government Photo).

19   U.S. Army truck convoy in Iranian snow storm, 1943 (U.S. Library of Congress LC-USW3-028327-E DLC, U.S. Government Photo).

20   American, British, and Russian engineers in train in Iran, World War II (U.S. Library of Congress LC-USW3-028370-E DLC, Official U.S. Government Photo).

21   American aircraft assembly plant in Iran, World War II (U.S. National Archives RG 342-FH/Box 5, Official U.S. Government Photo).

22   Readying U.S. aircraft for delivery to Soviet Union – painting the white American star a Soviet red color (U.S. National Archives RG 342-FH/Box 5, Official U.S. Government Photo).

23   U.S. Air Transport Command aircraft in Salalah, Oman, World War II (U.S. National Archives RG 342 Series FH Box 5, Official U.S. Government Photo).

24   Changing of the guards, U.S. Air Transport Command Ferry Squadron, Aden (U.S. National Archives RG 342 Series FH Box 5, Official U.S. Government Photo).

25   Sharjah Airfield, World War II (U.S. National Archives RG 342 Series FH Box 5, Official U.S. Government Photo).

26   Habbaniya, Iraq, World War II (U.S. National Archives RG 342 Series FH Box 5, Official U.S. Government Photo).

27   Headquarters building of the Basra, Iraq detachment of the U.S. Persian Gulf Command, World War II (U.S. National Archives, RG 111SC – New Box 760, Official U.S. Government Photo).

28   Members of the 2nd U.S. Army Airways Communication Wing, radio receiving station, Bahrain, World War II (U.S. National Archives RG 342 Series FH Box 5, Official U.S. Government Photo).

29   British and American shared air facilities, Bahrain,

World War II (U.S. National Archives, RG 342 Series FH Box 5, Official U.S. Government Photo).

30 Shah with U.S. Persian Gulf Command's Commanding General, 1944 (U.S. Library of Congress LC-USZ62–53247, Official U.S. Government Photo).

31 Shah plays ping pong with U.S. serviceman, 1945 (U.S. Library of Congress Call Number LOT 5178–13, 13-5E-3, Official U.S. Government Photo).

32 Col. Norman Schwarzkopf, Sr. trains the Iranian Gendarmerie, World War II (U.S. National Archives RG 111SC – New Box 715, Official U.S. Government Photo).

33 Saudi desert soldiers, 1943 (U.S. National Archives 111-SC New Box 203, Official U.S. Photo).

34 Saudi Princes Faisal and Khalid in U.S. aircraft, World War II (U.S. National Archives RG 342-FH Box 193, Official U.S. Government Photo).

35 Sheikh of Bahrain presents pair of aviator wings to American pilot, World War II (U.S. National Archives RG 342 Series FH Box 5, Official U.S. Government Photo).

36 King Abdul Aziz Al Saud (Ibn Saud) walks through U.S. Navy honor guard, to confer with FDR, 1945 (U.S. National Archives, RG 111-SC New Box 472, Official U.S. Government Photo).

37 Ibn Saud and FDR, USS *Quincy*, Great Bitter Lake, Egypt, 1945 (U.S. National Archives 111-SC New Box 472, Official U.S. Government Photo).

38 Ibn Saud's desert tent pitched aboard USS *Murphy*, 1945 (Official U.S. Navy Photo, courtesy of the U.S. Naval Institute).

39 Slaughtering Ibn Saud's sheep, USS *Murphy*, 1945 (Official U.S. Navy Photo).

40 Egypt's King Farouk boards U.S. Navy warship to meet with President Roosevelt, 1945 (U.S. National Archives 111-SC New Box 472, Official U.S. Government Photo).

41 Ethiopian Emperor Haile Selassie on board U.S. Navy ship, 1945 (U.S. National Archives, RG111-SC New Box 472, Official U.S. Government Photo).

42 Iranian rifleman on the Azerbaijani border, 1946 (U.S. National Archives, RG 306NT).

43 British Political Resident Burrows with Bahraini Ruler, 1956 (Official U.S. Navy Photo).

44 Traditional Iranian nomad with camel, next to U.S.-supplied armored vehicle, 1956 (Official U.S. Government Photo).

45 U.S. and Saudi personnel at U.S.-built Dhahran air base, c. 1947 (U.S. National Archives RG 342-FH, Box 5005, Official U.S. Government Photo).

46 Saudi Bedouin inspects B-29 intercontinental bomber at

Dhahran, c. 1947 (U.S. National Archives RG 342-FH Box 5005, Official U.S. Government Photo).

47   U.S. Navy's Middle East Force flagship on diplomatic mission to Oman, c. 1956 (Official U.S. Navy Photo).

48   Abadan refinery, 1951 (BP Photographic Archives).

49   Tehran riots, encouraged by covert Anglo-American campaign to overthrow Prime Minister Mohammed Mossadegh, 1953 (U.S. National Archives, RG 306 PS, Box 196, FC1218898).

50   Aircraft carrier transits Suez Canal, 1948 (U.S. National Archives, RG 80G, 401914. Official U.S. Navy Photo).

51   U.S. military aircraft in Beirut, 1958 (U.S. National Archives RG 342-B Box 207, Official U.S. Air Force Photo).

52   U.S. Army troops in Beirut, 1958 (U.S. National Archives RG 342-B Box 207, Official U.S. Air Force Photo).

53   Iranian students in U.S.-funded English class, village near Tehran, 1951 (U.S. National Archives, RG 306PSD Box 7, U.S. State Department Photo).

54   Operation *Hard Surface* in Saudi Arabia during Yemeni Civil War, 1963 (U.S. National Archives RG 342-B Box 1033, Official U.S. Air Force Photo).

55   British soldiers threaten local boy in Aden, 1967 (Hulton Archive/Getty Images 2642659).

56   Dhofar rebels train with Chinese weapons, c. 1971 (U.S. National Archives, RG 306 PS, USIS, #201271).

57   British seconded troops in Oman, Dhofar rebellion (courtesy U.S. Naval Institute).

58   Hut and native on Diego Garcia, prior to Anglo-American defense improvements, c. early 1960s (Official U.S. Navy Photo).

59   U.S. trained Royal Saudi Air Force pilot straps in to jet aircraft, 1963 (U.S. National Archives RG 342-B Box 1496, Official U.S. Air Force Photo).

60   U.S. military trainers teach Saudis about aircraft engines, c. 1957 (U.S. National Archives RG 342-B Box 1496, Official U.S. Air Force Photo).

61   USS *La Salle*, flagship for the U.S. Middle East Force (Official U.S. Navy Photo).

62   U.S. military aircraft unloads self-propelled howitzer, 1973 Yom Kippur War (U.S. National Archives RG 342-B Box 1461, Official U.S. Air Force Photo).

63   The Imperial Iranian Ships IIS *Babr* and IIS *Palang*, former U.S. Navy ships, in drydock at the Philadelphia Naval Shipyard, c. 1973 (U.S. Naval Academy Nimitz Library Collection, Official U.S. Photo).

64   Diego Garcia improvements, 1980 (Official U.S. Navy Photo).

65   Operation *Earnest Will* – USS *Jarrett* escorts re-flagged

Kuwaiti tanker, August 1987 (U.S. Naval Institute, Official U.S. Navy Photo).

66 British Armilla patrol – HMS *Andromeda* accompanies British-flagged tanker during the Iran–Iraq War, 1980s (U.S. Naval Institute).

67 In amphibious assault vehicles, U.S. Marines advance toward Kuwait City, Operation *Desert Storm*, February 1991 (U.S. Department of Defense photograph by Lance Corporal R. Price).

68 U.S. Air Force tanker aircraft refuels Navy attack aircraft, Operation *Southern Watch*, over Saudi Arabia, April 1996 (Official U.S. Government Photo).

69 USS *Fletcher* conducts post-*Desert Storm* Maritime Intercept Operations aboard a container ship en route to Iraq, November 2000 (Official U.S. Navy Photo by Photographer's Mate 3rd Class Michael A. Meyers).

70 U.S. aircraft carrier during routine port call in United Arab Emirates, 1994 (Donald Bray, U.S. Naval Institute Photo Archives).

71 Aftermath of bomb explosion at Khobar Towers military housing complex in Dhahran, June 1996 (Official U.S. Government Photo).

72 Defending Prince Sultan Air Base in Saudi Arabia, August 1996 (Official U.S. Government Photo).

73 British communications team deploys to Al Kharj in Saudi Arabia, August 1996 (Official Department of Defense Photo by Senior Airman Richard M. Heileman, U.S. Air Force, 960816-F-0954H-007).

74 U.S. Army troops scan horizon, Al Najaf, Operation *Iraqi Freedom*, March 2003 (Official U.S. Army Photo by Staff Sergeant Kyle Davis).

75 U.S. Navy sailors apprehend suspected pirates in Gulf of Aden, February 2009 (U.S. Navy Photo by Mass Communications Specialist 2nd Class Jason R. Zalasky).

Index